Documents
of
Western Civilization

Volume II: 1550 to Present

M. Gregory Kendrick
Loretta Goldy
Janice Archer

D1312437

 **Wadsworth**
Thomson Learning

Australia • Canada • Mexico • Singapore • Spain • United Kingdom • United States

COPYRIGHT © 1999 Wadsworth, a division of Thomson Learning, Inc. Thomson Learning™ is a trademark used herein under license.

ALL RIGHTS RESERVED. No part of this work covered by the copyright hereon may be reproduced or used in any form or by any means—graphic, electronic, or mechanical, including photocopying, recording, taping, Web distribution, or information storage and retrieval systems—without the prior written permission of the publisher.

Printed in the Canada
2   3   4   5   6   7   03   02   01   00   99

For permission to use material from this text, contact us by **Web**: http://wwwthomsonrights.com **Fax:** 1-800-730-2215 **Phone:** 1-800-730-2214

ISBN 0-314-22100-X

For more information, contact
Wadsworth/Thomson Learning
10 Davis Drive
Belmont, CA 94002-3098
USA
http://www.wadsworth.com

International Headquarters
Thomson Learning
International Division
290 Harbor Drive, 2nd Floor
Stamford, CT 06902-7477
USA

UK/Europe/Middle East/South Africa
Thomson Learning
Berkshire House
168-173 High Holborn
London WC1V 7AA
United Kingdom

Asia
Thomson Learning
60 Albert Complex, #15-01
Singapore 189969

Canada
Nelson Thomson Learning
1120 Birchmount Road
Toronto, Ontario M1K 5G4
Canada

Documents of Western Civilization

Introduction

In an introductory math class, students work out the answers to math problems. In a first sociology class, they may construct and carry out simple sociological surveys. Students learn, by doing, what it means to be a mathematician or a sociologist. In education courses all over the country, prospective teachers are being taught that students learn best not by hearing or by observing, but by doing. Based upon that premise, we have collected primary documents so that students can actively engage in the exploration and analysis of past events.

This goes to the heart of what history is and what historians do. Historians consult the record of the past to attempt to determine what happened. From the results, we construct an interpretation of the past that will help us to understand how the experiences and acts of our predecessors have helped to make us what we are and how our acts and experiences will, in turn, help to shape the future.

In the middle of this century, an attempt was made to make history one of the social sciences—to invest it with the rigor of scientific method. In one sense this can never happen. Though science has opened new approaches for acquiring information about the past, such as radio-carbon dating and computer-based analysis of numerical data, we cannot prove that particular historical events happened in a certain way; we cannot reenact the Battle of Actium or the burning of Joan of Arc. Historical method is, rather, the method of the detective. We search for clues, we compare the stories of witnesses, we analyze the physical evidence, and we construct a narrative that best fits the results of our search. We even "try" our cases. We publish our results, along with the evidence, and wait for our colleagues, like opposing lawyers, to cross-examine us or bring out evidence pointing to a different conclusion.

Detecting history is fun! The purpose of this collection of documents is to allow students to participate in the fun. Using the documents provided, you can question your professor's description or explanation, or you can construct another narrative. Or you can find clues that support his or her position.

What are the raw materials of history? Where do we find our clues? Traditionally they have come from written sources, which make up most of the documents in this collection. You should ask several questions to help you evaluate the reliability of a written account. Was the writer an eyewitness to or a participant in the event? If not, where did he or she get the information? Who is the intended audience? What does the writer stand to gain by putting a particular "slant" on a description? Are the people being described friends or foes of the writer? A second series of questions one needs to ask of a written source concerns how it relates to other documents. Are the writer's statements supported or contradicted by other accounts?

For example, in collecting documents relevant to the Holocaust, we have included records that reveal various aspects of this complex event. Some of the accounts reflect the perspective of the various victims while others reveal the views of some of the perpetrators. Other documents relate to the Nazi party's program and ideology. Comparing intent, outcome, and perspective allow us to explore the complexities of this tragic event.

This collection of documents was put together following the plan of the Western Civilization textbook by Jackson Spielvogel, second edition, published by West Publishing Company. Its organization into units should, however, make it suitable for use with other texts or standing alone. We had several goals in mind when we suggested yet another collection of documents for Western Civilization. One goal was to integrate social history, the history of women, of working people, and of minorities into the more traditional political, intellectual, and religious history. A second goal was to avoid a mere collection of the most important documents. This book is not the "Greatest Hits of Western Civilization." To create a book of manageable size means finding a balance between the need for many documents, to provide context and continuity, and the need for length, so that an author's words are not misrepresented by being broken into pithy bits. We have chosen to limit the number of topics so that we could include, for each, at least one fairly lengthy segment, accompanied by shorter items that reflect the milieu in which it was created.

Chapter 15: Discovery and Crisis

Unit: 34: European Exploration

From the Diary of Columbus' First Voyage to America, 1492-93

> This is the first voyage and the courses and way that the Admiral Don Christóbal Colón took when he discovered the Indies, summarized except for the prologue that he composed for the king and queen, which is given in full and begins this way:[1]

IN THE NAME OF OUR LORD JESUS CHRIST

Whereas, Most Christian and Very Noble and Very Excellent and Very Powerful Princes, King and Queen of the Spains and of the Islands of the Sea, our Lords: This present year of 1492, after Your Highnesses had brought to an end the war with the Moors who ruled in Europe and had concluded the war in the very great city of Granada, where this present year on the second day of the month of January I saw the Royal Standards of Your Highnesses placed by force of arms on the towers of the Alhambra, which is the fortress of the said city; and I saw the Moorish King come out to the gates of the city and kiss the Royal Hands of Your Highnesses and of the Prince my Lord; and later in that same month, because of the report that I had given to Your Highnesses about the lands of India and about a prince who is called "Grand Khan," which means in our Spanish language "King of Kings"; how, many times, he and his predecessors had sent to Rome to ask for men learned in our Holy Faith in order that they might instruct him in it and how the Holy Father had never provided them; and thus so many peoples were lost, falling into idolatry and accepting false and harmful religions; and Your Highnesses, as Catholic Christians and Princes, lovers and promoters of the Holy Christian Faith, and enemies of the false doctrine of Mahomet and of all idolatries and heresies, you thought of sending me, Christóbal Colón, to the said regions of India to see the said princes and the peoples and the lands, and the characteristics of the lands and of everything, and to see how their conversion to our Holy Faith might be undertaken. And you commanded that I should not go to the East by land, by which way it is customary to go, but by the route to the West, by which route we do not know for certain that anyone previously has passed.

So, after having expelled all the Jews from all of your Kingdoms and Dominions, in the same month of January Your Highnesses commanded me to go, with a suitable fleet, to the said regions of India. And for that you granted me great favors and ennobled me so that from then on I might call myself "Don" and would be Grand Admiral of the Ocean Sea and Viceroy and perpetual Governor of all the islands and lands that I might discover and gain and [that] from now on might be discovered and gained in the Ocean Sea; and likewise my eldest son would succeed me and his son him, from generation to generation forever.

And I left the city of Granada on the twelfth day of May in the same year of 1492 on Saturday, and I came to the town of Palos, which is a seaport, where I fitted out three vessels very well suited for such exploits; and I left the said port, very well provided with supplies and with many seamen, on the third day of August of the said year, on a Friday, half an hour before sunrise; and I took the route to Your Highnesses' Canary Islands, which are in the said Ocean

---

[1] The diary was abstracted by Fray Bartolomé de las Casas. This is his introduction.

Sea, in order from there to take my course and sail so far that I would reach the Indies and give Your Highnesses' message to those princes and thus carry out that which you had commanded me to do.

And for this purpose I thought of writing on this whole voyage, very diligently, all that I would do and see and experience, as will be seen further along. Also, my Lord Princes, besides writing down each night whatever I experience during the day and each day what I sail during the night, I intend to make a new sailing chart. In it I will locate all of the sea and the lands of the Ocean Sea in their proper places under their compass bearings and, moreover, compose a book and similarly record all of the same in a drawing, by latitude from the equinoctial line and by longitude from the west; and above all it is very important that I forget sleep and pay much attention to navigation in order thus to carry out these purposes, which will be great labor.

FRIDAY, AUGUST 3

We departed Friday the third day of August of the year 1492 from the bar of Saltés at the eighth hour. We went south with a strong sea breeze 60 miles, which is 15 leagues, until sunset; afterward to the southwest and south by west, which was the route for the Canaries...

SUNDAY, SEPTEMBER 9

He made 15 leagues that day and he decided to report less than those actually traveled so in case the voyage were long the men would not be frightened and lose courage. In the night they made 120 miles at ten miles per hour, which is 30 leagues. The sailors steered badly, straying to the west by north and even to the half division [west-northwest], because of which the Admiral rebuked them many times.

WEDNESDAY, OCTOBER 10

He steered west-southwest; they traveled ten miles per hour and at times 12 and for a time seven and between day and night made 59 leagues; he told the men only 44 leagues. Here the men could no longer stand it; they complained of the long voyage. But the Admiral encouraged them as best he could, giving them good hope of the benefits that they would be able to secure. And he added that it was useless to complain since he had come to find the Indies and thus had to continue the voyage until he found them, with the help of Our Lord.

After thirty-three days of sailing, Columbus landed at an island the natives called Guanahani, which he named San Salvador.

THURSDAY, OCTOBER 11

He steered west-southwest. They took much water aboard, more than they had taken in the whole voyage. They saw petrels and a green bulrush near the ship. The men of the caravel Pinta saw a cane and a stick, and took on board another small stick that appeared to have been worked with iron, and a piece of cane, and other vegetation originating on land, and a small plank. The men of the caravel Niña also saw other signs of land and a small stick loaded with barnacles. With these signs everyone breathed more easily....

What follows are the very words of the Admiral in his book about his first voyage to, and discovery of, these Indies. I, he says, in order that they would be friendly to us—because I recognized that they were people who would be better freed [from error] and converted to our Holy Faith by love than by force—so some of them I gave red caps, and glass beads which they put on their chests, and many other things of small value, in which they took so much pleasure and became so much our friends that it was a marvel. Later they came swimming to the ships' launches where we were and brought us parrots and cotton thread in balls and javelins and many other things, and they traded them to us for other things which we gave them, such as small glass beads and bells. In sum, they took everything and gave of what they had very willingly. But it seemed to me that they were a people very poor in everything. All of them go around as naked as their mothers bore them; and the women also, although I did not see more than one quite young girl.

And all those that I saw were young people, for none did I see of more than 30 years of age. They are very well formed, with handsome bodies and good faces. Their hair [is] coarse—almost like the tail of a horse—and short. They wear their hair down over their eyebrows except for a little in the back which they wear long and never cut. Some of them paint themselves with black, and they are of the color of the Canarians, neither black nor white; and some of them paint themselves with white, and some of them with red, and some of them with whatever they find. And some of them paint their faces, and some of them the whole body, and some of them only the eyes, and some of them only the nose. They do not carry arms nor are they acquainted with them, because I showed them swords and they took them by the edge and through ignorance cut themselves. They have no iron. Their javelins are shafts without iron and some of them have at the end a fish tooth and others of other things. All of them alike are of good-sized stature and carry themselves well. I saw some who had marks of wounds on their bodies and I made signs to them asking what they were; and they showed me how people from other islands nearby came there and tried to take them, and how they defended themselves; and I believed and believe that they come here from *tierra firme* to take them captive. They should be good and intelligent servants, for I see that they say very quickly everything that is said to them; and I believe that they would become Christians very easily, for it seemed to me that they had no religion. Our Lord pleasing, at the time of my departure I will take six of them from here to Your Highnesses in order that they may learn to speak. No animal of any kind did I see on this island except parrots. All are the Admiral's words.

SATURDAY, OCTOBER 13

As soon as it dawned, many of these people came to the beach—all young as I have said, and all of good stature—very handsome people, with hair not curly but straight and coarse, like horsehair; and all of them very wide in the forehead and head, more so than any other race that I have seen so far. And their eyes are very handsome and not small; and none of them are black, but of the color of the Canary Islanders. Nor should anything else be expected since this island is on an east-west line with the island of Hierro in the Canaries. All alike have very straight legs and no belly but are very well formed. They came to the ship with dugouts that are made from the trunk of one tree, like a long boat, and all of one piece, and worked marvelously in the fashion of the land, and so big that in some of them 40 and 45 men came. And others smaller, down to some in which came one man alone. They row with a paddle like that of a baker and go marvelously. And if it capsizes on them they then throw themselves in the water, and they right and empty it with calabashes that they carry. They brought balls of spun cotton and parrots and javelins and other little things that it would be tiresome to write down, and they gave everything for anything that was given to them. I was attentive and labored to find out if there was any gold; and I saw that some of them wore a little piece hung in a hole that they have in their noses. And by signs I was able to understand that, going to the south or rounding the island to the south, there was there a king who had large vessels of it and had very much gold. I strove to get them to go there and later saw that they had no intention of going. I decided to wait until the afternoon of the morrow and then depart for the southwest, for, as many of them showed me, they said there was land to the south and to the southwest and to the northwest and that these people from the northwest came to fight them many times. And so I will go to the southwest to seek gold and precious stones…

translated by Oliver Dunn and James E. Kelley, Jr. *The Diario of Christopher Columbus's First Voyage to America 1492-1493*. Norman and London: University of Oklahoma Press, 1989.

Michele Soriano: The Gold of the Indies, 1559

From New Spain are obtained gold and silver, cochineal (little insects like flies), from which crimson dye is made, leather, cotton, sugar and other things; but from Pero nothing is obtained except minerals. The fifth part of all that is produced goes to the king, but since the gold and silver is brought to Spain and he has a tenth part of that which goes to the mint and is refined and coined, he eventually gets one-fourth of the whole sum, which fourth does not exceed in all four or five hundred thousand ducats, although it is reckoned not alone at millions, but at millions of pounds. Nor is it likely that it will long remain at this figure, because great quantities of gold and silver are no longer found upon the surface of the earth, as they have been in past years; and to penetrate into the bowels of the earth requires greater effort, skill and outlay, and the Spaniards are not willing to do the work themselves, and the natives cannot be forced to do so, because the Emperor has freed them from all obligation of service as soon as they accept the Christian religion. Wherefore it is necessary to acquire negro slaves, who are brought from the coasts of Africa, both within and without the Straits, and these are selling dearer every day, because on account of their natural lack of strength and the change of climate, added to the lack of discretion upon the part of their masters in making them work too hard and giving them too little to eat, they fall sick and the greater part of them die.

from *Translations and Reprints from the Original Sources of European History*. vol. 3, #3. Philadelphia: University of Pennsylvania Press. 1896.

Unit 35: Disorderly Women and Witchcraft

In the sixteenth and seventeenth centuries, between 60,000 and 100,000 people, most of them women, were executed for alleged witchcraft. Carlo Ginsburg, in his book The Night Walkers, has demonstrated how a benign folk belief could be transformed, by the questions and accusations of officials, into a belief in worship of the devil, accompanied by supernatural acts of malice toward the enemies of the alleged witch. Throughout Europe, folk healers used herbs and incantations to treat illness. In the popular view, a person who could cure illness might also cause it. A particularly malevolent person with such powers might even cause death or failure of crops. Prosecutions for such acts focused on the act itself. A different view of witchcraft developed among theologians who claimed that a human could not do these evils without the aid of the devil. Accusations switched from a focus on actions performed to the condition of being a witch—of having made a pact with the devil. The stereotypical witch was an independent adult woman, often a widow, who did not conform to male ideas of proper female behavior. She was assertive and not under the authority of a male relative.

Innocent VIII: The Witch-Bull of 1484

Desiring with supreme ardor, as pastoral solicitude requires, that the catholic faith in our days everywhere grow and flourish as much as possible, and that all heretical pravity be put far from the territories of the faithful, we freely declare and anew decree this by which our pious desire may be fulfilled, and, all errors being rooted out by our toil as with the hoe of a wise laborer, zeal and devotion to this faith may take deeper hold on the hearts of the faithful themselves.

It has recently come to our ears, not without great pain to us, that in some parts of upper Germany, as well as in the provinces, cities, territories, regions, and dioceses of Mainz, Köln, Trier, Salzburg, and Bremen, many persons of both sexes, heedless of their own salvation and forsaking the catholic faith, give themselves over to devils male and female, and by their incantations, charms, and conjurings, and by other abominable superstitions and sortileges, offences, crimes, and misdeeds, ruin and cause to perish the offspring of women, the foal of animals, the products of the earth, the grapes of vines, and the fruits of trees, as well as men and women, cattle and flocks and herds and animals of every kind, vineyards also and orchards, meadows, pastures, harvests, grains and other fruits of the earth; that they afflict and torture with dire pains and anguish, both internal and external, these men, women, cattle, flocks, herds, and animals, and hinder men from begetting and women from conceiving, and prevent all consummation of marriage; that, moreover, they deny with sacrilegious lips the faith they received in holy baptism; and that, at the instigation of the enemy of mankind, they do not fear to commit and perpetrate many other abominable offences and crimes, at the risk of their own souls, to the insult of the divine majesty and to the pernicious example and scandal of multitudes. And, although our beloved sons Henricus Institoris and Jacobus Sprenger, of the order of Friars Preachers, professors of theology, have been and still are deputed by our apostolic letters as inquisitors of heretical pravity, the former in the aforesaid parts of upper Germany, including the provinces, cities, territories, dioceses, and other places as above, and the latter throughout certain parts of the course of the Rhine; nevertheless certain of the clergy and of the laity of those parts, seeking to be wise above what is fitting, because in the said letter of deputation the aforesaid provinces, cities, dioceses, territories, and other places and the persons and offences in question were not individually and specifically named, do not blush obstinately to assert that these are not at all included in the said parts and that therefore it is illicit for the aforesaid inquisitors to exercise their office of inquisition in the provinces, cities, dioceses, territories, and other places aforesaid, and that they ought not to be permitted to proceed to the punishment, imprisonment, and correction of the aforesaid persons for the offences and crimes above named. Wherefore in the provinces, cities, dioceses, territories, and places aforesaid such offences and crimes, not without evident damage to their souls and risk of eternal salvation, go unpunished.

We, therefore, desiring, as is our duty, to remove all impediments by which in any way the said inquisitors are hindered in the exercise of their office, and to prevent the taint of heretical pravity and of other like evils from spreading their infection to the ruin of others who are innocent, the zeal of religion especially impelling us, in order that the provinces, cities, dioceses, territories, and places aforesaid in the said parts of upper Germany may not be deprived of the office of inquisition which is their due, do hereby decree, by virtue of our apostolic authority, that it shall be permitted to the said inquisitors in these regions to exercise their office of inquisition and to proceed to the correction, imprisonment, and punishment of the aforesaid persons for their said offences and crimes, in all respects and altogether precisely as if the provinces, cities, territories, places, persons, and offences aforesaid were expressly named in the said letter. and, for the greater sureness, extending the said letter and deputation to the provinces, cities, dioceses, territories, places, persons, and crimes aforesaid, we grant to the said inquisitors that they or either of them, joining with them our beloved son Johannes Gremper, cleric of the dioceses of Constance, master of arts, their present notary, or any other notary public who by them or by either of them shall have been temporarily delegated in the provinces, cities, dioceses, territories, and places aforesaid, may exercise against all persons, of whatsoever condition and rank, the said office of inquisition, correcting, imprisoning, punishing, and chastising, according to their deserts, those persons whom they shall find guilty as aforesaid.

And they shall also have full and entire liberty to propound and preach to the faithful the word of God, as often as it shall seem to them fitting and proper, in each and all of the parish churches in the said provinces, and to do all things necessary and suitable under the aforesaid circumstances, and likewise freely and fully to carry them out...

from *Translations and Reprints from the Original Sources of European History*. vol. 3, #4.
Philadelphia: University of Pennsylvania Press. 1896.

Heinrich Krämer and Jacob Sprenger: Malleus Maleficarum, 1486

The "Hammer of Witches" was a handbook compiled by the two inquisitors named in the previous selection (Institoris is the Latinized version of Krämer's name). It is an extensive collection of beliefs about witches, with a code of procedure for detecting and punishing them.

DIRECTIONS FOR THE TORTURE OF A WITCH

The method of beginning an examination by torture is as follows: First, the jailers prepare the implements of torture, then they strip the prisoner (if it be a woman, she has already been stripped by other women, upright and of good report.) This stripping is lest some means of witchcraft may have been sewn into the clothing—such as often, taught by the Devil, they prepare from the bodies of unbaptized infants, (murdered) that they may forfeit salvation. And when the implements of torture have been prepared, the judge, both in person and through other good men zealous in the faith, tries to persuade the prisoner to confess the truth freely; but, if he will not confess, he bids attendants make the prisoner fast to the *strappado*[2] or some other implement of torture. The attendants obey forthwith, yet with feigned agitation. Then, at the prayer of some of those present, the prisoner is loosed again and is taken aside and once more persuaded to confess, being led to believe that he will in that case not be put to death.

Here it may be asked whether the judge, in the case of a prisoner much defamed, convicted both by witnesses and by proofs, nothing being lacking but his own confession, can properly lead him to hope that his life will be spared—when, even if he confess his crime, he will be punished with death.

It must be answered that opinions vary. Some hold that even a witch of very ill repute, against whom the evidence justifies violent suspicion, and who, as a ringleader of the witches, is accounted very dangerous, may be assured her life, and condemned instead to perpetual imprisonment on bread and water, in case she will give sure and convincing testimony against other witches; yet this penalty of perpetual imprisonment must not be announced to her, but only that her life will be spared, and that she will be punished in some other fashion, perhaps by exile.

---

[2] See note 3, below.

And doubtless such notorious witches, especially those who prepare witch-potions or who by magical methods cure those bewitched, would be peculiarly suited to be thus preserved, in order to aid the bewitched or to accuse other witches, were it not that their accusations cannot be trusted, since the Devil is a liar, unless confirmed by proofs and witnesses.

Others hold, as to this point, that for a time the promise made to the witch sentenced to imprisonment is to be kept, but that after a time she should be burned.

A third view is, that the judge may safely promise witches to spare their lives, if only he will later excuse himself from pronouncing the sentence and will let another do this in his place...

But if, neither by threats nor by promises such as these, the witch can be induced to speak the truth, then the jailers must carry out the sentence, and torture the prisoner according to the accepted methods, with more or less of severity as the delinquent's crime may demand. And, while he is being tortured, he must be questioned on the articles of accusation, and this frequently and persistently, beginning with the lighter charges—for he will more readily confess the lighter than the heavier. And, while this is being done, the notary must write down everything in his record of the trial—how the prisoner is tortured, on what points he is questioned, and how he answers.

And note that, if he confesses under the torture, he must afterward be conducted to another place, that he may confirm it and certify that it was not due alone to the force of the torture.

But, if the prisoner will not confess the truth satisfactorily, other sorts of tortures must be placed before him, with the statement that, unless he will confess the truth, he must endure these also. But, if not even thus he can be brought into terror and to the truth, then the next day or the next but one is to be set for a continuation of the tortures—not a repetition,[3] for they must not be repeated unless new evidences by produced.

The judge must then address to the prisoners the following sentence: We, the judge, etc., do assign to you, _____, such and such a day for the continuation of the tortures, that from your own mouth the truth may be heard, and that the whole may be recorded by the notary.

And during the interval, before the day assigned, the judge, in person or through approved men, must in the manner above described try to persuade the prisoner to confess, promising her (if there is ought to be gained by this promise) that her life shall be spared.

The judge shall see to it, moreover, that throughout this interval guards are constantly with the prisoner, so that she may not be left alone; because she will be visited by the Devil and tempted into suicide.

from *Translations and Reprints from the Original Sources of European History*. vol. 3, #4.
Philadelphia: University of Pennsylvania Press. 1896.

---

[3] The law prohibited repeated torture. Inquisitors got around this by claiming that a series of tortures were simply one long session, with periods of respite.

Chapter 16: Absolute and Limited Monarchies

Unit 36: The Growth of Absolutism

Busbecq: Letters from France

Living as we do under a democratic representative system of federal government, it is often difficult for Americans to understand why a great many French men and women during the sixteenth and seventeenth centuries were attracted to the idea of a strong centralized state under the absolute rule of a monarch like Louis XIV. To appreciate the appeal of absolutism, we must first try to understand the situation in which the French found themselves in the late sixteenth century. Divided by the Reformation into mutually antagonistic Protestant and Catholic communities, the French endured three civil wars during the 1500s, as well as a nationwide massacre of thousands of Huguenots[1] on St. Bartholomew's Day in 1572. What these wars and massacres meant for the people of France is vividly described in the following passage selected from a letter written in 1575 by Ogier Ghiselin de Busbecq, the ambassador of the Holy Roman Empire to France.

LETTER XII

I will not weary your Majesty with a full description of the state of France, but content myself with a sketch.

Ever since the commencement of the civil wars which are distracting the country, there has been a terrible change for the worse. So complete is the alteration, that those who knew France before would not recognize her again. Everywhere are to be seen shattered buildings, fallen churches, and towns in ruins, while the traveller gazes horror-stricken on spots which have but lately been the scenes of murderous deeds and inhuman cruelties. The fields are left untilled: the farmer's stock and tools have been carried off by the soldier as his booty, he is plundered alike by Frenchman and by foreigner. Commerce is crippled; the towns lately thronged with merchants and customers are now mourning their desolation in the midst of closed shops and silent manufactories. Meanwhile, the inhabitants, ground down by ceaseless exactions, are crying out at the immense sums which are being squandered for nought, or applied to purposes for which they were never intended. They demand a reckoning in tones which breathe a spirit of rebellion. Men of experience, members of the oldest families in France, are in many cases regarded with suspicion, and either not allowed to come to Court, or left to vegetate at home. Besides the two parties into which Frenchmen are divided by their religious differences, there are also feuds and quarrels which affect every grade of society.... The feuds which separate the leading families of France are more bitter than those described in ancient tragedy; this is the state of feeling which exists between the Houses of Guise, Vendôme and Bourbon, not to mention that of Montmorency, which, through its alliances and connections, has a considerable party of its own.

The Bourbons are the strongest; the Guises have most influence at Court, but this is an advantage which they may lose any day by the death of the King, and then their fall is inevitable....

The district in which the rebellion on religious grounds has struck its deepest roots begins at Rochelle and reaches to the Rhone, comprising the whole of Guienne and Languedoc: it includes Saintonge, Poitou, the Limousin, Perigord, Gascony, the country round Narbonne, &c., &c. Nor

---
[1] French Protestants

is this all; across the Rhone, in Dauphiny itself, Montbrun has seized places, as for instance, Livron, which is now besieged by the Royalists.

In making the statement that the rebels are powerful in Laguedoc and Guienne, I must not be understood to say that the principal cities of those provinces do not obey the King; by meaning is that the insurgents occupy posts of vantage throughout the country, which enable them to render both life and property insecure; there is no peace or quiet for those who are loyal to the King. To drive them from their fortresses would be a most difficult task, for they have formidable positions and strong fortifications, garrisoned by veteran soldiers, who have made up their minds to die rather than trust the King's word. Such, undoubtedly, is their determination, for though peace, which is the only cure for these ills, has lately been freely mentioned, and certain men were at Avignon from Condé and his party, still, up to the present moment, no arrangement has been concluded. True, the King is ready to pledge his word that, if his towns are restored to him, no one shall be troubled on account of his religion; but the memory of Saint Bartholomew is a fatal obstacle; they will place no confidence in his promise, and believe that it is only a stratagem to destroy the survivors of that night.

Such acts of treachery, it would seem, never answer in the long run, whatever the advantage at the time may be!...

It is not that I should regard the situation as hopeless, if there were a prospect of matters taking a turn for the better, but bad as is the present state of things, it is nothing compared to what we may expect any day to see....

from Charles Thornton Forster and F. H. Blackburne Daniell, *The Life and Letters of Ogier Ghiselin de Busbecq*, vol. 2 London, 1881.

Questions:
1. What are the consequences of the French civil wars for the economy and social order of France?
2. What motives does Busbecq suggest were behind these civil wars?
3. How might this kind of violence and turmoil make the idea of a strong royal state an attractive one to the French people?
4. As we will see in the following unit, which deals with constitutional government in England, absolutism is not the only way of dealing with domestic turmoil and civil war. How might a constitutional government have addressed the deep divisions that were destroying France in the sixteenth century?

The Edict of Nantes, 1598

A key figure in the development of absolutism in France was the grandfather of Louis XIV, the Protestant king of Navarre, Henry of Bourbon (1553-1610). Following the assassination of Henry III in 1589, Henry was named heir to the French throne, provided that he would convert to Catholicism. Believing that "Paris is well worth a mass," Henry became a Catholic, ascended the throne as Henry IV, defeated his enemies among the French aristocracy, and ended a century of religious warfare by issuing the Edict of Nantes, a decree which granted the Huguenots a measure of political and religious freedom in France. Aside from restoring to France a degree of stability and internal peace that it had not known for almost a century, the reign of Henry IV also gave further credence to the idea that only a strong royal government could keep the French House in order.

HENRY, BY THE GRACE OF GOD KING OF FRANCE AND OF NAVARRE, TO ALL TO WHOM THESE PRESENTS COME, GREETING:

Among the infinite benefits which it has pleased God to heap upon us, the most single and precious is his granting us the strength and ability to withstand the fearful disorders and troubles which prevailed in our advent in this kingdom. The realm was so torn by innumerable factions and sects that the most legitimate of all the parties was fewest in numbers. God has given us strength to stand out against this storm; we have finally surmounted the waves and made our port of safety,—peace for our state....

We have, by this perpetual and irrevocable edict, established and proclaimed and do establish and proclaim:

1. First, that the recollection of everything done by one party or the other between March, 1585, and our accession to the crown, and during all the preceding period of troubles, remain obliterated and forgotten, as if no such things had ever happened.

3. We ordain that the Catholic Apostolic and Roman religion shall be restored and reestablished in all places and localities of this our kingdom and countries subject to our sway, where the exercise of the same has been interrupted, in order that it may be peaceably and freely exercised, without any trouble or hindrance; forbidding very expressly all persons, of whatsoever estate, quality, or condition, from troubling, molesting, or disturbing ecclesiastics in the celebration of divine service, in the enjoyment or collection of tithes, fruits, or revenues of their benefices, and all other rights and dues belonging to them; and that all those who during the troubles have taken possession of churches, houses, goods or revenues, belonging to the said ecclesiastics, shall surrender to them entire possession and peaceable enjoyment of such rights, liberties and sureties as they had before they were deprived of them.

6. And in order to leave no occasion for troubles or differences between our subjects, we have permitted, and herewith permit, those of the said religion called Reformed to live and abide in all the cities and places of this our kingdom and countries of our sway, without being annoyed, molested, or compelled to do anything in the matter of religion contrary to their consciences, ... upon condition that they comport themselves in other respects according to that which is contained in this our present edict.

8. It is permitted to all lords, gentlemen, and other persons making profession of the said religion called Reformed, holding the right of high justice, to exercise the said religion in their houses.

9. We also permit those of the said religion to make and continue the exercise of the same in all villages and places of our dominion where it was established by them and publicly enjoyed several and divers times in the year 1597, up to the end of the month of August, notwithstanding all decrees and judgments to the contrary.

13. We very expressly forbid to all those of the said religion its exercise, either in respect to ministry regulation, discipline, or the public instruction of children, or otherwise, in this our kingdom and lands of our dominion, otherwise than in the places permitted and granted by the present edict.

14. It is forbidden as well to perform any function of the said religion in our court or retinue, or in our lands and territories beyond the mountains, or in our city of Paris, or within five leagues of the said city.

18. We also forbid all our subjects, of whatever quality and condition, from carrying off by force or persuasion, against the will of their parents, the children of the said religion, in order to cause them to be baptized or confirmed in the Catholic Apostolic and Roman

Church; and the same is forbidden to those of the said religion called Reformed, upon penalty of being punished with especial severity.

21. Books concerning the said religion called Reformed may not be printed and publicly sold, except in cities and places where the public exercise of the said religion is permitted.

22. We ordain that there shall be no difference or distinction made in respect to the said religion, in receiving pupils to be instructed in universities, colleges, and schools; nor in receiving the sick and poor into hospitals, retreats, and public charities....

from Readings in European History, ed. J. H. Robinson. Boston: Ginn, 1906.

Questions:
1. Does the Edict of Nantes grant complete freedom of religious belief and practice in France? If not, how is freedom of religion restricted?
2. What is the position of the Catholic Church under the Edict of Nantes?
3. The Edict of Nantes is a royal decree made by the king alone without either the advice or consent of any other governmental institution. What does that reveal about Henry's attitude toward government in France? What does this tell us about the power of the French monarch and his role in religious affairs?

The Demolition of Feudal Castles, 1626

The French "Wars of Religion" were not fought only over religious differences. They were also a part of the struggle of many of the high nobles of the kingdom against the increasing centralization of authority. In 1626 Louis XIII ordered the destruction of all fortresses in the interior of France, from which these nobles had often defied royal power.

Whereas formerly the assemblies of the states of this realm and those of notable persons chosen to give advice to ourselves, and to the late king, our very honorable lord and father, on important affairs of this realm, and likewise the assembly of the estates of the province of Brittany held by us in the year 1614, have repeatedly requested and very humbly supplicated our said lord and father and ourselves to cause the demolition of many strongholds in divers places of this realm, which, being neither on hostile frontiers nor in important passes or places, only serve as retreats for divers persons who on the least provocation disturb the provinces where they are located;...

For these reasons, we announce, declare, ordain, and will that all the strongholds, either towns or castles, which are in the interior of our realm or provinces of the same, not situated in places of importance either for frontier defense or other considerations of weight, shall be razed and demolished; even ancient walls shall be destroyed so far as it shall be deemed necessary for the well-being and repose of our subjects and the security of this state, so that our said subjects henceforth need not fear that the said places will cause them any inconvenience, and so that we shall be freed from the expense of supporting garrisons in them.

from Readings in European History, ed. J. H. Robinson. Boston: Ginn, 1906.

Questions:
1. What are the reasons that Louis XIII gives for ordering the demolition of the "many strongholds" in the "diverse places" of his realm? What other reasons might have moved Louis to want these fortified areas destroyed?
2. How might Louis XIII have viewed the idea that the different states of the U.S. have the right to maintain forts, arsenals, and state militias?

Cardinal Richelieu: The Political Testament, 1638

No one was more committed to the idea that France's problems could best be solved by concentrating power in the hands of an absolute monarch than Armand Jean de Plessis, Cardinal and Duke of Richelieu (1585-1642). Though he was trained to be a churchman, Richelieu's abiding passions in life were politics and the exercise of power. In 1616, he entered the service of Louis XIII and by 1624 had become not only the favorite of that king but his chief minister as well. From that moment until his death in 1642, Richelieu dedicated himself to the establishment of royal absolutism in France and the expansion of French influence throughout Europe. As Louis XIII's chief minister, he worded tirelessly to make France's nobility and urban elites subject to the will of his royal employer in Paris. And as the king's Secretary of State, he also controlled French foreign policy and was principally responsible for bringing Catholic France into the Thirty Years' War as an ally of the Protestant foes of France's principal European rival, Hapsburg Spain.

Nowhere is Richelieu's grasp of French politics and his acumen for the acquisition of power more pronounced than in his *Political Testament*. Written as an instruction for Louis XIII and his heirs, Richelieu's testament is both an assessment of his accomplishments in office and a collection of shrewd observations regarding how a king should govern his people, increase his power, and hold on to his throne.

When Your Majesty resolved to admit me both to your council and to an important place in your confidence for the direction of your affairs, I may say that the Huguenots shared the state with you; that the nobles conducted themselves as if they were not your subjects, and the most powerful governors of the provinces as if they were sovereign in their offices.

I may say that the bad example of all of these was so prejudicial to the welfare of this realm that even the best courts were affected by it, and endeavored, in certain cases, to diminish your legitimate authority as far as it was possible in order to carry their own powers beyond the limits of reason.

I may say that everyone measured his own merit by his audacity; that in place of esteeming the benefits which they received from Your Majesty at their proper worth, they all valued them only as they satisfied the demands of their imaginations; that the most scheming were held to be the wisest, and often found themselves the most prosperous.

In broadest outline, Sire, these have been the matters with which Your Majesty's reign has thus far been concerned. I would consider them most happily concluded if they were followed by an era of repose during which you could introduce into your realm a wealth of benefits of all types. In order to present the problem to you, it is necessary to look into the nature of the various classes in your realm and the state which it comprises, together with your own role, both as a private and a public person. In sum, what will be indicated is the need for a competent and faithful council, whose advice should be listened to and followed in governing the state. It is to the detailed explanation and urging of this that the remainder of my testament will be devoted.

While the nobility merits to be generously treated if it does well, it is necessary at the same time to be severe with it if it ever fails in what its status demands of it. I do not hesitate to say that those nobles who, degenerating from the virtuous conduct of their forebears, fail to serve the crown constantly an courageously with both their swords and their lives, as the laws of the state require, deserve the loss of the privileges of their birth and should be reduced to sharing the burdens of the common people. Since honor should be more dear to them than life itself, it would be much more of a punishment to them to be deprived of the former than the latter.

All students of politics agree that when the common people are too well off it is impossible to keep them peaceable. The explanation for this is that they are less well informed than the members of the other orders in the state, who are much more cultivated and enlightened, and so if not preoccupied with the search for the necessities of existence, find it difficult to remain within the limits imposed by both common sense and the law.

It would not be sound to relieve them of all taxation and similar charges, since in such a case they would lose the mark of their subjection and consequently the awareness of their station. Thus being free from paying tribute, they would consider themselves exempted from obedience. One should compare them with mules, which being accustomed to work, suffer more when long idle than when kept busy. But just as this work should be reasonable, with the burdens placed upon these animals proportionate to their strength, so it is likewise with the burdens placed upon the people. If they are not moderate, even when put to good public use, they are certainly unjust. I realize that when a king undertakes a program of public works it is correct to say that what the people gain from it is returned by paying the taille. In the same fashion it can be maintained that what a king takes from the people returns to them, and that they advance it to him only to draw upon it for the enjoyment of their leisure and their investments, which would be impossible if they did not contribute to the support of the state....

Power being one of the things most necessary to the grandeur of kings and the success of their governments, those who have the principal management of states are particularly obliged to omit nothing which could contribute to making their masters fully and universally respected. As goodness is the object of love, so power is the cause of fear. It is certain that of all the forces capable of producing results in public affairs, fear, if based on both esteem and reverence, is the most effective, since it can drive everyone to do his duty. If this principle is of great efficacy with regard to internal affairs, it is of no less value externally, since both foreigners and subjects take the same view of redoubtable power and both refrain from offending a prince whom they recognize as being able to hurt them if he so wishes. I have said already that this power of which I speak should be based on esteem and respect. I hasten to add that this is so necessary that if it is based on anything else there is the grave danger that instead of producing a reasonable fear the result will be hatred of princes, for whom the worst possible fate is to incur public disapprobation.

There are several kinds of power which can make princes respected and feared—it is a tree with various branches, all nourished by the same root. The prince ought to be powerful because of his good reputation, because of a reasonable number of soldiers kept continuously under arms, because of a sufficient revenue to meet his ordinary expenses, plus a special sum of money in his treasury to cover frequent but unexpected contingencies, and finally, because of the possession of the hearts of his subjects, as we will clearly demonstrate.—

translated by Henry Bertram Hill. *The Political Testament of Cardinal Richelieu: The Significant Chapters and Supporting Selections.* © 1961. Reprinted by permission of the University of Wisconsin Press.

Questions:
1. What were the principal problems confronting France when Richelieu was named chief minister of Louis XIII? Does Richelieu's assessment bear out Busbecq's observation?
2. How does Richelieu counsel the king with regard to his relationship with his nobles? What function does Richelieu feel that the nobility should play in a royal state?
3. Why does Richelieu refer to the common people as "mules," and what does this reflect about the society and social values of his time?
4. According to Richelieu, what is the most important thing that a king must bear in mind during his reign?

5. How do you think Richelieu would have responded to our society and its representative form of government?

Revocation of the Edict of Nantes, 1685

One of the major problems with absolutism is that everything is ultimately subject to the prejudices of the reigning prince. This was made painfully clear to France's Protestant minority in 1685 when Louis XIV decided to revoke the Edict of Nantes, the decree that his grandfather had issued guaranteeing France's Huguenots a measure of political and religious freedom. Why Louis took this step, after having tolerated this Protestant subjects for the majority of his reign, remains a hotly debated issue. Some have pointed to the influence of his devoutly Catholic mistress, Mme. de Maintenon, while others have pointed to Louis" fear of a future recurrence of the religious wars in France. Whatever the reason behind his decision to turn France's Protestant minority into criminals and to violently persecute them, Louis' revocation of the Edict of Nantes merely served to underscore that in an absolutist state what the king gives he can also take away.

LOUIS, BY THE GRACE OF GOD KING OF FRANCE AND NAVARRE, TO ALL PRESENT AND TO COME, GREETING:

King Henry the Great, our grandfather of glorious memory, being desirous that the peace which he had procured for his subjects after the grievous losses they had sustained in the course of domestic and foreign wars, should not be troubled on account of the religion called Reformed, as had happened in the reigns of the kings, his predecessors, by his edict, granted at Nantes in the month of April, 1598, regulated the procedure to be adopted with regard to those of the said religion, and the places in which they might meet for public worship, established extraordinary judges to administer justice to them, and, in fine, provided in particular articles for whatever could be thought necessary for maintaining the tranquillity of his kingdom and for diminishing mutual aversion between the members of the two religions, so as to put himself in a better position to labor, as he had resolved to do, for the reunion to the Church of those who had so lightly withdrawn from it.

As the intention of the king, our grandfather, was frustrated by his sudden death, and as the execution of the said edict was interrupted during the minority of the late king, our most honored lord and father of glorious memory, by new encroachments on the part of the adherents of the said religion known as Reformed, which gave occasion for their being deprived of diverse advantages accorded to them by the said edict; nevertheless the king, our late lord and father, in the exercise of his usual clemency, granted them yet another edict at Nîmes, in July, 1629, by means of which, tranquillity being established anew, the said late king, animated by the same spirit and the same zeal for religion as the king, our said grandfather, had resolved to take advantage of this repose to attempt to put his said pious design into execution. But foreign wars having supervened soon after, so that the kingdom was seldom tranquil from 1635 to the truce concluded in 1684 with the powers of Europe, nothing more could be done for the advantage of religion beyond diminishing the number of places for the public exercise of the religion known as Reformed, interdicting such places as were found established to the prejudice of the dispositions made by the edicts, and suppressing of the bi-partisan courts, these having been appointed provisionally only.

God having at last permitted that our people should enjoy perfect peace, we, no longer absorbed in protecting them from our enemies, are able to profit by this truce (which we have ourselves facilitated), and devote our whole attention to the means of accomplishing the designs of our said grandfather and father, which we have consistently kept before us since our succession to the crown.

And now we perceive, with thankful acknowledgment of God's aid, that our endeavors have attained their proposed end, inasmuch as the better and the greater part of our subjects of the religion known as Reformed have embraced the Catholic faith. And since by this fact the execution of the Edict of Nantes and of all that has ever been ordained in favor of the said religion known as Reformed has been rendered nugatory, we have determined that we can do nothing better, in order wholly to obliterate the memory of the troubles, the confusion, and the evils which the progress of this false religion has caused in this kingdom, and which furnished occasion for the said edict and for so many previous and subsequent edicts and declarations, than entirely to revoke the said Edict of Nantes, with the special articles granted as a sequel to it, as well as all that has since been done in favor of the said religion.

1. Be it known that for these causes and others us hereunto moving, and of our certain knowledge, full power, and royal authority, we have, by this present perpetual and irrevocable edict, suppressed and revoked, and do suppress and revoke, the edict of our said grandfather, given at Nantes in April, 1598, in its whole extent, together with the particular articles agreed upon in the month of May following, and the letters patent issued upon the same date; and also the edict given at Nîmes in July, 1629; we declare them null and void, together with all concessions, of whatever nature they may be, made by them as well as by other edicts, declarations, and orders, in favor of the said persons of the religion known as Reformed, the which shall remain in like manner as if they had never been granted; and in consequence we desire, and it is our pleasure, that all the temples of those of the said religion known as Reformed situate in our kingdom, countries, territories, and the lordships under our crown, shall be demolished without delay.

2. We forbid our subjects of the religion known as Reformed to meet anymore for the exercise of the said religion in any place or private house, under any pretext whatever, …

3. We likewise forbid all noblemen, of what condition soever, to hold such religious exercises in their houses or fiefs, under penalty to be inflicted upon all our said subjects who shall engage in the said exercises, of imprisonment and confiscation.

4. We enjoin all ministers of the said religion known as Reformed, who do not choose to become converts and to embrace the Catholic, apostolic, and Roman religion, to leave our kingdom and the territories subject to us within a fortnight of the publication of our present edict, without leave to reside therein beyond that period, or, during the said fortnight, to engage in any preaching, exhortation, or any other function, on pain of being sent to the galleys…

7. We forbid private schools for the instruction of children of the religion known as Reformed, and in general all things whatever which can be regarded as a concession of any kind in favor of the said religion.

8. As for children who may be born of persons of the religion known as Reformed, we desire that from henceforth they be baptized by the parish priests. We enjoin parents to send them to the churches for that purpose, under penalty of five hundred livres fine, to be increased as circumstances may demand; and thereafter the children shall be brought up in the Catholic, apostolic, and Roman religion, which we expressly enjoin the local magistrates to see done.

10. We repeat our most express prohibition to all our subjects of the said religion known as Reformed, together with their wives and children, against leaving our kingdom, lands, and territories subject to us, or transporting their goods and effects therefrom under penalty, as respects the men, of being sent to the galleys, and as respects the women, of imprisonment and confiscation.

12. As for the rest, liberty is granted to the said persons of the religion known as Reformed, pending the time when it shall please God to enlighten them as well as others, to remain in the cities and places of our kingdom, lands, and territories, subject to us, and there to continue their commerce, and to enjoy their possessions, without being subjected to molestation or hindrance on account of the said religion known as Reformed, on condition of not engaging in the exercise of the said religion, or of meeting under pretext of prayers or religious services, of whatever nature these may be, under the penalties above mentioned of imprisonment and confiscation. This do we give in charge to our trusty and well-beloved counselors, etc.

Given at Fontainbleau in the month of October, in the year of grace 1685, and of our reign the forty-third.

from *Readings in European History*, edited by J. H. Robinson. Boston: Ginn, 1906.

Questions:
1. How does Louis XIV justify his revocation of the Edict of Nantes?
2. What do the measures announced in this decree mean for those French men and women who were followers of the Reformed faith?
3. How might this historical episode have influenced the religious views of our own Founding Fathers?

Bossuet: from "Politics Drawn from the Very Words of Holy Scripture"

If there is one constant of political life in history, it is the ongoing effort of those in power to justify their right to govern. Typically, this is done by laying claim to a "mandate of heaven," or some divinely ordained right to rule. In the case of Louis XIV, such a claim of divine right was argued most forcefully by Jacques Benigne Bossuet (1627-1704), a member of the French clergy who was appointed Bishop of Meaux in 1681 and achieved fame as a preacher at the court of Versailles. In 1679, he penned a tract entitled "Politics Drawn from the Very Words of Holy Scripture," in which he laid out for his student, the son of Louis XIV, a biblically-justified basis for the absolutist state.

We have already seen that all power is of God. The ruler, adds St. Paul, "is the minister of God to thee for good. But if thou do that which is evil, be afraid; for he beareth not the word in vain: for he is the minister of God, a revenger to execute wrath upon him that doeth evil."[2] Rulers then act as the ministers of God and as his lieutenants on earth. It is through them that God exercises his empire. Think ye "to withstand the kingdom of the Lord in the hand of the sons of David"?[3] Consequently, as we have seen, the royal throne is not the throne of a man, but the throne of God himself. The Lord "hath chosen Solomon my son to sit upon the throne of the

---

[2] See Romans 13:1-7.

[3] II Chronicles 13.8.

kingdom of the Lord over Israel."[4] And again, "Solomon sat on the throne of the Lord."[5]

Moreover, that no one may assume that the Israelites were peculiar in having kings over them who were established by God, note what is said in Ecclesiasticus: "God has given to every people its ruler, and Israel is manifestly reserved to him."[6] He therefore governs all peoples and gives them their kings, although he governed Israel in a more intimate and obvious manner.

It appears from all this that the person of the king is sacred, and that to attack him in any way is sacrilege. God has the kings anointed by his prophets with the holy unction in like manner as he has bishops and altars anointed. But even without the external application in thus being anointed, they are by their very office the representatives of the divine majesty deputed by Providence for the execution of his purposes. Accordingly God calls Cyrus his anointed. "Thus saith the Lord to his anointed, to Cyrus, whose right hand I have holden, to subdue nations before him."[7] …Kings should be guarded as holy things, and whosoever neglects to protect them is worthy of death.…

There is something religious in the respect accorded to a prince. The service of God and the respect for kings are bound together. St. Peter unites these two duties when he says, "Fear God. Honour the king."[8]…

But kings, although their power comes from on high, as has been said, should not regard themselves as masters of that power to use it at their pleasure;…they must employ it with fear and self-restraint, as a thing coming from God and of which God will demand an account.… "It is God who gives you the power. Your strength comes from the Most High, who will question your works and penetrate the depths of your thoughts.…for those who command is the heaviest punishment reserved."[9]

The royal power is absolute. With the aim of making this truth hateful and insufferable, many writers have tried to confound absolute government with arbitrary government. But no two things could be more unlike, as we shall show when we come to speak of justice.

The prince need render account of his acts to no one. "I counsel thee to keep the king's commandment, and that in regard of the oath of God. Be not hasty to go out of his sight; stand not on an evil thing for he doeth whatsoever pleaseth him. Where the word of a king is, there is power; and who may say unto him, What doest thou? Whoso keepeth the commandment shall feel no evil thing."[10] Without this absolute authority the king could neither do good nor repress evil. It is necessary that his power be such that no one can hope to escape him, and, finally, the only protection of individuals against the public authority should be their innocence. This

---

[4] I Chronicles 28.5.

[5] I Chronicles 29.23.

[6] Ecclesiasticus 17:14,15.

[7] Isaiah 14:1.

[8] I Peter 2:17.

[9] Book of Wisdom vi. 2 ff.

[10] Ecclesiasticus 8:2-5.

conforms with the teaching of St. Paul: "Wilt thou then be afraid of power? Do that which is good."[11]

I do not call majesty that pomp which surrounds kings or that exterior magnificence which dazzles the vulgar. That is but the reflection of majesty and not majesty itself. Majesty is the image of the grandeur of God in the prince.

God is infinite, God is all. The prince, as prince, is not regarded as a private person; he is a public personage, all the state is in him; the will of all the people is included in his. As all perfection and all strength are united in God, so all the power of individuals is united in the person of the prince. What grandeur that a single man should embody so much!

The power of God makes itself felt in a moment from one extremity of the earth to another. Royal power works at the same time throughout all the realm. It holds all the realm in position, as God holds the earth. Should God withdraw his hand, the earth would fall to pieces; should the king's authority cease in the realm, all would be in confusion....

Finally, let us put together the things so great and so august which we have said about royal authority. Behold an immense people united in a single person; behold this holy power, paternal and absolute; behold the secret cause which governs the whole body of the state, contained in a single head: you see the image of God in the king, and you have the idea of royal majesty. God is holiness itself, goodness itself, and power itself. In these things lies the majesty of God. In the image of these things lies the majesty of the prince....

from Readings in European History, ed. J. H. Robinson. Boston: Ginn, 1906.

Questions:
1. How is divine kingship justified by Bossuet? Are there any limits on the monarch's power?
2. Given the historical context of seventeenth-century France, what aspects of Bossuet's political theory might have been appealing or objectionable to the French? How might social class have affected one's reaction to Bossuet's ideas?

Louis XIV: Letter to the Officials of Marseilles, 1664

"My glory," "my greatness," and "my reputation" are three phrases that recur constantly in the writings of Louis XIV. Nor were these empty phrases for France's Sun King. In order to achieve glory, greatness, and a reputation that would be remembered by posterity, Louis patronized scores of artists and writers, constructed lavish palaces such as Versailles, and engaged in almost incessant warfare with his neighbors. Not surprisingly, all of these glorious, reputation-enhancing activities cost a considerable amount of money, and Louis spend a good part of his reign looking for way to finance his legacy of greatness.

Fortunately for Louis, he was able to call on the services of Jean-Babtiste Colbert (1619-1683), a cloth merchant's son who by dint of ambition, hard work, competence, and financial acumen managed to get himself ennobled in 1658 and appointed France's Controller-General of finance in 1664. From the time of this appointment until his death, Colbert dedicated himself to finding the money that Louis needed to pay for his foreign campaigns and costly court. Towards that end, he practiced an economic policy known as mercantilism, by which the French state played a significant role in protecting, regulating, and stimulating the economy. This letter was written by Colbert but released under the name of Louis XIV (reigned 1643-1715) to the officials of Marseilles, France's principal port on the Mediterranean.

Considering how advantageous it would be to this realm to reestablish its foreign and domestic commerce,...we have resolved to establish a council particularly devoted to commerce, to be held every fortnight in our presence, in which all the interests of merchants and the means

---

[11] Romans 13:3.

conducive to the revival of commerce shall be considered and determined upon, as well as all that which concerns manufactures.

We also inform you that we are setting apart, in the expenses of our state, a million livres each year for the encouragement of manufactures and the increase of navigation, to say nothing of the considerable sums which we cause to be raised to supply the companies of the East and West Indies;

That we are working constantly to abolish all the tolls which are collected on the navigable rivers;

That there has already been expended more than a million livres for the repair of the public highways, to which we shall also devote our constant attention;

That we will assist by money from our royal treasury all those who wish to reestablish old manufactures or to undertake new ones;

That we are giving orders to all our ambassadors or residents at the courts of the princes, or allies, to make, in our name, all proper efforts to cause justice to be rendered in all cases involving our merchants, and to assure for them entire commercial freedom;

That we will comfortably lodge at our court each and every merchant who has business there during all the time that he shall be obliged to remain there, having given orders to the grand marshal of our palace to indicate a proper place for the purpose, which shall be called the House of Commerce;...

That all merchants and traders by sea who purchase vessels, or who build new ones, for traffic or commerce shall receive from us subsidies for each ton of merchandise which they export or import on the said voyages.

We desire, in this present letter, not only to inform you concerning all these things, but to require you, as soon as you have received it, to cause to be assembled all the merchants and traders of your town of Marseilles, and explain to them very particularly our intentions in all matters mentioned above, in order that, being informed of the favorable treatment which we desire to give them, they may be more desirous of applying themselves to commerce. Let them understand that for everything that concerns the welfare and advantage of the same they are to address themselves to Sieur Colbert...

from *Readings in European History*, edited by J. H. Robinson. Boston: Ginn, 1906.

Questions:
1. What do you think was Colbert's motivation in writing this letter to the officials of Marsielles?
2. What advantages or disadvantages would there have been for the Marseilles officials, merchants and traders under Colbert's policy?
3. How would you, living under a capitalistic economic system, compare or contrast Colbert's policy with the relationship between the government and the business world in the United States?

From the Memoires of the Duke of St. Simon

Louis XIV, no less than his father and grandfather, was keenly aware of the danger that the French nobility posed to both the internal unity of France and his own untrammeled exercise of power. Consequently, he required his aristocracy to spend a considerable amount of time at his court in Versailles. By involving them in tedious court ceremonies and encouraging their rivalries, Louis kept his noble peers from plotting against him, and he also managed to increase their dependence on him.

Given the fact that attendance at court was the best way of influencing state policy and acquiring further wealth and privilege, most of France's nobles were more than willing to play the role that Louis assigned to them at Versailles. One of the noblemen who competed for influence and appointments at the Versailles palace was Louis de Rouvroy, the Duke of Saint-Simon (1675-1755). In this selection from Saint-Simon's *Memoires*, we are treated to a glimpse of what life was like for the rich and famous at the court of the Sun King in the seventeenth century.

The king's great qualities shone more brilliantly by reason of an exterior so unique and incomparable as to lend infinite distinction to his slightest actions; the very figure of a hero, so impregnated with a natural but most imposing majesty that it appeared even in his most insignificant gestures and movements, without arrogance but with simple gravity; proportions such as a sculptor would choose to model; a perfect countenance and the grandest air and mien ever vouchsafed to man; all these advantages enhanced by a natural grace which enveloped all his actions with a singular charm which has never perhaps been equaled. He was as dignified and majestic in his dressing gown as when dressed in robes of state, or on horseback at the head of his troops.

He excelled in all sorts of exercise and liked to have every facility for it. No fatigue nor stress of weather made any impression on that heroic figure and bearing; drenched with rain or snow, pierced with cold, bathed in sweat or covered with dust, he was always the same. I have often observed with admiration that except in the most extreme and exceptional weather nothing prevented his spending considerable time out of doors every day.

A voice whose tones corresponded with the rest of his person; the ability to speak well and to listen with quick comprehension; much reserve of manner adjusted with exactness to the quality of different person; a courtesy always grave, always dignified, always distinguished, and suited to the age, rank, and sex of each individual, and, for the ladies, always an air of natural gallantry. So much for his exterior, which has never been equaled nor even approached.

In whatever did not concern what he believed to be his rightful authority and prerogative, he showed a natural kindness of heart and a sense of justice which made one regret the education, the flatteries, the artifice which resulted in preventing him from being his real self except on the rare occasions when he gave way to some natural impulse and showed that,—prerogative aside, which choked and stifled everything,—he loved truth, justice, order, reason,—that he loved even to let himself be vanquished.

Nothing could be regulated with greater exactitude than were his days and hours. In spite of all his variety of places, affairs, and amusements, with an almanac and a watch one might tell, three hundred leagues away, exactly what he was doing…. Except at Marly, any man could have an opportunity to speak to him five or six times during the day; he listened, and almost always replied, "I will see," in order not to afford or decide anything lightly. Never a reply or a speech that would give pain; patient to the last degree in business and matters of personal service; completely master of his face, manner, and bearing; never giving way to impatience or anger. If he administered reproof, it was rarely, in few words, and never hastily. He did not lose control of himself ten times in his whole life, and then only with inferior persons, and not more than four or five times seriously.

Louis XIV's vanity was without limit or restraint; it colored everything and convinced him that no one even approached him in military talents, in plans and enterprises, in government. Hence those pictures and inscriptions in the gallery at Versailles which disgust every foreigner;

those opera prologues that he himself tried to sing; that flood of prose and verse in his praise for which his appetite was insatiable; those dedications of statues copied from pagan sculpture, and the insipid and sickening compliments that were continually offered to him in person and which he swallowed with unfailing relish; hence his distaste for all merit, intelligence, education, and most of all, for all independence of character and sentiment in others; his mistakes of judgement in matters of importance, his familiarity and favor reserved entirely for those to whom he felt himself superior in acquirements and ability; and above everything else, a jealously of his own authority which determined and took precedence of every other sort of justice, reason, and consideration whatever.

from *Readings in European History*, ed. J. H. Robinson. Boston: Ginn, 1906.

Questions:
1. What do you learn about life at the Versailles royal court as described by Saint-Simon? How might Saint-Simon's description be biased?
2. How does this document add to your understanding of absolutism?
3. Imagine yourself as a White House news correspondent. How would your description of the President of the United States compare to Saint-Simon's description of Louis XIV?

Isabel Charras: Renewed Persecution, 1707

Among the Huguenots who fled France because of the renewed persecution after the revocation of the Edict of Nantes were a group who experienced visions. One of them here describes the deaths she witnessed while still in France.

ISABEL CHARRAS OF LES ROCHES, HALF A LEAGUE FROM ST. GREVE, IN THE VELLAY, DECLARED THE 19TH OF FEBRUARY 1706 (MARCH 5, 1707, NEW STYLE)

I left France in the Year 1696. From the beginning of 1689, for seven years complete, until my leaving that country, I saw in the Vellay abundance of people of every age and sex, that fell into violent agitations of body, in an extraordinary manner; during which they uttered large discourses, very pious, and strongly hortatory of repentance. They had also predictions of the ruin of mystical Babylon, with assurances that the Church would speedily be delivered out of affliction. They were forewarned and directed in a multitude of things, relating either to their own particular conduct, or to the religious assemblies (held almost daily in secret) for their safety. They always spoke good French in the inspiration, though they never could at other times; and during their discourses then, they spoke in the manner as if the Divine Spirit has spoken in them, saying "I tell thee," "I declare to thee," "my child," etc.

As 'tis many years ago, that I have left that country, I will not fix the times of several remarkable particulars here recited, though the certainty of them be no ways the less for it, for I relate nothing, but what I heard and saw, and what I well remember.

One John Heraut of our neighbourhood, and four or five of his children, had all of them the gift of inspiration, the two youngest were, one of five and a half, and the other seven years old, when they first had it. I have seen these many a time, in their ecstasies. Another of our neighbours, named Marliant, had two sons and three daughters in the same state. One of his daughters being big, and within a month of her time, went with the rest of her brothers and sisters, and a boy of her own about seven, to an assembly for worship. In that assembly, she with her child, a brother and sister, were massacred. The brother that escaped was wounded, but recovered. The youngest sister was left for dead among the slaughtered bodies, but had no harm. One of the two sisters butchered was brought home to her father's yet alive, but she died of her wounds a few days after. I was not at that assembly, but saw the sad spectacles of the slain and wounded. What was most remarkable on that occurrence is that the father, the surviving brother and sister, a nephew, and the whole family assured me that those martyrs were forewarned of their death by the inspiration. They acquainted their father as much, in taking leave of him, and asking him blessing, the same evening, when they went out of doors, to go to that assembly, which was by right. When the father beheld these lamentable objects, he did not abandon himself and sink under grief, but on the contrary only said, with pious resignation "The Lord gave, and the Lord has taken away. Blessed be the name of the Lord."

from *A Cry from the Desart*, ed. François-Maximilien Misson, translated by John Lacy. London: B. Bragg, 1707.

Questions:
1. What recourse did a member of France's Protestant minority have if they chose to defy the king's decree? What were the consequences if they chose to stay in France and practice their faith?
2. What does this document reveal about the belief system of these Huguenots?

Fénelon: The Condition of the French Army, 1710

Unfortunately for France and Europe, Louis XIV was inordinately fond of war. Indeed, for Louis, glory and bloodshed appear to have been synonymous with one another. From 1661 until his death in 1715, Louis was almost constantly at war with his neighbors in an effort to extend his kingdom's frontiers and make France the preeminent power in Europe. What this meant for the people of France is vividly described by François de Salignac de la Mothe-Fénelon (1651-1715), an intelligent, ambitious and influential member of the French clergy who served as tutor to Louis XIV's grandson.

If I were to take the liberty of judging the condition of France by the portions of the government that I imperfectly see on this frontier, I would conclude that we survive only because of miracles and that the government is a dilapidated machine that continues to run only on momentum and will collapse at the first shock. I would be tempted to believe that our greatest weakness is that no one perceives the essence of our condition; there even seems to be a desire to avoid seeing it. They do not dare face up to the exhaustion of our forces. Everything is reduced to blind grasping without knowing what is to be had; today's miracle only serves to answer for the one that will be needed tomorrow. They do not wish to perceive the facts and the extent of our ills and to take appropriate steps until it is too late.

This is what I see and intend to say constantly to the wisest and most informed persons.

The soldiers are often unpaid. Often they may even go several days without bread; it is made almost entirely out of oats, badly cooked and full of dirt. These poorly nourished soldiers will fight badly, in all likelihood, and are heard to mutter and say things that should be alarming. The junior officers suffer proportionally even more than the soldiers. The majority, having exhausted all the credit of their families, eat the bad bread and drink the water of the camp. There are a great many of them who lack the means to return from their provinces; many others languish in Paris where they fruitlessly ask help of the minister of war. Others who are in the army are in a state of discouragement and despair that causes us to fear the worst.

The general of our army is unable to prevent disorder among the troops. Can one punish soldiers who are being made to die of hunger and who pillage only to avoid complete exhaustion? Do we wish that they not be in condition to fight? But on the other hand, how many evils are to be expected when they go unpunished? They ravage the whole countryside. The peasants fear the troops that should defend them as much as those of the enemy that seek to attack them. The army can hardly move from one position because it usually has bread for only one day. It is even obliged to remain near the area through which it may receive supplies, that is, Hainaut. It lives only on grain that comes to it from the Dutch.

Our fortifications, which we thought the strongest, have achieved nothing. In Menin and Tournai, we even say that the king was deceived by their masonry, which was worthless. Every stronghold also lacks munitions. If we lose another battle, these places will fall like a house of cards.

The peasants no longer live like human beings, and it is impossible to count on their patience when it is put to such terrible tests. Those who lost their wheat, which was sown in the spring, have no other resources. Others, somewhat more remote, are also about to lose their wheat. Since they have nothing to hope for, they have nothing to fear.

The funds of all the cities are exhausted. Their revenues of ten years hence have been taken for the king, and demands are shamelessly being made, with threats, for new advances that are double those already taken. All the hospitals are filled to overflowing; they refuse the townsmen for whom they were built and are filled with soldiers. Great sums are owed these hospitals but instead of being paid, they are more overcrowded every day.

The French prisoners in Holland are dying of hunger or lack of payment by the king. Those who have had permission to come back to France dare not return to Holland, although they are honor bound to do so, because they cannot pay the cost of the journey or meet the debt that they owe in enemy territory.

Our wounded lack nourishment, linen, and medication. They cannot even find shelter because they are sent to hospitals that are already overcrowded by the king, entirely filled with injured soldiers. Who would risk being wounded in battle, knowing that he will neither be treated nor helped? Soldiers have been heard to say in their despair that if the enemy comes they will lay down their arms. We may judge from this what is to be expected of a battle that will decide the fate of France.

The whole province is damaged by confiscating wagons and killing the peasants' horses. This destroys the tillage for years to come and leaves neither peasants nor troops any hope of surviving. We may judge from this how odious French domination has become to the entire province.

In spite of themselves, the intendants ravage almost as much as the marauders. They steal even from public depots, openly deplore the shameful necessity that reduced them to this, and admit that they cannot keep the promises that they have been ordered to make. They cannot do their duty without cheating on all sides; it is the way of beggars rather than governors. The nation seems completely bankrupt. Notwithstanding violence and fraud, many important transactions must be abandoned whenever they cannot be carried out without advancing two hundred *pistoles* to meet the most pressing needs.

The nation is falling into disrepute and becoming an object of ridicule. Our enemies openly say that the Spanish government which we so despised never fell as low as ours. Our common people, soldiers, and officers no longer evince loyalty, respect, confidence, hope of rising again or fear of authority; everyone seeks only to evade the laws and wait for the end of the war regardless of its price.

If we lose a battle in Dauphiné, the Duke of Savoy will invade an area filled with Huguenots; he could raise several provinces of the realm in revolt. If we lose one in Flanders, the enemy will advance to the gates of Paris. What succor will remain? I know not. God grant that someone knows!

translated by William F. Church, in *The Impact of Absolutism in France: National Experience Under Richelieu, Mazarin, and Louis XIV.* New York: John Wiley & Sons, 1969. Reprinted by permission of John Wiley & Sons, Inc.

Questions:
1. What social, economic, and political consequences did these wars have on France?
2. What do you think were Fénelon's concerns?
3. What similarities and differences do you find between the conduct of war in the eighteenth century and in the present?

Unit 37: Royalists, Roundheads, and Regicides: The Struggle for Power in Seventeenth Century England

James I on the Divine Right of Kings, 1609

Elizabeth I was the last of the English Tudor dynasty, and when she died in 1603 her throne passed to the Stuart king of Scotland, James VI (reigned 1603-1625), the son of the ill-fated Mary, Queen of Scots. Styling himself James I, England's first Stuart monarch promoted peace in Europe, English colonial expansion in North America, and royal absolutism at home. While James' new subjects favored peace and colonies abroad, they were less than enthusiastic about his views on the powers of a monarch. Why this was the case become abundantly clear in the following selection from a speech that James made to the English parliament in 1609. James was, in effect, challenging a centuries-old English governmental tradition. Indeed, James' speech would prove to be the first salvo in an exchange that would plunge England into nearly a century of discord and bloody civil war.

The state of the monarchy is the supremest thing upon earth; for kings are not only God's lieutenants upon earth, and sit upon God's throne, but even by God himself they are called gods. There be three principal similitudes that illustrate the state of monarchy: one taken out of the word of God; and the two other out of the grounds of policy and philosophy. In the Scriptures kings are called gods, and so their power after a certain relation compared to the divine power. Kings are also compared to fathers of families; for a king is truly *parens patriae*, the politic father of his people. And lastly, kings are compared to the head of this microcosm of the body of man.

Kings are justly called gods, for that they exercise a manner or resemblance of divine power upon earth; for if you will consider the attributes to God, you shall see how they agree in the person of the king. God hath power to create or destroy, make or unmake at his pleasure, to give life or send death, to judge all and to be judged by nor accountable to none, to raise low things and to make high things low at his pleasure, and to God are both soul and body due. And the like power have kings: they make and unmake their subjects, they have power of raising and casting down, of life and of death, judges over all their subjects and in all causes and yet accountable to none but God only. They have power to exalt low things and abase high things, and make of their subjects, as they do their money. And to the king is due both the affection of the soul and the service of the body of his subjects....

from *Reading in European History*, ed. J. H. Robinson. Boston: Ginn, 1906.

Questions:
1. How did James challenge English governmental traditions in his speech?
2. What justification did James give to support his position?
3. Compare and contrast James' speech with Bossuet's writing. What similarities or differences to you find?

4. If you were 1) a peasant, 2) a nobleman, and 3) a bishop in England, how might you have reacted to James' speech?

From "The Petition of Right," 1628

James' son, Charles I (reigned 1625-1649) found himself in conflict with the English Parliament from the very beginning of his reign. Like his father, Charles I believed that he was answerable only to God for his actions, and that people and Parliament should unquestioningly follow his divinely-guided lead. Unlike his father, however, Charles was also fond of war and subsequently embroiled England in a conflict with both Spain and France. As is usually the case, wars are expensive and Charles soon found himself in desperate need of tax revenues that required parliamentary approval. When Parliament demanded reforms in exchange for the required revenue, Charles dissolved the legislature, demanded that property owners give him the money that he needed, and then arrested more than seventy knights and gentlemen who refused to comply. When Parliament reconvened in March 1628, is issued "The Petition of Right," a document that condemned the king's actions and demanded that he recognize certain fundamental principles that would later become cornerstones of both the British and American constitutions.

TO THE KING'S MOST EXCELLENT MAJESTY:

We humbly show unto our sovereign lord the king, the lords spiritual and temporal, and commons in Parliament assembled, that whereas it is declared and enacted by a statute made in the time of the reign of King Edward I, commonly "*Statutum de Tallagio non Concedendo*," that no tallage or aid shall be laid or levied by the king or his heirs in this realm without the good will and assent of the archbishops, bishops, earls, barons, knights, burgesses, and the other freemen of the commonality of this realm; and by authority of Parliament holden in the five-and-twentieth year of the reign of King Edward III, it is declared and enacted, that from thenceforth no person should be compelled to make any loans to the king against his will, because such loans were against reason and the franchise of the land; and by other laws of this realm it is provided, that none should be charged by any charge or imposition called a benevolence, nor by any such like charge; by which statutes before mentioned, and other the good laws and statutes of this realm, your subjects have inherited this freedom, that they should not be compelled to contribute to any tax, tallage, aid, or other like charge not set by common consent in Parliament.

2. Yet nevertheless of late divers commissions, directed to sundry commissioners in several counties with instructions, have issued; by means whereof your people have been in divers places assembled and required to lend certain sums of money unto your Majesty, and many of them upon their refusal so to do…have been constrained to make appearance before your privy council and in other places, and others of them have been therefore imprisoned, confined, and sundry other ways molested and disquieted.…

3. And whereas also, by the statute called "The Great Charter of the Liberties of England," it is declared and enacted, that no freeman may be taken or imprisoned or be disseized of his freehold or liberties, or his free customs, or be outlawed or exiled, or in any manner destroyed but by the lawful judgment of his peers, or by the law of the land.…

5. Nevertheless, against the tenor of the said statues, and other the good laws and statutes of your realm, to that end provided, divers of your subjects have of late been imprisoned without any cause showed;…and whereas of late great companies of soldiers and mariners have been dispersed into divers counties of this realm, and the inhabitants, against their will, have been compelled to receive them into their houses,

and there to suffer them to sojourn, against the laws and customs of this realm, and to the great grievance and vexation of the people....

10. They [Parliament] do therefore humbly pray your most excellent Majesty that no man hereafter be compelled to make or yield any loan, benevolence, tax, or such like charge, without common consent by act of Parliament; and that none be called to make answer, or take such oath, or to give attendance, or be confined, or otherwise molested or disquieted concerning the same, or for refusal thereof; and that no freeman, in any such manner as is before mentioned, be imprisoned or detained; and that your Majesty would be pleased to remove the said soldiers and mariners, and that your people may not be so burdened in time to come; and that the foresaid commissions for proceeding by martial law may be revoked and annulled; and that hereafter no commissions of like nature may issue forth to any person or persons whatsoever, to be executed as aforesaid, lest by color of them any of your Majesty's subjects be destroyed or put to death, contrary to the laws and franchise of the land.

11. All which they most humbly pray of your most excellent Majesty, as their rights and liberties according to the laws and statutes of this realm; and that your Majesty would also vouchsafe to declare, that the awards, doings, and proceedings to the prejudice of your people, in any of the premises, shall not be drawn hereafter into consequence or example; and that your Majesty would be also graciously pleased, for the further comfort and safety of your people, to declare your royal will and pleasure, that in the things aforesaid all your officers and ministers shall serve you, according to the laws and statutes of this realm, as they tender the honor of your Majesty and the prosperity of this kingdom.

from *The Constitutional Documents of Constitutional History*, edited by G. Adams and H. Stephens.
New York: Macmillan, 1916

Questions:
1. What rights was Parliament demanding that the king recognize?
2. What does this document tell us about the relationship between England's Parliament and King?
3. If you were a confidant of the King, what advice would you have given him in response to this petition?

A Pamphlet on the Civil War

Charles I's response to the parliamentary demand that he respect traditional English rights was to adjourn the House of Commons and not summon it back into session for eleven years. A rebellion in Scotland, however, forced Charles to summon a new parliament in 1640 for the purpose of approving taxes that were needed to raise an army to defeat the Scottish rebels. This Parliament, which would become known as the "Long Parliament" because it would remain in session for the next thirteen years, made it clear from the moment it convened that Charles would see no money until he accepted a number of constitutional reforms, such as accepting the right of the House of Commons to meet on a regular basis, approve taxes, and make laws. For a monarch imbued with the idea that he need answer to no one but the Almighty, such demands were unacceptable, and in 1642 Charles declared the leaders of Parliament rebels and traitors and plunged England into a civil war. Compare the following selection from a pamphlet of the time with an account written by a Puritan named Wallington.

The war went on with horrid rage in many palaces at one time; and the fire, when once kindled, cast forth, through every corner of the land, not only sparks but devouring flames; insomuch that the kingdom of England was divided into more seats of war than counties; nor has she more fields than skirmishes, nor cities than sieges; and almost all the palaces of lords, and other great houses, were turned everywhere to garrisons of war. They fought at once by sea and land; and through all England (who could but lament the miseries of his country!) sad spectacles were seen of plundering and firing villages; and the fields, otherwise and desolate, were rich only and terribly glorious in camps and armies.

from *Readings in European History*, edited by J. H. Robinson. Boston: Ginn. 1906.

Wallington's Account of the Battle of Edgehill

1642. October the 23rd, being the Lord's day in the forenoon, both the armies met in the midway between Banburn and Stratford-upon-Avon. And they had a very hot skirmish, their ordinance playing very hot from twelve o'clock till three in the afternoon, and made a great slaughter, and then the main forces joined battle, both horse and foot, and had a furious skirmish on both sides, which continued for all that day.

But that which I would take notice of is God's great mercy and providence, which was seen to his poor despised children, that although the enemy came traitorously and suddenly upon them, and unexpectedly, and four of our regiments falling from us, and our soldiers being a company of despised, inexperienced youths which never used to lie in the fields on the cold ground before the enemy, they being strong, old, experienced soldiers. But herein we see God's great mercy, for all that to give us the victory; for, as I hear, the slaughter was in all five thousand five hundred and seventeen; but ten of the enemy's side were slain to one of ours. And observe God's wonderful works, for those that were slain of our side were mostly of them that ran away; but those that stood most valiantly to it, they were most preserved; so that you may see the Lord stands for them that stand for him.

If I could but relate how admirably the hand of Providence ordered our artillery and bullets for the destruction of the enemy; when a piece of ordinance was shot off, what a lane was made in their army! Oh, how God did guide the bullets [of the enemy] also (as I wrote afore at Southam), that some fell down before them, some grazed along, some bullets went over their heads, and some one side of them! Oh, how seldom or never almost were they hurt that stood valiant to it, by their bullets! You would stand and wonder....

from *Readings in European History*, edited by J. H. Robinson. Boston: Ginn, 1906.

Questions:
1. What do we learn about the nature of warfare from these two accounts?
2. What does the Puritan's account of this conflict reveal to us about the religious tensions underlying the English Civil War?

Death Warrant of Charles I, 1649

Civil wars usually do not produce the results that were desired by the people who start them. In the case of the English Civil War, Charles I not only watched the royal cause go down in defeat, but he also found himself a prisoner of parliamentarians he had hoped to dispense with once and for all. As for the parliamentary party, years of warfare and deep divisions among the various factions in Parliament led to a military *coup d'etat* in 1647, which brought the commander of the popular army, one Oliver Cromwell (ruled 1649-1658) to power. A devout Puritan and anti-royalist, Cromwell considered Charles I to be little more than a "papist" and a tyrant. After purging the "Long Parliament" of those who opposed military rule, Cromwell and his supporters compelled the remaining members of the so-called "Rump Parliament" to pass a death warrant ordering the beheading of Charles I on January 30, 1649. Charles' last address merely served to underscore once more the chasm that separated Royalists from Roundheads in seventeenth-century England.

Whereas Charles Stuart, king of England, is, and standeth convicted, attainted, and condemned of high treason, and other high crimes; and sentence upon Saturday last was pronounced against him by this Court, to be put to death by the severing of his head from his body; of which sentence, execution yet remaineth to be done; these [presents] are therefore to will and require you to see the said sentence executed in the open street before Whitehall, upon the morrow, being the thirtieth day of this instant month of January, between the hours of ten in the morning and five in the afternoon of the same day, with full effect. And for so doing this shall be your sufficient warrant. And these are to require all officers, soldiers, and others, the good people of the nation of England, to be assisting unto you in this service.

To Colonel Francis Hacker, Colonel Huncks, and Lieutenant Colonel Phayre, and to every of them.

> Given under our hands and seals.
> John Bradshaw
> Thomas Grey
> Oliver Cromwell
> Etc., etc.

from Readings in European History, edited by J. H. Robinson. Boston: Ginn, 1906.

Charles I: At His Execution, 1649

...[As for the people,] truly I desire their liberty and freedom as much as anybody whomsoever, but I must tell you that their liberty and freedom consist in having of government, those laws by which their life and their goods may be most their own. It is not for having share in government, sirs; that is nothing pertaining to them; a subject and a sovereign are clearly different things. And therefore until they do that, I mean that you do put the people in that liberty, as I say, certainly they will never enjoy themselves. Sirs, it was for this that now I am come here. If I would have given way to an arbitrary way, for to have all laws changed according to the power of the sword, I needed not to have come here; and therefore I tell you (and I pray God it be not laid to your charge) that I am the martyr of the people....

from Readings in European History, edited by J. H. Robinson. Boston: Ginn, 1906.

The Act Abolishing the Office of King in England and Ireland, March 17, 1649

Having horrified the crowned heads of Europe by executing an anointed king, England's "Rump Parliament" went a step further and abolished both the monarchy and the House of Lords. While these actions appeared to leave the House of Commons as England's sole government, real power remained in the hands of the army and its commander, Oliver Cromwell. This fact was underscored in no uncertain way in 1653 when Cromwell, who believed himself an instrument of God's will, forcibly dissolved what he considered to be a hopelessly corrupt Parliament and declared Britain a Commonwealth with himself as its dictatorial Lord Protector. Doubtless, Charles I would have found it ironic that after ten years of bloodshed, England was once more in the hands of a man who believed that his actions were answerable to no one but God.

Whereas Charles Stuart, late king of England, Ireland, and the territories and dominions thereunto belonging, hath, by authority derived from Parliament, been and is hereby declared to be justly condemned, and judged to die, and put to death, for many treasons, murders, and other heinous offenses committed by him, but which judgment he stood, and is hereby declared to be, attained of high treason, whereby his issue and posterity, and all others pretending title under him, are become incapable of the said crowns or of being king or queen of the said kingdom or dominions, or either or any of them, be it therefore enacted and ordained, and it is enacted, ordained, and declared, by this present Parliament and by the authority thereof, that all the people ordained, and declared, by this present Parliament and by the authority thereof, that all the people of England and Ireland, and the dominions and territories thereunto belonging, of what degree or condition soever, are discharged of all fealty, homage, and allegiance which is or shall be pretended to be due unto any of the issue and posterity of the said late king, or any claiming under him, and that Charles Stuart, eldest son, and James, called Duke of York, second son, and all other the issue and posterity of him the said late king, and all and every person and persons pretending title from, by, or under him, are and be disabled to hold or enjoy the said crown of England and Ireland....

And whereas it is and hath been found by experience that the office of a king in this nation and Ireland, and to have the power thereof in any single person, is unnecessary, burdensome, and dangerous to the liberty, safety, and public interest of the people, and that for the most part use hath been made of the regal power and prerogative to oppress and impoverish and enslave the subject; and that usually and naturally any one person in such power makes it his interest to encroach upon the just freedom and liberty of the people, and to promote the setting up of their own will and power above the laws, that so they might enslave these kingdoms to their own lust; be it therefore enacted and ordained by this present Parliament, and by authority of the same, that the office of a king in this nation shall not henceforth reside in, or be exercised by, any one single person; and that no one person whatsoever shall or may have or hold the office, style, dignity, power, or authority of king of the said kingdoms and dominions....

from *Readings in European History*, edited by J. H. Robinson. Boston: Ginn, 1906.

Questions:
1. Both the king and Parliament felt their views were justified. Considering the historical context, what alternatives to warfare existed in trying to resolve this conflict? If you were a member of Parliament, what alternatives would you have recommended?
2. Are there more advantages or disadvantages to resolving conflicts by use of force? What are they?
3. There is an assumption on Parliament's part that by its very nature kingship is contrary to liberty and that only a legislative form of government is conducive to freedom. What do you think of this idea? Is it true that kingship leads to enslavement and parliamentary government equals freedom?

A Leveller's Petition to Cromwell, 1652

As we will continue to see in our survey of modern European history, revolutions often end up betraying their ideals and devouring their supporters. In the case of Commonwealth England, this tendency was best illustrated by the fate of the Levellers, a radical religious group that had enthusiastically supported the anti-royalist cause, the execution of Charles I, and Cromwell's dissolution of Parliament. Nevertheless, Leveller demands were regarded as too radical by Cromwell and his generals, and so the group was suppressed and its leaders imprisoned. As the following selection from a Leveller petition makes clear, this kind of repression was a bitter blow to individuals who had sacrificed so much for the parliamentarian cause.

Sir: God hath honored you with the highest honor of any man since Moses' time, to be head of a people, who have cast out an oppressing Pharaoh....Now you know, Sir, that the kingly conqueror was not beaten by you only as you are a single man, nor by the officers of the army joined to you; but by the hand and assistance of the Commoners; whereof some came in person and adventured their lives with you, others stayed at home, and planted the earth and paid taxes and free-quarter to maintain you that went to war. So that whatsoever is recovered from the Conqueror, is recovered by a joint consent of the Commoners. And now you have the power of the land in your hand, you must do one of these things: First, either set the land free to the oppressed Commoners who assisted you, paid the army their wages, and then you will fulfill the Scriptures and your own [promises]. Or secondly, you must only remove the Conqueror's power out of the kingly hand into other men, maintaining the old laws still....And it is our desire, that the commonwealth's Land, and the lands newly got in, by the Armies victories, out of the oppressors hands, as parks, forests, chases [hunting areas] and the like, may be set free to all who have lent assistance, either of person or purse, to obtain it, and to all that are willing to come in the practice of the government, and be obedient to the Laws thereof.

As for my own part, I am a free man, yea a denizen of England and I have been in the field with my sword in my hand to adventure my life and my blood [against tyrants], for the preservation of my just freedom...and by virtue of my being a freeman [I conceive] I have as a right to all the privileges that do belong to a freeman, as the greatest man in England, whatsoever he be; and the ground and foundation of my freedom I build upon the Grand Charter of England...which I humbly crave to illustrate as follows: that no freeman shall be taken or imprisoned; or be deprived of his freehold or liberties, or be outlawed or exiled, or any wise destroyed, nor we will not pass upon him, nor condemn him but by lawful judgment of his peers, or by the law of the land; we will sell to no man, we will not deny or defer to any man either justice or right. And the privileges contained herein are my birthright and inheritance, which privileges have been ratified and confirmed to the free people of England by the Parliament assembled...

from *The Levellers' Remonstrance Sent in a Letter to His Excellency Lord General Cromwell together with Their Propositions and Desires in the Name of All the Commoners of England.* London: George Morton, 1652.

Questions:
1. What rights were the Levellers demanding of Cromwell?
2. How did the Levellers justify their demands?
3. What comparisons or contrasts do you find between the Levellers' demands and those listed in the Petition of Right (1628)?
4. Why might this document be perceived as revolutionary in its time?

From *The Diary of John Evelyn,* 1652-1655

The Commonwealth was not only a disappointment to the Levellers. As the diary entries of John Evelyn make clear, the Lord Protector's promises of greater freedom and religious toleration also proved illusory. Indeed, Evelyn's chronicle cannot help but remind one of the famous quote by Alphonse Karr, "*Plus ça change, plus ç'est la même chose.*" (The more things change, the more they remain the same.) Unfortunately, as we will see, this will become an all-too-common refrain in the political history of the modern era.

[1652, December] 25 *Christmas day* (no sermon anywhere, so observed it at home, the next day) we sent to *Lewsham,* where was an honest divine preach'd on 21. *Matt: 9.* celebrating the Incarnation, for on the day before, no Churches were permitted to meete: to that horrid passe were they come: 31 I adjusted all accompts, & rendered thanks to God for his mercys to me the yeare past....

[1655, October] 21 A young stranger preach'd on 8: *Luke* 18. showing our greate concerne to take care of what we heard: That the Word was our pardon, our portion, & that by which we should be judg'd. In the Afternoones I frequently stay'd at home to Catechize & Instruct my Familie, those exercises universally ceasing in the parish churches, so as people had no Principles, & grew very ignorant of even the common points of Christianity, all devotion being now plac'd in hearing Sermons and discourses of Speculative & notional things: & our owne *Viccar* very tedious in repeating....

[December] 30 I went to *Lond*: where Dr. *Wild* (at St. *Greg*) preached the funeral Sermon of Preaching, this being the last day, after which *Cromwells* Proclamation was to take place, that none of the Ch: of England should dare either to Preach, administer Sacraments, Teach Schoole &c. on paine of Imprisonment or Exile; so this was the mournfullest day that in my life I had seene, or the Church of *Engl*: her selfe, since the *Reformation*: to the greate rejoicing of both *Papist & Presbyter*:...

> from *The Diary of John Evelyn*, edited by E. S. de Beer. London: Oxford University Press, 1959.
> By permission of Oxford University Press.

Questions:
1. How do these excerpts from John Evelyn's diary support the claim that religion played a role in England's seventeenth-century conflicts? Specifically, how is Evelyn being restricted and why?
2. Based upon the above excerpts, compare and contrast Cromwell's goals and their implementation with those of Charles I.
3. Is it true that "the more things change, the more they remain the same"? Think of a present-day example that would support or reject this argument.

The Restoration: Excerpts from the Memoires of Reresby and the Diary of Evelyn regarding James II, 1685-1686

The Commonwealth outlived its Protector by little more than a year. In 1660, Cromwell's generals invited Charles I's son to return home from exile in France and ascend the English throne as Charles II (reigned 1660-1685). While Charles II shared his father's views on the prerogatives of the monarchy, he wisely avoided conflicts with Parliament by respecting its role in the governance of the country. The same cannot be said of Charles' brother and heir, James II (reigned 1685-1688). Raised in the court of Louis XIV, where his family had sought refuge during the civil war, James had imbibed a great many of the Sun King's political and religious views. Not only was James a committed absolutist, but he was also a devout Catholic. As the following selections make clear, for a country like England which had been Protestant for well over a century, the prospect of a Roman Catholic absolute king did not sit well with a great many of James' English subjects.

RERESBY

November 20, 1685. The popish party at this time behaved themselves with an insolence which did them a prejudice. The king of France continued to practice all the cruelties imaginable towards the Protestants in France to make them turn papists, commanding that all extremities should be used but death,—as seizing their lands, razing their temples and houses, taking all their goods, putting them into prisons, quartering dragoons with them to eat up their estates and to watch them that they should not sleep till they changed their religion. Many of them fled into all parts as they could escape, poor and naked; for their estates were stopped and themselves condemned to the gallows if they were taken attempting to fly.

March 1, 1686. Though it could not be said that there was as yet any remarkable invasion upon the rights of the Church of England, yet the king gave all the encouragement he could to the increase of his own, by putting more papists into office, but especially in Ireland; by causing or allowing popish books to be printed and sold and cried publicly; by publishing some popish papers found in the late king's closet and the declaration of his dying a papist and the manner of it;…by sending my Lord Castlemain upon a solemn embassy to the pope, and many other such things; which made all men expect that more would follow of a greater concern.

EVELYN

December 29, 1686. I went to hear the musiq of the Italians in the New Chapel, now first open'd publickly at Whitehall for the Popish service.… The throne where the King and Queene sit is very glorious, in a closet above, just opposite to the altar. Here was saw the Bishop in his mitre and rich copes, with 6 or 7 Jesuits and others in rich copes, sumptuously habited, often taking off and putting on the Bishop's mitre, who satte in a chair with arms pontifically, was ador'd and cens'd by 3 Jesuits in their copes; then he went to the altar and made divers cringes, then censing the images and glorious tabernacle plac'd on the altar, and now and then changing place: the crosier which was of silver was put into his hand with a world of mysterious ceremony, the musiq playing with singing. I could not have believed I should ever have seene such things in the King of England's Palace, after it had pleas'd God to enlighten this Nation; but owr greate sin has, for the present, eclips'd the blessing, which I hope He will in mercy and his good time restore to it purity.…

from *Readings in European History*, edited by J. H. Robinson. Boston: Ginn, 1906.

Questions:
1. How were Protestants being treated in France under Louis XIV (reigned 1643-1715)?
2. Why might the treatment of French Protestants be a concern for British Anglicans and Puritans?
3. What actions was James II taking to strengthen Catholicism in England and Ireland?
4. Why did Evelyn find the church services he described so offensive?

The Glorious Revolution of 1688: The Bill of Rights, 1689

Probably no monarch has been better at arousing the worst feats of his subjects than James II. Aside from openly practicing his Catholicism, James also began to elevate Catholics to leading posts in the military and in the central government. Furthermore, he began a series of maneuvers that were aimed at packing Parliament with his supporters. All of this proved too much for the English gentry, who entered into negotiations with William of Orange, the husband of James' eldest daughter, Mary, and the champion of Protestant Europe against Louis XIV of France. In 1688, William and Mary landed in England with a small army and marched, unopposed, to London, where they were proclaimed king and queen of Britain. James II fled to France and spent the rest of his life engaged in futile efforts to regain his throne.

Due to the fact that William and Mary's invasion had resulted in little bloodshed or social disorder, this event became known as the Glorious Revolution. Aside from ridding England of the last of the absolutist Stuarts, this revolution also produced the Declaration (or Bill) of Rights, which was presented to, and accepted by, William and Mary before they took the throne. As you will see from the selection of that Declaration printed below, this Bill is one of the great landmarks in the development of limited constitutional government.

And thereupon (in response to letters from William of Orange) the said lords spiritual and temporal and commons, pursuant to their respective letters and elections, being now assembled in a full and free representation of this nation, taking into their most serious consideration the best means for attaining the ends aforesaid, do in the first place (as their ancestors in like case have usually done), for the vindicating and asserting their ancient rights and liberties, declare:

1. That the pretended power of suspending laws, or the execution of laws, by regal authority, without consent of parliament, is illegal.

2. That the pretended power of dispensing with laws, or the execution of laws, by regal authority, as it hath been assumed and exercised of late, is illegal.

4. That levying money for or to the use of the crown by pretense of prerogative, without grant of parliament, for longer time or in other manner than the same is or shall be granted, is illegal.

5. That it is the right of the subjects to petition the king, and all commitments and prosecutions for such petitioning are illegal.

6. That the raising or keeping of a standing army within the kingdom in time of peace, unless it be with consent of parliament, is against law.

7. That the subjects which are Protestants may have arms for their defense suitable to their conditions, and as allowed by law.

8. That election of members of parliament ought to be free.

9. That the freedom of speech, and debates or proceedings in parliament, ought not to be impeached or questioned in any court or place out of parliament.

10. That excessive bail ought not to be required, nor excessive fines imposed, nor cruel and unusual punishments inflicted.

11. That jurors ought to be duly impaneled and returned, and jurors which pass upon men in trials for high treason ought to be freeholders.

13. And that for redress of all grievances, and for the amending, strengthening, and preserving of the laws, parliament ought to be held frequently....

The said lords spiritual and temporal, and commons, assembled at Westminster, do resolve that William and Mary, prince and princess of Orange, be, and be declared king and queen of England, France, and Ireland, and the dominions thereunto belonging,...

from *Readings in English History Drawn from the Original Sources*, edited by Edward P. Cheyney. Boston: Ginn, 1922.

Questions:
1. What rights did this document secure for Parliament? List some historical examples that would demonstrate how these rights had been violated in the past and how this justified Parliament's need to have these powers guaranteed in writing?
2. Both England and France had experienced political crises in the seventeenth century. What was the outcome of these crises? Compare and contrast the distribution of political power in England and France on the eve of the eighteenth century.
3. Imagine that you are living in 1700. Would you rather be an English or a French nobleman? Give specific examples to justify your choice.

John Locke: Two Treatises on Civil Government, 1690

Even though England was no stranger to revolutions, the deposing of an anointed and crowned king was still a highly controversial and problematic act in the seventeenth and eighteenth centuries. Fortunately for the English revolutionaries of 1688, they had an able defender of their actions in John Locke (1632-1704). A philosopher, scientist, Lord Ashley, the Earl of Shaftesbury, Locke shared his employer's views of James and as a result was declared a traitor and forced to flee to Holland (1683-1689). When William and Mary ascended the English throne, Locke returned home and penned the "Two Treatises on Civil Government," an essay that provided an intellectual justification for both constitutional government and revolutionary actions against its foes. Indeed, Locke's Treatises, which would go on to inspire the American Founding Fathers, have continued to exercise a powerful influence on the political life and thought of the West to the present day.

OF THE BEGINNING OF POLITICAL SOCIETIES

...Men being, as has been said, by nature all free, equal, and independent, no one can be put out of this condition and subjected to the political power of another without his own consent. The only way whereby any one divests himself of his natural liberty, and puts on the bonds of civil society, is by agreeing with other men to join and unite into a community for their comfortable, safe, and peaceable living one among another, in a secure enjoyment of their properties and a greater security against any that are not of it. This any number of men may do, because it injures not the freedom of the rest; they are left as they were in the liberty of the state of nature. When any number of men have so consented to make one community or government, they are thereby incorporated and make one body politic wherein the majority have a right to act and govern the rest.

For when any number of men have, by the consent of every individual, made a community, they have thereby made that community one body, with a power to act as one body, which is only by the will and determination of the *majority*. For that which moves any community, which is the consent of the individuals of it, and it being necessary to that which is one body to move one way, it is necessary the body should move that way where the greater force carries it, which is the consent of the majority; or else it is impossible it should act or continue one body, one community, which the consent of every individual that united into it agree that it should. Therefore, every one is bound by that consent to be governed by the majority. And therefore we see that in assemblies empowered by positive laws, where no other number is set by that positive law which empowers them, the act of the majority passes for the act of the whole....

Whosoever, therefore, out of a state of nature unite into a community must be understood to give up all the power necessary for the purposes for which they unite into society to the majority of the community, unless they expressly agreed in any number greater than the majority. And this is done by simply agreeing to unite into one political society, which is all the compact that is, or needs be, between the individuals that enter into or make up a commonwealth. As thus that which begins and actually constitutes any political society is nothing but the consent of any number of freemen capable of a majority to unite and incorporate into such a society. And this is that, and that only, which did or could give beginning to any lawful government in the world....

OF THE ENDS OF POLITICAL SOCIETY AND GOVERNMENT

If man in the state of nature be so free, as has been said, if he be absolute lord of his own person and possessions, equal to the greatest, and subject to nobody, why will he part with his freedom, why will he give up his independence and subject himself to the rule and control of any other power? To which it is obvious to answer that though in the state of nature he has such a right, yet the enjoyment of it is very uncertain and constantly exposed to the attacks of others; for all being kings as much as he, every man his equal, and the greater part not strict observers of equity and justice, the enjoyment of the property he has in this state is very unsafe, very insecure. This makes him willing to give up a condition which, however free, is full of fears, and continual dangers; and it is not without reason that he seeks out and is willing to join in society with others, who are already united, or have mind to unite, for the mutual preservation of their lives, liberties, and estates, which I call by the general name "property."

from *Readings in European History*, edited by J. H. Robinson. Boston: Ginn, 1906.

Questions:
1. What did Locke mean by the "state of nature"? What are the disadvantages of living in the state of nature?
2. According to Locke, what is a "civil society" and how is it formed?
3. What restrictions are placed on the legislative power under Locke's political system?
4. Why should an individual give up one's liberties as exist in the state of nature and be restricted by civil society? What protections does an individual have against an abusive government, according to Locke? What potential violations of the trust given to the government did Locke outline?
5. If individuals have a right to rebel against an abusive government, wouldn't this potentially result in chaos? How did Locke respond to such concerns? Do you agree with him?
6. What is the historical context of this document? That is, what relationship is between John Locke's political theory and what was happening in England?

Thomas Hobbes, *Leviathan*, 1651

The royalist party in England also had its apologists. Foremost among them was Thomas Hobbes (1588-1679). Hobbes was a noted scientist and teacher who had traveled widely. Indeed, during his lifetime, Hobbes met and befriended such intellectual luminaries as Ben Johnson, Francis Bacon, Galileo, and Rene Descartes. With regard to politics, Hobbes did not believe in the "sweet reason" of his fellow men, nor was he convinced of the wisdom of vesting sovereign power in the hands of the people. These political views were shaped in no small way by the fact that he was the protégé of the Cavendishes, a powerful aristocratic English family that was loyal to the Stuart cause during the civil war. Living through the horrors of that conflict, Hobbes became convinced that there was only one way to restore peace and order in England. In his essay, *Leviathan*, Hobbes presents his solution to the problem of civil disorder in a forceful and compelling way. It is an argument that we will come across again, albeit in different clothing, throughout the modern period.

Nature has made men so equal in the faculties of the body and mind, as that, though there be found one man sometimes manifestly stronger in body or of quicker mind than another, yet, when all is reckoned together, the difference between man and man is not so considerable that one man can thereupon claim to himself any benefit to which another may not pretend as well as he. For, as to the strength of body, the weakest has strength enough to kill the strongest, either by secret machination or by confederacy with others that are in the same danger with himself.

And, as to the faculties of the mind, setting aside the arts grounded upon words and especially that skill of proceeding upon general and infallible rules called science, which very few have and but in few things, as being not a native faculty born with us, nor attained, as prudence, while we look after somewhat else, I find yet a greater equality amongst men than that of strength. For prudence is but experience, which equal time equally bestows on all men in those things they equally apply themselves unto. That which may perhaps make such equality incredible is but a vain conceit of one's own wisdom, which almost all men think they have in a greater degree than the vulgar, that is, than all men but themselves, and a few others whom by fame or for concurring with themselves they approve. For such is the nature of men that, howsoever they may acknowledge many others to be more witty or more eloquent or more learned, yet they will hardly believe there be many so wise as themselves, for they see their own wit at hand and other men's at a distance. But this proveth rather that men are in that point more equal than unequal. For there is not a greater sign of the equal distribution of anything than that every man is contented with his share.

From this equality of ability arises equality of hope in the attaining of our ends. And therefore if any two men desire the same thing, which nevertheless they cannot both enjoy, they become enemies; and in the way to their end, which is principally their own preservation, and sometimes their pleasure only, endeavor to destroy or subdue one another. And from hence it comes to pass that where an invader has no more to fear than another man's single power, if one plant, sow, build, or possess an estate, others may be expected to come prepared with forces united to dispossess and deprive him, not only of the fruit of his labor, but also of his life or liberty. And the invader again is in the like danger of another....

It is certain, that during the time men live without a common power to keep them all in awe, they are in that condition which is called war; and such a war is of every man against every man. For war consists not in battle only, or the act of fighting, but in a time span, where the will to fight is sufficiently known; and therefore the notion of time is to be considered in the nature of war as it is in the nature of weather. For as the nature of war consists not in actual fighting but in the known disposition thereto during all the time there is no assurance to the contrary. All other time is peace.

Whatsoever therefore is consequent to a time of war where every man is enemy to every man, the same is consequent to the time wherein men live without other security than what their own strength and their own invention shall furnish them withal. In such condition there is no place for industry, because the fruit thereof is uncertain, and consequently no culture of the earth, no navigation nor use of the commodities that may be imported by sea, no commodious building, no instruments of moving and removing such things as require much force, no knowledge of the face of the earth; no account of time, no arts, no letters, no society, and which is worst of all, continual fear and danger of violent death, and the life of man solitary, poor, nasty, brutish, and short.

It may seem strange to some man that has not well weighed these things that Nature should thus dissociate and render men apt to invade and destroy one another; and he may therefore, not trusting to this inference made from the passions, desire perhaps to have the same confirmed by experience. Let him therefore consider with himself, when taking a journey, he arms himself and seeks to go well accompanied; when going to sleep, he locks his doors; when even in his house, he locks his chests; and this when he knows there are laws and public officers armed to revenge all injuries done to him; what opinion he has of his fellow-subjects, when he rides armed; of his fellow-citizens, when he locks his doors; and of his children and servants, when he locks his chests. Does he not there as much accuse mankind by his actions as I do by my words? But neither of us accuse man's nature in it. The desires and other passions of man are in themselves no sin. Nor more are the actions that proceed from those passions, till they know a law that forbids them; which, till laws be made, they cannot know, nor can any law be made till they have agreed upon the person that shall make it.

It may perhaps be thought there was never such a time nor condition of war as this; and I believe it was never generally so over all the world, but there are many places where they live so now. For the savage people in many places of America, except the government of small families the concord whereof depends on natural lust, have no government at all, and live at this day in that brutish manner as I said before. However, it may be perceived what manner of life there would be where there were no common power to fear, by the manner of life which men that have formerly lived under a peaceful government use to degenerate into, in a civil war.

But, though there had never been any time wherein particular men were in a condition of war one against another, yet in all times kings and persons of sovereign authority, because of their independence, are in continual jealousies and in the state and posture of gladiators, having their weapons pointing, and their eyes fixed on one another, that is, their forts, garrisons, and guns, upon the frontiers of their kingdoms, and continual spies upon their neighbours: which is a posture of war. But because they uphold thereby the industry of their subjects, there does not follow from it that misery which accompanies the liberty of particular men.

To this war of every man against every man this also is consequent, that nothing can be unjust. The notions of right and wrong, justice and injustice, have there no place. Where there is no common power, there is no law; where no law, no injustice. Force and fraud are in war the two cardinal virtues. Justice and injustice are none of the faculties neither of the body nor mind. If they were, they might be in a man that were alone in the world, as well as his senses and passions. They are qualities that relate to men in society, not in solitude. It is consequent also to the same condition that there be no propriety, no dominion, no 'mine,' and 'thine,' distinct, but only that to be every man's that he can get, and for so long as he can keep it. And thus much for the ill condition which man by mere nature is actually placed in, though with a possibility to come out of it, consisting partly in the passions, partly in his reason.

The passions that incline men to peace are fear of death, desire of such things as are necessary to commodious living, and a hope by their industry to obtain them. And reason suggests convenient articles of peace, upon which men may be drawn to agreement. These articles are they which otherwise are called the Laws of Nature, whereof I shall speak more particularly in the two following chapters....

from *The Harvard Classics*, vol. 34. Edited by Charles W. Eliot. New York: F. F. Collier & Sons, 1910.

Questions:
1. What does Hobbes think is man's natural state of being? Do you agree or disagree with him and why?
2. According to Hobbes, what are the origins of a civil society and why would an individual choose to live in one?
3. How is our social organization different from that of other creatures in nature?
4. How might the historical context have influenced Hobbes' political views?
5. If you have read William Golding's *Lord of the Flies*, how would you compare or contrast that novel with Hobbes' perspective?
6. Imagine that John Locke and Thomas Hobbes participated in a debate on the role of the state and its relationship to individuals' rights. What points would they have made? Be sure to consider historical events they may have used to support their positions.

Chapter 17: Skepticism, Science, and the Supernatural: The Search for "Truth" in the Seventeenth Century

Unit 38: The Scientific Revolution

In our time, the term "revolution" has a predominantly political meaning. It connotes the overthrow of an existing status quo and it evokes images of palaces being stormed by mobs, guerilla warfare in the countryside, or large-scale civil disobedience against oppressive regimes. In the seventeenth century, however, "revolution" was normally used to indicate the recurrent circular orbits of various physical bodies in space and time.

It is important to bear in mind both the modern and seventeenth-century senses of "revolution" when examining the "new science" of the 1600s. For the "Scientific Revolution" of this century was often concerned with questions about the orbits and movements of physical objects in space and time, and the ideas that came out of these disputes quite literally overturned the accepted notions of how our world operates. Indeed, much of the so-called "new science" of this time period was not so much about revolutionary inventions or discoveries, but about seeing pre-existing evidence from a different perspective and in a completely new light.

Galileo Galilei: *Letters to Johannes Kepler*

Nowhere was this new world view more evident than in the work of the Italian astronomer, mathematician, and physicist, Galileo Galilei (1564-1642). Inspired by the heliocentric theories of the Polish mathematician-astronomer, Nicolaus Copernicus, and using the just-invented telescope, Galileo confirmed the Copernican theory that our earth is one of several planets that revolve around a stationary sun. This discovery, in tandem with others about the moon, sunspots, gravity, and planetary movement, completely contravened the seventeenth-century European view of the universe and forced the West to look at the sky above in a new way. In the selections below, we not only get a sense of Galileo's revolutionary approach to science but also of the dangers that await someone who dares to turn the accepted view of the world on its head.

On the Hazards of publishing his Views

I count myself happy, in the search after truth, to have so great an ally as yourself, and one who is so great a friend of the truth itself. It is really pitiful that there are so few who seek truth, and who do not pursue a perverse method of philosophizing. But this is not the place to mourn over the miseries of our times, but to congratulate you on your splendid discoveries in conformation of truth. I shall read your book to the end, sure of finding much that is excellent in it. I shall do so with the more pleasure, because *I have been for many years an adherent of the Copernican system*, and it explains to me the causes of many of the appearances of nature which are quite unintelligible on the commonly accepted hypothesis. *I have collected many arguments for the purpose of refuting the latter;* but I do not venture to bring them to the light of publicity, for fear of sharing the fate of our master, Copernicus, who, although he has earned immortal fame with some, yet with very many (so great is the number of fools) has become an object of ridicule and scorn. I should certainly venture to publish my speculations if there were more people like you. But this not being the case, I refrain from such an undertaking.

ON THE TELESCOPE

You must know that about two months ago a report was spread here that in Flanders a spy-glass had been presented to Prince Maurice, so ingeniously constructed that it made the most distant objects appear quite near, so that a man could be seen quite plainly at a distance of two *miglia*. This result seemed to me so extraordinary that it set me thinking; and as it appeared to me that it depended upon the theory of perspective, I reflected on the manner of constructing it, in which I was at length so entirely successful that I made a spy-glass which far surpasses the report of the Flanders one. As the news had reached Venice that I had made such an instrument, six days ago I was summoned before their highnesses the signoria, and exhibited it to them, to the astonishment of the whole senate. Many noblemen and senators, although of a great age, mounted the steps of the highest church towers at Venice, in order to see sails and shipping that were so far off that it was two hours before they were seen steering full sail into the harbor without my spy-glass, for the effect of my instrument is such that it makes an object fifty *miglia* off appear as large and near as if it were only five.

ON HIS CRITICS

You are the first and almost the only person who, even after but a cursory investigation, has, such is your openness of mind and lofty genius, given entire credit to my statements.... We will not trouble ourselves about the abuses of the multitude, for against Jupiter even giants, to say nothing of pigmies, fight in vain. Let Jupiter stand in the heavens, and let the sycophants bark at him as they will.... In Pisa, Florence, Bologna, Venice, and Padua many have seen the planets; but all are silent on the subject and undecided, for the greater number recognize neither Jupiter nor Mars and scarcely the moon as planets. At Venice one man spoke against me, boasting that he knew for certain that my satellites of Jupiter, which he had several times observed, were not planets because they were always to be seen with Jupiter, and either all or some of them now followed and now preceded him. What is to be done? Shall we decide with Democritus or Heraclitus? I think, my Kepler, we will laugh at the extraordinary stupidity of the multitude. What do you say to the leading philosophers of the faculty here, to whom I have offered a thousand times of my own accord to show my studies, but who with the lazy obstinacy of a serpent who has eaten his fill have never consented to look at planets, nor moon, nor telescope? Verily, just as serpents close their ears, so do these men close their eyes to the light of the truth. These are great matters; yet they do not occasion me any surprise. People of this sort think that philosophy is a kind of book like the Aeneid or the Odyssey, and that the truth is to be sought, not in the universe, nor in nature, but (I use their own words) *by comparing texts!* How you would laugh if you heard the things the first philosopher of the faculty at Pisa brought against me in the presence of the Grand Duke, for he tried, now with logical arguments, now with magical adjurations, to tear down and to argue the new planets out of heaven.

from *The Ideas that Have Influenced Civilization, in the Original Documents*. Volume 5.
Edited by Oliver J. Thatcher. Milwaukee: Roberts-Manchester, 1901.

Questions:
1. Copernicus published his *Revolutions of the Heavenly Spheres*, setting forth the theory of a heliocentric universe, in 1542, nearly a century before Galileo wrote these letters. What do Galileo's letters reveal about his fellow philosophers and their willingness to entertain such new ideas?
2. Does Galileo foresee his new theories eventually triumphing over the old? If so, how does he suggest it will happen?

From Galileo: *Dialogue on the Two Chief Systems of the World,* 1632

SALVIATI: Whenever you wish to reconcile what your senses show you with the soundest teachings of Aristotle, you will have no trouble at all. Does not Aristotle say that because of the great distance, celestial matters cannot be treated very definitely?

SIMPLICIO: He does say so, quite clearly.

SALVIATI: Does he not also declare that what sensible experience shows ought to be preferred over any argument, even one that seems to be extremely well founded? And does he not say this positively and without a bit of hesitation?

SIMPLICIO: He does.

SALVIATI: Then of the two propositions, both of them Aristotelian doctrines, the second—which says it is necessary to prefer the senses over arguments—is a more solid and definite doctrine than the other, which holds the heavens to be inalterable. Therefore it is better Aristotelian philosophy to say, "Heaven is alterable because my senses tell me so," than to say, "Heaven is inalterable because Aristotle was so persuaded by reasoning." Add to this that we possess a better basis for reasoning about celestial things than Aristotle did. He admitted such perceptions to be very difficult for him by reason of the distance from his senses, and conceded that one whose senses could better represent them would be able to philosophize about them with more certainty. Now we, thanks to the telescope, have brought the heavens thirty or forty times closer to us than they were to Aristotle, so that we can discern many things in them that he could not see; among other things these sunspots, which were absolutely invisible to him. Therefore we can treat of the heavens and the sun more confidently than Aristotle could.

from *Dialogue Concerning the Two Chief World Systems—Ptolemaic & Copernican,*
translated by Stillman Drake. Berkeley: University of California Press. 1967.

Questions:
1. Seventeenth-century natural philosophy, with its roots in Aristotle's ideas (384-322 BCE) along with modifications made during the medieval period and Renaissance, still made a distinction between the physical nature of the heavenly bodies and of earth. While the earth was subject to decay, the other bodies of the universe were perfect and unchanging. Therefore, irregularly-moving bodies, like comets, were believed to be in the earth's atmosphere or between the earth and moon. Given these perceptions, what is so "revolutionary" about Galileo's discussion of sunspots? Give some specific examples from Salviati's discussion.
2. How did Galileo try to use Aristotle's ideas to support the new view of the heavenly bodies?
3. What reasons did Galileo cite to justify modifying Aristotle's views of the universe?

The Papal Inquisition of Galileo and His Abjuration, 1633

Some view science as a politically-neutral field of activity. However, as the selection below makes clear, scientific inquiry is often a politically charged minefield. Galileo's contention that the earth was not the center of the universe called into question the reputations of his more orthodox colleagues in the sciences and also contravened the world view of the Roman Catholic Church. Indeed, the Church was so perturbed by Galileo's *Dialogue Concerning the Two Chief World Systems* that it summoned the astronomer before a Papal Inquisition in 1633, forced him to recant his views, and held him under house arrest until his death nine years later.

WEDNESDAY, JUNE 22, 1633: THE SENTENCE

...Whereas you, Galileo, son of the late Vincenzo Galilei, Florentine, aged seventy years, were in the year 1615 denounced to this Holy Office for holding as true the false doctrine taught by some that the Sun is the center of the world and immovable and that the Earth moves, and also with a diurnal motion; for having disciples to whom you taught the same doctrine; for holding correspondence with certain mathematicians of Germany concerning the same; for having printed certain letters, entitled "On the Sunspots," wherein you developed the same doctrine as true; and for replying to the objections from the Holy Scriptures, which from time to time were urged against it, by glossing the said Scriptures according to your own meaning: and whereas there was thereupon produced the copy of a document in the form of a letter, purporting to be written by you to one formerly your disciple, and in this divers propositions are set forth, following the position of Copernicus, which are contrary to the true sense and authority of Holy Scripture:

This Holy Tribunal being therefore of intention to proceed against the disorder and mischief thence resulting, which went on increasing to the prejudice of the Holy Faith, by command of His Holiness and of the Most Eminent Lords Cardinals of this supreme and universal Inquisition, the two propositions of the stability of the Sun and the motion of the Earth were by the theological Qualifiers qualified as follows:

The proposition that the Sun is the center of the world and does not move from its place is absurd and false philosophically and formally heretical, because it is expressly contrary to the Holy Scripture.

The proposition that the Earth is not the center of the world and immovable but that it moves, and also with a diurnal motion, is equally absurd and false philosophically and theologically considered at least erroneous in faith....

We say; pronounce, sentence, and declare that you, the said Galileo, by reason of the matters adduced in trial, and by you confessed as above, have rendered yourself in the judgment of this Holy Office vehemently suspected of heresy, namely, of having believed and held the doctrine—which is false and contrary to the sacred and divine Scriptures—that the Sun is the center of the world and does not move from east to west and that the Earth moves and is not the center of the world; and that an opinion may be held and defended as probably after it has been declared and defined to be contrary to the Holy Scripture; and that consequently you have incurred all the censures and penalties imposed and promulgated in the sacred canons and other constitutions, general and particular, against such delinquents. From which we are content that you be absolved, provided that, first, with a sincere heart and unfeigned faith, you abjure, curse, and detest before us the aforesaid errors and heresies and every other error and heresy contrary to the Catholic and Apostolic Roman Church in the form to be prescribed by us for you.

And, in order that this your grave and pernicious error and transgression may not remain altogether unpunished and that you may be more cautious in the future and an example to others that they may abstain from similar delinquencies, we ordain that the book of the "Dialogue of Galileo Galilei" be prohibited by public edict.

We condemn you to the formal prison of this Holy Office during our pleasure, and by way of salutary penance we enjoin that for three years to come you repeat once a week the seven penitential Psalms. Reserving to ourselves liberty to moderate, commute, or take off, in whole or in part, the aforesaid penalties and penance.

And so we say, pronounce, sentence, declare, ordain, and reserve in this and in any other better way and form which we can and may rightfully employ....

FORMULA OF ABJURATION, READ ALOUD BY GALILEO:

I, Galileo, son of the late Vincenzo Galilei, Florentine, aged seventy years, arraigned personally before this tribunal and kneeling before you, Most Eminent and Reverend Lord Cardinals Inquisitors-General against heretical pravity throughout the entire Christian commonwealth, having before my eyes and touching with my hands the Holy Gospels, swear that I have always believed, do believe, and by God's help will in the future believe all that is held, preached, and taught by the Holy Catholic and Apostolic Church. But, whereas—after an injunction had been judicially intimated to me by this Holy Office to the effect that I must altogether abandon the false opinion that the Sun is the center of the world and immovable and that the Earth is not the center of the world and moves and that I must not hold, defend, or teach in any way whatsoever, verbally or in writing, the said false doctrine, and after it had been notified to me that the said doctrine was contrary to Holy Scripture—I wrote and printed a book in which I discuss this new doctrine already condemned and adduce arguments of great cogency in its favor without presenting any solution of these, I have been pronounced by the Holy Office to be vehemently suspected of heresy, that is to say, of having held and believed that the Sun is the center of the world and immovable and that the Earth is not the center and moves:

Therefore, desiring to remove from the minds of your Eminences, and of all faithful Christians, this vehement suspicion justly conceived against me, with sincere heart and unfeigned faith I abjure, curse, and detest the aforesaid errors and heresies and generally every other error, heresy, and sect whatsoever contrary to the Holy Church, and I swear that in future I will never again say or assert, verbally or in writing, anything that might furnish occasion for a similar suspicion regarding me; but, should I know any heretic or person suspected of heresy, I will denounce him to this Holy Office or to the Inquisitor or Ordinary of the place where I may be. Further, I swear and promise to fulfil and observe in their integrity all penances that have been, or that shall be, imposed upon me by this Holy Office. And, in the event of my contravening (which God forbid!) any of these my promises and oaths, I submit myself to all the pains and penalties imposed and promulgated in the sacred canons and other constitutions, general and particular, against such delinquents. So help me God and these His Holy Gospels, which I touch with my hands.

SIGNED ATTESTATION:

I, the said Galileo Galilei, have abjured, sworn, promised, and bound myself as above; and in witness of the truth thereof I have with my own hand subscribed the present document of my abjuration and recited it word for word at Rome, in the convent of the Minerva, this twenty-second day of June, 1633.

I, Galileo Galilei, have abjured as above with my own hand.

from *The Crime of Galileo*, Giorgio de Santillana. University of Chicago Press, 1955

Questions:
1. What were the specific charges brought against Galileo by the Papal Inquisition? What evidence did the Church use to support its allegations/
2. What actions did the Church take against Galileo?
3. What was Galileo's response? Considering the historical context, how might you explain his reaction?
4. Ultimately, Galileo is proposing a new paradigm or model of the universe that shakes the foundations of orthodox views. While his conclusions are now commonplace, in his time they were revolutionary and difficult to accept, as evidenced by the above documents. Have you ever experienced a situation where your "paradigm"

was shaken (whether it be your view of art, of a career, of parenthood, etc.)? What convinced you to modify your views?

Discourse on Method, René Descartes, 1637

One of the most commonplace complaints of our century is that we live in a time of uncertainty where truth is elusive and doubt reigns supreme. What is missing from this analysis, however, is that we are now probably more "certain" about how our world operates than at any other time in human history, and that much of this "certainty" is owed to a method of approaching the world that accepts nothing as true until it has been subjected to rigorous critical examination. This idea of contesting, or "questioning authority" as a means of achieving the "truth" owes much to the work of a French soldier-of-fortune by the name of René Descartes (1596-1650). A minor nobleman, Descartes studied philosophy, mathematics, and law prior to joining the Dutch army in 1616 in order to see the world. While campaigning during the Thirty Years' War, Descartes experienced an "epiphany," or moment of truth, in 1619. As you will see in the excerpt from Descartes' *Discourse*, this revelation would not only change his life, but would create a new approach to seeking the truth and acquiring knowledge.

Part 1: From my childhood, I have been familiar with letters; and as I was given to believe that by their help a clear and certain knowledge of all that is useful in life might be acquired, I was ardently desirous of instruction. But as soon as I had finished the entire course of study, at the close of which it is customary to be admitted into the order of the learned, I completely changed my opinion. For I found myself involved in so many doubts and errors, that I was convinced I had advanced no farther in all my attempts at learning, than the discovery at every turn of my own ignorance. And yet I was studying in one of the most celebrated Schools in Europe, in which I thought there must be learned men, if such were anywhere to be found. I had been taught all that others learned there; and not contented with sciences actually taught us, I had, in addition, read all the books that had fallen into my hands, treating of such branches as are esteemed the most curious and rare. I knew the judgment which others had formed of me; and I did not find that I was considered inferior to my fellows, although there were among them some who were already marked out to fill the places of our instructors. And, in fine, our age appears, to me, as flourishing, and as fertile in powerful minds as any preceding one. I was thus led to take the liberty of judging of all other men by myself, and of concluding that there was no science in existence that was of such a nature as I had previously been given to believe.

I still continued, however, to hold in esteem the studies of the Schools. I was aware that the Languages taught in them are necessary to the understanding of the writings of the ancients; that the grace of Fable stirs the mind; that the memorable deeds of History elevate it; and, if read with discretion, aid in forming the judgment; that the perusal of all excellent books is, as it were, to interview with the noblest men of past ages, who have written them, and even a studied interview, in which are discovered to us only their choicest thoughts; that Eloquence has incomparable force and beauty; that Poesy has its ravishing graces and delights; that in the Mathematics there are many refined discoveries eminently suited to gratify the inquisitive, as well as further all the arts and lessen the labour of man; that numerous highly useful precepts and exhortations to virtue are contained in treatises on Morals; that Theology points out the path to heaven; that Philosophy affords the means of discoursing with an appearance of truth on all matters, and commands the admiration of the more simple; that Jurisprudence, Medicine, and the other Sciences, secure for their cultivators honours and riches; and in fine, that it is useful to bestow some attention upon all, even upon those abounding the most in superstition and error, that we may be in a position to determine their real value, and guard against being deceived.

But I believed that I had already given sufficient time to Languages, and likewise to the reading of the writings of the ancients, to their Histories and Fables. For to hold converse with those of other ages and to travel, are almost the same thing. It is useful to know something of the manners of different nations, that we may be enabled to form a more correct judgment regarding our own, and be prevented from thinking that everything contrary to our customs is ridiculous and irrational,—a conclusion usually come to by those whose experience has been limited to their own country. On the other hand, when too much time is occupied in travelling, we become strangers to our native country; and the over curious in the customs of the past are generally ignorant of those of the present. Besides, fictitious narratives lead us to imagine the possibility of many events that are impossible; and even the most faithful histories, if they do not wholly misrepresent matters, or exaggerate their importance to render the account of them more worthy of perusal, omit, at least, almost always the meanest and least striking of the attendant circumstances; hence it happens that the remainder does not represent the truth, and that such as regulate their conduct by examples drawn from this source, are apt to fall into the extravagances of the knight-errants of Romance, and to entertain projects that exceed their powers....

I esteemed Eloquence highly, and was in raptures with Poesy; but I thought that both were gifts of nature rather than fruits of study. Those in whom the faculty of Reason is predominant, and who most skillfully dispose their thoughts with a view to render them clear and intelligible, are always the best able to persuade others of the truth of what they lay down, though they should speak only in the language of Lower Brittany, and be wholly ignorant of the rules of Rhetoric; and those whose minds are stored with the most agreeable fancies and who can give expression to them with the greatest embellishment and harmony, are still the best poets, though unacquainted with the Art of Poetry.

I was especially delighted with the Mathematics, on account of the certitude and evidence of their reasonings; but I had not as yet a precise knowledge of their true use; and thinking that they but contributed to the advancement of the mechanical arts, I was astonished that foundations, so strong and solid, should have had no loftier superstructure reared on them. On the other hand, I compared the disquisitions of the ancient Moralists to very towering and magnificent palaces with no better foundation than sand and mud; they laud the virtues very highly, and exhibit them as estimable far above anything on earth; but they give us no adequate criterion of virtue, and frequently that which they designate with so fine a name is but apathy, or pride, or despair, or parricide.

I revered our Theology, and aspired as much as any one to reach heaven; but being given assuredly to understand that the way is not less open to the most ignorant than to the most learned, and that the revealed truths which lead to heaven are above our comprehension, I did not presume to subject them to the impotency of my Reason; and I thought that in order competently to undertake their examination, there was need of some special help from heaven, and of being more than man.

Of philosophy I will say nothing, except that when I saw that it had been cultivated for many ages by the most distinguished men, and that yet there is not a single matter within its sphere which is not still in dispute, and nothing, therefore, which is above doubt, I did not presume to anticipate that my success would be greater in it that that of others; and further, when I considered the number of conflicting opinions touching a single matter that may be upheld by learned men, while there can be but one true, I reckoned as well-nigh false all that was only probable.

As to the other Sciences, inasmuch as these borrow their principles from Philosophy, I judged that no solid superstructures could be reared on foundations so infirm;…

For these reasons, as soon as my age permitted me to pass from under the control of my instructors, I entirely abandoned the study of letters, and resolved no longer to seek any other science than the knowledge of myself, or of the great book of the world. I spent the remainder of my youth in travelling, in visiting courts and armies, in holding intercourse with men of different dispositions and ranks, in collecting varied experience, in proving myself in the different situations into which fortune threw me, and, above all, in making such reflection on the matter of my experience as to secure my improvement.… In addition, I had always a most earnest desire to know how to distinguish the true from the false, in order that I might be able clearly to discriminate the right path in life, and proceed in it with confidence.

Part 2: …Among the branches of Philosophy, I had, at an earlier period, given some attention to Logic, and among those of the Mathematics to Geometrical Analysis and Algebra,—three Arts or Sciences which ought, as I conceived, to contribute something to my design. But, on examination, I found that, as for Logic, its syllogisms and the majority of its other precepts are of avail rather in the communication of what we already know, or even as the Art of Lully, in speaking without judgment of things of which we are ignorant, than in the investigation of the unknown; and although this Science contains indeed a number of correct and very excellent precepts, there are nevertheless, so many others, and these either injurious or superfluous, mingled with the former, that it is almost quite as difficult to effect a severance of the true from the false as it is to extract a Diana or a Minerva from a rough block of marble. Then as to the Analysis of the ancients and the Algebra of the moderns, besides that they embrace only matters highly abstract, and to appearance, of no use, the former is so exclusively restricted to the consideration of figures, that it can exercise the Understanding only on condition of greatly fatiguing the Imagination; and, in the latter, there is so complete a subjection to certain rules and formulas, that there results an art full of confusion and obscurity calculated to embarrass, instead of a science fitted to cultivate the mind. By these considerations I was induced to seek some other Method which would comprise the advantages of the three and be exempt from their defects. And as a multitude of laws often only hampers justice, so that a state is best governed when, with few laws, these are rigidly administered; in like manner, instead of the great number of precepts of which Logic is composed, I believed that the four following would prove perfectly sufficient for me, provided I took the firm and unwavering resolution never in a single instance to fail in observing them.

The *first* was never to accept anything for true which I did not clearly know to be such; that is to say, carefully to avoid precipitancy and prejudice, and to comprise nothing more in my judgment than what was presented to my mind so clearly and distinctly as to exclude all ground of doubt.

The *second*, to divide each of the difficulties under examination into as many parts as possible, and as might be necessary for its adequate solution.

The *third*, to conduct my thoughts in such order that, by commencing with objects the simplest and easiest to know, I might ascend by little and little, and, as it were, step by step, to the knowledge of the more complex; assigning in thought a certain order even to those objects which in their own nature do not stand in a relation of antecedence and sequence.

And the *last*, in every case to make enumerations so complete, and reviews so general, that I might be assured that nothing was omitted.

The long chains of simple and easy reasonings by means of which geometers are accustomed to reach the conclusions of their most difficult demonstrations, had led me to imagine that all things, to the knowledge of which man is competent, are mutually connected in the same way, and that there is nothing so far removed from us as to be beyond our reach, or so hidden that we cannot discover it, provided only we abstain from accepting the false for the true, and always preserve in our thoughts the order necessary for the deduction of one truth from another....

Part 4: I am in doubt as to the propriety of making my first meditations in the place above mentioned a matter of discourse; for these are so metaphysical, and so uncommon, as not, perhaps, to be acceptable to every one. And yet, that it may be determined whether the foundations that I have laid are sufficiently secure, I find myself in a measure constrained to advert to them. I had long before remarked that, in practice, it is sometimes necessary to adopt, as if above doubt, opinions which we discern to be highly uncertain, as has been already said; but as I then desired to give my attention solely to the search after truth, I thought that a procedure exactly the opposite was called for, and that I ought to reject as absolutely false all opinions in regard to which I could suppose the least ground for doubt, in order to ascertain whether after that there remained aught in my belief that was wholly indubitable. Accordingly, seeing that our senses sometimes deceive us, I was willing to suppose that there existed nothing really such as they presented to us; and because some men err in reasoning, and fall into paralogisms, even on the simplest matters of Geometry, I, convinced that I was as open to error as any other, rejected as false all the reasonings I had hitherto taken for demonstrations; and finally, when I considered that the very same thoughts which we experience when awake may also be experienced when we are asleep, while there is at that time not one of them true, I supposed that all the objects that had ever entered into my mind when awake, had in them no more truth than the illusions of my dreams. But immediately upon this I observed that, whilst I thus wished to think that all was false, it was absolutely necessary that I, who thus thought, should be somewhat; and as I observed that this truth, *I think, hence, I am*, was so certain and of such evidence, that no ground of doubt, however extravagant, could be alleged by the Skeptics capable of shaking it, I concluded that I might, without scruple, accept it as the first principle of the Philosophy of which I was in search....

In *The Harvard Classics*, vol. 34. New York: P. F. Collier & Son, 1910

Questions:
1. What was Descartes' opinion of the education he had received in school and from established authorities? Why did he hold these opinions?
2. What methods of learning did Descartes propose?
3. Ultimately Descartes concludes, "I think, therefore I am." What is the significance of this conclusion? Why would his path to this conclusion have been seen as revolutionary?

Sir Isaac Newton: *Rules of Reasoning in Philosophy,* 1687

There is an episode of "Star Trek: The Next Generation" that opens with a Holosuite[1] poker game between the Starship Enterprise's android science officer, Commander Data, and three giants of modern

---

[1] A simulated reality chamber

physics, Dr. Stephen W. Hawking (current occupant of Newton's Chair of Mathematics at Cambridge University), Albert Einstein (father of the Relativity Theory) and Sir Isaac Newton. As this scene plays out, we are made aware of the fact that Newton does not find poker either amusing or interesting, nor is he impressed with his fellow physicists. Now while this entire scene is a cleverly written piece of fiction, the real Sir Isaac Newton (1642-1727) would probably have responded in much the same way as did the actor impersonating him in this humorous Star Trek scene. Not only did Newton find cards to be a frivolous waste of time, but he was also convinced that there was no such thing as "chance" in the universe. Furthermore, it is unlikely that Newton would have been unduly impressed by either Einstein or Hawking. After all, as both of these men would freely admit, their own work was only possible because Newton had essentially invented physics in the seventeenth century. Indeed, many scientists look to Newton as the father of modern science, and few would argue with them on this point, particularly in light of the fact that it was Sir Isaac who discovered the binomial theorem, differential calculus, and the laws of gravity. In the following selection, Newton lays out the principles that made both his remarkable work and his vaunted reputation possible.

RULE 1: WE ARE TO ADMIT NO MORE CAUSES OF NATURAL THINGS THAN SUCH AS ARE BOTH TRUE AND SUFFICIENT TO EXPLAIN THEIR APPEARANCES.

To this purpose the philosophers say that Nature does nothing in vain, and more is in vain when less will serve; for Nature is pleased with simplicity, and affects not the pomp of superfluous causes.

RULE 2: THEREFORE TO THE SAME NATURAL EFFECTS WE MUST, AS FAR AS POSSIBLE, ASSIGN THE SAME CAUSES.

As to respiration in a man and in a beast; the descent of stones in Europe and in America; the light of our culinary fire and of the sun; the reflection of light in the earth, and in the planets.

RULE 3: THE QUALITIES OF BODIES, WHICH ADMIT NEITHER INTENSIFICATION NOR REMISSION OF DEGREES, AND WHICH ARE FOUND TO BELONG TO ALL BODIES WITHIN THE REACH OF OUR EXPERIMENTS, ARE TO BE ESTEEMED THE UNIVERSAL QUALITIES OF ALL BODIES WHATSOEVER.

For since the qualities of bodies are only known to us by experiments, we are to hold for universal all such as universally agree with experiments; and such as are not liable to diminution can never be quite taken away. We are certainly not to relinquish the evidence of experiments for the sake of dreams and vain fictions of our own devising; nor are we to recede from the analogy of Nature, which is wont to be simple, and always consonant to itself. We no other way know the extension of bodies than by our senses, nor do these reach it in all bodies; but because we perceive extension in all that are sensible, therefore we ascribe it universally to all others also. That abundance of bodies are hard, we learn by experience; and because the hardness of the whole arises from the hardness of the parts, we therefore justly infer the hardness of the undivided particles not only of the bodies we feel but of all others. That all bodies are impenetrable, we gather not from reason, but from sensation. The bodies which we handle we find impenetrable, and thence conclude impenetrability to be an universal property of all bodies whatsoever. That all bodies are movable, and endowed with certain powers (which we call the inertia) of persevering in their motion, or in their rest, we only infer from the like properties observed in the bodies which we have seen. The extension, hardness, impenetrability, mobility, and inertia of the whole, result from the extension, hardness, impenetrability, mobility, and inertia of the parts; and hence we conclude the least particles of all bodies to be also all extended, and hard and impenetrable, and movable, and endowed with their proper inertia. And this is the foundation of all philosophy. Moreover, that the divided but contiguous particles of bodies may be separated from one another, is matter of observation; and, in the particles that remain undivided, our minds are able to distinguish yet lesser parts, as is mathematically demonstrated. But whether the parts so distinguished, and not yet divided, may, by the powers of Nature, be actually divided and separated from one another, we cannot certainly determine. Yet, had we the proof of but one experiment that any undivided particle, in breaking a hard and solid body, suffered a division, we might by virtue of this rule conclude that the undivided as well as the divided particles may be divided and actually separated to infinity.

Lastly, if it universally appears, by experiments and astronomical observations, that all bodies about the earth gravitate towards the earth, and that in proportion to the quantity of matter which they severally contain; that the moon likewise, according to the quantity of its matter, gravitates towards the earth; that, on the other hand, our sea gravitates towards the moon; and all the planets one towards another; and the comets in like manner towards the sun; we must, in consequence of this rule, universally allow that all bodies whatsoever are endowed with a principle of mutual gravitation. For the argument from the appearances concludes with more force for the universal gravitation of all bodies than for their impenetrability; of which, among those in the celestial regions, we have no experiments, nor any manner of observation. Not that I affirm gravity to be essential to bodies: by their *vis insita* I mean nothing but their inertia. This is immutable. Their gravity is diminished as they recede from the earth.

RULE 4: IN EXPERIMENTAL PHILOSOPHY WE ARE TO LOOK UPON PROPOSITIONS INFERRED BY GENERAL INDUCTION FROM PHENOMENA AS ACCURATELY OR VERY NEARLY TRUE, NOTWITHSTANDING ANY CONTRARY HYPOTHESES THAT MAY BE IMAGINED, TILL SUCH TIME AS OTHER PHENOMENA OCCUR, BY WHICH THEY MAY EITHER BE MADE MORE ACCURATE, OR LIABLE TO EXCEPTIONS.

This rule we must follow, that the argument of induction may not be evaded by hypotheses...

Isaac Newton, *Principia Mathematica*. Translated Andrew Motte 1729. Translation revised Florian Cajori. Berkeley: University of California Press. 1934. Reprinted by permission of the Regents of the University of California.

Questions:
1. In your own words, what were Newton's rules for understanding the physical world? What methods did he propose we use?
2. Recall that the orthodox view of the universe differentiated between the qualities of heavenly bodies and the earth. How did Newton's investigations and mathematical calculations overturn the traditional view of the physical world as having qualitatively distinct regions?
3. One effect of writings like Newton's was that some drew an analogy between the universe and a clock. How might you explain such an analogy? Cite some examples from Newton's "Rules of Reasoning" to support such a comparison. Do you find such a metaphor convincing?

Sir Isaac Newton, *General Scholium*, 1687

While Sir Isaac Newton believed that a scientist must be guided by concrete, observable evidence, he did not think that the scientific method was at odds with religion and the quest for spiritual truth. Indeed, from Newton to Hawking, scientific inquiry has often deepened one's religious convictions. In the following selection, Newton shares with us his own feelings with regard to science and the supernatural.

...The six primary planets are revolved about the sun in circles concentric with the sun, and with motions directed towards the same parts, and almost in the same plane. Ten moons are revolved about the earth, Jupiter, and Saturn, in circles concentric with them, with the same direction of motion, and nearly in the planes of the orbits of those planets; but it is not to be conceived that mere mechanical causes could give birth to so many regular motions, since the comets range over all parts of the heavens in very eccentric orbits; for by that kind of motion they pass easily through the orbs of the planets, and with great rapidity; and in their aphelions[2], where they move the slowest, and are detained the longest, they recede to the greatest distances from each other, and hence suffer the least disturbance from their mutual attractions. This most beautiful system of the sun, planets, and comets, could only proceed from the counsel and dominion of an intelligent and powerful Being. And if the fixed stars are the centres of other like systems, these, being formed by the like wise counsel, must be all subject to the dominion of One; especially since the light of the fixed stars is of the same nature with the light of the sun, and from every system light passes into all the other systems: and lest the systems of the fixed stars should, by their gravity, fall on each other, he hath placed those systems at immense distances from one another.

This Being governs all things, not as the soul of the world, but as Lord over all,…He is eternal and infinite, omnipotent and omniscient; that is, his duration reaches from eternity to eternity; his presence from infinity to infinity; he governs all things, and knows all things that are or can be done. He is not eternity and infinity, but eternal and infinite; he is not duration or space, but he endures and is present. He endures forever, and is everywhere present; and, by existing always and everywhere, he constitutes duration and space…. We have ideas of his attributes, but what the real substance of anything is we know not. In bodies, we see only their figures and colors, we hear only the sounds, we touch only their outward surfaces, we smell only the smells, and taste the savors; but their inward substances are not to be known either by our senses, or by any reflex act of our minds: much less, then, have we any idea of the substance of God….

Hitherto we have explained the phenomena of the heavens and of our sea by the power of gravity, but have not yet assigned the cause of this power. This is certain, that it must proceed from a cause that penetrates to the very centres of the sun and planets, without suffering the least diminution of its force; that operates not according to the quantity of the surfaces of the particles upon which it acts (as mechanical causes used to do), but according to the quantity of the solid matter which they contain, and propagates its virtue on all sides to immense distances, decreasing always as the inverse square of the distances. Gravitation towards the sun is made up out of the gravitations towards the several particles of which the body of the sun is composed; and in receding from the sun decreases accurately as the inverse square of the distances as far as the orbit of Saturn, as evidently appears from the quiescence of the aphelion of the planets; nay, and even to the remotest aphelion of the comets, if those aphelions are also quiescent. But hitherto I have not been able to discover the cause of those properties of gravity from phenomena, and I frame no hypotheses; for whatever is not deduced from the phenomena is to be called an hypothesis; and hypotheses, whether metaphysical or physical, whether of occult qualities or mechanical, have no place in experimental philosophy. In this philosophy particular propositions are inferred from the phenomena, and afterwards rendered general by induction. Thus it was that the impenetrability, the mobility, and the impulsive force of bodies, and the laws of motion and of gravitation, were discovered. And to us it is enough that gravity does really exist, and act according to the laws which we have explained, and abundantly serves to account for all the motions of the celestial bodies, and of our sea.

---

[2] Point of the orbit farthest from the sun

Isaac Newton, *Principia Mathematica*. Translated Andrew Motte 1729. Translation revised Florian Cajori. Berkeley: University of California Press. 1934.

Questions:
1. Newton is known for having outlined certain "universal laws" including the law of gravity, which could be used to explain the motions of heavenly bodies. What does Newton say about the cause of gravity?
2. As evidenced in Galileo and the Papal Inquisition, some interpreted the new scientific findings as heretical. Using the example of Newton, how might the new science have been seen to support Christianity?
3. Newton claims that "hypotheses...have no place in experimental philosophy." How does this claim help to define the essence of the "Scientific Revolution"?

Friedrich von Spee: The Methods of the Witch Persecutions, 1631

One thing that the new science did not end was the very old fear of witchcraft. In fact, the persecution, torture, and cruel murder of people accused of sorcery and consorting with Satan reached its height during the seventeenth century. Tens of thousands of individuals, most of them women, were burned at the stake throughout the 1600s as a veritable "witch craze" swept Europe.

As the following selection makes clear, however, not everyone was caught up in this murderous frenzy. Friedrich von Spee (1591-1635) was a German Jesuit priest who was appointed the confessor of those sentenced to death for witchcraft in the Bavarian province of Franconia. His remarks attest not only to the horrors that were visited upon those unfortunates who found themselves accused of being witches, but also to the rising tide of critical thinking that would, in time, unmask these proceedings for the travesties of justice that they were. The selection below is the last of fifty-one doubts into which Spee divided his work.

WHAT , NOW, IS THE OUTLINE AND METHOD OF THE TRIALS AGAINST WITCHES TODAY IN GENERAL USE?—A THING WORTHY GERMANY'S CONSIDERATION.

I answer:

1. Incredible among us Germans and especially (I blush to say it) among Catholics are the popular superstition, envy, calumnies, backbitings, insinuations, and the like, which, being neither punished by the magistrates nor refuted by the pulpit, first stir up suspicion of witchcraft. All the divine judgments which God has threatened in Holy Writ are now ascribed to witches. No longer do God or nature do aught, but witches everything.

2. Hence it comes that all at once everybody is clamoring that the magistrates proceed against the witches—those witches whom only their own clamor has made seem so many.

3. Princes, therefore, bid their judges and counselors to begin proceedings against the witches.

4. These at first do not know where to begin, since they have no testimony or proofs, and since their conscience clearly tells them that they ought not to proceed in this rashly.

5. Meanwhile they are a second time and a third admonished to proceed. The multitude clamors that there is something suspicious in this delay; and the same suspicion is, by one busybody or another, instilled into the ear of the princes.

6. To offend these, however, and not to defer at once to their wishes, is in Germany a serious matter: most men, and even clergymen, approve with zeal whatever is but pleasing to the princes, not heeding by whom these (however good by nature) are often instigated.

7. At last, therefore, the judges yield to their wishes, and in some way contrive at length a starting-point for the trials.

8. Or, if they still hold out and dread to touch the ticklish matter, there is sent to them a commissioner [Inquisitor] specially deputed for this. And, even if he brings to his task something of inexperience or of haste, as is wont to happen in things human, this takes on in this field another color and name, and is counted only zeal for justice. This zeal for justice is no whit diminished by the prospect of gain, especially in the case of a commissioner of slender means and avaricious, with a large family, when there is granted him as salary so many dollars per head for each witch burned, besides the fees and assessments which he is allowed to extort at will from the peasants.

9. If not some utterance of a demoniac or some malign and idle rumor ten current (for proof of the scandal is never asked) points especially to some poor and helpless Gaia[3], she is the first to suffer.

10. And yet, lest it appear that she is indicted on the basis of rumor alone, without other proofs, as the phrase goes, lo a certain presumption is at once obtained against her by posing the following dilemma: Either Gaia has led a bad and improper life, or she has led a good proper one. If a bad one, then, say they, the proof is cogent against her; for from malice to malice the presumption is strong. If, however, she has led a good one, this also is none the less a proof; for thus, they say, are witches wont to cloak themselves and try to seem especially proper.

11. Therefore it is ordered that Gaia be haled away to prison. And lo now a new proof is gained against her by this other dilemma: Either she then shows fear or she does not show it. If she does show it (hearing forsooth of the grievous tortures wont to b used in this matter), this is of itself a proof; for conscience, they say, accuses her. If she does not show it (trusting forsooth in their innocence), this too is a proof; for it is most characteristic of witches, they say, to pretend themselves peculiarly innocent and wear a bold front.

12. Lest, however, further proofs against her should be lacking, the Commissioner has his own creatures, often depraved and notorious, who question into all her past life. This, of course, cannot be done without coming upon some saying or doing of hers which evil-minded men can easily twist or distort into ground for suspicion of witchcraft.

13. If, too, there are any who have borne her ill will, these, having now a fine opportunity to do her harm, bring against her such charges as it may please them to devise; and on every side there is a clamor that the evidence is heavy against her.

14. And so, as soon as possible, she is hurried to the torture, if indeed she be not subjected to it on the very day of her arrest, as often happens.

15. For in these trials there is granted to nobody an advocate or any means of fair defense, for the cry is that the crime is an excepted one[4], and whoever ventures to defend the prisoner is brought into suspicion of the crime—as are all those who dare to utter a

---

[3] woman. Gaia was the generic name used for a female culprit by the Roman law, like Jane Doe in our time.

[4] *Criminia excepta* were those in which, because of their enormity, all restraints on procedure were suspended. Such were treason and, by analogy, treason against heaven—heresy, that is, and especially witchcraft.

protest in these cases and to urge the judges to caution; for they are forthwith dubbed patrons of the witches. Thus all mouths are closed and all pens blunted, lest they speak or write.

16. In general, however, that it may not seem that no opportunity of defense has been given to Gaia, she is brought out and the proofs are first read before her and examined—if examine it can be called.

17. But, even though she then denies these and satisfactorily makes answer to each, this is neither paid attention to nor even noted down: all the proofs retain their force and value, however perfect her answer to them. She is only ordered back into prison, there to bethink herself more carefully whether she will persist in her obstinacy—for, since she has denied her guilt, she is obstinate.

18. When she has bethought herself, she is next day brought out again, and there is read to her the sentence of torture—just as if she had before answered nothing to the charges, and refuted nothing.

19. Before she is tortured, however, she is led aside by the executioner, and, lest she may by magical means have fortified herself although up to this time nothing of the sort was ever found....

21. Then, when Gaia has thus been searched and shaved, she is tortured that she may confess the truth, that is to say, that she may simply declare herself guilty; for whatever else she may say will not be the truth and cannot be....

25. So, whether she confesses or does not confess, the result is the same. If she confesses, the thing is clear, for, as I have said and as is self-evident, she is executed: all recantation is in vain, as I have shown above. If she does not confess, the torture is repeated—twice, thrice, four times: anything one pleases is permissible, for in an excepted crime there is no limit of duration or severity or repetition of the tortures. As to this, think the judges, no sin is possible which can be brought up before the tribunal of conscience.

26. If now Gaia, no matter how many times tortured, has not yet broken silence—if she contorts her features under the pain, if she loses consciousness, or the like, then they cry that she is laughing or has bewitched herself into taciturnity, and hence deserves to be burned alive, as lately has been done to some who though several times tortured would not confess.

27. And then they say—even clergymen and confessors—that she died obstinate and impenitent, that she would not be converted or desert her paramour (the Devil), but rather kept her faith with him.

28. If, however, it chances that under so many tortures one dies, they say that her neck has been broken by the Devil....

29. Wherefore justly, forsooth, the corpse is dragged out by the executioner and buried under the gallows.

30. But if, on the other hand, Gaia does not die and some exceptionally scrupulous judge hesitates to torture her further without fresh proofs or to burn her without a confession,

she is kept in prison and more harshly fettered, and there lies for perhaps an entire year to rot until she is subdued....

36. If, now, any under stress of pain has once falsely declared herself guilty, her wretched plight beggars description. For not only is there in general no door for her escape, but she is also compelled to accuse others, of whom she knows no ill, and whose names are not seldom suggested to her by her examiners or by the executioner, or of whom she has heard as suspected or accused or already once arrested and released. These in their turn are forced to accuse others, and these still others, and so it goes on: who can help seeing that it must go on without end?...

46. From all which there follows this corollary, worthy to be noted in red ink: that, if only the trials be steadily pushed on with, there is nobody in our day, of whatsoever sex, fortune, rank, or dignity, who is safe, if he have but an enemy and slanderer to bring him into suspicion of witchcraft.

from *Translations and Reprints from the Original Sources of European History*.
University of Pennsylvania. 1902.

Questions:
1. What does von Spee suggest might be the source of increasing number of accusations of witchcraft?
2. Why might officials have agreed to bring charges against "alleged" witches even against their better judgement?
3. What were the methods used to bring charges against "alleged" witches, and how were their trials conducted? How did von Spee challenge the logic of such proceedings?
4. Is this topic strictly historical, or do you think we might be guilty of modern-day witch-hunts? Give some examples to support your view.

Chapter 18: The Enlightenment

Unit 39: The Best of All Possible Worlds: The European Quest for a New World Order

The ideas and discoveries of Galileo, Newton, and the other natural philosophers of the seventeenth century electrified the intellectuals of the eighteenth century. Not only did the achievements of the "new science" inspire the educated classes of the 1700s, but it also fostered a hope among them that the rational scientific method, which had been so successful in explaining the operations of the material world, might be able to uncover laws that governed human societies as well. Indeed, for the "philosophes" of the eighteenth century, science appeared to be an all-purpose panacea that would eventually banish war, tyranny, ignorance, crime, and poverty from the human condition.

However, even though they were optimistic about the benefits that would accrue to humanity from the new science, the intellectuals of the eighteenth century were not naive. They were fully aware of the fact that for most of European society, life was a "short, brutish" affair characterized by high mortality rates, hunger, widespread illiteracy, superstition, and cruel oppression. Nevertheless, they believed, with an almost religious zeal, that most of these ills could be rectified if only human beings were encouraged and allowed to develop their "sweet reason," i.e. their innate capacity to observe, learn, and think critically.

Voltaire: from *Candide,* 1759

There is a very famous statue of François Marie Arouet (1694-1778), better known by his pen name Voltaire, that was sculpted in 1781 by one of France's greatest portrait sculptors, Houdon. While the painstaking realistic detail of this statue make it a superb example of Neoclassical sculpture, its most striking feature is the smile that dominates the face of its subject. Witty, humane, and full of life, it is a smile that conveys not only the personality of Voltaire, but also the fact that humor and satire were the principal weapons that he used in his lifelong war against intolerance, ignorance, superstition, and tyranny.

Both Voltaire's disdain for the status quo of his time and his decision to pit his wit and pen against it stemmed from his youthful decision to abandon his father's law practice and become a playwright. His early success with the Parisian stage was cut short when a witticism on his part about a dissolute nobleman resulted in his imprisonment in the Bastille and exile to England. The relative political freedom and religious toleration that Voltaire witnessed while residing in England impressed him deeply and upon his return to France he committed himself to the struggle for freedom, reason, and science. Thereafter, he spent a considerable part of his life in flight, exile, or seclusion writing a profusion of plays, poems, pamphlets, histories, novels, and encyclopedia articles, all of which lambasted superstition, intolerance, religious fanaticism, and tyranny. Of these many works, the one for which Voltaire is most famous is *Candide,* or *Optimism,* a novel that he wrote when he was sixty-five. In the selected chapters from that work, as well as in the excerpt of Voltaire's critique of religion that is taken from his *Philosophical Dictionary,* you can get some sense of the wit, humanity, and savagely funny humor that Houdon sought to immortalize in his sculpture of the man that many consider the embodiment of the Enlightenment spirit.

CHAPTER 1: HOW CANDIDE WAS BROUGHT UP IN A NOBLE CASTLE AND HOW HE WAS EXPELLED FROM THE SAME

In the country of Westphalia, in the castle of the most noble baron of Thunder-ten-tronckh[1] lived a youth whom nature had endowed with a sweet disposition. His face was a true reflection of his mind. He had a solid judgment and an unaffected simplicity; this, I presume, was the reason he was called Candide.[2] The old servants of the house suspected him to have been the son of the baron's sister, by a very good sort of a gentleman of the neighborhood, whom that young lady refused to marry, because he could produce no more than seventy-one quarterings[3] in his arms, the rest of his genealogical tree having been lost through the injuries of time.

The baron was one of the most powerful lords in Westphalia; for his castle had not only a gate, but even windows; and his great hall was hung with tapestry. He used to hunt with his mastiffs and spaniels instead of greyhounds; his groom served him for huntsman; and the parson of the parish was his grand almoner. He was called My Lord by all his people, and when he told a story everyone laughed.

The baroness weighed three hundred and fifty pounds, so she was a person of no small consideration; and she did the honors of the house with a dignity that commanded universal respect. Her daughter was about seventeen years of age, fresh colored, comely, plump, and desirable. The baron's son seemed to be in every way a worthy son of his father. Pangloss[4], the tutor, was the oracle of the family, and little Candide listened to his instructions with all the simplicity appropriate to his age and disposition.

Pangloss taught metaphysico-theolo-cosmolo-nigology.[5] He proved admirably that there is no effect without a cause and that, in this best of all possible worlds, the baron's castle was the most magnificent of all castles, and my lady the best of all possible baronesses.

It is demonstrable, said he, that things cannot be otherwise than as they are; for as all things have been created for some end, they must necessarily be created for the best end. Observe, for instance, that the nose is shaped for spectacles, and so we wear spectacles. The legs are designed for stockings, and so we wear stockings. Stones were made to be quarried and to construct castles, therefore My Lord has a magnificent castle; for the greatest baron in the province ought to have the best lodging. Pigs were made to be eaten; therefore we eat pork all the year round; and they who assert that everything is *right* do not express themselves correctly; they should say that everything is *best*.

Candide listened attentively, and believed implicitly; for he thought Miss Cunegund very beautiful, though he never had the courage to tell her so. He concluded that next to the happiness

---

[1] Voltaire is making fun of the lesser German nobles. Voltaire saw them as ignorant, with minuscule holdings, yet inordinately proud.

[2] Literally, "glowing white," or pure.

[3] As noble families intermarried, the coat of arms was divided so that the antecedents of both husband and wife could be shown. Each quartering represented a generation; thus, 71 quarterings would mean that the family had been of the nobility for more than 2,000 years.

[4] Literally (in Greek), all tongue

[5] Voltaire uses Pangloss as a foil for his ridicule of the optimistic assumptions and statements of the English poet Alexander Pope (1688-1744), the German philosopher Gottfried Wilhelm von Leibnitz (1646-1716), and Christian von Wolff (1679-1754), who developed and popularized Leibnitz' philosophy.

of being baron of Thunder-ten-tronckh, the next best thing was to be Miss Cunegund, the next seeing her every day, and the last hearing the teachings of Master Pangloss, the greatest philosopher in the whole province, and consequently in the whole world.

One day when Miss Cunegund was taking a walk in a little neighboring wood which was called a park, she saw, through the bushes, the wise Doctor Pangloss giving a lecture in experimental physics to her mother's chambermaid, a little brown wench, very pretty and very docile. As Miss Cunegund loved the sciences, she observed the experiments with the utmost attention as they were repeated. She understood perfectly well the force of the doctor's reasoning upon causes and effects. She returned home excited, pensive, and filled with desire to learn, imagining that she might be the *sufficient reason* for young Candide, and he for her.

On her way back she happened to meet the young man; she blushed, and so did he. She wished him a good morning in a flattering tone. He returned the greeting without knowing what he was saying. The next day, as they were rising from dinner, Cunegund and Candide slipped behind a screen. She dropped her handkerchief; he picked it up. She innocently took hold of his hand; he as innocently kissed hers with a singular warmth, sensitivity, and grace. Their lips met. Their eyes sparkled. Their knees trembled. Their hands strayed. The baron happened to come by. Observing this cause and effect, he drove him out of the castle with memorable kicks on his backside. Miss Cunegund fainted away; as soon as she recovered, the baroness boxed her ears. Thus a general consternation was spread over this most magnificent and most agreeable of all possible castles.

CHAPTER 2: WHAT HAPPENED TO CANDIDE AMONG THE BULGARIANS

Candide, thus driven out of this terrestrial paradise, rambled a long time without knowing where he went; sometimes he raised his eyes, wet with tears, towards heaven, and sometimes he cast a melancholy look towards the magnificent castle, where dwelt the fairest of young baronesses. He laid himself down to sleep in a furrow, heartbroken, and supperless. The snow fell in great flakes, and, in the morning when he awoke, he was almost frozen to death; however, he made shift to crawl to the next town, which was called Wald-berghoff-trabkdikdorff, without a penny in his pocket, and half dead with hunger and fatigue. He took up his stand at the door of an inn. He had not been long there, before two men dressed in blue, fixed their eyes on him.

Candide, expelled from the earthly paradise, wandered for a long time without knowing where he was going, turning up his eyes to Heaven, gazing back frequently at the noblest of castles which held the most beautiful of young Baronesses; he lay down to sleep supperless between two furrows in the open fields; it snowed heavily in large flakes. The next morning the shivering Candide, penniless, dying of cold and exhaustion, dragged himself toward the neighboring town, which was called Kaklberghorr-trarbkdikdorff.[6] He halted sadly at the door of an inn. Two men dressed in blue[7] noticed him.

"Comrade," said one, "there's a well-built young man of the right height."

They went up to Candide and, with the greatest civility and politeness, invited him to dine with them.

---

[6] Voltaire is ridiculing the sound of the German language.

[7] Uniforms of Prussian recruiting officers. As the army suffered heavy losses in many battles, Prussian recruiters were incessantly searching for replacements.

"Gentlemen," said Candide with charming modesty, "you do me a great honor, but I have no money to pay my share."

"Money, Sir!" said one of the men in blue, "young persons of your appearance and merit never pay anything; are you not five feet five inches tall?"

"Yes, gentlemen," said he, bowing, "that is my height."

"Come, then, sir; sit down with us; we will not only pay your expenses, we will never allow such a clever young man as you to be short of money. Men were born to assist each other."

"You are perfectly right, gentlemen" said Candide, "that is what Dr. Pangloss was always telling me, and I am convinced that everything is for the best."

His generous companions begged him to accept a few crowns; he took them and wished to give them a note of repayment; they refused to take it and all sat down to table.

"Do you not have great affection for…"

"Oh, yes," said he. "I have a great affection for the lovely Miss Cunegund."

"Maybe so," replied one of the gentlemen. "but that is not the question! We were asking if you do not have a great affection for the King of the Bulgarians."[8]

"Not at all," said he, "why I never saw him in my life."

"Is it possible! He is the most charming of kings. Come, we must drink his health."

"Oh, gladly, gentlemen."

And he drank.[9]

"Bravo!" cry the blues. "You are now the support, the aid, the defender, the hero of the Bulgarians; your fortune is made; you are on the high road to glory."

So saying, they handcuffed him and carried him away to the regiment. There he was made to wheel about to the right, to the left, to draw his rammer, to return his rammer, to present, to fire, to march, and they gave him thirty blows with a cane. The next day he performed his exercise a little better, and they gave him only twenty. The day following he got by with ten, and was looked on as a young man of surprising genius by all his comrades.

Candide was completely mystified and could not make out how he was a hero. One fine spring day he thought he would take a walk, going straight ahead, in the belief that to use his legs as he pleased was a privilege of the human species as well as of animals. He had not gone two leagues when four other heroes, each six feet tall, fell upon him, bound him and carried him to a dungeon. He was tried in a court-martial, and was asked which he preferred—to run the gauntlet thirty-six times or to have his brains blown out with a dozen musket-balls? He protested vainly that the human will is free, and that he chose neither. They forced him to make a choice and he decided, by virtue of that divine gift called free will, to run the gauntlet thirty-six times. He had run it twice; since the regiment consisted of 2000 men, he received 4000 strokes, which laid bare all his muscles and nerves from the nape of his neck to his rump. As they were

---

[8] Frederick II (or Frederick the Great), king of Prussia from 1740 to 1786.

[9] Accepting the toast of the recruiters and having a drink with them took the place of signing up.

preparing to make him set out the third time our young hero, unable to bear it any longer, begged that they would be so obliging as to shoot him in the head. The favor was granted; a bandage was tied over his eyes, and he was made to kneel down. At that very instant, his Bulgarian majesty, happening to pass by, made a stop, and inquired into the delinquent's crime. Since he was king of great genius, he found, from what he had heard of Candid, that he was a young philosopher, entirely ignorant of the world. Out of his great clemency, he condescended to pardon him, for which his name will be celebrated in every journal, and in every age. A skillful surgeon cured the flagellated Candide in three weeks by means of emollient unguents prescribed by Dioscorides. His sores were now scabbed over and he was able to march when the king of the Bulgarians went to war with the king of the Abares.

CHAPTER 3: HOW CANDIDE ESCAPED FROM THE BULGARIANS AND WHAT BECAME OF HIM

Never was anything so gallant, so well accoutred, so brilliant, and so finely disposed as the two armies. The trumpets, fifes, oboes, drums, and cannon made such harmony as never was heard in hell itself. The entertainment began by a discharge of cannon, which, in the twinkling of an eye, laid flat about 6000 men on each side. The musket bullets swept away, out of the best of all possible worlds, nine or ten thousand scoundrels that infested its surface. The bayonet was next the sufficient reason of the deaths of several thousands. The whole might amount to thirty thousand souls. Candide trembled like a philosopher, and concealed himself as well as he could during this heroic butchery.

At last, while the two kings commanded *Te* Deums to be sung in their camps, Candide decided to go and reason somewhere else upon causes and effects. After passing over heaps of dead or dying men, the first place he came to was a neighboring village, in the Abarian territories, which had been burned to the ground by the Bulgarians, in accordance with the laws of war. Here lay a number of old men covered with wounds, who beheld their wives dying with their throats cut, and hugging their children to their breasts, all stained with blood. There several young virgins, whose bellies had been ripped open, after they had satisfied the natural appetites of the Bulgarian heroes, breathed their last, while others, half burned in the flames, begged to be put to death. The ground around them was covered with the brains, arms, and legs of dead men.

Candide fled as quickly as he could to another village, which belonged to the Bulgarians, and there he found the heroic Abares had enacted the same tragedy. Stumbling over quivering limbs and through ruined buildings, Candide at last arrived beyond the theatre of war, with a little provision in his budget and Miss Cunegund's image in his heart. When he arrived in Holland his provisions ran out. Having heard that the inhabitants of that country were all rich and Christians, he felt sure he would be treated by them in the same manner as at the baron's castle, before he had been driven from there through the power of Miss Cunegund's bright eyes.

He asked charity of several grave-looking people, each of whom answered him that, if he continued to follow this trade, they would have him sent to the house of correction, where he should be taught to earn his bread.

He next addressed a person who had just come from haranguing a large assembly for a whole hour on the subject of charity. The orator, squinting at him under his broad-brimmed hat, asked him sternly

"What are you doing here? Are you for the good old cause?"

"Sir," said Candied in a submissive manner, "There can be no effect without a cause; everything is necessarily concatenated and arranged for the best. It was necessary that I should be banished from the presence of Miss Cunegund; that I should run the gauntlet; and it is necessary that I should beg my bread, till I am able to earn it. All this could not have been otherwise."

"My friend," said the orator, "do you believe that the pope is the Antichrist?"

"Truly, I never heard anything about it," said Candide, "but whether he is or not, I am hungry."

"You don't deserve to eat or drink," replied the orator, "you wretch! you monster! Hence! Out of my sight! And don't come near me again as long as you live!"

The orator's wife happened to put her head out of the window at that instant. Seeing a man who doubted whether the pope was Antichrist, she emptied a chamber pot full of — on his head. Good heavens, to what excess religious zeal drives women!

A man who had never been christened, an honest anabaptist named James, witnessed the cruel and ignominious treatment shown to one of his brothers, a rational, two-footed, featherless creature. Moved with pity he carried him to his own house, had him cleaned up, fed him, and gave him two florins. He even offered to teach him his own trade of weaving Persian silks, which are made in Holland. Candide, overwhelmed by so much goodness, threw himself at his feet, crying, "Now I am convinced that my master Pangloss told me the truth when he said that everything was for the best in this world; for I am infinitely more touched by your extraordinary generosity than by the inhumanity of that gentleman in the black cloak, and his wife."

The next day, as Candide was walking out, he met a beggar all covered with scabs, his eyes sunk in his head, the end of his nose eaten off, his mouth drawn on one side, his teeth as black as a cloak, snuffling and coughing most violently, and every time he attempted to spit, out dropped a tooth.

adapted from the translation of William F. Fleming, in *The Works of Voltaire*.
New York: E.R. DuMont, 1901.

Questions:
1. Who is Pangloss, and what is Candide's view of him? What was Voltaire's purpose in his introductory depiction of these characters?
2. What is Voltaire's description of the Prussian military recruitment process, training, and discipline?
3. In his characterization of a battle, what do you learn about Voltaire's views on war, military rituals and strategies?
4. How was Voltaire critical of religion and religious practices?
5. According to Voltaire, what else is wrong with "the best of all possible worlds"?

Voltaire: from *Philosophical Dictionary,* 1764

"RELIGION"

...Last night I was meditating; I was absorbed in the contemplation of nature, admiring the immensity, the courses, the relations of those infinite globes, which are above the admiration of the vulgar.

I admired still more the intelligence that presides over this vast machinery. I said to myself: A man must be blind not to be impressed by this spectacle; he must be stupid not to recognize its author; he must be mad not to adore him. What tribute of adoration ought I to render him?

Should not this tribute be the same throughout the extent of space, since the same Supreme Power reigns equally in all that extent?

Does not a thinking being, inhabiting a star of the Milky Way, owe him the same homage as the thinking being on this little globe where we are? Light is the same to the dog-star as to us; morality, too, must be the same.

If a feeling and thinking being in the dog-star is born of a tender father and mother, who have labored for his welfare, he owes them as much love and duty as we here owe to our parents. If any one in the Milky Way sees another lame and indigent, and does not relieve him, though able to do it, he is guilty in the sight of every globe.

The heart has everywhere the same duties; on the steps of the throne of God, if He has a throne, and at the bottom of the great abyss, if there by an abyss.

I was wrapt in these reflections, when one of those genii who fill the spaces between worlds, came down to me. I recognized the same aerial creature that had formerly appeared to me, to inform me that the judgments of God are different from ours, and how much a good action is preferable to controversy.

He transported me into a desert covered all over with bones piled one upon another; and between these heaps of dead there were avenues of evergreen trees, and at the end of each avenue a tall man of august aspect gazing with compassion on these sad remains.

"Alas! my archangel," said I, "whither have you brought me?" "To desolation," answered he. "And who are those fine old patriarchs whom I see motionless and melancholy at the end of those green avenues, and who seem to weep over this immense multitude of dead?" "Poor human creature! thou shalt know," replied the genius; "but, first, thou must weep."

He began with the first heap. "These," said he, "are the twenty-three thousand Jews who danced before a calf, together with the twenty-four thousand who were slain while ravishing Midianitish women; the number of the slaughtered for similar offences or mistakes amounts to nearly three hundred thousand.

"At the following avenues are the bones of Christians, butchered by one another on account of metaphysical disputes. They are divided into several piles of four centuries each; it was necessary to separate them; for had they been all together, they would have reached the sky."

"What!" exclaimed I, "have brethren thus treated their brethren; and have I the misfortune to be one of this brotherhood?"

"Here," said the spirit, "are the twelve millions of Americans slain in their own country for not having been baptized." "Ah! my god! why were not these frightful skeletons left to whiten in the hemisphere where the bodies were born, and where they were murdered in so many various ways? Why were all these abominable monuments of barbarity and fanaticism assembled here?" "For thy instruction."...

Here I beheld a man of mild and simple mien, who appeared to me to be about thirty-five years old. He was looking with compassion upon the distant heaps of whitened skeletons through which I had been led to the abode of the sages. I was astonished to find his feet swelled and bloody, his hands in the same state, his side pierced, and his ribs laid bare by flogging "Good God!" said I, "is it possible that one of the just and wise should be in this state? I have just seen one who was treated in a very odious manner;[10] but there is no comparison between his punishment and yours. Bad priests and bad judges poisoned him. Was it also by priests and judges that you were so cruelly assassinated?

With great affability he answered—"Yes."

"And who were those monsters?"

"They were hypocrites."

"Ah! you have said all! by that one word I understand that they would condemn you to the worst of punishments. You then had proved to them, like Socrates, that the moon was not a goddess, and that Mercury was not a god?"

"No; those planets were quite out of the question. My countrymen did not even know what a planet was; they were all arrant ignoramuses. Their superstitions were quite different from those of the Greeks."

"Then you wished to teach them a new religion?"

"Not at all; I simply said to them—'Love God with all your hearts, and your neighbor as yourselves; for that is all.' Judge whether this precept is not as old as the universe; judge whether I brought them a new worship...." Why, then, did they put you in the state in which I now see you?"

"Must I tell you?—They were proud and selfish; they saw that I knew them; they saw that I was making them known to the citizens; they were the strongest; they took away my life; and such as they will always do the same, if they can, to whoever shall have done them too much justice."

"But did you say nothing; did you do nothing, that could serve them as a pretext?"

"The wicked find a pretext in everything." "Did you not once tell them that you were come to bring, not peace, but the sword?"

"This was an error of some scribe. I told them that I brought, not the sword, but peace. I never wrote anything; what I said might be miscopied without any ill intent."

"You did not then contribute in anything, by your discourses, either badly rendered or badly interpreted, to those frightful masses of bones which I passed on my way to consult you?"

"I looked with horror on those who were guilty of all these murders."

"And those monuments of power and wealth—of pride and avarice—those treasures, those ornaments, those ensigns of greatness, which, when seeking wisdom, I saw accumulated on the way—do they proceed from you?"

"It is impossible; I and mine lived in poverty and lowliness; my greatness was only in virtue."

I was on the point of begging of him to have the goodness just to tell me who he was; but my guide warned me to refrain. He told me that I was not formed for comprehending these sublime mysteries. I conjured him to tell me only in what true religion consisted.

---

[10] He had just encountered Socrates in this spiritual journey.

"Have I not told you already?—Love God and your neighbor as yourself."

"What! Can we love God and yet eat meat on a Friday?"

"I always ate what was given me; for I was too poor to give a dinner to any one."

"Might we love God and be just, and still be prudent enough not to intrust all the adventures of one's life to a person one does not know?"

"Such was always my custom."

"Might not I, while doing good, be excused from making a pilgrimage to St. James of Compostello?"

"I never was in that country."

"Should I confine myself in a place of retirement with blockheads?"

"For my part, I always made little journeys from town to town."

"Must I take part with the Greek or with the Latin Church?"

"When I was in the world, I never made any difference between the Jew and the Samaritan."

"Well, if it be so, I take you for my only master."

Then he gave me a nod, which filled me with consolation. The vision disappeared, and I was left with a good conscience.

> from *Voltaire: A Philosophical Dictionary.* translated by E. R. DuMont. New York: St. Hubert Guild, 1901

Questions:
1. From this entry on religion, Voltaire gives us a glimpse of his view of the universe and thinking beings' relationship with their Creator. What were his views? How might they have been seen as "radical" in the eighteenth century?
2. What are some of the sources and the results of religious conflict according to Voltaire? What point was he trying to make?
3. Who is the individual of "gentle countenance" that Voltaire depicts in this conversation? What is that individual's message according to Voltaire? What religious practices and beliefs was Voltaire criticizing/
4. Voltaire was suggesting that the remains of victims of religious wars should serve as instructive monuments to future generations. What kinds of war monuments have you observed? How did they affect you, and what do you believe were their purposes?

Voltaire: "Women," from *Philosophical Dictionary*, 1764

Women played no small role in the propagation of the ideas and projects of the Enlightenment philosophes. Indeed, in Paris it was women such as Mme. Marie Thérèse de Geoffrin (1699-1777), Marquise de Deffand (1697-1780), and her niece Julie de Lespinasse (1733-1776), who took the lead in organizing the fashionable salons that brought together the brightest men and women of the day to discuss and promote the latest plays, pamphlets, discoveries and discourses that were calling into question the orthodoxies of the time. Not only did these salons provide a refuge for ideas and opinions that were condemned by the political and religious authorities of the eighteenth century, but they also influenced existing opinion and set literary and artistic standards. Nevertheless, as Voltaire's essay on women makes clear, women continued to be regarded as second-class citizens within the "enlightened" world that they worked so hard to create.

Woman is in general less strong than man, smaller, and less capable of lasting labor. Her blood is more aqueous; her flesh less firm; her hair longer; her limbs more rounded; her arms less muscular; her mouth smaller; her hips more prominent; and her belly larger. These physical points distinguish women all over the earth, and of all races, from Lapland unto the coast of Guinea, and from America to China…

Women live somewhat longer than men; that is to say, in a generation we count more aged women than aged men. This fact has been observed by all who have taken accurate accounts of births and deaths in Europe; and it is thought that it is the same in Asia, and among the negresses, the copper-colored, and olive-complexioned, as among the white. "*Natura est semper sibi consona.*"[11]

We have elsewhere adverted to an extract from a Chinese journal, which states, that in the year 1725, the wife of the emperor Yontchin made a distribution among the poor women of China who had passed their seventieth year; and that, in the province of Canton alone, there were 98,222 females aged more than seventy, 40,893 beyond eighty, and 3,453 of about the age of a hundred. Those who advocate final causes say, that nature grants them a longer life than men, in order to recompense them for the trouble they take in bringing children into the world and rearing them. It is scarcely to be imagined that nature bestows recompenses, but it is probable that the blood of women being milder, their fibres harden less quickly.

No anatomist or physician has ever been able to trace the secret of conception. Sanchez has curiously remarked; "*Mariam et spiritum sanctum emisisse semen in copulation, et ex semine amborum natum esse Jesum*[12]." This abominable impertinence of the most knowing Sanchez is not adopted at present by any naturalist.

The periodical visitations which weaken females, while they endure the maladies which arise out of their suppression, the times of gestation, the necessity of suckling children, and of watching continually over them, and the delicacy of their organization, render them unfit for the fatigue of war, and the fury of the combat. It is true, as we have already observed, that in almost all times and countries women have been found on whom nature has bestowed extraordinary strength and courage, who combat with men, and undergo prodigious labor; but, after all, these examples are rare. On this point we refer to the article on "Amazons."

Physics always govern morals. Women being weaker of body than we are, there is more skill in their fingers, which are more supple than ours. Little able to labor at the heavy work of masonry, carpentering, metalling, or the plough, they are necessarily intrusted with the lighter labors of the interior of the house, and, above all, with the care of children. Leading a more sedentary life, they possess more gentleness of character than men, and are less addicted to the commission of enormous crimes—a fact so undeniable, that in all civilized countries there are always fifty men at least executed to one woman….

It is not astonishing, that in every country man has rendered himself the master of woman, dominion being founded on strength. He has ordinarily, too, a superiority both in body and mind. Very learned women are to be found in the same manner as female warriors, but they are seldom or ever inventors.

A social and agreeable spirit usually falls to their lot; and, generally speaking, they are adapted to soften the manners of men. In no republic have they ever been allowed to take the

---

[11] "Nature is always in harmony with itself."

[12] "Semen was emitted by Mary and the Holy Spirit during copulation, and from the semen of both Jesus was born."

least part in government; they have never reigned in monarchies purely elective; but they may reign in almost all the hereditary kingdoms of Europe—in Spain, Naples, and England, in many states of the North, and in many grand fiefs which are called "feminines."

Custom, entitled the Salic law,[13] has excluded them from the crown of France; but it is not, as Mézeray remarks, in consequence of their unfitness for governing, since they are almost always intrusted with the regency.

It is pretended, that Cardinal Mazarin confessed that many women were worthy of governing a kingdom; but he added, that it was always to be feared they would allow themselves to be subdued by lovers who were not capable of governing a dozen pullets. Isabella in Castile, Elizabeth in England, and Maria Theresa in Hungary, have, however, proved the falsity of this pretended *bon-mot*, attributed to Cardinal Mazarin; and at this moment we behold a legislatrix in the North as much respected as the sovereign of Greece, of Asia Minor, of Syria, and of Egypt, is disesteemed....

from *Voltaire: A Philosophical Dictionary*. translated by E. R. DuMont. New York: St. Hubert Guild, 1901

Questions:
1. In *Candide*, Voltaire criticized outdated medical practices and was promoting a more scientific and objective approach to medicine. In what ways might Voltaire be challenged for not doing the same in his physical description of women?
2. Giving some examples from the document, how might you argue that Voltaire's description of women's bodies, morals, and intelligence was socially constructed? That is, were women's bodies, morals, and intelligence restricted by nature in the way that Voltaire claims, or did the limitations he described result from social constraints placed on women?

Cesare Beccaria: On Crimes and Punishments, 1764

As some international humanitarian organizations continue to remind us, torture, imprisonment without due process of law, and harsh punishments for victimless crimes remain a very real part of life for countless millions around the globe. The fact that such practices have largely vanished throughout most of Europe is due in no small way to the work of Cesare Beccaria (1738-1794), an aristocrat from Milan, Italy, who was deeply inspired by the writings of the "enlightened" authors of England and France. Emulating the philosophes of Paris and London, Beccaria and a group of friends formed their own salon in Milan in 1760 and dedicated themselves to the fight for political, social, and cultural reform. Out of the discussions of this group emerged Beccaria's work *On Crimes and Punishments*, which examined and critiqued the legal practices, punishments, and prisons of the time. This work made Beccaria an international *cause célèbre* at the age of 26 and inspired the monarchs of Russia, Sweden, Prussia, and Austria, as well as several states in the then American colonies, to effect wide-ranging judicial and penal reforms.

If we look into history we shall find that laws, which are, or ought to be, conventions between men in a state of freedom, have been, for the most part, the work of the passions of a few, or the consequences of a fortuitous or temporary necessity; not dictated by a cool examiner of human nature, who knew how to collect in one point the actions of a multitude, and had this only end in view, *the greatest happiness of the greatest number*....

Observe that by *justice* I understand nothing more than that bond which is necessary to keep the interest of individuals united, without which men would return to their original state of barbarity. All punishments which exceed the necessity of preserving this bond are in their nature unjust....

---

[13] The legal code of the Salic Franks excluded females from succeeding to the throne.

The end of punishment, therefore, is no other than to prevent the criminal from doing further injury to society, and to prevent others from committing the like offence. Such punishments, therefore, and such a mode of inflicting them, ought to be chosen, as will make the strongest and most lasting impressions on the minds of others, with the least torment to the body of the criminal.

The torture of a criminal during the course of his trial is a cruelty consecrated by custom in most nations. It is used with an intent either to make him confess his crime, or to explain some contradiction into which he had been led during his examination, or discover his accomplices, or for some kind of metaphysical and incomprehensible purgation of infamy, or, finally, in order to discover other crimes of which he is not accused, but of which he may be guilty.

No man can be judged a criminal until he be found guilty; nor can society take from him the public protection until it have been proved that he has violated the conditions on which it was granted. What right, then, but that of power, can authorise the punishment of a citizen so long as there remians any doubt of his guilt? This dilemma is frequent. Either he is guilty, or not guilty. If guilty, he should only suffer the punishment ordained by the laws, and torture becomes useless, as his confession is unnecessary. If he be not guilty, you torture the innocent; for, in the eye of the law, every man is innocent whose crime has not been proved....

In proportion as punishments become more cruel, the minds of men, as a fluid rises to the same height with that which surrounds it, grow hardened and insensible; and the force of the passions still continuing, in the space of an hundred years the *wheel* terrifies no more than formerly the *prison*. That a punishment may produce the effect required, it is sufficient that the evil it occasions should exceed the *good* expected from the crime, including in the calculation the certainty of the punishment, and the privation of the expected advantage. All severity beyond this is superfluous, and therefore tyrannical.

The punishment of death is pernicious to society, from the example of barbarity it affords. If the passions, or the necessity of war, have taught men to shed the blood of their fellow creatures, the laws, which are intended to moderate the ferocity of mankind, should not increase it by examples of barbarity, the more horrible as this punishment is usually attended with formal pageantry. Is it not absurd, that the laws, which detest and punish homicide, should, in order to prevent murder, publicly commit murder themselves?...

It is better to prevent crimes than to punish them. This is the fundamental principle of good legislation, which is the art of conducting men to the *maximum* of happiness, and to the *minimum* of misery, if we may apply this mathematical expression to the good and evil of life....

Would you prevent crimes? Let the laws be clear and simple, let the entire force of the nation be united in their defence, let them be intended rather to favour every individual than any particular classes of men; let the laws be feared, and the laws only. The fear of the laws is salutary, but the fear of men is a fruitful and fatal source of crimes.

translated by E. D. Ingraham. *An Essay on Crimes and Punishments*. Philadelphia: H. Nicklin, 1819.

Questions:
1. Beccaria asked, "Are torture and torments *just*, and do they attain the *end* for which laws are instituted?" How did he answer this question? Give some specific examples from the document which illustrate his argument and reasoning.
2. How is Beccaria's writing an example of Enlightenment thought? What Enlightenment principles are illustrated in his work?

Jean Jaques Rousseau: *Social Contract* and *Emile*, 1762

Not all of the French philosophes were enamored with reason, science, and civilization. Jean Jacques Rousseau (1712-1778) was a case in point. The son of a Swiss watchmaker and dance instructor, Rousseau was abandoned by his family at an early age and spent his youth as an itinerant wanderer and jack-of-all-trades. In 1733, Rousseau was fortunate enough to catch the fancy of Mme. de Warens, an unmarried wealthy woman who paid him for his romantic attentions and sent him back to school where he studied music and the classics. Moving to Paris in 1742, Rousseau was befriended by Denis Diderot, who introduced him to the intellectual life of the French capital. Though he contributed articles to the *Encyclopedia*, Rousseau was never comfortable with his fellow philosophes and came to detest what he regarded as the stifling and artificial life of Paris. In 1750, he formally broke with the Parisian intelligentsia when he published "A Discourse on the Arts and Sciences," an essay which essentially attacked reason, science, and the arts as instruments of corruption that dull our instincts and imaginations, and make it impossible for us to live virtuous lives.

In all of his works that followed this essay, Rousseau reiterated his belief that property and civilization are the roots of all evil, and that humanity must find a more natural and democratic way of life it if is to survive. In his *Social Contract* and *Emile*, Rousseau presented his ideas with regard to education and the ideal organization of a society's political life. Both of these works would have an enormous impact on the intellectual life of the modern period. *Emile* would become one of the foundation stones of both modern pedagogical practice and the Romantic movement, and the *Social Contract* has found its way into the lexicon of many revolutionaries, including Robespierre and Mao-tse-tung.

Social Contract

BOOK 1, CHAPTER 1

Man is born free, and everywhere he is in chains. One thinks himself the master of others, and still remains a greater slave than they. How did this change come about? I do not know. What can make it legitimate? That question I think I can answer.

If I took into account only force, and the effects derived from it, I should say: "As long as a people is compelled to obey, and obeys, it does well; as soon as it can shake off the yoke, and shakes it off, it does still better; for, regaining its liberty by the same right as took it away, either it is justified in resuming it, or there was no justification for those who took it away." But the social order is a sacred right which is the basis of all rights. Nevertheless, this right does not come from nature, and must therefore be founded on conventions....

BOOK 1, CHAPTER 6

I suppose men to have reached the point at which the obstacles in the way of their preservation in the state of nature show their power of resistance to be greater than the resources at the disposal of each individual for his maintenance in that state. That primitive condition can then subsist no longer; and the human race would perish unless it changed its manner of existence.

But, as men cannot engender new forces, but only unite and direct existing ones, they have no other means of preserving themselves than the formation, by aggregation, of a sum of forces great enough to overcome the resistance. These they have to bring into play by means of a single motive power, and cause to act in concert.

This sum of forces can arise only where several persons come together: but, as the force and liberty of each man are the chief instruments of his self-preservation, how can he pledge them without harming his own interests, and neglecting the care he owes to himself? This difficulty, in its bearing on my present subject, may be stated in the following terms:

"The problem is to find a form of association which will defend and protect with the whole common force the person and goods of each associate, and in which each, while uniting himself with all, may still obey himself alone, and remain as free as before." This is the fundamental problem of which the *Social Contract* provides the solution.

The clauses of this contract are so determined by the nature of the act that the slightest modification would make them vain and ineffective; so that, although they have perhaps never been formally set forth, they are everywhere the same and everywhere tacitly admitted and recognized, until, on the violation of the social compact, each regains his original rights and resumes his natural liberty, while losing the conventional liberty in favour of which he renounced it.

These clauses, properly understood, may be reduced to one—the total alienation of each associate, together with all his rights, to the whole community; for, in the first place, as each gives himself absolutely, the conditions are the same for all; and, this being so, no one has any interest in making them burdensome to others.

Moreover, the alienation being without reserve, the union is as perfect as it can be, and no associate has anything more to demand; for, if the individuals retained certain rights, as there would be no common superior to decide between them and the public, each, being on one point his own judge, would ask to be so on all; the state of nature would thus continue, and the association would necessarily become inoperative or tyrannical.

Finally, each man, in giving himself to all, gives himself to nobody; and as there is no associate over which he does not acquire the same right as he yields others over himself, he gains an equivalent for everything he loses, and an increase of force for the preservation of what he has.

If then we discard from the social compact what is not of its essence, we shall find that it reduces itself to the following terms:

"Each of us puts his person and all his power in common under the supreme direction of the general will, and, in our corporate capacity, we receive each member as an indivisible part of the whole."…

In order then that the social compact may not be an empty formula, it tacitly includes the undertaking, which alone can give force to the rest, that whoever refuses to obey the general will shall be compelled to do so by the whole body. This means nothing less than that he will be forced to be free; for this is the condition which, by giving each citizen to his country, secures him against all personal dependence. In this lies the key to the working of the political machine; this alone legitimizes civil undertakings, which, without it, would be absurd, tyrannical, and liable to the most frightful abuses.

BOOK 2, CHAPTER 1

The first and most important deduction from the principles we have so far laid down is that the general will alone can direct the State according to the object for which it was instituted, i.e. the common good: for if the clashing of particular interests made the establishment of societies necessary, the agreement of these very interests made it possible. The common element in these different interests is what forms the social tie; and, were there no point of agreement between them all, no society could exist. It is solely on the basis of this common interest that every society should be governed.

I hold then that Sovereignty, being nothing less than the exercise of the general will, can never be alienated, and that the Sovereign, who is no less than a collective being, cannot be represented except by himself: the power indeed may be transmitted, but not the will.

BOOK 2, CHAPTER 3

It follows from what has gone before that the general will is always right and tends to the public advantage but it does not follow that the deliberations of the people are always equally correct. Our will is always for our own good, but we do not always see what that is; the people is never corrupted, but it is often deceived; and, on such occasions only does it seem to will what is bad.

There is often a great deal of difference between the will of all and the general will; the latter considers only the common interest, while the former takes private interest into account, and is no more than a sum of particular wills; but take away from these same wills the pluses and minuses that cancel one another, and the general will remains as the sum of the differences.

If, when the people, being furnished with adequate information, held its deliberations, the citizens had no communication one with another, the grand total of the small differences would always give the general will, and the decision would always be good. But when factions arise, and partial associations are formed at the expense of the great association, the will of each of these associations becomes general in relation to its members, while it remains particular in relation to the State; it may then be said that there are no longer as many votes as there are men, but only as many as there are associations. The differences become less numerous and gives a less general result. Lastly, when one of these associations is so great as to prevail over all the rest, the result is no longer a sum of small differences, but a single difference; in this case there is no longer a general will, and the opinion which prevails is purely particular.

It is therefore essential, if the general will is to be able to express itself, that there should be no partial society within the State, and that each citizen would think only his own thoughts; which was indeed the sublime and unique system established by the great Lycurgus. But if there are partial societies, it is best to have as many as possible and to prevent them from being unequal, as was done by Solon, Numa, and Servius. These precautions are the only ones that can guarantee that the general will shall be always enlightened, and that the people shall in no way deceive itself.

CHAPTER XV: DEPUTIES OR REPRESENTATIVES

As soon as public service ceases to be the chief business of the citizens and they would rather serve with their money than with their persons, the State is not far from its fall. When it is necessary to march out to war, they pay troops and stay at home: when it is necessary to meet in council, they name deputies and stay at home. By reason of idleness and money, they end by having soldiers to enslave their country and representatives to sell it.

It is through the hustle of commerce and the arts, through the greedy self-interest of profit, and through softness and love of amenities that personal services are replaced by money payments. Men surrender a part of their profits in order to have time to increase them at leisure.

Make gifts of money, and you will not be long without chains. The word "finance" is a slavish work, unknown in the city-state. In a country that is truly free, the citizens do everything with their own arms and nothing by means of money; so far from paying to be exempted from their duties, they would even pay for the privilege of fulfilling them themselves....

...In a well-ordered city every man flies to the assemblies: under a bad government no one cares to stir a step to get to them, because no one is interested in what happens there. Because it is foreseen that the general will will not prevail, and lastly because domestic cares are all-absorbing. Good laws lead to the making of better ones; bad ones bring about worse. As soon as any man says of the affairs of the State *What does it matter to me*? the State may be given up for lost.

from *The Social Contract and Discourses* New York: E. P. Dutton, nd

Questions:
1. What is the political problem Rousseau is trying to address in the *Social Contract*?
2. What do you think Rousseau meant by the "general will"? He makes a distinction between the "will of all" and the "general will." What is the difference between these two concepts, and what is the significance of this distinction?
3. From this excerpt of the *Social Contract*, what do you think the government implementing Rousseau's ideas would look like?
4. What was Rousseau's position on factions? Do you agree or disagree with him? Are his observations on this topic relevant today?
5. Some claim that Rousseau was a supporter of democracy while others find the roots of a dictatorship in his ideas. What evidence do you find in this document that would support such diverse views of Rousseau's ideas?

Emile

Coming from the hand of the Author of all things, everything is good; in the hands of man, everything degenerates. Man obliges one soil to nourish the productions of another, one tree to bear the fruits of another; he mingles and confounds climates, elements, seasons; he mutilates his dog, his horse, his slave. He overturns everything, disfigures everything; he loves deformity, monsters; he desires that nothing should be as nature made it, not even man himself. To please him, man must be broken in like a horse; man must be adapted to man's own fashion, like a tree in his garden.

Were it not for all this, matters would be still worse. No one wishes to be a half-developed being; and in the present condition of things, a man left to himself among others from his birth would be the most deformed among them all. Prejudices, authority, necessities, example, all the social institutions in which we are submerged, would stifle nature in him, and would put nothing in its place. In such a man nature would be like a shrub sprung up by chance in the midst of a highway, and jostled from all sides, bent in every direction, by the passers-by....

We are born weak, we need strength; we are born destitute of all things, we need assistance; we are born stupid, we need judgment. All that we have not at our birth, and that we need when grown up, is given us by education.

This education comes to us from nature itself, or from other men, or from circumstances. The internal development of our faculties and of our organs is the education nature gives us; the use we are taught to make of this development is the education we get from other men; and what we learn, by our own experience, about things that interest us, is the education of circumstances....

On Swaddling Children

The new-born child needs to stretch and to move his limbs so as to draw them out of the torpor in which, rolled into a ball, they have so long remained. We do stretch his limbs, it is true, but we prevent him from moving them. We even constrain his head into a baby's cap. It seems as if we were afraid he might appear to be alive. The inaction, the constraint in which we keep his limbs, cannot fail to interfere with the circulation of the blood and of the secretions, to prevent the child from growing strong and sturdy, and to change his constitution. In regions where these extravagant precautions are not taken, the men are all large, strong, and well proportioned. Countries in which children are swaddled swarm with hunchbacks, with cripples, with persons crook-kneed, stunted, rickety, deformed in all kinds of ways....

Childhood is to be Loved

Although the longest term of human life, and the probability, at any given age, of reaching this term, have been computed, nothing is more uncertain than the continuance of each individual life: very few attain the maximum. The greatest risks in life are at its beginning; the less one has lived, the less prospect he has of living.

Of all children born, only about half reach youth; and it is probably that your pupil may never attain to manhood. What, then, must be thought of that barbarous education which sacrifices the present to an uncertain future, loads the child with every description of fetters, and begins, by making him wretched, to prepare for him some far-away indefinite happiness he may never enjoy! Even supposing the object of such an education reasonable, how can we without indignation see the unfortunate creatures bowed under an insupportable yoke, doomed to constant labor like so many galley-slaves, without any certainty that all this toil will ever be of use to them! The years that ought to be bright and cheerful are passed in tears amid punishments, threats, and slavery. For his own good, the unhappy child is tortured: and the death thus summoned will seize on him unperceived amidst all this melancholy preparation. Who knows how many children die on account of the extravagant prudence of a father or of a teacher? Happy in escaping his cruelty, it gives them one advantage; they leave without regret a life which they know only from its darker side.

O men, be humane! It is your highest duty; be humane to all conditions of men, to every age, to everything not alien to mankind. What higher wisdom is there for you than humanity? Love childhood; encourage its sports, its pleasures, its lovable instincts. Who among us has not at times looked back with regret to the age when a smile was continually on our lips, when the soul was always at peace? Why should we rob these little innocent creatures of the enjoyment of a time so brief, so transient, of a boon so precious, which they cannot misuse? Why will you fill with bitterness and sorrow these fleeting years which can no more return to them than to you? Do you know, you fathers, the moment when death awaits your children? Do not store up for yourselves remorse, by taking from them the brief moments nature has given them. As soon as they can appreciate the delights of existence, let them enjoy it. At whatever hour God may call them, let them not die without having tasted life at all....

Reasoning Should Not Begin Too Soon

Locke's great maxim was that we ought to reason with children, and just now this maxim is much in fashion. I think, however, that its success does not warrant its reputation, and I find nothing more stupid than children who have been so much reasoned with. Reason, apparently a compound of all other faculties, the one latest developed, and with most difficulty, is the one proposed as agent in unfolding the faculties earliest used! The noblest work of education is to make a reasoning man, and we expect to train a young child by making him reason! This is beginning at the end; this is making an instrument of a result. If children understood how to reason they would not need to be educated. But by addressing them from their tenderest years in a language they cannot understand, you accustom them to be satisfied with words, to find fault with whatever is said to them, to think themselves as wise as their teachers, to wrangle and rebel. And what we mean they shall do from reasonable motives we are forced to obtain from them by adding the motive of avarice, or of fear, or of vanity.

Nature intends that children shall be children before they are men. If we insist on reversing this order we shall have fruit early indeed, but unripe and tasteless, and liable to early decay; we shall have young savants and old children. Childhood has its own methods of seeing, thinking, and feeling. Noting shows less sense than to try to substitute our own methods for these....

from *Émile: or Concerning Education, Extracts*. Boston: D. C. Heath, 1883

Adam Smith: The Wealth of Nations, 1776

In the award-winning film, *Wall Street,* a ruthless corporate tycoon declares unabashedly and with great conviction that selfishness and greed are good. He goes on further to explain that by pursuing their own self-interests without regard for the welfare of others or the health of the environment, business people and investors are generating the wealth, jobs, and inventions that will eventually solve all of our problems, past, present, and future. Though the movie later goes on to demonstrate the many ways in which unabashed and unrestrained greed can undermine moral conduct and destroy countless lives, the Wall Street villain's belief in the positive nature of self-interest is, nevertheless, an article of faith among the political and economic leaders of most of the nations of the earth at the end of the twentieth century.

The origin of this widespread economic consensus is to be found in the work of Adam Smith (1723-1790), a Scottish professor of philosophy and the father of modern *laissez-faire* economics. Just as the natural world was seen as operating by certain laws, Smith argued that the law of "supply and demand" should be allowed to govern the economy. Like the laws of nature, this "invisible hand" would allow the economy to govern itself naturally. In the following selection from Smith's book, *An Inquiry into the Nature and Causes of the Wealth of Nations*, we are enlightened as to what these economic natural laws are and why he felt governments should refrain from interfering in the affairs of both domestic and foreign markets.

Every individual is continually exerting himself to find out the most advantageous employment for whatever capital he can command. It is his own advantage, indeed, and not that of the society, which he has in view. But the study of his own advantage, naturally, or rather necessarily, leads him to prefer that employment which is most advantageous to the society....

...The statesman who should attempt to direct private people in what manner they ought to employ their capitals, would not only load himself with a most unnecessary attention, but assume an authority which could safely be trusted, not only to no single person, but to no council or senate whatever, and which would nowhere be so dangerous as in the hands of a man who had folly and presumption enough to fancy himself fit to exercise it....

It is thus that every system which endeavours, either by extraordinary encouragements to draw towards a particular species of industry a greater share of the capital of the society than would naturally go to it, or, by extraordinary restraints, force from a particular species of industry some share of the capital which would otherwise be employed in it, is, in reality subversive to the great purpose which it means to promote. It retards, instead of accelerating, the progress of the society towards real wealth and greatness; and diminishes, instead of increasing, the real value of the annual produce of its land and labour.

All systems either of preference or of restraint, therefore, being thus completely taken away, the obvious and simply system of natural liberty establishes itself of its own accord. Every man, as long as he does not violate the laws of justice, is left perfectly free to pursue his own interest his own way, and to bring both his industry and capital into competition with those of any other man, or order of men. The sovereign is completely discharged from a duty, in the attempting to perform which he must always be exposed to innumerable delusions, and for the proper performance of which no human wisdom or knowledge could ever be sufficient; the duty of superintending the industry of private people, and of directing it towards the employments most suitable to the interest of the society. According to the system of natural liberty, the sovereign has only three duties to attend to; three duties of great importance, indeed, but plain and intelligible to common understandings: first, the duty of protecting the society from the violence and invasion of other independent societies: secondly, the duty of protecting, as far as possible, every member of the society from the injustice of oppression of every other member of it, or the duty of establishing an exact administration of justice; and, thirdly, the duty of erecting and maintaining certain public works and certain public institutions which it can never be fore the interest of any individual, or small number of individuals, to erect and maintain; because the profit could never repay the expense to any individual or small number of individuals, though it may frequently do much more than repay it to a great society.

London: Ward Lock, n.d. reprint of the edition of 1813, edited by J. R. McCulloch.

Questions:
1. What role does individualism play in Adam Smith's view of the economy and the "wealth of nations"? Do you agree with his reasoning? Why or why not?
2. In what capacity should the state function in regard to regulating individuals' economic activities? Why?
3. According to Smith, what duties should the sovereign have?
4. How might Smith's ideas fit into Enlightenment thought?

Antoine Nicolas de Condorcet, *The Progress of the Human Mind*, 1793

Of all the philosophes of the eighteenth century, none was a more enthusiastic proponent of the Enlightenment belief in progress and reason than Marie Jean Antoine Nicolas Caritat, Marquis de Condorcet (1743-1794). A philosopher, mathematician, and the secretary of the French Academy of Science under the monarchy, Condorcet was deeply committed to the idea that knowledge in general, and science in particular, could reshape the world for the better. Nor did Condorcet limit his interests to academic affairs. Though he was an aristocrat, he opposed noble privilege, supported social and political reform, and embraced the French Revolution, ultimately becoming a member of the Convention that abolished France's monarchy. Despite his commitment to the Enlightenment and its revolutionary offspring, however, Condorcet was condemned during the Reign of Terror as an enemy of the French Republic. While living as a fugitive, he penned a "passionate affirmation of the rationalist faith" in his *Sketch for a Historical Picture of the Progress of the Human Mind*. Arrested shortly after completing this work, Condorcet poisoned himself rather than suffer the final humiliation of being guillotined by a government that he had hoped would make terror a relic of an unenlightened past.

All the causes which contribute to the improvement of the human species, all the means we have enumerated that insure its progress, must, from their very nature, exercise an influence always active, and acquire an extent forever increasing. The proofs of this have been exhibited, and from their development in the work itself they will derive additional force: accordingly we may already conclude, that the perfectibility of man is indefinite. Meanwhile we have hitherto considered him as possessing only the same natural faculties, as endowed with the same organization. How much greater would be the certainty, how much wider the compass of our hopes, could we prove that these natural faculties themselves, that this very organization, are also susceptible of melioration? And this is the last question we shall examine.

The organic perfectibility or deterioration of the classes of the vegetable, or species of the animal kingdom, may be regarded as one of the general laws of nature.

This law extends itself to the human race; and it cannot be doubted that the progress of the sanative art, that the use of more wholesome food and more comfortable habitations, that a mode of life which shall develop the physical powers by exercise, without at the same time impairing them by excess; in fine that the destruction of the two most active causes of deterioration, penury and wretchedness on the one hand, and enormous wealth on the other, must necessarily tend to prolong the common duration of man's existence, and secure him a more constant health and a more robust constitution. It is manifest that the improvement of the practice of medicine, become more efficacious in consequence of the progress of reason and the social order, must in the end put a period to transmissible or contagious disorders, as well to those general maladies resulting from climate, aliments, and the nature of certain occupations. Nor would it be difficult to prove that this hope might be extended to almost every other malady, of which it is probable we shall hereafter discover the most remote causes. Would it even be absurd to suppose this quality of melioration in the human species as susceptible of an indefinite advancement; to suppose that a period must one day arrive when death will be nothing more than the effect either of extraordinary accidents, or of the flow and gradual decay of the vital powers; and that the duration of the middle space, of the interval between the birth of man and this decay, will itself have no assignable limit? Certainly man will not become immortal; but may not the distance between the moment in which he draws his first breath and the common term when, in the course of nature, without malady, without accident, he finds it impossible any longer to exist, be necessarily protracted?...

May not our physical faculties, the force, the sagacity, the acuteness of the senses, be numbered among the qualities, the individual improvement of which it will be practicable to transmit? An attention to the different breeds of domestic animals must lead us to adopt the affirmative of this question, and a direct observation of the human species itself will be found to strengthen the opinion.

Lastly, may we not include in the same circle the intellectual and moral faculties? May not our parents, who transmit to us the advantages or defects of their conformation, and from whom we receive our features and shape, as well as our propensities to certain physical affections, transmit to us also that part of organization upon which intellect, strength of understanding, energy of soul or moral sensibility depend? Is it not probable that education by improving these qualities will at the same time have an influence upon, will modify and improve this organization itself? Analogy, an investigation of the human faculties, and even some facts, appear to authorize these conjectures, and thereby to enlarge the boundary of our hopes.

Such are the questions with which we shall terminate the last division of our work. And how admirably calculated is this view of the human race, emancipated from its chains, released alike from the dominion of chance, as well as from that of the enemies of its progress, and advancing with a firm and indeviate step in the paths of truth, to console the philosopher lamenting the errors, the flagrant acts of injustice, the crimes with which the earth is still polluted? It is the contemplation of this prospect that rewards him for all his efforts to assist the progress of reason and the establishment of liberty.

from Marquis de Condorcet, *Outlines of a Historical View of the Progress of the Human Mind.*
Philadelphia, 1796.

Question:
According to Condorcet, what does the future hold for humankind? Give some examples from the document.

Chapter 19: The Eighteenth Century

Unit 40: Society: Elite and Ordinary

Two hundred years of republican government and a longstanding distrust of monarchy have left most Americans profoundly skeptical of the idea that any prince or dictator could be relied upon to pursue policies that would restrict their authority and privilege in order to advance the freedom and wealth of their citizens. For the philosophes of the eighteenth century, however, it was an article of faith that Europe's monarchs could be convinced to support policies of reform that would ultimately secure the welfare and prosperity of their subjects. In part, this conviction was born out of desperation. After all, monarchical despotism was the rule rather than the exception throughout Europe in the eighteenth century, and, if one wanted to achieve anything, it had to be done through the princely courts of the time. This political reality aside, however, there were also some rather exceptional monarchs sitting on Europe's thrones at this time, and they were not only aware of the Enlightenment project, but eager to play the role that the philosophes had in mind for them.

Two of these would-be "enlightened despots" were King Frederick II (the Great) of Prussia (ruled 1740-1786) and Empress Catherine II (the Great) of Russia (rules 1762-1796). These monarchs had a great many things in common. They were close political and military allies, able administrators, deft diplomats, ruthless rulers, and they were both painfully conscious of the fact that they governed states that were regarded as "backward" and "unenlightened" by their neighbors in western Europe. In an effort to rectify this latter problem, both Frederick and Catherine invested a considerable amount of time cultivating friendships with the French philosophes and pursuing policies that were aimed at making their domains models of benign despotism. Indeed, Frederick went so far as to give Voltaire refuge at his palace at Sans Souci outside of Berlin, and Catherine supported Diderot by purchasing his library and then allowing him to use it until his death. In the selections below, you can get some idea of how these two monarchs sought to govern in an enlightened manner. The first of these documents represents Frederick II's thinking on the nature of an enlightened state and the best way to govern it. The second selection is a collection of excerpts from Catherine the Great's instructions to an elected assembly that she had convened for the purpose of drawing up a new and more "enlightened" law code for Russia.

The Political Testament of Frederick II, 1752

A sovereign must possess an exact and detailed knowledge of the strong and of the weak points of his country. He must be thoroughly acquainted with its resources, the character of the people, and the national commerce....

Rulers should always remind themselves that they are men like the least of their subjects. The sovereign is the foremost judge, general, financier, and minister of his country, not merely for the sake of his prestige. Therefore, he should perform with care the duties connected with these offices. He is merely the principal servant of the state. Hence, he must act with honesty, wisdom, and complete disinterestedness in such a way that he can render an account of his stewardship to the citizens at any moment. Consequently, he is guilty if he wastes the money of the people, the taxes which they have paid, in luxury, pomp, and debauchery. He who should improve the morals of the people, be the guardian of the law, and improve their education should not pervert them by his bad example.

Princes, sovereigns, and king have not been given supreme authority in order to live in luxurious self-indulgence and debauchery. They have not been elevated by their fellow-men to enable them to strut about and to insult with their pride the simple-mannered, the poor, and the suffering. They have not been placed at the head of the State to keep around themselves a crowd of idle loafers whose uselessness drives them towards vice. The bad administration which may be found in monarchies springs from many different causes, but their principal cause lies in the character of the sovereign. A ruler addicted to women will become a tool of his mistresses and favourites, and these will abuse their power and commit wrongs of every kind, will protect vice, sell offices, and perpetrate every infamy....

The sovereign is the representative of his State. He and his people form a single body. Ruler and ruled can be happy only if they are firmly united. The sovereign stands to his people in the same relation in which the head stands to the body. He must use his eyes and his brain for the whole community, and act on its behalf to the common advantage. If we wish to elevate monarchical above republican government, the duty of sovereigns is clear. They must be active, hard-working, upright and honest, and concentrate all their strength upon filling their office worthily. That is my idea of the duties of sovereigns.

translated by J. Ellis Barker in The Foundations of Germany. New York: E. P. Dutton, 1916.

Questions:
What Enlightenment ideals are reflected in Frederick II's "Political Testament"? What part should the ruler play in implementing these ideals? Give some examples from the document, including some of Frederick's justifications for the ruler's role.

Catherine the Great: "Instructions to the Commissioners," 1768

1. The Christian law teaches us to do mutual good to one another, as much as possibly we can.

2. Laying this down as a fundamental rule prescribed by that religion, which has taken, or ought to take root in the hearts of the whole people; we cannot but suppose, that every honest man in the community is, or will be, desirous of seeing his native country at the very summit of happiness, glory, safety, and tranquillity.

3. And that individual citizen in particular must wish to see himself protected by laws, which should not distress him in his circumstances, but, on the contrary, should defend him from all attempts of others, that are repugnant to this fundamental rule.

4. In order therefore to proceed to a speedy execution of what we expect from such a general wish, *we,* fixing the foundation upon the above first-mentioned rule, ought to begin with an inquiry into the natural situation of this empire.

5. For those laws have the greatest conformity with nature, whose particular regulations are best adapted to the situation and circumstances of the people, for whom they are instituted.

This natural situation is described in the three following chapters.

6. Russia is an European state.

7. This is clearly demonstrated by the following observations: the alterations which Peter the Great undertook in Russia succeeded with the greater ease, because the manners, which prevailed at that time, and had been introduced amongst us by a mixture of different nations, and the conquest of foreign territories, were quite unsuitable to the climate. Peter the First, by introducing the manners and customs of Europe among the European people in his dominions, found at that time such means as even he himself was not sanguine enough to expect.

8. The possessions of the Russian empire extend upon the terrestrial globe to 32 degrees of latitude, and to 165 of longitude.

9. The sovereign is absolute; for there is no other authority but that which centers in his single person, that can act with a vigour proportionate to the extent of such a vast dominion.

10. The extent of the dominion requires an absolute power to be vested in that person who rules over it. It is expedient so to be, that the quick dispatch of affairs, sent from distant parts, might make ample amends for the delay occasioned by the great distance of the places.

11. Every other form of government whatsoever would not only have been prejudicial to Russia, but would even have proved its entire ruin.

12. Another reason is; that it is better to be subject to the laws under one master, than to be subservient to many.

13. What is the true end of monarchy? Not to deprive people of their natural liberty; but to correct their actions, in order to attain the *supreme good*.

14. The form of government, therefore, which best attains this end, and at the same time sets less bounds than others to natural liberty, is that which coincides with the views and purposes of rational creatures, and answers the end, upon which we ought to fix a steadfast eye in the regulations of civil polity.

15. The intention and the end of monarchy, is the glory of the citizens, of the state, and of the sovereign.

16. But, from this glory, a sense of liberty arises in a people governed by a monarch; which may produce in these states as much energy in transacting the most important affairs, and may contribute as much to the happiness of the subjects, as even liberty itself....

81. The love of our country, shame, and the dread of publick censure, are motives which restrain, and may deter mankind from the commission of a number of crimes.

82. The greatest punishment for a bad action, under a mild administration, will be for the party to be convinced of it. The civil laws will there correct vice with the more ease, and will not be under a necessity of employing more rigorous means.

83. In these governments, the legislature will apply itself more to prevent crimes, than to punish them, and should take more care to instill good manners into the minds of the citizens, by proper regulations, than to dispirit them by the terror of corporal and capital punishment.

84. In a word, whatever is termed punishment in the law, is, in fact, nothing but pain and suffering.

85. Experience teaches us, that, in those countries, where punishments are mild, they operate with the same efficacy upon the minds of the citizens, as the most severe in other places....

123. The usage of torture is contrary to all the dictates of nature and reason; even mankind itself cries out against it, and demands loudly the total abolition of it. We see, at this very time, a people greatly renowned for the excellence of their civil polity, who reject it without any sensible inconveniences. It is, therefore, by no means necessary by its nature. We will explain this more at large here below....

129. The sentence ought to be as clear and distinct as possible; even so far as to preserve the very identical words of the law. But if they should include the private opinion of the judge, the people will live in society, without knowing exactly the reciprocal obligations they lie under to one another in that State....

205. ...For this reason, such punishments and such a mode of inflicting them, ought to be selected, as will make the deepest and most durable Impression on the minds of the people, and at the same time with the least cruelty to the body of the criminal.

206. Who can read, without being struck with horror, the history of so many barbarous and useless tortures, invented and executed without the least remorse of conscience, by people who assumed to themselves the name of sages? Who does not feel within himself a sensible palpitation of the heart, at the sight of so many thousands of unhappy wretches, who have suffered, and still suffer: frequently accused of crimes, which are difficult, or impossible to happen, proceeding often from ignorance, and some-times from superstitions? Who can look, I say, upon the dismembering of these people, who are executed with slow and studied barbarity, by the very persons who are their brethren? Countries and times, in which the most cruel punishments were made use of, are those in which the most inhuman villainies were perpetrated.

207. That a punishment may produce the desired effect, it will be sufficient; when the evil it occasions exceeds the good expected from the crime, including in the calculation the excess of the evil over the good, the undoubted certainty of the punishment, and the privation of all the advantages hoped for from the crime. All severity exceeding these bounds is useless, and consequently tyrannical....

240. It is better to prevent crimes, than to punish them.

241. To prevent crimes, is the intention, and the end of every good legislation; which is nothing more than the art of conducting people to the greatest good, or to leave the least evil possible amongst them, if it should prove impracticable to exterminate the whole.

242. If we forbid many actions, which are termed indifferent by the moralist, we shall not prevent the crimes, of which they may be productive, but shall create still new ones.

243. Would you prevent crimes? order it so, that the laws might rather favour every individual, than any particular rank of citizens, in the community.

244. Order it so, that the people should feat the laws, and nothing but the laws.

245. Would you prevent crimes? order it so, that the light of knowledge may be diffused among the people....

from *Documents of Catherine the Great*, edited by W. F. Reddaway. London: Cambridge University Press, 1931.

Questions:
1. What principles in Catherine's *Instructions* reflect Enlightenment thought? Do you find any examples that contradict Enlightenment ideals?
2. Compare Catherine's philosophy with that of Frederick II.

John Howard: On Penal Law in Russia, 1777

One of the principal problems with attempting to reform a society from the top down is that everything is dependent on the competence and good will of whoever happens to be sitting on the throne at a given time. Nowhere was this more evident than in the case of Enlightenment Europe during the eighteenth century. While a monarch like Frederick II of Prussia was an energetic and able administrator who left his kingdom with an efficient and honest bureaucracy, a full treasury, fair taxes, a unified code of law, and religious toleration, Louis XV of France was an indolent and incompetent ruler who bankrupted his country and bequeathed to his successor a chaotic and corrupt government.

Moreover, even when a nation was fortunate enough to have a strong, energetic, and reform-minded ruler, there was no guarantee that their policies would be put into effect by the nobility that they relied on for support. The enlightened despotism of Catherine II of Russia perhaps best exemplified this problem. Brought to the throne by a palace coup, Catherine's position as Russian empress was ultimately dependent on the good will of her allies among the country's aristocratic landowners and military officers. As such, some historians argue that her efforts to initiate enlightened social reforms largely remained an impressive, albeit empty, gesture. Nowhere is this more evident than in the following selections from the eighteenth-century Russian travel diaries of the English penal reformer, John Howard, and the commentary on Catherine's reign that was penned by the nineteenth century Russian liberal, Alexander Herzen.

In *Russia* the peasants and servants are bondmen or slaves, and their lords (or masters) may inflict on them any corporal punishment; or banish them to *Siberia* on giving notice of their offence to the police. But they are not permitted to put them to death. Should they, however, die by the severity of their punishment, the penalty of the law is easily evaded.

Debtors in this country are often employed as *slaves* by government, and allowed twelve *roubles* yearly wages, which goes towards discharging the debt. In some cases of private debts, if any person will give sufficient security to pay twelve *roubles* a year, as long as the slave lives, or till the debt is paid off; as also to produce the slave when he is demanded; such person may take him out of confinement: but if he fails to produce him when demanded, is liable to pay the whole debt immediately.

There are no regular gaolers appointed in *Russia,* but all the prisons are guarded by the *military*. Little or no attention is paid to the reformation of prisoners.

There is no capital punishment for any crime but treason: but the common punishment of the *knoot* is often dreaded more than death, and sometimes a criminal has endeavoured to bribe the executioner to kill him. This punishment seldom causes immediate death, but death is often the consequence of it.

The governor of the *police* at *Petersburg* was so kind as to fix a time for shewing me all the instruments commonly used for punishment—the axe and block—-the machine (now out of use) for breaking the arms and legs—the instrument for slitting or lacerating the nostrils—and that for marking criminals, (which is done by punctuation, and then rubbing a black powder on the wounds)— the *knoot* whip—and another called the *cat,* which consists of a number of thongs from two to ten.

The *knoot* whip is fixed to a wooden handle a foot long, and consists of several thongs about two feet in length twisted together, to the end of which is fastened a single tough thong of a foot and half, tapering towards a point, and capable of being changed by the executioner, when too much softened by the blood of the criminal.

August 10, 1781, I saw two criminals, a man and a woman, suffer the punishment of the *knoot.* They were conducted from prison by about fifteen hussars and ten soldiers. When they arrived at the place of punishment, the hussars formed themselves into a ring round the whipping-post, the drum beat a minute or two, and then some prayers were read, the populace taking off their hats. The woman was taken first, and after being roughly script to the waist, her hands and feet were bound with cords to a post made for the purpose, a man standing before the post, and holding the cords to keep them tight. A servant attended the executioner, and both were stout men. The servant first marked his ground and struck the woman five times on the back. Every stroke seemed to penetrate deep into her flesh. But his master thinking him too gentle, pushed him aside, took his place, and gave all the remaining strokes himself, which were evidently more severe. The woman received twenty-five, and the man sixty:

I pressed through the hussars, and counted the number as they were chalked on a board; and both seemed but just alive, especially the man, who yet had strength enough to receive a small donation with some signs of gratitude. They were conducted back to prison in a little waggon. I saw the woman in a very weak condition some days after, but could not find the man any more.

from *The State of the Prisons in England and Wales, With Preliminary Observations on some Foreign Prisons.*
London, 1777.

Alexander Herzen: On Empress Catherine, 1858

In reading these memoirs one is surprised that one thing is constantly forgotten, to the point of being nowhere mentioned,—it is *Russia* and *the people.* And this is the characteristic trait of the period.

The Winter Palace, with its administrative and military machinery, was a world apart. Like a ship floating on the water's surface, the only intercourse it had with the inhabitants of the Ocean was to eat them. It was *the State for the State's sake.* Organized in the German fashion, it imposed itself upon the people as a victor would. In this monstrous barracks, in this enormous chancellery, there was a dry sort of rigidity, as in a camp. The one gave or transmitted the orders, the others obeyed in silence. There was only one point where human passions reappeared, stormy and agitated, and this point was, in the Winter Palace, the domestic focus not of the nation but of the State. Behind the triple line of guards, in these heavily ornate *salons*, a feverish life fermented with its intrigues and its struggles, its drama and its tragedies. It was there that

Russia's destinies were plotted in the obscurity of the alcove, in the midst of orgies, beyond the reach of police and spies.

from the preface to Memoirs of Empress Catherine II. London, 1859.

Questions:
1. In Catherine's *Instructions* to the Legislative Commission, she addresses the issue of punishments. Considering Howard's observations, how would you compare her Enlightenment beliefs on this topic with actual practices in Russia?
2. What criticisms did Herzen have of Catherine? What evidence from Catherine's *Instructions* might be used to support his interpretation of her reign?

Madame Campan: from Memoirs of Marie Antoinette

In the eighteenth century, aristocratic life was increasingly associated with wasteful luxury, sloth, meaningless rituals, and frivolous pastimes. One can get some sense of why this was the case in the following selection from the recollections of a member of Queen Marie Antoinette's entourage regarding court life at Versailles on the eve of the French Revolution.

It will he seen that the admission of a milliner into the house of the Queen was followed by evil consequences to Her Majesty. The skill of the milliner, who was received into the household in spite of the usual custom which kept all persons of her description out of it, afforded her the means of introducing some new fashion every day. Up to this time the Queen had shown but a very plain taste in dress; she now began to make it an occupation of moment, and she *was,* of course, imitated by other women.

Everyone instantly wished to have the same dress as the Queen, and to wear the feathers and flowers to which her beauty, then in its brilliancy, lent an indescribable charm. The expenditure of young women was necessarily much increased, and mothers and husbands murmured at it; some giddy women contracted debts, and unpleasant domestic scenes occurred; in many families quarrels arose; in another affection was extinguished, and the general report was that the Queen would be the ruin of all the French ladies.

Fashion continued its fluctuating progress; and head-dresses, with their superstructures of gauze, flowers and feathers, arose to such a degree of loftiness that the women could not find carriages high enough to admit them; and they were often seen either stooping, or holding their heads out at the windows. Others knelt down in order to manage these elevated objects of ridicule with the less danger. Innumerable caricatures, exhibited in all directions— and some of which artfully gave the features of the Queen—attacked the extravagance of fashion, but with very little effect. It changed only, as is always the case, through the influence of inconstancy and time.

The Princess's toilette was a masterpiece of etiquette; everything done on the occasion was in a prescribed form. Both the lady of honour and the tire-woman usually attended and officiated, assisted by the first *femme de chambre* and two inferior attendants. The tire-woman put on the petticoat and handed the gown to the Queen. The lady of honour poured out the water for her hands and put on her body linen. When a Princess of the Royal Family happened to be present while the Queen was dressing, the lady of honour yielded to her the latter act of office, but still did not yield it directly to the Princess of the Blood; in such a case the lady of honour was accustomed to present the linen to the chief lady in waiting, who, in her turn, handed it to the Princess of the Blood. Each of these ladies observed these rules scrupulously as affecting her rights. One winters day it happened that the Queen, who was entirely undressed, was just going to put on her body linen. I held it ready unfolded for her; the lady of honour came in, slipped off her gloves, and took it. A rustling was heard at the door—it was opened, and in came the Duchess d'Orleans; she took her gloves off, and came forward to take the garment; but as it would have been wrong in the lady of honour to hand it to her, she gave it to me, and I handed it to the Princess. A further noise; it was the Countess de Provence; the Duchess d'Orleans handed her the linen. All this while the Queen kept her arms crossed upon her bosom, and appeared to feel cold. Madame observed her uncomfortable situation, and merely laying down her handkerchief, without taking off her gloves, she put on the linen, and, in doing so, knocked the Queen's cap off. The Queen laughed to conceal her impatience, but not until she had muttered several times: "How disagreeable ! how tiresome!"

All this etiquette, however inconvenient, was suitable to the Royal dignity, which expects to find servants in all classes of persons, beginning even with the brothers and sisters of the monarch.

Speaking here of etiquette, I do not allude to that order of State laid down for days of ceremony in all Courts. I mean those minute ceremonies that were observed towards our Kings in their inmost privacies, in their hours of pleasure, in those of pain, and even during the most revolting of human infirmities.

These servile rules were drawn up in a kind of code; they offered to a Richelieu, a La Rochefoucauld, and a Duras, in the exercise of their domestic functions, opportunities of intimacy useful to their interests; and to humour their vanity they were pleased with customs which converted the right to give a glass of water, to put on a dress, and to remove a basin, into honourable prerogatives.

Princes thus accustomed to be treated as divinities naturally arrived at the belief that they were of a distinct nature, of a purer essence than the rest of mankind.

from *Secret Memoirs of the Courts of Europe from the 16th to the 19th Century*. Vol. I.
Philadelphia: George Barrie & Son, n.d.

Questions:
1. As evidenced in this excerpt, what effect did Marie Antoinette's attire have? On the topic of fashion, who are today's Marie Antoinette's?
2. What do you learn about court etiquette from the section on the rituals surrounding Marie's dressing? What effect do you think such rituals would have had? What do you think their purpose might have been?

Arthur Young, *Travels in France*, 1787-89

Europe's peasantry comprised roughly 85% of the continent's population. They tilled the soil, repaired the roads, built the cities, paid the priests, maintained the churches, and fought and died in the armies of their princes. In return for these critical services, they were compelled to pay most of the taxes, surrender up to a third of their crops to the nobility and church, pay a variety of dues and fees, and be humble and subservient to their social betters. As if this iniquitous social arrangement were not bad enough, Europe's peasants were also compelled to live in the kind of primitive and squalid conditions that are described in the following selection.

September 1. To Combourg, the country has a savage aspect; husbandry not much further advanced, at least in skill, than among the Hurons, which appears incredible amidst enclosures; the people almost as wild as their country, and their town of Combourg one of the most brutal filthy places that can be seen; mud houses, no windows, and a pavement so broken as to impede all passengers, but ease none—yet here is a chateau, and inhabited; who is this Monsieur de Chateaubriant, the owner, that has nerves strung for a residence amidst such filth and poverty?...

19th Turned aside to Auvergnac the seat of the Count de la Bourdonaye, to whom I had a letter from the Duchess d'Anville, as a person able to give me every species of intelligence relative to Bretagne, having for five-and-twenty years been first syndac of the noblesse. A fortuitous jumble of rocks and steeps could scarcely form a worse road than these five miles: could I put as much faith in two bits of wood laid over each other as the good folks of the country do, I should have crossed myself, but my blind friend with the most incredible sure-footedness carried me safe over such places, that if I had not been in the every-day habit of the saddle I should have shuddered at, though guided by eyes keen as Eclipse's; for I suppose a fine racer, on whose velocity so many fools have been ready to lose their money, must have good eyes as well as good legs. Such a road leading to several villages and one of the first noblemen of the province shows what the state of society must be;—no communication—no neighbourhood—no temptation to the expenses which flow from society; a mere seclusion to save money in order to spend it in towns....

I told M. de la Bourdonaye that his province of Bretagne seemed to me to have nothing in it but privileges and poverty, he smiled and gave me some explanations that are important; but no nobleman can ever probe this evil as it ought to be done, resulting as it does from the privileges going to themselves and the poverty to the people....

from Arthur Young, Travels in France & Italy During the Years 1787 1788 and 1789.
London: J. M. Dent, 1915.

Unit 41: Capital, Commerce, and Human Cargoes

During the eighteenth century, new methods of finance, industry, and trade heralded the advent of the modern capitalism that has come to dominate the economic thought and practice of our century. national banks, paper currency, government bonds, joint stock companies, and multinational trading companies were just a few of the financial innovations and commercial ventures that first made their appearance during the Enlightenment. It was also during this period that Europe's wholesale traders, merchant bankers, manufacturers, and entrepreneurs began to emerge as a distinct social class with interests, ideas, and principles that set them apart from the aristocrats, churchmen, peasants, artisans, and shopkeepers of the Old Regime.

Daniel Defoe: from *The Complete English Tradesman,* 1727

Many people in "respectable society" believed that one's income should be derived from agricultural enterprises, rents, and annuities, rather than from "base" commerce. They decried the growing importance of banking and merchandising in the economies of Western Europe. Englishman Daniel Defoe, the creator of *Robinson Crusoe*, (1660-1731) took issue with this prejudice.

CHAPTER XXV: OF THE DIGNITY OF TRADE IN ENGLAND, MORE THAN IN OTHER COUNTRIES. THAT ENGLAND IS THE GREATEST TRADING COUNTRY IN THE WORLD

As so many of our noble and wealthy families, as we have shown, are raised by and derived from trade, so it is true, and indeed it cannot well be otherwise, that many of the younger branches of our gentry, and even of the nobility itself, have descended again into the spring from whence they flowed, and have become tradesmen; and thence it is that, as I said above, our tradesmen in England are not, as it generally is in other countries, always of the meanest of our people. Nor is trade itself in England, as it generally is in other countries, the meanest thing the men can turn their hand to; but, on the contrary, trade is the readiest way for men to raise their fortunes and families; and therefore it is a field for men of figure and of good families to enter upon.

N.B. By trade we must be understood to include navigation and foreign discoveries; because they are, generally speaking, all promoted and carried on by trade, and even by tradesmen, as well as merchants; and the tradesman, as owners, are at this time as much concerned in shipping as the merchants, only the latter may be said to be the chief employers of the shipping....

As to the wealth of the nation, that undoubtedly lies chiefly among the trading part of the people; and though there are a great many families raised within few years, in the late war, by great employments and by great actions abroad, to the honour of the English gentry, yet how many more families among the tradesmen have been raised to immense estates, even during the same time, by the attending circumstances of the war; such as the clothing, the paying, the victualling and furnishing, &c., both army and navy. And by whom have the prodigious taxes been paid, the loans supplied, and money advanced upon all occasions? By whom are the customs and excises levied? Have not the trade and tradesmen borne the burden of the war? And do they not still pay four millions a year interest for the public debts? On whom are the funds levied, and by whom the public credit supported? Is no trade the inexhausted fund of all funds, and upon which all the rest depend?

As is the trade, so in proportion are the trades men; and how wealthy are tradesmen in almost all the several parts of England, as well as in London? How common is it to see a tradesman go off the stage, even but from mere shopkeeping, with from ten to forty thousand pounds' estate to divide among his family! when, on the contrary, take the gentry in England, from one end to the other, except a few here and there, what with excessive high living, which is of late grown so much into a disease, and the other ordinary circumstances of families, we find few families of the lower gentry, that is to say from six or seven hundred a year downwards, but they are in debt, and in necessitous circumstances, and a great many of greater estates also.

On the other hand, let any one who is acquainted with England, look but abroad into the several counties, especially near London, or within fifty miles of it; how are the ancient families worn out by time and family misfortunes, and the estates possessed by a new race of tradesmen, grown up into families of gentry, and established by the immense wealth gained, as I may say, behind the counter; that is, in the shop, the warehouse, and the counting-house....

Again; in how superior a port or figure (as we now call it) do our tradesmen live, to what the middling gentry either do or can support! An ordinary tradesman now, not in the city only, but in the country, shall spend more money by the year, than a gentleman of four or five hundred pounds a year can do, and shall increase and lay up every year too; whereas the gentleman shall at the best stand stock still just where he began, nay, perhaps, decline: and as for the lower gentry, from a hundred pounds a year to three hundred, or thereabouts, though they are often as proud and high in their appearance as the other; as to them, I say, a shoemaker in London shall keep a better house, spend more money, clothe his family better, and yet grow rich too. It is evident where the difference lies; an estate's a pond, but trade's a spring: the first, if it keeps full, and the water wholesome, by the ordinary supplies and drains from the neighbouring grounds, it is well, and it is all that is expected; but the other is an inexhausted current, which not only fills the pond, but is continually running over, and fills all the lower ponds and places about it.

This being the case in England, and our trade being so vastly great, it is no wonder that the tradesmen in England fills the lists of our nobility and gentry; no wonder that the gentlemen of the best families marry tradesmen's daughters, and put their younger sons apprentices to tradesmen; and how often do these younger sons come to buy the elder sons' estates, and restore the family, when the elder and head of the house, proving rakish and extravagant, has wasted his patrimony, and is obliged to make out the blessing of Israel's family, where the younger son bought the birthright, and the elder was doomed to serve him!

Trade is so far here from being inconsistent with a gentleman, that, in short, trade in England makes gentlemen, and has peopled this nation with gentlemen; for, after a generation or two, the tradesman's children, or at least their grandchildren, come to be as good gentlemen, statesmen, parliamentmen, privy-counsellors, judges, bishops, and noblemen, as those of the highest birth and the most ancient families; as we have shown. Nor do we find any defect either in the genius or capacities of the posterity of tradesmen, arising from any remains of mechanic blood, which, it is pretended, should influence them; but all the gallantry of spirit, greatness of soul, and all the generous principles that can be found in any of the ancient families, whose blood is the most untainted, as they call it, with the low mixtures of a mechanic race, are found in these; and, as is said before, they generally go beyond them in knowledge of the world, which is the best education....

from *The Complete English Tradesman.* Vol. 1. 1889. Reprinted New York: Burt Franklin, 1970.

Questions:
1. What social prejudices was Defoe arguing against in his book on trade? What points did he make to support his convictions?
2. In what ways did Defoe claim that England was different from other countries in its view of trade-related occupations?
3. What biases exist toward certain kinds of business activities and occupations today? Are there certain kinds of work that are considered "honorable" for people who either have money or who want to be considered "professional"?

Unit 42: Bringing Up Baby: Family and Education in the Old Regime

Earl of Chesterfield: from Letters to His Son

Among the aristocracy of the eighteenth century, a person's standing in "good society" was very much dependent on his social behavior. An individual's manners, wit, conversational ability, and social graces were often the critical factors in determining his access to the dinner parties and evening soirees where much of the private and public business of the Old Regime was conducted. Indeed, as the following letter from the Earl of Chesterfield to his son demonstrates, teaching one's children the "art" of proper behavior in society was regarded as the most important skill one could impart to one's offspring.

Having, in my last, pointed out what sort of company you should keep, I will now give you some rules for your conduct in it; rules which my own experience and observation enable me to lay down and communicate to you with some degree of confidence. I have often given you hints of this kind before, but then it has been by snatches; I will now be more regular and methodical. I shall say nothing with regard to your bodily carriage and address, but leave them to the care of your dancing-master, and to your own attention to the best models; remember however, that they are of consequence.

Talk often, but never long; in that case, if you do not please at least you are sure not to tire your hearers. Pay your own reckoning, but do not treat the whole company; this being one of the very few cases in which people do not care to be treated, every one being fully convinced that he has wherewithal to pay.

Tell stories very seldom, and absolutely never but where they are very apt, and very short. Omit every circumstance that is not material, and beware of digressions To have frequent recourse to narrative betrays great want of imagination.

Never hold anybody by the button, or the hand, in order to be heard out; for, if people are not willing to hear you, you had much better hold your tongue than them.

Most long talkers single out some one unfortunate man in company (commonly him whom they observe to be the most silent, or their next neighbour) to whisper, or at least, in a half voice, to convey a continuity of words to. This is excessively ill-bred, and, in some degree, a fraud; conversation-stock being a joint and common property. But, on the other hand, if one of these unmerciful talkers lays hold of you, hear him with patience, and at least seeming attention, if he is worth obliging; for nothing will oblige him more than a patient hearing, as nothing would hurt him more than either to leave him in the midst of his discourse, or to discover your impatience under your affliction

Take, rather than give, the tone of the company you are in. If you have parts, you will show them, more or less, upon every subject; and, if you have not, you had better talk sillily upon a subject of other people's than of your own choosing. Avoid as much as you can, in mixed companies, argumentative polemical conversations; which, though they should not, yet certainly do, indispose, for a time, the contending parties towards each other; and, if the controversy grows warm and noisy, endeavour to put an end to it by some genteel levity or joke. I quieted such a conversation hubbub once, by representing to them that, though I was persuaded none there present would repeat, out of company, what passed in it, yet I could not answer for the discretion of the passengers in the street, who must necessarily hear all that was said.

Above all things, and upon all occasions, avoid speaking of yourself, if it be possible. Such is the natural pride and vanity of our hearts, that it perpetually breaks out, even in people of the best parts, in all the various modes and figures of the egotism.

…Always look people in the face when you speak to them; the not doing it is thought to imply conscious guilt; besides that, you lose the advantage of observing by their countenances what impression your discourse makes upon them. In order to know people's real sentiments, I trust much more to my eyes than to my ears; for they can say whatever they have a mind I should hear; but they can seldom help looking what they have no intention that I should know.

Neither retail nor receive scandal willingly; for though the defamation of others may for the present gratify the malignity of the pride of our hearts, cool reflection will draw very disadvantageous conclusions from such a disposition; and in the case of scandal, as in that of robbery, the receiver is always thought as bad as the thief.

Mimicry, which is the common and favourite amusement of little low minds, is in the utmost contempt with great ones. It is the lowest and most illiberal of all buffoonery. Pray, neither practise it yourself, nor applaud it in others. Besides that, the person mimicked is insulted; and, as I have often observed to you before, an insult is never forgiven.

I need not, I believe, advise you to adapt your conversation to the people you are conversing with; for I suppose you would not, without this caution, have talked upon the same subject and in the same manner to a Minister of state, a Bishop, a philosopher, a Captain, and a woman. A man of the world must, like the cameleon, be able to take every different hue, which is by no means a criminal or abject, but a necessary complaisance, for it relates only to manners, and not to morals.

One word only as to swearing; and that I hope and believe is more than is necessary. You may sometimes hear some people in good company interlard their discourse with oaths, by way of embellishment, as they think; but you must observe, too, that those who do so are never those who contribute in any degree to give that company the denomination of good company. They are always subalterns, or people of low education; for that practice, besides that it has no one temptation to plead, is as silly and as illiberal as it is wicked.

Loud laughter is the mirth of the mob, who are only pleased with silly things; for true wit or good sense never excited a laugh since the creation of the world A man of parts and fashion is therefore only seen to smile, but never heard to laugh....

from *The Letters of Philip Dormer Stanhope, Earl of Chesterfield,* vol. 1. Edited by John Bradshaw.
London: Swan Sonnenschein, 1892

Questions:
1. What specific advice did Chesterfield give to his son? What social values and customs are revealed in this document?
2. If you were at a dinner party given by your employer, a computer programming company, how much of this advice would you try to practice? In general, what principles of Chesterfield do you accept, and which do you reject?

John Howard On The Education of Noble Women in Russia, 1777

It may strike one as odd that the English penal reformer, John Howard, would include a description of a girl's boarding school in St. Petersburg in his book on European prisons. Howard's decision, however, to include a description of this school in his book did not stem from a belief on his part that it was like a prison. Instead, this school struck him as a model for the sort of enlightened educational system that he believed would make prisons an odious relic of the past. Whatever his reasons, however, one can see in Howard's commentary on Catherine the Great's boarding school the basis for a more modern educational system.

On a rising ground at a little distance from *Petersburg*, and on the south side of the river *Neva*, there is a stately pile of buildings, originally designed for a *Convent*, but ever since 1764 converted by the Empress *Catharine* the Second, into a public establishment for educating the female *nobility* of *Russia*, and a limited number of the children of *commoners.* The sleeping rooms and dining-halls in these buildings are remarkably lofty and airy, having large galleries round them; and adjoining to the buildings there are spacious gardens and lawns, which extend to the banks of the river.—The number of the children of *nobility* on this establishment is two hundred; and the number of the children of commoners or *peasants* was, till 1770, limited to two hundred and forty: but since this year it has been increased to two hundred and eighty, by a fund provided by the munificence of general *De Betskoi*, the enlightened and liberal head and director-general of this, and all the other institutions of the same kind established by her *imperial majesty.*

The principal regulations for conducting this institution are the following.—The children are admitted between five and six years of age, and continued on the establishment twelve years. They are divided into classes according to their ages, *four* of *nobles* with fifty in each class, and *four* of *commoners* with seventy in each class.— In every third year on the 21st of April, (the birthday of the Empress,) fifty children of the *nobility*, and seventy of *commoners* are taken in, to replace the same numbers discharged.—Before they rise every morning, the windows of their rooms are thrown open to purify them with fresh air.—The *first* class (dressed in *brown*, and consisting of children of the youngest ages,) rise at seven in winter, and at six in summer.—After being washed and attending prayers, they are taken into the garden where they breakfast, and play about in the coldest weather till nine. During their first year, each of them is allowed for breakfast, a small loaf of white bread, and a glass of milk and water; but after their first year, they are allowed no other drink than water.—At nine they are called back to the house, and from this hour to eleven are employed in learning the *French* and *Russian* languages, and in knitting, sewing &c. but care is taken to render all the instruction they receive agreeable, nothing being taught in this establishment by compulsion.—Twice in the week they receive lessons in dancing; and this is a part of education common to all the classes, and never discontinued, because reckoned conducive to health.—After *eleven* they return to their play in the garden where they continue till noon, at which time they are called to dinner, which consists of soup, vegetables &c. For some months at first they are allowed meat; but they are gradually weaned from it, till at last, while in this and the next class, it comes to be entirely withheld from them (except in soups,) in order to cure them of some cutaneous distempers to which at this age they are subject, and also to prepare them for passing with less danger through the hooping-cough, measles and small-pox. After dinner they return to the garden, and at four, have a repast similar to that in the morning, viz. a loaf of brad and a glass of water. Here they continue to divert themselves till at seven they are called to supper, which consists in winter of dried fruit, milk and grain; and in summer of preparations of milk, and some provisions from the garden.—It may be proper to add, that they read and write standing, and are not allowed to sit down, except to needle-work.— In consequence of this management, and of living so much in the air, and being used to exercise, and cleanliness and a simple diet, they are seldom known to take cold; and become capable of bearing the severest weather of the climate without receiving any harm, their clothing being only a short wadded cloak, whilst others are loaded with furs.

The *second* class (dressed in *blue*) enter it about eight years of age, and are obliged to apply more closely to writing, drawing, dancing &c.

The *third* class (dressed in *grey*) enter it at eleven or twelve years of age. They rise at five, in the summer, and six, in winter; but are called to the house (after breakfasting in the garden,) an hour sooner than the children in the first and second classes; because more time is wanted for instructing and improving them. They are now taught (besides drawing, dancing, turning, needle-work &c.) vocal and instrumental music. They are allowed a ball and concert every week; and a taste for books is inspired, by putting them upon copying and reciting select passages from the best authors.

The *fourth* class (dressed in *white*) enter it at fourteen or fifteen years of age. They are taught tambour-work, house-keeping, the management of a family &c. and initiated into history, geography and natural philosophy. In order to acquire a just elocution, and to exercise themselves in politeness, and vocal and instrumental music, they occasionally give balls and little operas to company from *Petersburg*.

The children of the nobility and of commoners are distinguished from one another, only by wearing a finer camlet of the colours appropriated to the different classes; and as far as diet, exercise, regimen &c. are concerned, the method of managing them is the same; but the instruction given the latter, is confined to needle-work, reading, house-keeping and such other occupations and improvements as are suitable to the humbler walks of life, for which they are intended.

from John Howard, *The State of the Prisons in England and Wales, with Preliminary Observations on Some Foreign Prisons*. Volume 2. London, 1777.

Questions:
1. Recalling the unit on Enlightened Despotism, how might one use this document to argue in support of or against Catherine being an "enlightened" ruler?
2. What would Rousseau have thought of this school?

Chapter 20: The French Revolution

Unit 43: Prelude to the Revolution

In his historical romance, *A Tale of Two Cities*, Charles Dickens described the late eighteenth century as both the best and the worst of times, and nowhere was this more true than in Old Regime France. Possessed of a population of some 27 million people, a steadily expanding industrial and commercial economy, and a sizable army and navy, late eighteenth-century France remained one of the most populous, wealthy, and militarily strong nations in Europe. Moreover, France's language was the *lingua franca* of all educated Europeans, and the salons and shops of Paris continued to be the final arbiters of all that was considered fashionable, elegant, and civilized in Europe. Impressive as all of these achievements were, however, France was an extremely troubled country at the end of the eighteenth century. On the eve of the French Revolution, France was a nation that was burdened with an enormous public debt, an inept monarch, and a deeply divided society grounded in gross inequalities of wealth, privilege and opportunity. Indeed, France in the years immediately prior to 1789 was a tragedy waiting to happen.

Protest by the *Cour des Aides*, 1775

PRESENTED TO THE KING, OUR MOST HONORED SOVEREIGN AND LORD, BY THOSE WHO HOLD HIS COUR DES AIDES AT PARIS.

Sire:

Your *Cour des aides* had just protested on its own part, and on the part of the whole Magistracy, against certain articles of the act by which it has been re-established; but another and more important duty still remains to be fulfilled. It is the cause of the people which we must now plead before the tribunal of Your Majesty. We must present a faithful picture to you of the taxes and dues which are levied in your kingdom, and which constitute the subject-matter of the jurisdiction confided to us; we must make known to Your Majesty at the beginning of your reign the real condition of the people, whom the spectacle of a brilliant court can never call to your mind....

[8] Neither can Your Majesty be unaware that in addition to the taxation on individual commodities the production of certain of them is either forbidden or embarrassed throughout the country in the interest of the Farm. Your subjects are, for instance, forbidden to cultivate tobacco, while millions are paid for it each year to foreigners; salt, too, would prove one of the most precious gifts which nature has bestowed upon France if only the hand of the Financier did not constantly reject what the sea as constantly brings to our shores. Your Majesty cannot be ignorant that there are regions where the manufacture of salt is confined to certain privileged persons, and where, at certain seasons of the year, the agents of the Farm call together the peasants to throw back into the sea the salt which been deposited on the shore; that on other coasts salt manufacture, although ostensibly permitted, is nevertheless subject to such restraints that the Farmer can ruin, and ruin effectively, whoever undertakes it against his wishes; that almost everywhere the exorbitant price of salt deprives the people of the benefits that they might derive from this precious commodity, by using it as seasoning and as a preservative, or for their cattle, or in innumerable useful ways, even for the enrichment of the soil.

[9] Your Majesty knows also that all the other taxes on commodities are prejudicial to production and to commerce; that France would produce more wine were it not for the excises; that it would manufacture more merchandise were it not for the interior customs duties. The list of these disadvantages is interminable; we are well aware, Sire that we cannot give you a complete account of them, because every day we hear of new ones; but this sketch will suffice to show you the injury done to your kingdom by the farming of the taxes, independently of the sums paid by the people for the cost of administration and as profit to the Farmers of the revenue....

[11] But there is still another sort of tyranny, of which it is possible that Your Majesty has never heard. Although it does not afford so cruel a spectacle as that of which we have been speaking, it is none the less insupportable to the people, since it affects all the citizens of the lowest class, those who live quietly by labor or trade. It is due to the circumstance that every man belonging to the people is forced to submit daily to the caprices, the insolence, even the insults of the minions of the Tax-farmer. This particular kind of annoyance has never received much attention, because it is only experienced by the obscure and unknown. In fact, if a Clerk shows a want of regard for persons of consideration the heads of the financial administration hasten to disavow their subordinate and to satisfy the complainant; and it is precisely by means of this consideration for the Great that the Farm has been able to subject the defenceless people to an unrestrained and unlimited despotism. Yet this unprotected class is the largest in your realm, and the defenceless certainly have the first claim to the direct protection of Your Majesty.

[12] It devolves upon us, therefore, to explain to Your Majesty the real cause of the servitude to which the people are reduced throughout the provinces. That cause, Sire, is to be sought in the nature of the power exercised by the officers of the Farm—a power arbitrary in many respects, which makes it only too easy for them to render themselves formidable.

[13] In the first place, the General Farm[1] has an enormous body of rules and regulations, which have never been collected and codified. It is an occult science which no one except the Financiers themselves has studied, or can study, so that the individual against whom action is brought can neither know the law himself nor consult any one else; he is obliged to rely on the very same Clerk who is his enemy and persecutor. How can a laborer or an artisan help trembling and humbling himself continually before an adversary who has such terrible weapons to turn against him?

[14] In the second place, the laws of the Farm are not only unknown but are sometimes uncertain. There are many doubtful prerogatives which the Farmer will exercise according to circumstances. It will readily be surmised that the employees of the Farm make their experiments by preference upon those who have had the misfortune to displease them. It is natural, too, that they are never made except upon those who have not means enough to defend themselves.

[15] Finally, there are other laws which are unfortunately only too definite, but which it is impossible to execute literally, by reason of their extreme severity. The Farmer procures their adoption well knowing that he will not carry them into execution, and he reserves the right to exempt from them when he wishes, but on condition that such exemption, without which the

---

[1] The company called "the General Farm" had been given the privilege of raising the majority of the indirect taxes, including the salt tax, the excises, and the customs duties. They paid the government a lump sum and had a lot of latitude in apportioning the tax between the taxpayers.

individual subject to the taxes would be ruined, shall be a favor granted arbitrarily either by him or his employees. This is a favorite expedient of the financial administration which should be fully exposed to Your Majesty. Yes, Sire, the Farmer has been known to say to the citizen: "The Farm must have certain favors to grant and to refuse you; it is essential that you should be obliged to come and ask for them." This is equivalent to saying, "It is not enough that you bring your money to satisfy our greed—you must gratify the insolence of our Clerks by your servility." Now, even if it be true that the greed of the Farmer can be turned to the advantage of the King, it is certain that the insolence of the army of Clerks who overrun the provinces cannot profit him in the least....

[84] In France the nation has always been profoundly conscious of its rights and of its freedom. Our traditions have been more than once recognized by our Kings, who have even gloried in being the sovereigns of a free people. Nevertheless the articles of that freedom have never been duly drawn up, and the real power, the power of arms, which under the feudal system was in the hands of the nobles, has been entirely concentrated in the sovereign.

[85] When, therefore, there have been cases of grievous abuse of authority, the representatives of the Nation have not been satisfied with complaining of mal-administration, they have felt obliged to vindicate the national rights. They have talked not merely of justice, but of liberty; and the consequence of their efforts has been that the Ministers, who were always ready to seize every possible means of shielding their administration from examination, have been artful enough to arouse suspicion in regard both to the governmental bodies which protested and to the protests themselves. Recourse to the King against his Ministers has been represented as an attack upon his authority. The grievances of the Estates, the remonstrances of the Magistrates, have been distorted into dangerous measures, against which the government should protect itself. The most powerful of Kings have been persuaded that they must fear even the tears of a submissive people. Upon this pretext a government has been introduced into France which is more fatal than despotism and is worthy of Oriental barbarism, namely, the clandestine system of administration, which under the eyes of a just ruler and in the midst of an enlightened nation permits injustice to show herself, nay more, to flaunt herself openly. Entire departments of the administration are founded upon principles of injustice, and no recourse either to public opinion or to a superior authority is possible.

[89] General assemblies of the Nation have not been convened for a hundred and sixty years, and for a long time before that they were very infrequent, and, we venture to say, almost useless, since what should have rendered their presence especially necessary, namely, the fixing of the taxes, was accomplished without them....

from *Translations and Reprints from the Original Sources of European History*, vol. 5 # 2. University of Pennsylvania Press, 1899.

Unit 44: The Revolution

The immediate cause of the French Revolution was the disastrous state of the country's finances in 1788. The only solution to this financial crisis was a complete reform of the nation's public finances and, of course, new taxes to pay off the government's enormous debt. Initially, Louis XVI's finance ministers attempted to win over France's notables in the First and Second Estates to the rather novel idea of paying a larger share of the country's taxes. When this suggestion was rebuffed at an Assembly of Notables in 1787, Louis XVI found himself compelled to issue, on August 8, 1788, a call to the communities of France to elect and send to Versailles their representatives for the purpose of forming an Estates-General, or parliament, that would give him advice and support in meeting the financial problems of the realm. The Estates General had last met nearly two centuries before, in 1614. Unbeknownst to Louis, the calling of the Estates-General would be the first scene in a drama that would cost him first his throne and then his head.

The *Cahiers de doleances*

In addition to calling on the country to elect representatives to an Estates-General, Louis XVI also asked France's electoral assemblies to submit to him so-called *cahiers de doleances*, or "notebooks of grievances," which would outline the problems and needs of the different estates in each district of the nation. Louis also requested that these *cahiers* recommend possible remedies or reforms to take care of these problems.

One key area of discord that you will find running through all of these *cahiers* was the whole question of whether voting in the Estates-General should be by order or by head (i.e., each delegate would have one vote on all issues.) According to the procedures that had been used by the Estates-General in 1614, each order had voted separately on issues and each could veto the actions of the other two, an arrangement that favored the nobility and the clergy, who had far fewer representatives than the commoners of the Third Estate. Ultimately, this question of voting would be the first salvo in the events that would lead to the French Revolution.

CLERGY OF THE BAILLIAGE OF BLOIS AND OF ROMORANTIN

Constitution: The clergy of the *bailliage* of Blois have never believed that the constitution needed reform. Nothing is wanting to assure the welfare of king and people except that the present constitution should be religiously and inviolably observed.

The constitutional principles concerning which no doubt can be entertained are:

1. That France is a true monarchy, where a single man rules and is ruled by law alone.

2. That the general laws of the kingdom may be enacted only with the consent of the king and the nation. If the king proposes a law, the nation accepts or rejects it; if the nation demands a law, it is for the king to consent or to reject it; but in either case it is the king alone who upholds the law in his name and attends to its execution.

3. That in France we recognize as king him to whom the crown belongs by hereditary right according to the Salic law.

4. That we recognize the nation in the States General, composed of the three orders of the kingdom, which are the clergy, the nobility and the third estate.

5. That to the king belongs the right of assembling the States General, whenever he considers it necessary.

For the welfare of the kingdom we ask, in common with the whole nation, that this convocation be periodical and fixed, as we particularly desire, at every five years, except in the case of the next meeting, when the great number of matters to be dealt with makes a less remote period desirable.

6. That the States General should not vote otherwise than by order.

7. That the three orders are equal in power and independent of each other, in such a manner that their unanimous consent is necessary to the expression of the nation's will.

8. That no tax may be laid without the consent of the nation.

9. That every citizen has, under the law, a sacred and inviolable right to personal liberty and to the possession of his goods....

Taxes: After having observed that the clergy have never enjoyed other privileges in the imposition of taxes than those which were anciently common to all orders of the state, the clergy of the bailliage of Blois declare that for the future they desire to sustain the burden of taxation in common with other subjects of the king....

Justice: For the purpose of securing a reform of the principal abuses in the administration of justice we very humbly present to His Majesty what appears to us of first importance:

5. To authorize vassals to refuse the jurisdiction of their *seigneurs* in suits against the said *seigneurs;*

6. To establish in the principal rural places justices of the peace for the trial of minor cases;

7. To do away with the sale of judicial and magisterial offices;

10. To reform the civil and criminal codes and to diminish the number of customary codes which prevail in various parts of the kingdom, in order to hasten the day, if possible, when there shall be but one national code;

from *Translations and Reprints from the Original Sources of European History*, vol. 4.
Philadelphia: University of Pennsylvania Press, 1897.

Questions:
1. From this *cahier*, what do you learn about the relationship of the Catholic clergy of Blois with the monarch? That is, what was the relationship between church and state in France on the revolution's eve?
2. What procedure was recommended by this group for voting in the Estates General?

THE NOBILITY OF THE BAILLIAGE OF BLOIS

Deep and established ills cannot be cured with a single effort: the destruction of abuses is not the work of a day. Alas! of what avail to reform them if their causes be not removed? The misfortune of France arises from the fact that it has never had a fixed constitution. A virtuous and sympathetic king seeks the counsels and cooperation of the nation to establish one: let us hasten to accomplish his desires; let us hasten to restore to his soul that peace which his virtues merit. The principles of this constitution should be simple; they may be reduced to two: *Security for person, security for property;* because, in fact, it is from these two fertile principles that all organization of the body politic takes its rise.

On Personal Liberty

Article 1. In order to assure the exercise of this first and most sacred of the rights of man, we ask that no citizen may be exiled, arrested or held prisoner except in cases contemplated by the law and in accordance with a decree originating in the regular courts of justice.

That in case the States General determine that provisional detention may be necessary at times, it ought to be ordained that every person so arrested shall he delivered, within twenty-four hours, into the hands of appropriate judges, to be judged with the least possible delay, in conformity with the laws of the kingdom; that evocations be abolished, and that no extraordinary commission be established in any instance; finally that no person be deprived of his position, civil or military, without judgment in due form.

Since individual liberty is a right equally sacred for citizens of all ranks and classes, without distinction or precedence, the States General are invited to interest themselves in the suppression of all forced service in the militia and of acts of authority which involve the violation of personal rights, and which are the more intolerable in a century of intelligence, when it is possible to accomplish the same end with less oppressive means. The application of these principles ought to suffer exception only in the case of an urgent necessity, when the safety of the country is at stake, in which case the extent of the executive power should be enlarged.

From the right of personal liberty arises the right to write, to think; to write and to publish, with the names of authors and publishers, all kinds of complaints and reflections upon public and private affairs, limited by the right of every citizen to seek in the established courts legal redress against author or publisher, in case of defamation or injury; limited also by all restrictions which the States General may see t to impose in that which concerns morals and religion.

The violation of the secrecy of letters is still an infringement upon the liberty of citizens; and since the sovereign has assumed the exclusive right of transporting letters throughout the kingdom, and this has become a source of public revenue, such carriage ought to be made under the seal of confidence.

We indicate further a number of instances in which natural liberty is abridged:

1. The abuse of police regulations, which every year, in an arbitrary manner and without regular process, thrusts a number of artisans and useful citizens into prisons, work-houses and places of detention, often for trivial faults and even upon simple suspicion;

2. The abuse of exclusive privileges which fetter industry;

3. The gilds and corporations which deprive citizens of the right of using their faculties;

4. The regulations governing manufactures, the rights of inspection and *marque,* which impose restrictions that have lost their usefulness, and which burden industry with a tax that yields no profit to the public treasury.

Taxes

Article 2. A tax is a partition of property.

This partition ought not to be otherwise than voluntary; in any other case the rights of property are violated: Hence it is the indefeasible and inalienable right of the nation to consent to its taxes.

According to this principle, which has been solemnly recognized by the king, no tax, real or personal, direct or indirect, nor any contribution whatsoever, under whatsoever name or form, may be established except with the consent and free and voluntary approval of the nation. Nor may said power of consenting to a tax he transferred or delegated by the nation to any magistracy or other body, or exercised by the provincial estates nor by the provincial, city or communal assemblies: superior and inferior courts shall be especially charged to attend to the execution of this article, and to prosecute as exactors those who may undertake to levy a tax which has not received the proper sanction.

All public loans are, properly speaking, taxes in disguise, since the property of the kingdom is affected and hypothecated for the payment of capital and interest. Therefore no loan, under whatsoever form or denomination, may be effected without the consent and will of the nation assembled.

Since the greater number of the taxes and imposts established up to this time have not received the sanction of the nation, the first business of the assembled estates will be to abolish all without exception; at the same time, in order to avoid the inconvenience resulting from an interruption in the payment of interest on the public debt and the expenses of government, the nation assembled, by virtue of the same authority, shall re-establish them, collecting them under the title of a free gift during the session of the States General and up to the time when they shall have established such other taxes as may seem to them desirable.

A tax is no other thing than a voluntary sacrifice which each person makes of his particular property in favor of the public power which protects and guarantees all. It is therefore evident that the tax ought to be proportioned to the interest which each has in preserving his property, and consequently to the value of this property. In accordance with this principle the nobility of the *bailliage* of Blois believes itself in duty bound to lay at the feet of the nation all the pecuniary exemptions which it has enjoyed or might have enjoyed up to this time, and it offers to contribute to the public needs in proportion with other citizens, upon condition that the names of *taille* and *corvée* be suppressed and all direct taxes be comprised in a single land tax in money.

The nobility of the bailliage of Blois, in making this surrender of its ancient privileges, has been unable to suppress a sentiment of interest in favor of that portion of the nobility which a modest fortune confines to the rural districts. It believes that. a proprietor, who fulfils the obligation of his heritage, spreads about him prosperity and happiness; that the efforts he makes to increase his revenues increase at the same time the mass of the agricultural products of the realm; that the country districts are covered with chateaux and manors, formerly inhabited by the French nobility, but to-day abandoned; that a great public interest would be subserved by inducing proprietors to seek again, so far as possible, their interests in the country.

Animated by these motives we believe that it is our duty to solicit the especial protection of the States General in favor of that respectable portion of the nation, which divides its time between the culture of the fields and the defence of the state; and we hope that means will be found to reconcile that which is due to their interests and needs with the absolute renunciation which is about to be made of the pecuniary exemptions of nobility.

If as has been said, a tax is the price paid for the protection which government accords to property, it follows that all property which the government protects ought to be subject to the tax; that the tax, as a necessary consequence, ought to affect incomes from bonds and interest upon the royal funds in the same proportion as land.

It is useless to urge that such an extension of the tax would be a violation of the public faith: property in bonds is no more sacred than property in land: and if the nation can consent to a tax upon one it can also tax the other. The same contribution should be exacted from the emoluments derived from all financial positions and from all lucrative employments.

The order of nobility has no doubt that the national assembly will concern itself with the examination and reformation of that mass of taxes, the collection of which, thanks to the financial spirit which necessity has imparted to the administration, has been rendered intolerable to the people; such as the *gabelle*, the *aides* and others.

While awaiting the suppression of these taxes, their simplification, condensation, conversion or assessment by provinces, we ask that at least their collection be made less burdensome; that lists be drawn up and given to the public, in order that each may know the amount of his obligation; that over-assessments be avoided and abuses reformed....

The free and voluntary renunciation which the order of nobility is about to make of its pecuniary privileges gives it the right to demand that no exemption whatsoever shall be retained in favor of any class of citizens. We have no doubt that the clergy will voluntarily consent to bear all taxes in common with citizens of other orders, in proportion to their possessions; and we demand that the privileges of free cities, of stage masters, of sealers of weights and measures and of all other persons be abolished; in order that the tax shall affect all persons and places in proportion to the net product of their incomes....

Concerning the National Constitution and the Means of Obtaining the Abolition of Abuses

Article 8. Up to this point we have merely indicated the abuses which have accumulated in France during a long succession of centuries; we have made it evident that the rights of citizens have been abridged by a multitude of laws which attack property, liberty and personal safety....

It is not sufficient to suppress these abuses; it is necessary to prevent their return; there must be established an ever active influence, moving without interruption in the direction of public prosperity, which shall bear in itself the germ of all good, a principle destructive of all evil.

In order to accomplish this great object the nobility of the *bailliage* of Blois demand:

That the States General about to assemble shall be permanent and shall not be dissolved until the constitution be established; but in case the labors connected with the establishment of the constitution be prolonged beyond a space of two years, the assembly shall be reorganized with new deputies freely and regularly elected.

That a fundamental and constitutional law shall assure forever the periodical assembly of the States General at frequent intervals, in such a manner that they may assemble and organize themselves at a fixed time and place, without the concurrence of any act emanating from the executive power.

That the legislative power shall reside exclusively in the assembly of the nation, under the sanction of the king, and shall not be exercised by any intermediate body during the recess of the States General.

That the king shall enjoy the full extent of executive power necessary to insure the execution of the laws; hut that he shall not be able in any event to modify the laws without the consent of the nation.

That the form of the military oath shall be changed, and the troops promise obedience and fidelity to the king and the nation.

That taxes may not be imposed without the consent of the nation;

That taxes may he granted only for a specified time, and for no longer than the next meeting of the States General.

[The question of how voting should be conducted in the States Genera called forth a variety of opinions, and it was decided to insert in the cahier the minutes of the meeting of March 28, in so far as they bore upon the matter. The substance of the discussion is as follows:

Upon the first ballot the assembly stood 51 for the vote by order and 48 for the vote per capita.

It was suggested however that many present favored a mixed system of voting, viz: that in matters of general welfare, or which involved the granting of subsidies and the maintenance of the national honor, voting should be per capita; that in matters touching the rights and interests of the individual orders, voting should be by order.

Upon ballot, 68 signified their approval of this system and 28 still adhered to the vote by order.]

There shall be established this year, if possible, and before the adjournment of the States General, provincial estates, which shall superintend the levy of taxes approved by the nation,…have charge of highways and public works and of all that concerns the special local interests of the provinces, as well as all matters of administration confided to them by the States General, especially the administration of the domains and forests belonging to the king and to communes.

With respect to the organization of the provincial estates the nobility of the *bailliage* of Blois will aquiesce in whatever the States General may be pleased to determine.

That a part of the magisterial and judicial powers hitherto possessed by intendants shall be entrusted to a court established in each *généralité*

It has been determined to grant absolute powers to delegates; but that notice he given them that the unanimous desire of the nobility of the *bailliage* of Blois has never swerved from this principle: No subsidies without a constitution; no tax to be legal, unless decreed and determined by the States General.

[The cahier is signed by 7 marquises, 7 counts, 3 viscounts, S barons, 9 knights, and 64 persons without special title.]

from *Translations and Reprints from the Original Sources of European History*, vol. 4.
Philadelphia: University of Pennsylvania Press, 1897.

Questions:
1. What rights did this group of nobles want to secure? What abuses did they want to eliminate? Cite specific examples from the document.
2. What position did these nobles take in relation to taxes? Is this what you would have expected? Why do you think they took this position?

THE THIRD ESTATE OF THE BAILLIAGE OF VERSAILLES

The Constitution

Article 1. The power of making laws resides in the king and the nation.

Article 2. The nation being too numerous for a personal exercise of this right, has confided its trust to representatives freely chosen from all classes of citizens. These representatives constitute the national assembly.

Article 3. Frenchmen should regard as laws of the kingdom those alone which have been prepared by the national assembly and sanctioned by the king....

Article 11. Personal liberty, proprietary rights and the security of citizens shall be established in a clear, precise and irrevocable manner. All *lettres de cachet* shall be abolished for ever, subject to certain modifications which the States General may see fit to impose.

Article 13. All persons accused of crimes not involving the death penalty shall be released on bail within twenty-four hours. This release shall be pronounced by the judge upon the decision of the jury.

Article 14. All persons who shall have been imprisoned upon suspicion, and afterwards proved innocent, shall be entitled to satisfaction and damages from the state, if they are able to show that their honor or property has suffered injury.

Article 15. A wider liberty of the press shall be accorded, with this provision alone: that all manuscripts sent to the printer shall be signed by the author, who shall be obliged to disclose his identity and bear the responsibility of his work; and to prevent judges and other persons in power from taking advantage of their authority, no writing shall be held a libel until it is so determined by twelve jurors, chosen according to the forms of a law which shall be enacted upon this subject.

Article 17. All distinctions in penalties shall be abolished; and crimes committed by citizens of the different orders shall be punished irrespectively, according to the same forms of law and in the same manner. The States General shall seek to bring it about that the effects of transgression shall be confined to the individual, and shall not be reflected upon the relatives of the transgressor, themselves innocent of all participation.

Article 18. Penalties shall in all cases be moderate and proportionate to the crime. All kinds of torture, the rack and the stake, shall be abolished. Sentence of death shall be pronounced only for atrocious crimes and in rare instances, determined by the law.

Article 20. The military throughout the kingdom shall be subject to the general law and to the civil authorities, in the same manner as other citizens.

Article 21. No tax shall be legal unless accepted by the representatives of the people and sanctioned by the king.

Article 22. Since all Frenchmen receive the same advantage from the government, and are equally interested in its maintenance they ought to be placed upon the same footing in the matter of taxation.

Article 23. All taxes now in operation are contrary to these principles and for the most part vexatious, oppressive and humiliating to the people. They ought to be abolished as soon as possible, and replaced by others common to the three orders and to all classes of citizens, without exception.

Article 28. In case of war, or other exceptional necessity, no loan shall be made without the consent of the States General, and it shall be enacted that no loan shall be effected, without provision being made by taxation for the payment of interest, and of the principal at a specified time.

Article 29. The amount which each citizen shall be obliged to pay, in case of war, by reason of an increase in the existing taxes, at a certain rate per *livre*, shall be determined beforehand by the States General in conjunction with the king. The certainty of increase ought to have a marked effect in preventing useless and unjust wars, since it clearly indicates to Frenchmen the new burden they will have to bear, and to foreign nations the resources which the nation has in reserve and at hand to repulse unjust attacks.

Article 35. The present militia system, which is burdensome, oppressive and humiliating to the people, shall be abolished; and the States General shall devise means for its reformation.

Article 37. Since the nation undertakes to provide for the personal expenses of the sovereign, as well as for the crown and state, the law providing for the inalienability of the domain shall be repealed. As a result, all the domanial possessions immediately in the king's possession, as well as those already pledged, and the forests of his majesty as well, shall be sold, and transferred in small lots, in so far as possible, and always at public auction to the highest bidder; and the proceeds applied to the reduction of the public debt....

Article 40b. Ministers and all government officials shall be responsible to the States General for their conduct of affairs. They may be impeached according to fixed forms of law and punished according to the statute.

Article 46. All offices and positions, civil, ecclesiastical and military, shall be open to all orders; and no humiliating and unjust exception (in the case of the third estate), destructive to emulation and injurious to the interests of the state, shall be perpetuated.

Article 49. All relics of serfdom, agrarian or personal, still remaining in certain provinces, shall be abolished.

Article 50. New laws shall be made in favor of the negroes in our colonies; and the States General shall take measures toward the abolition of slavery. Meanwhile let a law be passed, that negroes in the colonies who desire to purchase their freedom, as well as those whom their masters are willing to set free, shall no longer be compelled to pay a tax to the domain.

Article 51. The three functions, legislative, executive and judicial, shall be separated and carefully distinguished.

The communes of the bailliage of Versailles have already expressed themselves in respect to the necessity of adopting the form of deliberation *per capita* in the coming States General. The reform of the constitution will be one of their principal duties. This magnificent monument of liberty and public felicity should be the work of the three orders in common session; if they are separated, certain pretensions, anxieties and jealousies are bound to arise; the tow upper orders are likely to oppose obstacles, perhaps invincible, to the reform of abuses and the enactment of laws destined to suppress such abuses. It seems indispensable that in this first assembly votes should be taken *per capita* and not by order. After the renunciation by the two upper orders of their pecuniary privileges; after all distinctions before the law have been abolished; when the exclusion of the third estate from certain offices and positions has been done away with,—then the reasons which today necessitate deliberation *per capita* will no longer exist.

The Executive

Article 52. It shall be ordained by the constitution that the executive power be vested in the king alone.

Article 55. His consent shall be necessary to all bills approved by the States General in order that they may acquire the force of law throughout the realm. He may reject all bills presented to him, without being obliged to state the reasons of his disapproval.

Article 56. He shall have the sole right of convening, progogueing and dissolving the States General.

The Judiciary

Article 57. The sale of the judicial office shall be suppressed as soon as circumstances will permit, and provision made for the indemnification of holders.

Article 64. Judges of all courts shall be obliged to adhere to the letter of the law and may never be permitted to change, modify, or interpret it at their pleasure.

Article 65. The fees received by all officers of justice shall be fixed at a moderate rate and clearly understood; and judges who extort fees in excess of the fixed rates shall be condemned to pay a fine of four times the amount they have received.

from *Translations and Reprints from the Original Sources of European History*, vol. 4.
Philadelphia; University of Pennsylvania Press, 1897.

Questions:
1. What rights were being demanded by these Third Estate members? What existing inequalities between the orders become evident in this document? What abuses were they trying to overcome?
2. What Estates-General voting procedure was recommended by this group? What was their justification for their stand?
3. Compare and contrast the *cahiers* of the three estates. What similarities and differences do you find in the directives that were given to their respective delegates? How would you account for the similarities and differences?

The Abolition of Feudalism, August 4-11, 1789

1. The National Assembly hereby completely abolishes the feudal system. It decrees that, among the existing rights and dues, both feudal and *censuel,* all those originating in or representing real or personal serfdom or personal servitude, shall be abolished without indemnification. All other dues are declared redeemable, the terms and mode of redemption to be fixed by the National Assembly. Those of the said dues which are not extinguished by this decree shall continue to be collected until indemnification shall take place.

2. The exclusive right to maintain pigeon-houses and dove-cotes is abolished. The pigeons shall be confined during the seasons fixed by the community. During such periods they shall be looked upon as game, and every one shall have the right to kill them upon his own land.

3. The exclusive right to hunt and to maintain unenclosed warrens is likewise abolished, and every land owner shall have the right to kill or to have destroyed on his own land all kinds of game, observing, however, such police regulations as may be established with a view to the safety of the public.

   All hunting *capitaineries,* including the royal forests, and all hunting rights under whatever denomination, are likewise abolished. Provision shall be made, however, in a manner compatible with the regard due to property and liberty, for maintaining the personal pleasures of the king.

The president of the assembly shall be commissioned to ask of the King the recall of those sent to the galleys or exiled, simply for violations of the hunting regulations, as well as for the release of those at present imprisoned for offences of this kind, and the dismissal of such cases as are now pending.

4. All manorial courts are hereby suppressed without indemnification. But the magistrates of these courts shall continue to perform their functions until such time as the National Assembly shall provide for the establishment of a new judicial system.

5. Tithes of every description, as well as the dues which have been substituted for them, under whatever denomination they are known or collected (even when compounded for), possessed by secular or regular congregations, by holders of benefices, members of corporations (including the Order of Malta and other religious and military orders,) as well as those devoted to the maintenance of churches, those impropriated to lay persons and those substituted for the *portion congrue,*[2] are abolished, on condition, however, that some other method be devised to provide for the expenses of divine worship, the support of the officiating clergy, for the assistance of the poor, for repairs and rebuilding of churches and parsonages, and for the maintenance of all institutions, seminaries, schools, academies, asylums, and organizations to which the present funds are devoted. Until such provision shall be made and the former possessors shall enter upon the enjoyment of an income on the new system, the National Assembly decrees that the said tithes shall continue to be collected according to law and in the customary manner.

    Other tithes, of whatever nature they may be, shall be redeemable in such manner as the Assembly shall determine. Until such regulation shall be issued, the National Assembly decrees that these, too, shall continue to be collected.

6. All perpetual ground rents, payable either in money or in kind, of whatever nature they may be, whatever their origin and to whomsoever they may be due, as to members of corporations, holders of the domain or appanages or to the Order of Malta, shall be redeemable. *Champarts*, of every kind and under all denominations, shall likewise be redeemable at a rate fixed by the Assembly. No due shall in the future be created which is not redeemable.

7. The sale of judicial and municipal offices shall be suppressed forthwith. Justice shall be dispensed *gratis*. Nevertheless, the magistrates at present holding such offices shall continue to exercise their functions and to receive their emoluments until the Assembly shall have made provision for indemnifying them.

8. The fees of the country priests are abolished, and shall be discontinued so soon as provision shall be made for increasing the minimum salary of the parish priests and the payment to the curates. A regulation shall be drawn up to determine the status of the priests in the towns.

---

[2] the minimum pay fixed for priests

9. Pecuniary privileges, personal or real, in the payment of taxes are abolished forever. Taxes shall be collected from all the citizens, and from all property, in the same manner and in the same form. Plans shall be considered by which the taxes shall be paid proportionally be all, even for the last six months of the current year.

10. Since a national constitution and public liberty are of more advantage to the provinces than the privileges which some of them enjoy, and inasmuch as the surrender of such privileges is essential to the intimate union of all parts of the realm, it is decreed that all the peculiar privileges, pecuniary or otherwise, of the provinces, principalities, districts, cantons, cities and communes, are once for all abolished and are absorbed into the law common to all Frenchmen.

11. All citizens, without distinction of birth, are eligible to any office or dignity, whether ecclesiastical, civil or military; and no profession shall imply any derogation.

12. Hereafter no remittances shall be made for annates or for any other purpose to the court of Rome, the vice-legation at Avignon, or to the nunciature at Lucerne. The clergy of the diocese shall apply to their bishops in regard to the filling of benefices and dispensations, the which shall be granted *gratis* without regard to reservations, expectancies and papal months, all the churches of France enjoying the same freedom....

17. The National Assembly solemnly proclaims King Louis XVI *Restorer of French Liberty*.

18. The National Assembly shall present itself in a body before the King, in order to submit to him the decrees which have just been passed, to tender to him the tokens of its most respectful gratitude and to pray him to permit the *Te Deum* to be chanted in his chapel, and to be present himself at this service.

19. The National Assembly shall consider, immediately after the constitution, the drawing up of the laws necessary for the development of the principles which it has laid down in the present decree. The latter shall be transmitted without delay by the deputies to all the provinces, together with the decree of the tenth of this month, in order that it may be printed, published, announced from the parish pulpits, and posted up wherever it shall be deemed necessary.

from *Translations and Reprints from the Original Sources of European History*, vol. 5.
Philadelphia; University of Pennsylvania Press, 1902.

Questions:
1. Compare and contrast the *cahiers* of the three estates with the points included in the August decrees. The interests of which estates are reflected in these reforms?
2. Do these decrees constitute a revolution? Why or why not?

Declaration of the Rights of Man and the Citizen, August 26, 1789

Having abolished feudalism, the National Assembly now proceeded to lay down what it regarded to be the basic and inalienable rights of human beings in general and of French citizens in particular. The Declaration of the Rights of Man and the Citizen embodied not only many of the fundamental ideas of the French Enlightenment, but also elements of the American Declaration of Independence. It remains one of the most important documents in the history of Western constitutional government.

The representatives of the French people, organized as a National Assembly, believing that ignorance, neglect, or contempt of the rights of man are the sole causes of public calamities and of the corruption of governments, have determined to set forth in a solemn declaration the natural, inalienable, and sacred rights of man, in order that this declaration, being constantly before all members of the social body, shall remind them continually of their rights and duties; in order that the acts of the legislative power, as well as those of the executive power, may be compared at any moment with the ends of every political institution and may thus be more respected; and lastly, in order that the demands of the citizens, based hereafter upon simple and incontestable principles, shall tend to the maintenance of the Constitution and redound to the happiness of all. Therefore, the National Assembly recognizes and proclaims, in the presence and under the auspices of the Supreme Being, the following rights of man and citizen.

1. Men are born and remain free and equal in rights; social distinctions only be founded upon the general good.

2. The aim of all political association is the preservation of the natural and inalienable rights of man; these rights are liberty, property, security, and resistance to oppression.

3. The source of all sovereignty resides essentially in the nation. No body nor individual may exercise any authority which does not proceed directly from the nation.

4. Liberty consists in the freedom to do everything which injures no one else; hence the exercise of the natural rights of every man has no limits except those that assure other members of society the enjoyment of those same rights. These limits may be determined only by law.

5. The law can only prohibit such actions as are injurious to society. Nothing may be prevented which is not forbidden by law, and no one may be forced to do anything not provided for by law.

6. Law is the expression of the general will. Every citizen has a right to participate personally, or through his representatives, in its formation. It must be the same for all, whether it protects or punishes. All citizens, being equal in the eyes of the law, are equally eligible to all dignities and to all public positions and occupations, according to their abilities, and without distinction other than that of virtues and talents.

7. No person shall be accused, arrested, or imprisoned except in the cases and according to the forms prescribed by law. Anyone soliciting, transmitting, executing or causing to be executed any arbitrary order shall be punished. But any citizen summoned or arrested in virtue of the law shall submit without delay, as resistance constitutes an offence.

8. The law shall provide for such punishments only as are strictly and obviously necessary; and no one may be punished except it be legally inflicted by virtue of a law passed and promulgated before the commission of the offense.

9. As all persons are held innocent until they shall have been declared guilty, if arrest shall be deemed indispensable, all harshness not essential to the securing of the prisoner's person shall be severely repressed by law.

10. No one shall be disquieted on account of his opinions, including his religious views, provided their manifestation does not disturb the public order established by law.

11. Free communication of ideas and opinions is one of the most precious of the rights of man. Every citizen may, accordingly, speak, write, and print with freedom, but shall be responsible for such abuses of this freedom as shall be defined by law.

12. The security of the rights of man and citizen requires public military force. These forces are, therefore, established for the good of all and not for the personal advantage of those to whom they shall be entrusted.

13. A common contribution is essential for the maintenance of the public forces and for the cost of administration. This must be assessed equally on all citizens in proportion to their means.

14. Citizens have the right to ascertain, by themselves or through their representatives, the necessity of the public tax, to consent to it freely, to supervise its use, and to determine its quota, assessment, payment, and duration.

15. Society has the right to require of every public agent an accounting of his administration.

16. Every society in which the guarantee of rights is not assured or the separation of powers not determined has no constitution at all.

17. Since property is a sacred and inviolable right, no one may be deprived thereof unless a legally established public necessity obviously requires it, and upon condition of a just and previous indemnity.

> from *Translations and Reprints from the Original Sources of European History*, vol. 5.
> Philadelphia; University of Pennsylvania Press, 1902.

Questions:
1. According to the National Assembly, what were the "Rights of Man"? What do you think are some of the more significant rights included in this document/ why?
2. Do you agree that these are the fundamental rights of humankind? Would you make any additions or deletions to this document if you were writing a contemporary declaration of human rights? Do you think such public statements are important? Why or why not?

Unit 45: The Revolution Devours its Children

Napoleon Bonaparte: "Upon Becoming Consul," November 10, 1799

Revolutions are chaotic affairs and even the politicians and parties that benefit from them eventually tire of their turmoil and violence. This was most certainly the case with the French Revolution. After five years, in which the French people witnessed the rise and fall of four governments, mob rule in Paris, a civil war, foreign invasion, and a reign of terror, a new constitutional arrangement was installed aimed at restoring order and stability to France. The Directory, which ruled from 1795 to 1799, was never terribly popular. It survived as long as it did because of the military skills and daring of one of its younger generals, a Corsican named Napoleon Bonaparte. Unfortunately for his employers, Bonaparte was also very ambitious and fully aware that the government he served was incompetent and without popular support On November 9, 1799, Napoleon lead a coup d'état that overthrew the Directory and set up a new government with himself at its head. In the following proclamation, Bonaparte justifies his seizure of power.

Frenchmen, on my return to France I found division reigning among all the authorities. They agreed only on this single point, that the constitution was half destroyed and was unable to protect liberty.

Each party in turn came to me, confided to me their designs, imparted their secrets, and requested my support. But I refused to be the man of a party.

The Council of Elders appealed to me. I answered their appeal. A plan of general restoration had been concerted by men whom the nation has been accustomed to regard as the defenders of liberty, equality, and property. This plan required calm deliberation, free from all influence and all fear. The Elders therefore resolved upon the removal of the legislative bodies to St. Cloud. They placed at my disposal the force necessary to secure their independence. I was bound, in duty to my fellow-citizens, to the soldiers perishing in our armies, and to the national glory acquired at the cost of so much blood, to accept the command.

The Council assembled at St. Cloud. Republican troops guaranteed their safety from without, but assassins created terror within. Many deputies in the Council of Five Hundred, armed with stilettos and pistols, spread the menace of death around them.

The plans which ought to have been developed were withheld. The majority of the Council was disorganized, the boldest orators were disconcerted, and the futility of submitting any salutary proposition was quite evident.

I proceeded, filled with indignation and chagrin, to the Council of the Elders. I besought them to carry their noble designs into execution. I directed their attention to the evils of the nation, which were their motives for conceiving those designs. They concurred in giving me new proofs of their unanimous good will.

I presented myself before the Council of the Five Hundred alone, unarmed, my head uncovered, just as the Elders had received and applauded me. My object was to restore to the majority the expression of its will and to secure to it its power.

The stilettos which had menaced the deputies were instantly raised against their deliverer. Twenty assassins rushed upon me and aimed at my breast. The grenadiers of the Legislative Body, whom I had left at the door of the hall, ran forward and placed themselves between me and the assassins. One of these brave grenadiers [Thomé] had his clothes pierced by a stiletto. They bore me out.

At the same moment cries of "Outlaw him!" were raised against the defender of the law. It was the horrid cry of assassins against the power destined to repress them. They crowded around the president [Lucien Bonaparte] uttering threats. With arms in their hands, they commanded him to declare me outlawed. I was informed of this. I ordered him to be rescued from their fury, and six grenadiers of the legislative body brought him out. Immediately afterwards some grenadiers of the legislative body charged the hall and cleared it.

The seditious, thus intimidated, dispersed and fled. The majority, freed from their assailants, returned freely and peaceably into the hail, listened to the propositions for the public safety, deliberated, and drew up the salutary resolution which will become the new and provisional law of the republic.

Frenchmen, you will doubtless recognize in this conduct the zeal of a soldier of liberty, of a citizen devoted to the republic. Conservative, judicial, and liberal ideas resumed their sway upon the dispersion of those seditious persons who had domineered in the councils and who proved themselves the most odious and contemptible of men.

BONAPARTE.

from *Readings in European History*, edited by J. H. Robinson, vol. II. Boston: Ginn, 1906.

Questions:
1. How did Napoleon Bonaparte justify his actions? How did he depict the situation in France?
2. How did Napoleon portray himself in this writing? What do you learn about him from this document?

Chapter 21: The Industrial Revolution and Its Impact

Unit 46: Machines, Muscles and Merchants

Living in an "electronic age" of automated production plants, personal computers, data nets, and supersonic transport, it is difficult to conceive of steam engines, coal-burning iron foundries, hand-operated power looms, and railroads as revolutionary technologies. Nevertheless, the appearance of these machines in Great Britain in the late eighteenth and early nineteenth centuries, and their application to the manufacturing and marketing of various goods and services profoundly affected every aspect of European life. Indeed, this "Industrial Revolution" dramatically increased the production of clothing, consumer goods, and machinery, replaced village shops and home-based cottage industries with large and impersonal factories, and also encouraged a mass migration of rural Europeans into urban areas. Furthermore, the need of this new industry for raw materials, cheap labor, and markets also sparked a renewed interest in exploration and colonialism, which would, in turn, wreak havoc on the cultures of non-European peoples, and also contribute to the great power rivalries and tensions that would lead to the outbreak of World War I.

While the profound impact of these eighteenth and nineteenth century industrial technologies and systems of production on European and world societies is incontestable, there remains the question of why this economic revolution originated in Great Britain. To answer that question, it is important to first understand what factors hindered economic expansion, entrepreneurship, and productivity on the European continent. The documents below touch on some of the problems that were noted by the eighteenth and nineteenth century European commentators who were looking for explanations for the lackluster economic performance of Britain's continental rivals.

Hodgskin: "On Tolls in Germany"

As cargoes passed through the territories of the continent's many kings, petty princes, and churchmen, tolls were levied in each jurisdiction. Indeed, one of Britain's key advantages over its European business rivals was the fact that British entrepreneurs, farmers, and tradesmen did business in a unified country free of the kinds of tolls that were a commonplace in the myriad principalities across the channel. No one captured the deadening effect of these tolls on European trade better than T. Hodgskin, a British writer who traveled throughout Germany in the early nineteenth century.

There are no less than twenty-two tolls on the Weser betwixt Münden and Bremen, seven of which belong to the sovereign of Hannover.... At every toll every vessel is stopped and her whole cargo examined. On an average, more than one hour is employed to examine each vessel; so that every one loses one whole day in passing between these two towns. This is mere waste, a loss of times to all the parties, more injurious probably than the duties which the merchants have also to pay. I have been informed that not one of these sovereigns who levy these tolls, except the King of Prussia, has ever employed one farthing of the money thus collected in clearing the river.... It is said the expense of collecting the tolls equals the receipts.

On the Leine, about twenty-four vessels capable of carrying eighty tons each, though they are seldom more than half loaded, pass and repass in a year between the towns of Bremen and Hannover. They are about sixty miles apart, and there are no less than five tolls in this distance.... On the average each vessel has to pay in descending the river about 200 Thalers, or more than £30 Sterling. In ascending the charge is double....

Similar tolls and impediments are known to exist on every river of Germany.... The cargo of the raft on which I passed from Munich to Vienna was nothing but trees, deals[1] and three bales of goods; yet we were frequently detained both in Bavaria and Austria for hours to have it examined. Boats whose cargoes were more complicated than ours were sometimes detained half a day.

Tolls on roads are perhaps not less numerous, though less pernicious, than tolls on rivers. The loading of a waggon is much sooner examined than the cargo of a ship...they are in general domanial tolls, the produce of which goes into the pocket of the sovereign, and he repairs the road or not as he pleases. I do not know what number of these may anywhere exist, but I can state that in Hannover they are numerous and rigidly levied.... Such domanial tolls are common on all the roads of Germany, and in some parts they belong to nobles.... Tolls are generally heavier for foreigners, under which term is included the subjects of other German powers, than for natives; and sometimes it appears that the sovereigns cannot agree on the conditions under which their respective subjects may be allowed to traverse the dominions of each other. Thus, the post which ought to go from Bremen direct through Oldenburg to Emden, a distance of seventy miles, goes all round by Osnabrück, which is at least twice as far; and it requires three days, without employing a messenger expressly for the purpose, to convey a letter from one of these two towns to the other.

Let any person conceive what would be the effect on the commerce of the Thames if there were twenty tolls between London Bridge and the Nore, and that every vessel...had to stop and be examined at every one of those tolls, and he may know accurately the extent of the impediments which the water tolls of the sovereigns of Germany throw in the way of the commerce of the country.... Let any person further conceive custom-houses placed at the border of every county in England, custom-house officers examining every loaded waggon...and he may then also know accurately the impediments which the land-tolls of the sovereigns throw in the way of commerce.

T. Hodgskin, Travels in the North of Germany. vol. II, Edinburgh, 1820.

Questions:
1. Where were tolls used in Germany? What regulations governed these tolls?
2. How was the income from the tolls used?
3. Overall, what disadvantages resulted from the use of tolls in Germany? How might Germany's political arrangement have contributed to this situation? What made Britain's situation different?

Marquis de Custine: "On Road Maintenance in Russia"

When the citizens of the Roman Empire boasted that "all roads lead to Rome," they were not only underscoring the fact that their city was at the heart of a worldwide empire, but that the key to a nation's power and prosperity lay in an extensive and well-maintained transportation system. In the eighteenth century, Britain's leaders and entrepreneurs were also keenly aware of the critical importance of transportation to the future security and economic well-being of their own empire, and subsequently invested in the construction of a national network of new roads and canals that were well-maintained and at the disposal of the entire nation. As the following selection from the Russian travel diaries of the French Marquis de Custine makes clear,

---

[1] boards or planks; fir or pine wood

however, Britain's continental neighbors often had rather different ideas with regard to the maintenance and uses of their roads.

To travel post on the road from Petersburg to Moscow is to treat one's self for whole days to the sensation experienced in descending the *montagnes Russes* at Paris. It would be well to bring an English carriage to Petersburg, if only for the pleasure of travelling, on really elastic springs, this famous road, the best chaussée[2] in Europe, according to the Russians, and, I believe, according to strangers also. It must be owned that it is well kept, although hard, by reason of the nature of the materials, which broken as they are in tolerably small pieces, form, in encrusting over the surface, little immovable asperities,[3] which shake the carriages to a degree that causes something to come out of place at every stage. As much time is thus lost as is gained by the speed at which they drive; for we rush along, in a whirlwind of dust, with the rapidity of a hurricane chasing the clouds before it. An English carriage is very pleasant for the few first stages; but in the long run, the necessity of a Russian equipage to withstand the pace of the horses and the hardness of the road, is discovered. The rails of the bridges are formed of handsome iron balustrades, and the granite pillars which support them are carved with the Imperial arms. This road is broader than those of England; it is also as even, although less easy: the horses are small, but full of muscle.

If we are to believe the Russians, all their roads are good during the summer season, even those that are not the great highways. I find them all bad. A road full of inequalities, sometimes as broad as a field, sometimes extremely narrow, passes through beds of sand in which the horses plunge above their knees, lose their wind, break their traces, and refuse to draw at every twenty yards; if these sands are passed, you soon plunge into pools of mud which conceal large stones and enormous stumps of trees, that are very destructive to the carriages. Such are the roads of this land, except during seasons when they become absolutely impassable, when the extreme of cold renders travelling dangerous, when storms of snow bury the country, or when floods, produced by the thaw, transform, for about three months in the year, the low plains into lakes; namely, for about six weeks after the summer, and for as many after the winter season; the rest of the year they continue marshes.

I had forgotten to mention a singular object which struck me at the commencement of the journey.

Between Petersburg and Novgorod, I remarked, for several successive stages, a second road that ran parallel to the principal highway, though at a considerable distance from it. It was furnished with bridges and every thing else that could render it safe and passable, although it was much less handsome, and less smooth, than the grand route. I asked the keeper of a posthouse the meaning of this singularity, and was answered, through my feldjäger[4] that the smaller road was destined for waggons, cattle, and travellers, when the Emperor, or other members of the Imperial family, proceeded to Moscow. The dust and obstructions that might incommode or retard the august travellers, if the grand route remained open to the public, were thus avoided. I cannot tell whether the innkeeper was amusing himself at my expense, but he spoke in a very serious manner, and seemed to consider it very natural that the sovereign should engross the road in a land where the sovereign is every thing. The king who said, 'I am France,' stopped to let a flock

---

[2] carriageway

[3] unevenness

[4] hunter

of sheep pass; and under his reign, the foot-passenger, the waggoner, and the clown who travelled the public road, repeated our old adage to the princes whom they met: 'the highway belongs to every body:' what really constitutes a law is, not its letter, but the manner in which it is applied.

Marquis de Custine, Russia, vol. 2. London, 1844.

Questions:
1. How would you describe the conditions of roads in nineteenth-century Russia? How might these circumstances have affected Russia's economic development?
2. How was the Imperial family affected by these road conditions? What does this reveal about Russia's political structure?

Adam Smith: "Increasing the Productive Power of Labor," 1904

In our survey of Enlightenment thinking, we were introduced to the laissez-faire economic theories of the Scottish social philosopher and political economist, Adam Smith (1723-1790). In addition to his commentaries on the economic benefits of free markets and self-interest, Smith was also keenly interested in systems of industrial production in which products were assembled in different stages by distinct groups of skilled and unskilled workers. In this selection from his *Wealth of Nations,* Smith described the advantages enjoyed by a factory where such a division of labor was put into operation.

The greatest improvement in the productive powers of labour, and the greater part of the skill, dexterity, and judgment with which it is any where directed, or applied, seem to have been the effects of the division of labour.

The effects of the division of labour, in the general business of society, will be more easily understood, by considering in what manner it operates in some particular manufactures.

To take an example, therefore, from a very trifling manufacture; but one in which the division of labour has been very often taken notice of, the trade of the pin-maker; a workman not educated to this business (which the division of labour has rendered a distinct trade), nor acquainted with the use of the machinery employed in it (to the invention of which the same division of labour has probably given occasion), could scarce, perhaps, with his utmost industry, make one pin in a day, and certainly could not make twenty. But in the way in which this business is now carried on, not only the whole work is a peculiar trade, but it is divided into a number of branches, of which the greater part are likewise peculiar trades. One man draws out the wire, another straights it, a third cuts it, a fourth points it, a fifth grinds it at the top for receiving the head; to make the head requires two or three distinct operations; to put it on, is a peculiar business, to whiten the pin is another; it is even a trade by itself to put them into the paper; and the important business of making a pin is, in this manner, divided into about eighteen distinct operations, which, in some manufactories, are all performed by distinct hands, though in others the same man will sometimes perform two or three of them. I have seen a small manufactory of this kind where ten men only were employed, and where some of them consequently performed two or three distinct operations. But though they were very poor, and therefore but indifferently accommodated with the necessary machinery, they could, when they exerted themselves, make among them about twelve pounds of pins in a day. There are in a pound upwards of four thousand pins of a middling size. Those ten persons, therefore, could make among them upwards of forty-eight thousand pins in a day. Each person, therefore, making a tenth part of forty-eight thousand pins, might be considered as making four thousand eight hundred pins in a day. But if they had all wrought separately and independently, and without any of them having been educated to this peculiar business, they certainly could not each of them have made twenty, perhaps not one pin in a day

This great increase of the quantity of work, which, in consequence of the division of labour, the same number of people are capable of performing, is owing to three different circumstances; first, to the increase of dexterity in every particular workman; secondly, to the saving of the time which is commonly lost in passing from one species of work to another; and lastly, to the invention of a great number of machines which facilitate and abridge labour, and enable one man to do the work of many.

Adam Smith *An Inquiry into the Nature and Causes of the Wealth of Nations*. London. 1904.

Questions:
1. What is meant by the "division of labor"? What example did Smith use?
2. What are the advantages of dividing production in this manner?
3. What are some possible social consequences of the "division of labor"? Have you ever worked in a factory that used this method of production? If so, how would you describe your workday?

Samuel Smiles: from *Self Help*

Not everyone attributed Britain's industrial success to its transportation system, machinery, factories, and trained workers. The Scottish journalist, Samuel Smiles (1812-1904), insisted that the nation's prosperity stemmed from its traditions of self-reliance, individual enterprise, and free trade. He propagated this belief in a whole series of inspirational self-improvement books that enjoyed widespread popularity. Of these works, the most popular was his book *Self-Help*, which sold over 250,000 copies and was translated into seventeen different languages.

"Heaven helps those who help themselves," is a well-worn maxim, embodying in a small compass the results of vast human experience. The spirit of self-help is the root of all genuine growth in the individual; and, exhibited in the lives of many, it constitutes the true source of national vigor and strength. Help from without is often enfeebling in its effects, but help from within invariably invigorates. Whatever is done for men or classes, to a certain extent takes away the stimulus and necessity of doing for themselves; and where men are subjected to over-guidance and over-government, the inevitable tendency is to render them comparatively helpless.

Even the best institutions can give a man no active aid. Perhaps the utmost they can do, is, to leave him free to develop himself and improve his individual condition. But in all times men have been prone to believe that their happiness and well-being were to be secured by means of institutions rather than by their own conduct. Hence the value of legislation as an agent in human advancement has always been greatly over-estimated. To constitute the millionth part of a legislature, by voting for one or two men once in three or five years, however conscientiously this duty may be performed, can exercise but little active influence upon any man's life and character. Moreover, it is every day becoming more clearly understood, that the function of government is negative and restrictive, rather than positive and active; being resolvable principally into protection,—protection of life, liberty and property. Hence the chief "reforms" of the last fifty years have consisted mainly of abolitions and disenactments. But there is no power of law that can make the idle man industrious, the thriftless provident, or the drunken sober; though every individual can be each and all of these if he will, by the exercise of his own free powers of action and self-denial....

Any class of men that lives from hand to mouth will ever be an inferior class. They will necessarily remain impotent and helpless, hanging on to the skirts of society, the sport of times and seasons. Having no respect for themselves, they will fail in securing the respect of others. In commercial crises, such men must inevitably go to the wall. Wanting that husbanded power which a store of savings, no matter how small, invariably gives them, they will be at every man's mercy, and, if possessed of right feelings, they cannot but regard with fear and trembling the future possible fate of their wives and children. "The world," once said Mr. Cobden to the working men of Huddersfield, "has always been divided into two classes,—those who saved, and those who have spent,—the thrifty and the extravagant. The building of all the houses, the mills, the bridges, and the ships, and the accomplishment of all other great works which have rendered man civilized and happy, has been done by the savers, the thrifty; and those who have wasted their resources have always been their slaves."…

from Samuel Smiles, *Self Help*. Boston, 1860.

Questions:
1. What values did Smiles promote as being of benefit to both the individual and to one's nation?
2. According to Smiles, what role should the government play in aiding individuals?
3. What class perspective does Smiles represent? Taking the historical context into consideration, do you feel Smiles' perspective was realistic? Give some examples to support your position.

Friedrich Engels: from *The Working Class in England in 1844*

Aside from being the long-time collaborator of Karl Marx and one of the founders of the modern socialist movement, Friedrich Engels (1820-1895) was also a very successful businessman. The son of a wealthy German manufacturer, Engels moved to Manchester in northern England in the early 1840s and successfully established himself in that city's thriving textile industry. As such, he had the perfect opportunity to observe firsthand how the new industrial system was radically changing the social patterns and lifestyles of the workers who were moving from the English countryside into the rapidly growing factory towns. In the following selection, Engels described the early nineteenth-century urban experience of Britain's industrial workers.

The history of the proletariat in England begins with the second half of the last century, with the invention of the steam engine and of machinery for weaving cotton. These inventions gave rise, as is well known, to an industrial revolution, a revolution which altered the whole civil society; one, the historical importance of which is only now beginning to be recognized. England is the classic soil of this transformation which was all the mightier, the more silently it proceeded; and England is, therefore, the classic land of its chief product also, the proletariat. Only in England can the proletariat be studied in all its relations and from all sides.

We have not, here and now, to deal with the history of this revolution, nor with its vast importance for the present and the future. Such a delineation must be reserved for a future, more comprehensive work. For the moment, we must limit ourselves to the little that is necessary for understanding the facts that follow, for comprehending the present state of the English proletariat.

Before the introduction of machinery, the spinning and weaving of raw materials was carried on in the workingman's home. Wife and daughter spun the yarn that the father wove or that they sold, if he did not work it up himself. These weaver families lived in the country in the neighborhood of the towns, and could get on fairly well with their wages, because the home market was almost the only one and the crushing power of competition that came later with the conquest of foreign markets and the extension of trade, did not yet press upon wages. There was, further, a constant increase in the demand of the home market, keeping pace with the slow increase in population and employing all the workers; and there was also the impossibility of vigorous competition of the workers among themselves, consequent upon the rural dispersion of their homes. So it was that the weaver was usually in a position to lay by something and rent a little piece of land that he cultivated in his leisure hours, of which he had as many as he chose to take, since he could weave whenever and as long as he pleased. True, he was a bad farmer and managed his land inefficiently, often obtaining but poor crops; nevertheless, he was no proletarian, he had a stake in the country, he was permanently settled, and stood one step higher in society than the English workman of to-day.

So the workers vegetated throughout a passably comfortable existence, leading a righteous and peaceful life in all piety and probity; and their material position was far better than that of their successors. They did not need to overwork; they did no more than they chose to do, and yet earned what they needed. They had leisure for healthful work in garden or field, work which, in itself, was recreation for them, and they could take part besides in the recreations and games of their neighbors, and all these games, bowling, cricket, football, etc., contributed to their physical health and vigor. They were, for the most part, strong, well-built people, in whose physique little or no difference from that of their peasant neighbors was discoverable. Their children grew up in the fresh country air and, if they could help their parents at work, it was only occasionally; while of eight or twelve hours work for them there was no question.

What the moral and intellectual character of this class was, may be guessed. Shut off from the towns which they never entered, their yarn and woven stuff being delivered to traveling agents for payment of wages—so shut off that old people who lived quite in the neighborhood of the town, never went thither until they were robbed of their trade by the introduction of machinery and obliged to look about them in the towns for work—the weavers stood upon the moral and intellectual plane of the yeomen with whom they were usually immediately connected through their little holdings. They regarded their squire, the greatest landholder of the region, as their natural superior; they asked advice of him, laid their small disputes before him for settlement, and gave him all honor, as this patriarchal relation involved. They were "respectable" people, good husbands and fathers, led moral lives because they had no temptation to be immoral, there being no groggeries or low houses in their vicinity and because the host, at whose inn they now and then quenched their thirst was also a respectable man, usually a large tenant farmer who had pride in his good order, good beer, and early hours. They had their children the whole day at home, and brought them up in obedience and the fear of God; the patriarchal relationship remained undisturbed so long as the children were unmarried. The young people grew up in idyllic simplicity and intimacy with their playmates until they married; and even though sexual intercourse before marriage almost unfailingly took place, this happened only when the moral obligation of marriage was recognized on both sides, and a subsequent wedding made everything good. In short, the English industrial workers of those days lived and thought after the fashion still to be found here and there in Germany, in retirement and seclusion, without mental activity and without violent fluctuations in their position in life. They could rarely read and far more rarely write; went regularly to church, never talked politics, never conspired, never bought, delighted in physical exercises, listened with inherited reverence when the Bible was read, and were, in their unquestioning humility, exceedingly well disposed towards the "superior" classes. But intellectually, they were dead; lived only for their petty, private interest, for their looms and gardens, and knew nothing of the mighty movement which, beyond their horizon, was sweeping through mankind. They were comfortable in their silent vegetation, and but for the industrial revolution they would never have emerged from this existence, which cosily romantic as it was, was nevertheless not worthy of human beings. In truth, they were not human beings; they were merely toiling machines in the service of the few aristocrats who had guided history down to that time. The industrial revolution has simply carried this out to its logical end by making the workers machines pure and simple, taking from them the last trace of independent activity, and so forcing them to think and demand a position worthy of men. As in France politics, so in England manufacture, and the movement of civil society in general drew into the whirl of history the last classes which had remained sunk in apathetic indifference to the universal interests of mankind.

The first invention which gave rise to a radical change in the state of the English workers was the jenny, invented in the year 1764 by a weaver, James Hargreaves, of Standhill, near Blackburn, in North Lancashire. This machine was the rough beginning of the later invented mule, and was moved by hand. Instead of one spindle like the ordinary spinning-wheel, it carried sixteen or eighteen manipulated by a single workman. This invention made it possible to deliver more yarn than heretofore, Whereas, though one weaver had employed three spinners, there had never been enough yarn and the weaver had often been obliged to wait for it, there was now more yarn to be had than could be woven by the available workers. The demand for woven goods, already increasing, rose yet more in consequence of the cheapness of these goods, which cheapness in turn, was the outcome of the diminished cost of producing the yarn. More weavers were needed, and weavers' wages rose. Now that the weaver could earn more at his loom, he gradually abandoned his farming, and gave his whole time to weaving. At that time a family of four grown persons and two children (who were set to spooling), could earn with eight hours' daily work four pounds sterling in a week, and often more if trade was good and work pressed. It happened often enough that a single weaver earned two pounds a week at his loom. By degrees the class of farming weavers wholly disappeared, and was merged in the newly arising class of weavers who lived wholly upon wages, had no property whatever, not even the pretended property of a holding, and so became workingmen, proletarians. Moreover, the old relation between spinner and weaver was destroyed. Hitherto, so far as this had been possible, yarn had been spun and woven under one roof. Now that the jenny as well as the loom required a strong hand, men began to spin and whole families lived by spinning, while others laid the antiquated, superseded spinning-wheel aside; and, if they had not means of purchasing a jenny, were forced to live upon the wages of the father alone. Thus began with spinning and weaving that division of labor which has since been so infinitely perfected.

translated by Florence Kelley Wischnewetzky in Frederick Engels, *The Working Class In England In 1884*.
New York: John W. Lovell Company, 1887.

Question:
According to Engels, how had life changed for the working class since the Industrial Revolution? That is, how did he compare life in the pre-industrial English countryside with industrialized urban life?

Charles Dickens: "What Cost Progress?" from *Hard Times*

There is probably no better chronicler of the trials and tribulations of the nineteenth-century British working class than the novelist Charles Dickens (1812-1870). Following his father's imprisonment for debt, Dickens was taken out of school at the age of twelve and sent to work in a blacking factory, where child labor was used to label bottles of polish and varnish. Laboring twelve to fourteen hours a day for six shillings a week, Dickens learned first-hand the drudgery of factory labor. He also became equally familiar with the beastly conditions in which his fellow workers were expected to live. He gives us some idea of this urban squalor in the following selection from his novel, *Hard Times*.

COKETOWN, to which Messrs. Bounderby and Gradgrind now walked, was a triumph of fact; it had no greater taint of fancy in it than Mrs. Gradgrind herself. Let us strike the key-note, Coketown, before pursuing our tune.

It was a town of red brick, or of brick that would have been red if the smoke and ashes had allowed it; but as matters stood it was a town of unnatural red and black like the painted face of a savage. It was a town of machinery and tall chimneys, out of which interminable serpents of smoke trailed themselves for ever and ever, and never got uncoiled. It had a black canal in it, and a river that ran purple with ill-smelling dye, and vast piles of building full of windows where there was a rattling and a trembling all day long, and where the piston of the steam-engine worked monotonously up and down like the head of an elephant in a state of melancholy madness. It contained several large streets all very like one another, and many small streets still more like one another, inhabited by people equally like one another, who all went in and out at the same hours, with the same sound upon the same pavements, to do the same work, and to whom every day was the same as yesterday and to-morrow, and every year the counterpart of the last and the next.

These attributes of Coketown were in the main inseparable from the work by which it was sustained; against them were to be set off, comforts of life which found their way all over the world, and elegancies of life which made, we will not ask how much of the fine lady, who could scarcely bear to hear the place mentioned. The rest of its features were voluntary, and they were these.

You saw nothing in Coketown but what was severely workful. If the members of a religious persuasion built a chapel there—as the members of eighteen religious persuasions had done— they made it a pious warehouse of red brick, with sometimes (but this is only in highly ornamental examples) a bell in a birdcage on the top of it. The solitary exception was the New Church: a stuccoed edifice with a square steeple over the door, terminating in four pinnacles like florid wooden legs. All the public inscriptions in the town were painted alike, in severe characters of black and white. The jail might have been the infirmary, the infirmary might have been the jail, the town-hall might have been either, or both, or anything else, for anything that appeared to the contrary in the graces of their construction. Fact, fact, fact, everywhere in the material aspect of the town; fact, fact, fact, everywhere in the immaterial. The M'Choakumchild school was all fact, and the school of design was all fact, and the relations between master and man were all fact, and everything was fact between the lying-in hospital and the cemetery, and what you couldn't state in figures, or show to be purchaseable in the cheapest market and saleable in the dearest, was not, and never should be, world without end, Amen....

In the hardest working part of Coketown; in the innermost fortifications of that ugly citadel, where Nature was as strongly bricked out as killing airs and gases were bricked in; at the heart of the labyrinth of narrow courts upon courts, and close streets upon streets, which had come into existence piecemeal, every piece in a violent hurry for some one man's purpose, and the whole an unnatural family, shouldering, and trampling, and pressing one another to death, in the last close nook of this great exhausted receiver, where the chimneys, for want of air to make a draught, were built in an immense variety of stunted and crooked shapes, as though every house put out a sign of the kind of people who might be expected to be born in it; among the multitude of Coketown, generically called "the Hands,"—a race who would have found more favour with some people, if Providence had seen fit to make them only hands, or, like the lower creatures of the seashore, only hands and stomachs—lived a certain Stephen Blackpool, forty years of age.

Stephen looked older, but he had had a hard life. It is said that every life has its roses and thorns; there seemed, however, to have been a misadventure or mistake in Stephen's case, whereby somebody else had become possessed of his roses, and he had become possessed of the same somebody else's thorns in addition to his own. He had known, to use his words, a peck of trouble. He was usually called Old Stephen, in a kind of rough homage to the fact.

A rather stooping man, with a knitted brow, a pondering expression of face, and a hard-looking head sufficiently capacious, on which his iron-grey hair lay long and thin, Old Stephen might have passed for a particularly intelligent man in his condition. Yet he was not, he took no place among those remarkable "Hands," who, piecing together their broken intervals of leisure through many years, had mastered difficult sciences, and acquired a knowledge of most unlikely things. He held no station among the Hands who could make speeches and carry on debates. Thousands of his compeers could talk much better than he, at any time. He was a good power-loom weaver, and a man of perfect integrity. What more he was, or what else he had in him, if anything, let him show for himself.

The lights in the great factories, which looked, when they were illuminated, like Fairy palaces—or the travellers by express-train said so—were all extinguished; and the bells had rung for knocking off for the night, and had ceased again; and the Hands, men and women, boy and girl, were clattering home. Old Stephen was standing in the street, with the old sensation upon him which the stoppage of the machinery always produced—the sensation of its having worked and stopped in his own head.

Charles Dickens, Hard Times. 1854.

Questions:
1. How is Coketown described by Dickens? How had the industrial revolution come to dominate the town?
2. According to Dickens, "fact, fact, fact" governed life in Coketown. What do you think he meant by this? What does this suggest about his perspective of the Industrial Revolution's social consequences? Do you agree or disagree with him? Do you feel that his observations have relevance to your life? Why or why not?
3. How does Dickens depict Stephen Blackpool and his living conditions?

Evidence Given Before The Sadler Committee and Ashley's Mines Commission, 1831 -1842

Surprisingly, much of the impetus in Britain for government intervention to regulate working conditions in the new industrial factories came from conservative members of Parliament. Two of the most effective British social and industrial reformers of the first half of the nineteenth century were Michael Thomas Sadler (1780-1835), a philanthropic businessman and Tory representative from Leeds in the north of England, and Anthony Ashley Cooper, seventh Earl of Shaftesbury (1801-1885), a Conservative member of the House of Commons and a leader of the evangelical movement within the Church of England. Both of these men launched parliamentary investigations of industrial working conditions in the first half of the nineteenth century, and the evidence that their committees produced not only shocked Britain, but resulted in the first laws regulating labor conditions in textile factories and mines and restricting the work hours of women and children.

SADLER COMMITTEE, 1831-1832

MR. MATTHEW CRABTREE, CALLED IN; AND EXAMINED.

What age are you? —Twenty-two.

What is your occupation? —A blanket manufacturer.

Have you ever been employed in a factory? —Yes.

At what age did you first go to work in one? —Eight.

How long did you continue in that occupation? —Four years.

Will you state the hours of labour at the period when you first went to the factory, in ordinary times? —From 6 in the morning to 8 at night.

Fourteen hours? —Yes.

With what intervals for refreshment and rest? —An hour at noon.

When trade was brisk what were your hours? —From 5 in the morning to 9 in the evening.

Sixteen hours? —Yes.

With what intervals at dinner? —An hour.

How far did you live from the mill? —About two miles.

Was there any time allowed for you to get your breakfast in the mill? —No.

Did you take it before you left your home? —Generally.

During those long hours of labour could you be punctual; how did you awake? —I seldom did awake spontaneously; I was most generally awoke or lifted out of bed, sometimes asleep, by my parents.

Were you always in time? —No.

What was the consequence if you had been too late? —I was most commonly beaten.

Severely? —Very severely, I thought.

In those mills is chastisement towards the latter part of the day going on perpetually? —Perpetually.

So that you can hardly be in a mill without hearing constant crying? —Never an hour, I believe.

Do you think that if the overlooker were naturally a humane person it would be still found necessary for him to beat the children, in order to keep up their attention and vigilance at the termination of those extraordinary days of labour? —Yes; the machine turns off a regular quantity of cardings, and of course they must keep as regularly to their work the whole of the day; they must keep with the machine, and therefore however humane the slubber[5] may be, as he must keep up with the machine or be found fault with, he spurs the children to keep up also by various means but that which he commonly resorts to is to strap them when they become drowsy.

At the time when you were beaten for not keeping up with your work, were you anxious to have done it if you possibly could? —Yes; the dread of being beaten if we could not keep up with our work was a sufficient impulse to keep us to it if we could.

When you got home at night after this labour, did you feel much fatigued? —Very much so.

---

[5] person who extends and twists fiber in carding

Had you any time to be with your parents, and to receive instruction from them? —No.

What did you do? —All that we did when we got home was to get the little bit of supper that was provided for us and go to bed immediately. If the supper had not been ready directly, we should have gone to sleep while it was preparing.

Did you not, as a child, feel it a very grievous hardship to be roused so soon in the morning? —I did.

Were the rest of the children similarly circumstanced? —Yes, all of them; but they were not all of them so far from their work as I was.

And if you had been too late you were under the apprehension of being cruelly beaten? —I generally was beaten when I happened to be too late; and when I got up in the morning the apprehension of that was so great, that I used to run, and cry all the way as I went to the mill.

ELIZABETH BENTLEY, CALLED IN; AND EXAMINED.

What age are you? —Twenty-three.

Where do you live? —At Leeds.

What time did you begin to work at a factory? —When I was six years old.

At whose factory did you work? —Mr. Busk's.

What kind of mill is it? —Flax-mill.

What was your business in that mill? —I was a little doffer.

What were your hours of labour in that mill? —From 5 in the morning till 9 at night, when they were thronged.

For how long a time together have you worked that excessive length of time? —For about half a year.

What were your usual hours of labour when you were not so thronged? —From 6 in the morning till 7 at night.

What time was allowed for your meals? —Forty minutes at noon.

Had you any time to get your breakfast or drinking? —No, we got it as we could.

And when your work was bad, you had hardly any time to eat it at all? —No; we were obliged to leave it or take it home, and when we did not take it, the overlooker took it, and gave it to his pigs.

Do you consider doffing a laborious employment? —Yes.

Explain what it is you had to do? —When the frames are full, they have to stop the frames, and take the flyers off, and take the full bobbins off, and carry them to the roller; and then put empty ones on, and set the frame going again.

Does that keep you constantly on your feet? —Yes, there are so many frames, and they run so quick.

Your labour is very excessive? —Yes; you have not time for any thing.

Suppose you flagged a little, or were too late, what would they do? —Strap us.

Are they in the habit of strapping those who are last in doffing? —Yes.

Constantly? —Yes.

Girls as well as boys? —Yes.

Have you ever been strapped? —Yes.

Severely? —Yes.

Could you eat your food well in that factory? —No, indeed I had not much to eat, and the little I had I could not eat it, my appetite was so poor, and being covered with dust; and it was no use to take it home, I could not eat it, and the overlooker took it, and gave it to the pigs.

You are speaking of the breakfast? —Yes.

How far had you to go for dinner? —We could not go home to dinner.

Where did you dine? —In the mill.

Did you live far from the mill? —Yes, two miles.

Had you a clock? —No, we had not.

Supposing you had not been in time enough in the morning at these mills, what would have been the consequence? —We should have been quartered.

What do you mean by that? —If we were a quarter of an hour too late, they would take off half an hour; we only got a penny an hour, and they would take a halfpenny more.

ASHLEY'S MINES COMMISSION, 1842

ISABELLA READ, 12 YEARS OLD, COAL-BEARER

Works on mother's account, as father has been dead two years. Mother bides at home, she is troubled with bad breath, and is sair weak in her body from early labour. I am wrought with sister and brother, it is very sore work; cannot say how many rakes or journeys I make from pit's bottom to wall face and back, thinks about 30 or 25 on the average; the distance varies from 100 to 250 fathom.

I carry about 1 cwt. and a quarter on my back; have to stoop much and creep through water, which is frequently up to the calves of my legs. When first down fell frequently asleep while waiting for coal from heat and fatigue.

I do not like the work, not do the lassies, but they are made to like it. When the weather is warm there is difficulty in breathing, and frequently the lights go out.

ISABEL WILSON, 38 YEARS OLD, COAL PUTTER

When women have children thick (fast) they are compelled to take them down early, I have been married 19 years and have had 10 bairns; seven are in life. When on Sir John's work was a carrier of coals, which caused me to miscarry five times from the strains, and was gai ill after each. Putting is not so oppressive; last child was born on Saturday morning, and I was at work on the Friday night.

Once met with an accident; a coal brake my cheek-bone, which kept me idle some weeks.

I have wrought below 30 years, and so has the guid man; he is getting touched in the breath now.

None of the children read, as the work is no regular. I did read once, but no able to attend to it now; when I go below lassie 10 years of age keeps house and makes the broth or stir-about.

Nine sleep in two bedsteads; there did not appear to be any beds, and the whole of the other furniture consisted of two chairs, three stools, a table, a kail-ot and a few broken basins and cups. Upon asking if the furniture was all they had, the guid wife said, furniture was of no use, as it was so troublesome to flit with.

from *Parliamentary Papers*, 1831-1832. vol XV-XVII.

Questions:
1. What do these interviews conducted by the Sadler Committee reveal about child labor? For example, how old were these workers? What hours were these children working? What were the working conditions under which these children labored?
2. What were the working conditions in England's mines as evidenced by Isabella Read's testimony to the Ashley's Mines Commission? How old were the miners? What ills did they suffer from this work?
3. What impact might working conditions in the mines and factories have had on family life and English society in general?

Fielden: from *The Curse of the Factory System*, 1836

One of the reasons for the success of the Sadler and Ashley reform initiatives stemmed in no small way from the fact that both men were able to call on the support of a large number of morally-minded British manufacturers. One of these manufacturers was John Fielden, a Lancashire textile factory owner, who was deeply committed to the cause of social reform. In the following excerpt from his work on the British industrial system, he talks about the problems faced by businessmen like himself, who were trying to make a profit and protect their workers at the same time.

Here, then, is the "curse" of our factory-system: as improvements in machinery have gone on, the "avarice of masters" has prompted many to exact more labour from their hands than they were fitted by nature to perform, and those who have wished for the hours of labour to be less for all ages than the legislature would even yet sanction, have had no alternative but to conform more or less to the prevailing practice, or abandon the trade altogether. This has been the case with regard to myself and my partners. We have never worked more than *seventy-one* hours a week before Sir JOHN HOBHOUSE'S Act was passed. We then came down to *sixty-nine;* and, since Lord ALTHORP'S Act was passed, in 1833, we have reduced the time of adults to *sixty-seven and a half hours* a week, and that of children under thirteen years of age to *forty-eight* hours in the week, though to do this latter, has, I must admit, subjected us to much inconvenience, but the elder hands to more, inasmuch as the relief given to the child is in some measure imposed on the adult. But the overworking does not apply to children only; the adults are also overworked. The increased speed given to machinery within the last thirty years, has, in very many instances, doubled the labour of both.

John Fielden, *The Curse of the Factory System*. London, 1836.

Questions:
1. According to Fielden, what factors contributed to the harsh working conditions in the early phases of the Industrial Revolution?
2. In your life, do you feel "advancements" in technology have improved your quality of life or not? Give some specific examples in supporting your opinion.

Chapter 22: An Era of Isms: Conservatism, Liberalism, Nationalism, and Romanticism

Unit 47: The Conservative Backlash

Following the fall of Napoleon Bonaparte, "order" and "legitimacy" became the watchwords of the day. After twenty-five years of social upheaval, costly wars, parvenu Bonapartist dynasties, and endless border changes, the crowned heads of Europe, and a goodly number of their subjects as well, desperately yearned for peace and stability. For Europe's conservative statesmen and their apologists, the peace and security of Europe and its citizens could best be preserved by adherence to tradition, and obedience to those political, social, and cultural institutions that had survived the test of time. While not opposed to change, Europe's nineteenth-century conservatives believed any reform should be a gradual process initiated and controlled by men of property, breeding, and education.

Nineteenth-century liberals, on the other hand, were committed to the principle of individual freedom. While they often disagreed on economic and political issues, they agreed that society exists to secure the rights and well-being of its individual members. In return, they believed, all of society would benefit from the unleashed talents and abilities of its individual members; the good of the many could best be insured by attending to the good of the one.

Edmund Burke: Reflections on the French Revolution, 1790

If one can speak of a "father" of modern conservatism, it would have to be Edmund Burke (1729-1797). A British politician and publicist, Burke served for many years in the House of Commons and became one of that body's most vociferous defenders of tradition and the preeminent position of aristocrats and men of property in the governance of the United Kingdom. Burke found the French Revolution, with its assault on the monarchy and its glorification of the individual, a horrifying event. In 1790, he responded to the events in France by penning his *Reflections on the French Revolution*, an essay that he wrote in the form of a letter to a resident of Paris.

WHO SHOULD GOVERN

…There is no qualification for government but virtue and wisdom, actual or presumptive. Wherever they are actually found, they have, in whatever state, condition, profession or trade, the passport of heaven to human place and honour. Woe to the country which would madly and impiously reject the service of the talents and virtues, civil, military or religious, that are given to grace and to serve it; and would condemn to obscurity everything formed to diffuse lustre and glory around a state. Woe to that country too, that, passing into the opposite extreme, considers a low education, a mean contracted view of things, a sordid, mercenary occupation, as a preferable title to command. Everything ought to be open; but not indifferently to every man. No rotation; no appointment by lot; no mode of election operating in the spirit of sortation, or rotation, can be generally good in a government conversant in extensive objects. Because they have no tendency, direct or indirect, to select the man with a view to the duty, or to accommodate the one to the other. I do not hesitate to say that the road to eminence and power, from obscure condition, ought not to be made too easy, nor a thing too much of course. If rare merit be the rarest of all rare things, it ought to pass through some sort of probation. The temple of honour ought to be seated on an eminence. if it be opened through virtue, let it be remembered too that virtue is never tried but by some difficulty and some struggle.

ON PROPERTY

Nothing is a due and adequate representation of a state that does not represent its ability, as well as its property. But as ability is a vigorous and active principle, and as property is sluggish, inert and timid, it never can be safe from the invasions of ability, unless it be, out of all proportion, predominant in the representation. It must be represented too in great masses of accumulation, or it is not rightly protected. The characteristic essence of property, formed out of the combined principles of its acquisition and conservation, is to be unequal. The great masses therefore which excite envy, and tempt rapacity, must be put out of the possibility of danger. Then they form a natural rampart about the lesser properties in all their gradations. The same quantity of property, which is by the natural course of things divided among many, has not the same operation. Its defensive power is weakened as it is diffused. In this diffusion each man's portion is less than what, in the eagerness of his desires, he may flatter himself to obtain by dissipating the accumulations of others. The plunder of the few would indeed give but a share inconceivably small in the distribution to the many. But the many are not capable of making this calculation; and those who lead them to rapine never intend this distribution.

The power of perpetuating our property in our families is one of the most valuable and interesting circumstances belonging to it, and that which tends the most to the perpetuation of society itself. It makes our weakness subservient to our virtue; it grafts benevolence even upon avarice. The possessors of family wealth, and of the distinction which attends hereditary possession, (as most concerned in it,) are the natural securities for this transmission. With us the House of Peers is formed upon this principle. It is wholly composed of hereditary property and hereditary distinction; and made therefore the third of the legislature; and in the last event, the sole judge of all property in all its subdivisions. The House of Commons too, though not necessarily, yet in fact, is always so composed, in the far greater part. Let those large proprietors be what they will, and they have their chance of being among the best, they are, at the very worst, the ballast in the vessel of the commonwealth. For though hereditary wealth, and the rank which goes with it are too much idolized by creeping sycophants, and the blind, abject admirers of power, they are too rashly slighted in shallow speculations of the petulant, assuming, short-sighted coxcombs of philosophy. Some decent, regulated pre-eminence, some preference (not exclusive appropriation), given to birth, is neither unnatural, nor unjust, nor impolitick.

It is said, that twenty-four millions ought to prevail over two hundred thousand. True; if the constitution of a kingdom be a problem of arithmetick. This sort of discourse does well enough with the lamp-post for its second: to men who *may* reason calmly, it is ridiculous. The will of the many, and their interest, must very often differ; and great will be the difference when they make an evil choice. A government of five hundred country attornies and obscure curates is not good for twenty-four millions of men, though it were chosen by eight and forty millions; nor is it the better for being guided by a dozen of persons of quality, who have betrayed their trust in order to obtain that power....

THE RIGHTS OF MEN

Far am I from denying in theory; full as far is my heart from withholding in practice (if I were of power to give or to withhold) the *real* rights of men. In denying their false claims of right, I do not mean to injure those which are real, and are such as their pretended rights would totally destroy. If civil society be made for the advantage of man, all the advantages for which it is made become his right. It is an institution of beneficence; and law itself is only beneficence acting by a rule. Men have a right to live by that rule; they have a right to do justice; as between their fellows, whether their fellows are in politick function or in ordinary occupation. They have a right to the fruits of their industry; and to the means of making their industry fruitful. They have a right to the acquisitions of their parents; to the nourishment and improvement of their offspring; to instruction in life, and to consolation in death. Whatever each man can separately do, without trespassing upon others, he has a right to do for himself; and he has a right to a fair portion of all which society, with all its combinations of skill and force, can do in his favour. In this partnership all men have equal rights; but not to equal things. He that has but five shillings in the partnership, has as good a right to it, as he that has five hundred pounds has to his larger proportion. But he has not a right to an equal dividend in the product of the joint stock; and as to the share of power, authority, and direction which each individual ought to have in the management of the state, that I must deny to be amongst the direct original rights of man in civil society;...

The science of constructing a commonwealth, or renovating it, or reforming it, is, like every other experimental science, not to be taught *a priori*. Nor is it a short experience that can instruct us in that practical science; because the real effects of moral causes are not always immediate; but that which in the first instance is prejudicial may be excellent in its remoter operation; and its excellence may arise even from the ill effects it produces in the beginning. The reverse also happens; and very plausible schemes, with very pleasing commencements, have often shameful and lamentable conclusion. It states there are often some obscure and almost latent causes, things which appear at first view of little moment, on which a very great part of its prosperity or adversity may most essentially depend. The science of government being therefore so practical in itself, and intended for such practical purposes, a matter which requires experience, and even more experience than any person can gain in his whole life, however sagacious and observing he may be, it is with infinite caution that any man ought to venture upon pulling down an edifice which has answered in any tolerable degree for ages the common purposes of society, or on building it up again, without having models and patterns of approved utility before his eyes....

The Effects of Revolution

It is now sixteen or seventeen years since I saw the queen of France, then the dauphiness, at Versailles; and surely never lighted on this orb, which she hardly seemed to touch, a more delightful vision. I saw her just above the horizon, decorating and cheering the elevated sphere the just began to move in,—glittering like the morning-star, full of life, and splendour, and joy. Oh! what a revolution! and what an heart must I have, to contemplate without emotion that elevation and that fall! Little did I dream when she added titles of veneration to those of enthusiastick, distant, respectful love, that she should ever be obliged to carry the sharp antidote against disgrace concealed in that bosom; little did I dream that I should have lived to see such disasters fallen upon her in a nation of gallant men, in a nation of men of honour and of cavaliers. I thought ten thousand swords must have leaped from their scabbards to avenge even a look that threatened her with insult. But the age of chivalry is gone. That of sophisters, economists, and calculators, has succeeded; and the glory of Europe is extinguished for ever. Never, never more, shall we behold that generous loyalty to rank and sex, that proud submission, that dignified obedience, that subordination of the heart, which kept alive, even in servitude itself, the spirit of an exalted freedom. The unbought grace of life, the cheap defence of nations, the nurse of manly sentiment and heroick enterprise is gone! It is gone, that sensibility of principle, that chastity of honour, which felt a stain like a wound, which inspired courage whilst it mitigated ferocity, which ennobled whatever it touched, and under which vice itself lost half its evil, by losing all its grossness.

This mixed system of opinion and sentiment had its origin in the ancient chivalry; and the principle, though varied in its appearance by the varying state of human affairs, subsisted and influenced through a long succession of generations, even to the time we live in. If it should ever be totally extinguished, the loss I fear will be great....

But now all is to be changed. All the pleasing illusions, which made power gentle, and obedience liberal, which harmonized the different shades of life, and which, by a bland assimilation, incorporated into politicks the sentiments which beautify and soften private society, are to be dissolved by this new conquering empire of light and reason. All the decent drapery of life is to be rudely torn off. All the superadded ideas, furnished from the wardrobe of a moral imagination, which the heart owns, and the understanding ratifies, as necessary to cover the defects of our naked shivering nature, and to raise it to dignity in our own estimation, are to be exploded as a ridiculous, absurd, and antiquated fashion.

On this scheme of things, a king is but a man, a queen is but a woman; a woman is but an animal; and an animal not of the highest order. All homage paid to the sex in general as such, and without distinct views, is to be regarded as romance and folly. Regicide, and parricide, and sacrilege, are but fictions of superstition, corrupting jurisprudence by destroying its simplicity. The murder of a king, or a queen, or a bishop, or a father, are only common homicide; and if the people are by any chance, or in any way gainers by it, a sort of homicide much the most pardonable, and into which we ought not to make too sever a scrutiny.

On the scheme of this barbarous philosophy, which is the offspring of cold hearts and muddy understandings, and which is as void of solid wisdom, as it is destitute of all taste and elegance, laws are to be supported only by their own terrours, and by the concern, which each individual may find in them, from his own private speculations, or can spare to them from his own private interests. In the groves of *their* academy, at the end of every visit, you see nothing but the gallows.

THE ENGLISH SCENE

...Four hundred years have gone over us. Thanks to our sullen resistance to innovation, thanks to the cold sluggishness of our national character, we still bear the stamp of our forefathers. We have not (as I conceive) lost the generosity and dignity of thinking of the fourteenth century; nor as yet have we subtilized ourselves into savages. We are not the converts of Rousseau; we are not the disciples of Voltaire; Helvetius has made no progress amongst us. Atheists are not our preachers; madmen are not our lawgivers. We know that *we* have made no discoveries; and we think that no discoveries are to be made, in morality; nor many in the great principles of government, nor in the ideas of liberty, which were understood long before we were born, altogether as well as they will be after the grave has heaped its mould upon our presumption, and the silent tomb shall have imposed its law on our pert loquacity. In England we have not yet been completely embowelled of our natural entrails; we still feel within us, and we cherish and cultivate, those inbred sentiments which are the faithful guardians, the active monitors of our duty, the true supporters of all liberal and manly morals. We have not been drawn and trussed, in order that we may be filled, like stuffed birds in a museum, with chaff and rags and paltry blurred shreds of paper about the rights of man. We preserve the whole of our feelings still native and intire, unsophisticated by pedantry and infidelity. We have real hearts of flesh and blood beating in our bosoms. We fear God; we look up with awe to kings; with affection to parliaments; with duty to magistrates; with reverence to priests; and with respect to nobility. Why? Because when such ideas are brought before our minds, it is *natural* to be so affected; because all other feelings are false and spurious, and tend to corrupt our minds, to vitiate our primary morals, to render us unfit for rational liberty; and by teaching us a servile, licentious, and abandoned insolence, to be our low sport for a few holidays, to make us perfectly fit for, and justly deserving of slavery, though the whole course of our lives.

You see, Sir, that in this enlightened age I am bold enough to confess, that we are generally men of untaught feelings; that instead of casting away all our old prejudices, we cherish them to a very considerable degree, and, to take more shame to ourselves, we cherish them because they are prejudices; and the longer they have lasted, and the more generally they have prevailed, the more we cherish them. We are afraid to put men to live and trade each on his own private stock of reason; because we suspect that the stock in each man is small, and that the individuals would do better to avail themselves of the general bank and capital of nations and of ages. Many of our men of speculation, instead of exploding general prejudices, employ their sagacity to discover the latent wisdom which prevails in them. If they find what they seek, and they seldom fail, they think it more wise to continue the prejudice, with the reason involved, than to cast away the coat of prejudice, and to leave nothing but the naked reason; because prejudice, with its reason, has a motive to give action to that reason, and an affection which will give it permanence. Prejudice is of ready application in the emergency; it previously engages the mind in a steady course of wisdom and virtue, and does not leave the man hesitating in the moment of decision, sceptical, puzzled, and unresolved. Prejudice renders a man's virtue his habit; and not a series of unconnected acts. Through just prejudice, his duty becomes a part of his nature.

Your literary men, and your politicians, and so do the whole clan of the enlightened among us, essentially differ in these points. They have no respect for the wisdom of others; but they pay it off by a very full measure of confidence in their own. With them it is a sufficient motive to destroy an old scheme of things, because it is an old one. As to the new, they are in no sort of fear with regard to the duration of a building run up in haste; because duration is no object to those who think little or nothing has been done before their time, and who place all their hopes in discovery. They conceive, very systematically, that all things which give perpetuity are mischievous, and therefore they are at inexpiable war with all establishments. They think that government may vary like modes of dress, and with as little ill effect: that there needs no principle of attachment, except a sense of present convenience, to any constitution of the state. They always speak as if they were of opinion that there is a singular species of compact between them and their magistrates, which binds the magistrate, but which has nothing reciprocal in it, but that the majesty of the people has a right to dissolve it without any reason, but his will. Their attachment to their country itself is only so far as it agrees with some of their fleeting projects; it begins and ends with that scheme of polity which falls in with their momentary opinion.

These doctrines, or rather sentiments, seem prevalent with your new statesmen. But they are wholly different from those on which we have always acted in this country....

from *The Works of the Right Honourable Edmund Burke.* vol. V. London: Rivington, 1808.

Questions:
1. According to Edmund Burke, what qualifications should an individual have in order to serve in government?
2. What rights do men have in Burke's eyes? Do you agree with him?

3. What do you think Burke's opinion would be of trying to implement a new form of government based upon an Enlightenment thinker's philosophical writing? Why might he support or oppose such an endeavor?
4. Why was Burke opposed to the French Revolution? In his eyes, what principles did the revolutionaries violate?
5. How did Burke view Britain as a preferable model of government and society to that in France?
6. What do you think Burke meant by "prejudice," and why did he support British "prejudices"?

Joseph de Maistre: from *Essay on the Generative Principle of Political Constitutions*, 1814

The French author, moralist, and diplomat Joseph de Maistre (1753-1821), wanted to go beyond the conservatism of Burke. He favored a resurrection of the institutions and principles that he believed had held sway in Europe during the Middle Ages: government by divine right monarchy, and a restoration of the absolute authority of the Pope. In an age of conservative reactionaries, Joseph de Maistre was a reactionary par excellence.

I. One of the greatest errors of a century which professed them all was to believe that a political constitution could be created and written *a priori*, whereas reason and experience unite in proving that a constitution is a divine work and that precisely the most fundamental and essentially constitutional of a nation's laws could not possibly be written....

IX. The more one examines the role of human agency in forming political constitutions, the more one becomes convinced that it enters only in an infinitely subordinate manner, or as a simple instrument, and I do not believe that the slightest doubt remains as to the unquestionable truth of the following propositions:

1. The fundamental principles of political constitutions exist prior to all written law.

2. Constitutional law (*loi)* is and can only be the development or sanction of a pre-existing and unwritten law. *(droit).*

3. What is most essential, most inherently constitutional and truly fundamental law is never written, and could not be, without endangering the State.

4. The weakness and fragility of a constitution are actually in direct proportion to the number of written constitutional articles....

XIX ....In their general sense, these ideas were known to the ancient philosophers, who clearly perceived the faint—indeed, almost total—insignificance of the written word for great institutions. No one has ever realized or expressed this truth better than Plato, who invariably was first on the way to finding all great truths. According to him, the man who acquires all his education from things written *will never have more than the appearance of wisdom*.... Thus he who believes himself able by writing alone to establish a clear and lasting doctrine IS A GREAT FOOL. If he really possessed the seeds of truth, he could never believe that a little black liquid and a pen could germinate them in the world, protect them from harsh weather, and make them sufficiently effective. As for whoever undertakes writing *laws or civil constitutions* in the belief that he can give them adequate conviction and stability because he has written them, he disgraces himself, whether or no other people say so. He shows an equal ignorance of the nature of inspiration and delirium, right and wrong, good and evil. This ignorance is shameful, even when approved by the whole body of the common people....

XXXII. The most famous nations of antiquity, especially the more serious and wise, such as the Egyptians, Etruscans, Lacedaemonians, and Romans, were precisely those with the most religious forms of government. And the duration of empires has always been proportionate to the degree of influence the religious element gained in the political constitution. *The cities and nations most attached to divine worship have always been the wisest and longest lasting, just as the most religious ages have always been the most distinguished by genius.*

XXXIII. Religion alone civilizes nations. No other known force can influence the savage. Without referring to antiquity's decisive proofs on this point, we can find tangible evidence in America. For three centuries we have been there with our laws, our arts, our sciences, our civilization, our commerce and luxuries. And what have we gained over the savage state? Nothing. We destroy these unfortunate beings with sword and alcohol. We gradually drive them into the middle of the wilderness until at last they wholly disappear, as much victims of our vices as of our callous superiority....

XXXVII. I have had to dwell principally on the formation of empires as being the most important subject. But all human institutions obey the same rule, being meaningless or dangerous unless they rest on the foundation of all existence. This principle being undeniable, what shall we think of a generation which has thrown everything to the winds, including the very foundations of the structure of society, by making education exclusively scientific? It was impossible to err more frightfully. For every educational system which does not have religion as its basis will collapse in an instant, or else diffuse only poisons throughout the State, *religion being*, as Bacon aptly says, *the spice which preserves the sciences from decay.*

XL. Creation is not man's province. Nor does his *unassisted* power even appear capable of improving on institutions already established. If anything is apparent to man, it is the existence of two opposing forces in the universe in continual conflict. Nothing good is unsullied or unaltered by evil. Every evil is repressed and assailed by good, which continually impels all existence towards a more perfect state. These two forces are present everywhere. We observe them equally in the growth of plants, the development of animals, the formation of languages and empires (two inseparable things), etc. Probably, human powers extend only to removing or resisting evil in order to separate from it the good, which may then develop freely according to its nature....

LXI ....Undoubtedly, vice has always existed in the world, but it can differ in quantity, essence, dominant characteristics, and intensity. Although impious men have always existed, there never was before the eighteenth century, and in the heart of Christendom, *an insurrection against God.* Never before, above all, has there been a sacrilegious conspiracy of every human talent against its Creator. For this is what we have witnessed in our time. Vaudeville has blasphemed, as well as tragedy, and the novel, along with history and the physical sciences. Men of this age have prostituted genius to irreligion and, according to the admirable phrase of Saint Louis on his deathbed, THEY HAVE WAGED WAR AGAINST GOD WITH HIS OWN GIFTS....

LXIV. Then that species of impiety which belongs only to the eighteenth century discloses itself for the first time. It is no longer the cold tone of indifference, of, at worst, the malignant irony of skepticism. It is a mortal hatred, the tone of anger and often of fury. The writers of that period, at least the most distinguished among them, no longer treat Christianity as an unimportant human error. They pursue it like a formidable enemy. They oppose it to the last extreme. It is a war to the death. What would seem incredible, if our own eyes had not seen the sad proofs of it, is that several of these men, who call themselves *philosophers*, advanced from hatred of Christianity to personal hatred of its Divine Author....

from the book *Joseph de Maistre: On God and Society.* © 1959 by Regnery Publishing. All rights reserved. Reprinted by special permission of Regnery Publishing, Inc., Washington, D.C.

Questions:

1. What was de Maistre's view of a constitution? How might his religious beliefs have affected de Maistre's perspective? What is his reaction to the movement toward secularization?
2. Compare and contrast the views of Burke and de Maistre. Using these documents as representatives of conservatism, how would you define this ideology?

Unit 48: The Many Faces of Liberalism

John Stuart Mill: On Liberty, 1859

No one embodied the liberal ideal and its contradictions better than the English philosopher, John Stuart Mill (1806-1873). In his essay *On Liberty* he expressed some basic principles of nineteenth-century liberalism.

…The struggle between Liberty and Authority is the most conspicuous feature in the portions of history with which we are earliest familiar, particularly in that of Greece, Rome, and England. But in old times this contest was between subjects, or some classes of subjects, and the Government. By liberty, was meant protection against the tyranny of the political rulers. The rulers were conceived (except in some of the popular governments of Greece) as in a necessarily antagonistic position to the people whom they ruled. They consisted of a governing One, or a governing tribe or caste, who derived their authority from inheritance or conquest, who, at all events, did not hold it at the pleasure of the governed, and whose supremacy men did not venture, perhaps did not desire, to contest, whatever precautions might be taken against it oppressive exercise. Their power was regarded as necessary, but also as highly dangerous; as a weapon which they would attempt to use against their subjects, no less than against external enemies. To prevent the weaker members of the community from being preyed upon by innumerable vultures, it was needful that there would be an animal of prey stronger than the rest, commissioned to keep them down. But as the king of the vultures would be no less bent upon preying on the flock than any of the minor harpies, it was indispensable to be in a perpetual attitude of defence against his beak and claws. The aim, therefore, of patriots was to set limits to the power which the ruler should be suffered to exercise over the community; and this limitation was what they meant by liberty. It was attempted in two ways. First, by obtaining a recognition of certain immunities, called political liberties or rights, which it was to be regarded as a breach of duty in the ruler to infringe, and which, if he did infringe, specific resistance, or general rebellion, was held to be justifiable. A second, and generally a later expedient, was the establishment of constitutional checks, by which the consent of the community, or of a body of some sort, supposed to represent its interests, was made a necessary condition to some of the more important acts of the governing power….

A time, however, came, in the progress of human affairs, when men ceased to think it a necessity of nature that their governors should be an independent power, opposed in the interest to themselves. It appeared to them much better that the various magistrates of the State should be their tenants or delegates, revocable at their pleasure. In that way alone, it seemed, could they have complete security that the powers of government would never be abused to their disadvantage. By degrees this new demand for elective and temporary rulers became the prominent object of the exertions of the popular party, wherever any such party existed; and superseded, to a considerable extent, the previous efforts to limit the power of rulers. As the struggle proceeded for making the ruling power emanate from the periodical choice of the ruled, some persons began to think that too much importance had been attached to the limitation of the power itself. *That* (it might seem) was a resource against rulers whose interests were habitually opposed to those of the people. What was now wanted was, that the rulers should be identified with the people; that their interest and will should be the interest and the will of the nation. The nation did not need to be protected against its own will. There was no fear of its tyrannizing over itself. Let the rulers be effectually responsible to it, promptly removable by it, and it could afford to trust them with power of which it could itself dictate the use to be made. Their power was but the nation's own power, concentrated, and in form convenient for exercise. This mode of thought, or rather perhaps of feeling, was common among the last generation of European liberalism, in the continental section of which it still apparently predominates. Those who admit any limit to what a government may do, except in the case of such governments as they think ought not to exist, stand out as brilliant exceptions among the political thinkers of the continent. A similar tone of sentiment might by this time have been prevalent in our own country, if the circumstances which for a time encouraged it, had continued unaltered.

But, in political and philosophical theories, as well as in persons, success discloses faults and infirmities which failure might have concealed from observation. The notion, that the people have no need to limit their power over themselves, might seem axiomatic, when popular government was a thing only dreamed about, or read of as having existed at some distant period of the past. Neither was that notion necessarily disturbed by such temporary aberrations as those of the French Revolution, the worst of which were the work of an usurping few, and which, in any case, belonged not to the permanent working of popular institutions, but to a sudden and convulsive outbreak against monarchical and aristocratic despotism. In time, however, a democratic republic came to occupy a large portion of the earth's surface, and made itself felt as one of the most powerful members of the community of nations; and elective and responsible government became subject to the observations and criticisms which wait upon a great existing fact. It was now perceived that such phrases as "self-government," and "the power of the people over themselves," do not express the true state of the case. The "people" who exercise the power are not always the same people with those over whom it is exercised; and the "self-government" spoken of is not the government of each by himself, but of each by all the rest. The will of the people, moreover, practically means the will of the most numerous or the most active *part* of the people; the majority, or those who succeed in making themselves accepted as the majority; the people, consequently, *may* desire to oppress a part of their number; and precautions are as much needed against this as against any other abuse of power....

Like other tyrannies, the tyranny of the majority was at first, and is still, vulgarly, held in dread, chiefly as operating through the acts of the public authorities. But reflecting persons perceive that when society is itself the tyrant—society collectively, over the separate individuals who compose it—its means of tyrannizing are not restricted to the acts which it may do by the hands of its political functionaries. Society can and does execute its own mandates: and if it issues wrong mandates instead of right, or any mandates at all in things with which it ought not to meddle, it practises a social tyranny more formidable than many kinds of political oppression, since, though not usually upheld by such extreme penalties, it leaves fewer means of escape, penetrating much more deeply into the details of life, and enslaving the soul itself. Protection, therefore, against the tyranny of the magistrate is not enough: there needs protection also against the tyranny of the prevailing opinion and feeling; against the tendency of society to impose, by other means than civil penalties, its own ideas and practices as rules of conduct on those who dissent from them; to fetter the development, and, if possible, prevent the formation, of any individuality not in harmony with its ways, and compel all characters to fashion themselves upon the model of its own. There is a limit to the legitimate interference of collective opinion with individual independence: and to find that limit, and maintain it against encroachment, is as indispensable to a good condition of human affairs, as protection against political despotism.

But though this proposition is not likely to be contested in general terms, the practical question, where to place the limit—how to make the fitting adjustment between individual independence and social control—is a subject on which nearly everything remains to be done. All that makes existence valuable to anyone, depends on the enforcement of restraints upon the actions of other people. Some rules of conduct, therefore, must be imposed, by law in the first place and by opinion on many things which are not fit subjects for the operation of law. What these rules should be, is the principal question in human affairs; but if we except a few of the most obvious cases, it is one of those which least progress has been made in resolving. No two ages, and scarcely any two countries, decided it alike; and the decision of one age or country is a wonder to another. Yet the people of any given age and country no more suspect any difficulty in it that if it were a subject on which mankind had always agreed. The rules which obtain among themselves appear to them self-evident and self-justifying. This all but universal illusion is one of the examples of the magical influence of custom, which is not only, as the proverb says, a second nature, but is continually mistaken for the first. The effect of custom, in preventing any misgiving respecting the rules of conduct which mankind impose on one another, is all the more complete because the subject is one on which it is not generally considered necessary that reasons should be given, either by one person to others, or by each to himself. People are accustomed to believe, and have been encouraged in the belief by some who aspire to the character of philosophers, that their feelings, on subjects of this nature, are better than reasons, and render reasons unnecessary. The practical principle which guides them to their opinions on the regulation of human conduct, is the feeling in each person's mind that everybody should be required to act as he, and those with whom he sympathizes, would like them to act. No one, indeed, acknowledges to himself that his standard of judgment is his own liking; but an opinion on a point of conduct, not supported by reasons, can only count as one person's preference; and if the reasons, when given, are a mere appeal to a similar preference felt by other people it is still only many people's liking instead of one. To an ordinary man, however, his own preference, thus supported, is not only a perfectly satisfactory reason, but the only one he generally has for any of his notions of morality, taste, or propriety, which are not expressly written in his religious creed; and his chief guide in the interpretation even of that. Men's opinions, accordingly, on what is laudable or blameable, are affected by all the multifarious causes which influence their wishes in regard to the conduct of others, and which are as numerous as those which determine their wishes on any other subject. Sometimes their reason—at other times their prejudices or superstitions: often their social affections, not seldom their anti-social ones, their envy or jealousy, their arrogance or contemptuousness: but more commonly, their desires or fears for themselves—their legitimate or illegitimate self-interest. Wherever there is an ascendant class, a large portion of the morality of the country emanates from its class-interests, and its feelings of class superiority. The morality between Spartans and helots, between planters and negroes, between princes and subjects, between nobles and roturiers,[1] between men and women, has been for the most part the creation of these class interests and feelings: and the sentiments thus generated, react in turn upon the moral feelings of the members of the ascendant class, in their

---

[1] non-nobles.

relations among themselves. Where, on the other hand, a class, formerly ascendant, has lost its ascendancy, or where its ascendancy is unpopular, the prevailing moral sentiments frequently bear the impress of an impatient dislike of superiority. Another grand determining principle of the rules of conduct, both in act and forbearance, which have been enforced by law or opinion, has been the servility of mankind towards the supposed preferences of aversions of their temporal master, or of their gods. This servility, though essentially selfish, is not hypocrisy; it gives rise to perfectly genuine sentiments of abhorrence; it made men burn magicians and heretics. Among so many baser influences, the general and obvious interest of society have of course had a share, and large one, in the direction of the moral sentiments: less, however, as a matter of reason, and on their own account, than as a consequence of the sympathies and antipathies which grew out of them: and sympathies and antipathies which had little or nothing to do with the interests of society, have made themselves felt in the establishment of moralities with quite as great force.

The likings and dislikings of society, or of some powerful portion of it, are thus the main thing which has practically determined the rule laid down for general observance under the penalties of law or opinion. And in general, those who have been in advance of society in thought and feeling, have left this condition of things unassailed in principle, however they may have come into conflict with it in some of its details. They have occupied themselves rather in inquiring what things society ought to like or dislike, than in questioning whether its likings or dislikings should be a law to individuals. They prefer endeavouring to alter the feelings of mankind on the particular points on which they were themselves heretical, rather than make common cause in defence of freedom, with heretics generally. The only case in which the higher ground has been taken on principle and maintained with consistency, by any but an individual here and there, is that of religious belief; a case instructive in many ways, and not least so as forming a most striking instance of the fallibility of what is called the moral sense; for the *odium theologicum*, in a sincere bigot, is one of the most unequivocal cases of moral feeling. Those who first broke the yoke of what called itself the Universal Church, were in general as little willing to permit difference of religious opinion as that church itself. But when the heat of the conflict was over, without giving a complete victory to any party, and each church or sect was reduced to limit its hopes to retaining possession of the ground it already occupied; minorities seeing that they had no chance of becoming majorities, were under the necessity of pleading to those whom they could not convert for permission to differ. It is accordingly on this battlefield, almost solely, that the rights of the individual against society have been asserted on broad grounds of principle, and the claim on society to exercise authority over dissentients, openly controverted. The great writers to whom the world owes what religious liberty it possesses, have mostly asserted freedom of conscience as an indefeasible right, and denied absolutely that a human being is accountable to others for his religious beliefs....

In England, from the peculiar circumstances of our political history, though the yoke of opinion is perhaps heavier, that of law is lighter than in most other countries of Europe and there is considerable jealousy of direct interference, by the legislative or executive power, with private conduct; not so much from any just regard for the independence of the individual, as from the still subsisting habit of looking on the government as representing an opposite interest to the public. The majority have not yet learned to feel the power of the government their power, or its opinions their opinions. When they do so, individual liberty will probably be as much exposed to invasion from the government, as it already is from public opinion. But, as yet, there is a considerable amount of feeling ready to be called forth against any attempt of the law to control individuals in things in which they have not hitherto been accustomed to be controlled by it; and this with very little discrimination as to whether the matter is, or is not, within the legitimate sphere of legal control; insomuch that the feeling, highly salutary on the whole, is perhaps quite as often misplaced as well grounded in the particular instances of its application. There is, in fact, no recognized principle by which the propriety or impropriety of government interference is customarily tested. People decide according to their personal preferences. Some, whenever they see any good to be done, or evil to be remedied, would willingly instigate the government to undertake the business; wile others prefer to bear almost any amount of social evil, rather than add one to the departments of human interests amenable to governmental control. And men range themselves on one or the other side in any particular case, according to this general direction of their sentiments; or according to the degree of interest which they feel in the particular thing which it is proposed that the government should do, or according to the belief they entertain that the government would, or would not, do it in the manner they prefer; but very rarely on account of any opinion to which they consistently adhere, as to what things are fit to be done by a government. And it seems to me that in consequence of this absence of rule or principle, one side is at present as often wrong as the other; the interference of government is, with about equal frequency, improperly invoked and improperly condemned.

The object of this Essay is to assert one very simple principle, as entitled to govern absolutely the dealings of society with the individual in the way of compulsion and control, whether the means used by physical force in the form of legal penalties, or the moral coercion of public opinion. That principle is, that the sole end for which mankind are warranted, individually or collectively, in interfering with the liberty of action of any of their number, is self-protection. That the only purpose for which power can be rightfully exercised over any member of a civilised community, against his will, is to prevent harm to others. His own good, either physical or moral, is not a sufficient warrant. He cannot rightfully be compelled to do or forbear because it will be better for him to do so, because it will make him happier, because, in the opinions of others, to do so would be wise, or even right. These are good reasons for remonstrating with him, or reasoning with him, or persuading him, or entreating him, but not for compelling him, or visiting him with any evil in case he do otherwise. To justify that, the conduct from which it is desired to deter him, must be calculated to produce evil to someone else. The only part of the conduct of anyone, for which he is amenable to society, is that which concerns others. In the part which merely concerns himself, his independence is, of right, absolute. Over himself, over his own body and mind, the individual is sovereign.

London, 1859.

Questions:
1. According to John Stuart Mill, how was liberty traditionally defined in relation to the ruler? How did this definition change through time?
2. How is it possible, according to Mill, that, under a democratic form of government, "the people" might "oppress a part of their number"?
3. Do you agree with Mill that prevailing opinions and feelings within a society can form a kind of tyranny over the individual? Why or why not?
4. According to Mill, what role should government play in relation to restricting an individual's freedom? Do you agree with him? Why or why not?

Charles Dickens: from *Hard Times,* 1854

While pinning down the exact tenets of liberalism was often a maddening exercise in the nineteenth century, pinpointing the kinds of people who regarded themselves as liberals was a relatively simple task.

With very few exceptions, liberalism was the creed of Britain's middle class businessmen, industrialists, and urban professionals. Indeed, liberal ideas regarding a utilitarian-based morality, individual freedom, and laissez-faire economics seemed ideally suited to a social class that was seeking to benefit from the new industrial technologies and obtain a voice for itself in the British government. Not everyone in the English middle classes, however, was enamored with the liberal project. In the following passage from his scathing critique of British society during the heyday of the Industrial Revolution, Charles Dickens takes aim at some of the shortcomings of liberal morality. The following is a conversation from *Hard Times*.

"But, if you please, Miss Louisa," Sissy pleaded, "I am—O so stupid!"

Louisa, with a brighter laugh than usual, told her she would be wiser by-and-by.

"You don't know," said Sissy, half crying, "what a stupid girl I am. All through school hours I make mistakes. Mr. and Mrs. M'Choakumchild call me up, over and over again, regularly to make mistakes. I can't help them. They seem to come natural to me."

"Mr. and Mrs. M'Choakumchild never make any mistakes themselves, I suppose, Sissy?"

"O no!" she eagerly returned. "They know everything."

"Tell me some of your mistakes."

"I am almost ashamed," said Sissy, with reluctance. "But today, for instance, Mr. M'Choakumchild was explaining to us about Natural Prosperity."

"National, I think it must have been," observed Louisa.

"Yes, it was.—But isn't it the same?" she timidly asked.

"You had better say, National, as he said so," returned Louisa, with her dry reserve.

"National Prosperity. And he said, Now, this schoolroom is a Nation. And in this nation, there are fifty millions of money. Isn't this a prosperous nation? Girl number twenty, isn't this a prosperous nation, and a'n't you in a thriving state?"

"What did you say?" asked Louisa

"Miss Louisa, I said I didn't know. I thought I couldn't know whether it was a prosperous nation or not, and whether I was in a thriving state or not, unless I knew who had got the money, and whether any of it was mine. But that had nothing to do with it. It was not in the figures at all," said Sissy, wiping her eyes.

"That was a great mistake of yours," observed Louisa.

"Yes, Miss Louisa, I know it was, now. Then Mr. M'Choakumchild said he would try me again. And he said, This schoolroom is an immense town, and in it there a million of inhabitants, and only five-and-twenty are starved to death in the streets, in the course of a year. What is your remark on that proportion? And my remark was—for I couldn't think of a better one—that I thought it must be just as hard upon those who were staved, whether the others were a million, or a million million. And that was wrong, too."

London: J. M. Dent, 1907.

Questions:
1. How did the student, Sissy, define "National Prosperity"? What was the teacher, Mr. M'Choakumchild's definition? What ideology do his ideas represent?
2. What do you think was Dicken's intent in including this passage?

Unit 49: People and Their Homelands: The Dream of National Self-Determination

We are so used to thinking of ourselves and others in national terms that it is difficult to conceive of a period when such a political arrangement was the exception rather than the rule. Nevertheless, prior to the French Revolution (and for a considerable time thereafter), most Europeans conceived of themselves as the subjects of one or more of the continent's multinational empires, rather than as the citizens of a distinct national community that shared a common homeland, language, culture, and history. it was only after the French Revolution and the Napoleonic Wars, two events that demonstrated what a sense of national brotherhood and solidarity could achieve in terms of unifying a people and defeating their enemies, that other European communities began to entertain the notion of themselves as distinctive nations with the right to independence. Indeed, much of the history of the nineteenth century is a chronicle of the struggles of Germans, Italians, Belgians, Greeks, and other European peoples for national liberation and unification.

Giuseppe Mazzini: from *On the Duties of Man,* 1864

One of the key figures in the European movement for national self-determination was the Italian patriot and revolutionary Giuseppe Mazzini (1805-1872). A passionate advocate of Italian unity and freedom from foreign occupation and control, Mazzini was involved in two revolutionary attempts to set up a Republic of Italy in the 1830s and 1840s. In the following selection, Mazzini explains what the idea of national self-determination meant for him. It is a moving affirmation not only of the right of every community to govern itself, but also a reminder that, in spite of our national differences, we owe our first allegiance to humanity.

DUTIES TO COUNTRY

Your first Duties—first, at least, in importance— are, as I have told you, to Humanity. You are *men* before you are *citizens* or *fathers*. If you do not embrace the whole human family in your love, if you do not confess your faith in its unity—consequent on the unity of God—and in brotherhood of the Peoples who are appointed to reduce that unity to fact—if wherever one of your fellowmen groans, wherever the dignity of human nature is violated by falsehood or tyranny, you are not prompt, being able, to succour that wretched one, or do not feel yourself called, being able, to fight for the purpose of relieving the deceived or oppressed—you disobey your law of life, or do not comprehend the religion which will bless the future.

But what can *each* of you, with his isolated power, *do* for the moral improvement, for the progress of Humanity? You can, from time to time, give sterile expression to your belief; you may, on some rare occasion, perform an act of *charity* to a brother not belonging to your own land, no more. Now, charity is not the watchword of the future faith. The watchword of the future faith is *association*, fraternal, co-operation towards a common aim, and this is as much superior to *charity* as the work of many uniting to raise with one accord a building for the habitation of all together would be superior to that which you would accomplish by raising a separate hut each for himself, and only helping one another by exchanging stones and bricks and mortar. But divided as you are in language tendencies, habits, and capacities, you cannot attempt this common aim, and this is as much superior to charity as the work of many uniting to raise with one accord a building for the habitation of all together would be superior to that which you would accomplish by raising a separate hut each for himself, and only helping one another by exchanging stones and bricks and mortar. But divided as you are in language tendencies, habits, and capacities, you cannot attempt this common work. The individual is too weak, the Humanity too vast. *My God*, prays the Breton mariner as he puts out to sea, protect me, my ship is so little, and *Thy ocean so great!* And this prayer sums up the condition of each of you, if no means is found of multiplying your forces and your powers of action indefinitely. But God gave you this means when he gave you a Country, when, like a wise overseer of labour, who distributes the different parts of the work according to the capacity of the workmen, he divided Humanity into distinct groups upon the face of our globe, and thus planted the seeds of nations. Bad governments have disfigured the design of God, which you may see clearly marked out, as far, at least, as regards Europe, by the courses of the great rivers, by the lines of the lofty mountains, and by other geographical conditions; they have disfigured it by conquest, by greed, by jealousy of the just sovereignty of others; disfigured it so much that to-day there is perhaps no nation except England and France whose confines correspond to this design. They did not, and they do not, recognize any country except their own families and dynasties, the egoism of caste. But the divine design will infallibly be fulfilled. Natural divisions, the innate spontaneous tendencies of the peoples will replace the arbitrary divisions sanctioned by bad governments. The map of Europe will be remade. The Countries of the People will rise, defined by the voice of the free, upon the ruins of the Countries of Kings and privileged castes. Between these countries there will be harmony and brotherhood.... O my Brothers! love your Country. Our Country is our home, the home which God has given us, placing therein a numerous family which we love and are loved by, and with which we have a more intimate and quicker communion of feeling and thought than with others; a family which by its concentration upon a given spot, and by the homogeneous nature of its elements, is destined for a special kind of activity. Our Country is our field of labour; the products of our activity must go forth from it for the benefit of the whole earth; but the instruments of labour which we can use best and most effectively exist in it, and we may not reject them without being unfaithful to God's purpose and diminishing our own strength. In labouring according to true principles for our Country we are labouring for Humanity; our Country is the fulcrum of the lever which we have to wield for the common good. If we give up this fulcrum we run the risk of becoming useless to our Country and to Humanity. Before *associating* ourselves with the Nations which compose Humanity we must exist as a Nation. There can be no association except among equals; and you have no recognised collective existence.

Humanity is a great army moving to the conquest of unknown lands, against powerful and wary enemies. The Peoples are the different corps and divisions of that army. Each has a post entrusted to it; each a special operation to perform; and the common victory depends on the exactness with which the different operations are carried out. Do not disturb the order of the battle. Do not abandon the banner which God has given you. Wherever you may be, into the midst of whatever people circumstances may have driven you, fight for the liberty of that people if the moment calls for it; but fight as Italians, so that the blood which you shed may win honour and love, not for you only, but for your Country. And may the constant thought of your soul be for Italy, may all the acts of your life be worthy of her, and may the standard beneath which you range yourselves to work for Humanity be Italy's. Do not say *I*; say *we*. Be every one of you an incarnation of your Country, and feel himself and make himself responsible for his fellow-countrymen; let each one of you learn to act in such a way that in him men shall respect and love his Country.

Your Country is one and indivisible. As the members of a family cannot rejoice at the common table if one of their number is far away, snatched from the affection of his brothers, so you should have no joy or repose as long as a portion of the territory upon which your language is spoken is separated from the Nation.

Your Country is the token of the mission which God has given you to fulfil in Humanity. The faculties, the strength of all its sons should be united for the accomplishment of this mission…A Country is a fellowship of free and equal men bound together in a brotherly concord of labour towards a single end. You must make it and maintain it such. A Country is not an aggregation, it is an association. There is no true Country without a uniform right. There is no true Country where the uniformity of that right is violated by the existence of caste, privilege, and inequality—where the powers and faculties of a large number of individuals are suppressed or dormant—where there is no common principle accepted, recognised, and developed by all…. Your Country should be your Temple. God at the summit, a People of equals at the base. Do not accept any other formula, any other moral law, if you do not want to dishonour your Country and yourselves. Let the secondary laws for the gradual regulation of your existence be the progressive application of this supreme law.

And in order that they should be so, it is necessary that *all* should contribute to the making of them. The laws made by one fraction of the citizens only can never by the nature of things and men do otherwise than reflect the thoughts and aspirations and desires of the fraction; they represent, not the whole country, but a third, a fourth part, a class, a zone of the country. The law must express the general aspiration, promote the good of all, respond to a beat of the nation's heart. The whole nation therefore should be, directly or indirectly, the legislator. By yielding this mission to a few men, you put the egoism of one class in the place of the Country, which is the union of *all* the classes.

A Country is not a mere territory; the particular territory is only its foundation. The Country is the idea which rises upon that foundation; it is the sentiment of love, the sense of fellowship which binds together all the sons of that territory. So long as a single one of your bothers is not represented by his own vote in the development of the national life—so long as a single one vegetates uneducated among the educated—so long as a single one able and willing to work languishes in poverty for want of work—you have not got a Country such as it ought to be, the Country of all and for all.

from Joseph Mazzini, *The Duties of Man and Other Essays*. London: J. M. Dent, 1907.

Questions:
1. After reading Mazzini's selection, how would you define nationalism? How does one identify him or herself as part of a national group?
2. Mazzini claimed that "In labouring for our own country on the right principle, we labour for Humanity." What do you think he meant by this statement? Do you agree with him? Why or why not?
3. What are the advantages of nationalism, according to Mazzini? What disadvantages might there be that Mazzini does not recognize?

Unit 50: Storm and Strife: The Romantic Sensibility

Not everyone in Europe's intellectual and artistic circles was enamored with the classical tastes and rational discourse of the eighteenth century Parisian salons. A whole generation of European artists and intellectuals followed in the footsteps of Jean-Jacques Rousseau, rejecting the cold, passionless reasoning of the Enlightenment for a philosophy that elevated feeling and sentiment. Labeled "romantics," they glorified emotion and passion over reason and logic, rejected agnosticism in favor of religion and mysticism, and embraced an artistic style that was guided by experimentation, impulse, fantasy, dreams, and mystery.

William Wordsworth: "The Tables Turned," 1798

William Wordsworth (1770-1850) is often regarded as the chief poet of the English Romantic movement. His lyrics were an unabashed celebration of nature and feeling. Raised in the hills and fields of the English Lake Country, Wordsworth preferred the solace of the countryside to the company of people his entire life. Indeed, he attributed humanity's few noble instincts to the moral force that he believed nature exerted over human character.

Up! up! my Friend, and quit your books;
Or surely you'll grow double:
Up! up! my Friend, and clear your looks;
Why all this toil and trouble?

The sun, above the mountain's head,
A freshening lustre mellow
Through all the long green fields has spread,
His first sweet evening yellow.

Books! 'tis a dull and endless strife:
Come, hear the woodland linnet,
How sweet his music! on my life,
There's more of wisdom in it.

And hark! how blithe the throstle sings!
He, too, is no mean preacher:
Come forth into the light of things,
Let Nature be your teacher.

She has a world of ready wealth,
Our minds and hearts to bless-
Spontaneous wisdom breathed by health,
Truth breathed by cheerfulness.

One impulse from a vernal wood
May teach you more of man,
Of moral evil and of good,
Than all the sages can.

from *Poems of Wordsworth*. Edited by Matthew
Arnold. London: Macmillan, 1920.

Questions:
1. What is your reaction to Wordsworth's claim that one can learn more from nature than from books? How does his poem fit into Enlightenment thinking?

Percy Bysse Shelley: "England in 1819"

An old, mad, blind, despised, and dying
king,—
Princes, the dregs of their dull race, who
flow
Through public scorn,—mud from a muddy
spring,—
Rulers who neither see, nor feel, nor know,
But leech-like to their fainting country cling,
Till they drop, blind in blood, without a
blow,—
A people starved and stabbed in the untilled
field,—

An army, which liberticide and prey
Makes as a two-edged sword to all who
wield
Golden and sanguine laws which tempt and
slay;
Religion Christless, Godless—a book
sealed;
A Senate,—Time's worst statute
unrepealed,—
Are graves, from which a glorious Phantom
may
Burst, to illumine our tempestuous day.

from *The Poetical Works of Percy Bysse Shelley*, vol. 1. London: J. M. Dent, 1907.

Questions:
1. In 1819 at St. Peter's Field in Manchester, England, thousands of protesters demonstrated against a perceived oppressive and less-than-representative British government. The military response ended in eleven deaths and several hundred wounded. As depicted in this piece, what was Shelley's response to this event?
2. What Romantic ideals are conveyed in this writing?

E.T.A. Hoffman: "Beethoven's Instrumental Music," 1813

After poetry, music was the Romantic art form par excellence, and of the many musicians of this period, none enraptured the Romantics more than the German composer, Ludwig van Beethoven (1770-1827). You can get some idea of why this was the case in the following paean of praise penned by the German writer, composer, and painter, Ernst Theodor Amadeus Hoffman.

...In singing, where the poetry suggests precise moods through words, the magical power of music acts like the philosopher's miraculous elixir, a few drops of which make any drink so much more wonderfully delicious. Any passion — love, hate, anger, despair, etc. — presented to us in an opera is clothed by music in the purple shimmer of romanticism, so that even our mundane sensations take us out of the everyday into the realm of the infinite. Such is the power of music's spell that it grows ever stronger and can only burst the fetters of any other art.

It is certainly not merely an improvement in the means of expression (perfection of instruments, greater virtuosity of players), but also a deeper awareness of the peculiar nature of music, that has enabled great composers to raise instrumental music to its present level.

Mozart and Haydn, the creators of modern instrumental music, first showed us the art in its full glory; but the one who regarded it with total devotion and penetrated to its innermost nature is Beethoven. The instrumental compositions of all three masters breathe the same romantic spirit for the very reason that they all intimately grasp the essential nature of the art; yet the character of their compositions is markedly different. Haydn's compositions are dominated by a feeling of childlike optimism. His symphonies lead us through endless, green forest-glades, through a motley throng of happy people. Youths and girls sweep past dancing the round; laughing children, lying in wait behind trees and rose-bushes, teasingly throw flowers at each other. A world of love, of bliss, of eternal youth, as though before the Fall; no suffering, no pain; only sweet, melancholy longing for the beloved vision floating far off in the red glow of evening, neither approaching nor receding; and as long as it is there the night will not draw on, for the vision is the evening glow itself illuminating hill and glade.

Mozart leads us deep into the realm of spirits. Dread lies all about us, but withholds its torments and becomes more an intimation of infinity. We hear the gentle spirit-voices of love and melancholy, the night dissolves into a purple shimmer, and with inexpressible yearning we follow the flying figures kindly beckoning to us from the clouds to join their eternal dance of the spheres. (Mozart's Symphony in E flat major, known as the 'Swan Song'.)

In a similar way Beethoven's instrumental music unveils before us the realm of the mighty and the immeasurable. Here shining rays of light shoot through the darkness of night and we become aware of giant shadows swaying back and forth, moving ever closer around us and destroying *us* but not the pain of infinite yearning, in which every desire, leaping up in sounds of exultation, sinks back and disappears. Only in this pain, in which love, hope, and joy are consumed without being destroyed, which threatens to burst our hearts with a full-chorused cry of all the passions, do we live on as ecstatic visionaries.

Romantic sensibility is rare, and romantic talent even rarer, which is probably why so few are able to strike the lyre whose sound unlocks the wonderful realm of the romantic.

Haydn romantically apprehends the humanity in human life; he is more congenial, more comprehensible to the majority.

Mozart takes more as his province the superhuman, magical quality residing in the inner self.

Beethoven's music sets in motion the machinery of awe, of fear, of terror, of pain, and awakens that infinite yearning which is the essence of romanticism. He is therefore a purely romantic composer....

translated by Martyn Clank in *E.T.A. Hoffman's Musical Writings,* edited by David Dharlton.
Cambridge University Press, 1989.

Questions:
1. According to Hoffman, what is "music's magic"? How does instrumental music differ from vocal music in capturing the essence of the Romantic movement?
2. What romantic images are evoked by Beethoven's music that distinguishes it from the works of such composers as Haydn or Mozart?

Chapter 23: Europe in an Age of Realism, 1850-1871

Unit 51: To Show Things as They Really Are

"Struggle" and "realism" were very much the "buzzwords" of mid-nineteenth century Europe. Not only did the principal philosophers and politicians of this period view existence as an ongoing struggle for survival, but they were also in agreement that the only guarantee of victory in this eternal conflict was a practical, "realistic" approach to life that was unfettered by the blinders of morality.

Karl Marx and Friedrich Engels: *The Communist Manifesto,* 1848

Born into well-to-do West German families, Karl Marx (1818-1883) and Friedrich Engels (1820-1895) met in Paris in 1842 and became lifelong friends and colleagues. In 1847, both men joined a small group of largely German socialist revolutionaries known as the Communist League. In 1848, both men penned for this Communist League a Communist Manifesto, which advocated the overthrow of capitalism and the establishment of a stateless, classless society.

This manifesto was largely unread in 1848, but it would go on to become one of the key political documents of the modern age. While many of Marx and Engels' prognostications for the future failed to materialize, their Manifesto's analysis of the development and operation of capital, and its assertion that history was essentially a predictable record of struggle between different economic classes, resonated strongly in an age of expanding industrial capitalism and growing class tensions. In the end, Marx and Engels' blend of philosophical, economic, and historical theory, in tandem with their call for pragmatic revolutionary action, captured the imagination of a generation of intellectuals and political activists who came of age in an era of realism and struggle.

BOURGEOIS AND PROLETARIANS

The history of all hitherto existing society is the history of class struggles.

Freeman and slave, patrician and plebeian, lord and serf, guild-master and journeyman, in a word, oppressor and oppressed, stood in constant opposition to one another, carried on uninterrupted, now hidden, now open fight, a fight that each time ended, either in a revolutionary reconstitution of society at large, or in the common ruin of the contending. classes.

In the earlier epochs of history we find almost everywhere a complicated arrangement of society into various orders, a manifold gradation of social rank. In ancient Rome we have patricians, knights, plebeians, slaves; in the middle ages, feudal lords, vassals, guild-masters, journeymen, apprentices, serfs; in almost all of these classes, again, subordinate gradations.

The modern bourgeois society that has sprouted from the ruins of feudal society has not done away with class antagonisms. It has but established new classes, new conditions of oppression, new forms of struggle in place of the old ones.

Our epoch, the epoch of the bourgeoisie, possesses, however, this distinctive feature; it has simplified the class antagonisms. Society as a whole is more and more splitting up into two great hostile camps, into two great classes directly facing each other: Bourgeoisie and Proletariat.

From the serfs of the Middle Ages sprang the chartered burghers of the earliest towns. From these burgesses the first elements of the bourgeoisie were developed.

The discovery of America, the rounding of the Cape, opened up fresh ground for the rising bourgeoisie. The East Indian and Chinese markets, the colonization of America, trade with the colonies, the increase in the means of exchange and in commodities generally, gave to commerce, to navigation, to industry, an impulse never before known, and thereby, to the revolutionary element in the tottering feudal society, a rapid development.

The feudal system of industry, under which industrial production was monopolized by close guilds, now no longer sufficed for the growing wants of the new market. The manufacturing system took its place. The guild-masters were pushed on one side by the manufacturing middle class; division of labor between the different corporate guilds vanished in the face of division of labor in each single workshop.

Meantime the markets kept ever growing, the demand ever rising. Even manufacture no longer sufficed. Thereupon, steam and machinery revolutionized industrial production. The place of manufacture was taken by the giant Modern Industry, the place of the industrial middle-class, by industrial millionaires, the leaders of whole industrial armies, the modern bourgeois.

Modern industry has established the world-market, for which the discovery of America paved the way. This market has given an immense development to commerce, to navigation, to communication by land. This development has, in its turn, reacted on the extension of industry; and in proportion as industry, commerce, navigation, railways extended, in the same proportion the bourgeoisie developed, increased its capital, and pushed into the background every class handed down from the Middle Ages.

We see, therefore, how the modern bourgeoisie is itself the product of a long course of development, of a series of revolutions in the modes of production and of exchange.

Each step in the development of the bourgeoisie was accompanied by a corresponding political advance of that class. An oppressed class under the sway of the feudal nobility; an armed and self-governing association in the medieval commune, (here independent urban republic, as in Italy and Germany, there taxable "third estate" of the monarchy, as in France); afterwards, in the period of manufacture proper, serving either the semi-feudal or the absolute monarchy as a counterpoise against the nobility, and in fact corner stone of the great monarchies in general—the bourgeoisie has at last, since the establishment of modern industry and of the world-market, conquered for itself, in the modern representative state, exclusive political sway. The executive of the modern state is but a committee for managing the common affairs of the whole bourgeoisie.

The bourgeoisie, historically, has played a most revolutionary part.

The bourgeoisie, wherever it has got the upper hand, has put an end to all feudal, patriarchal, idyllic relations. It has pitilessly torn asunder the motley feudal ties that bound man to his "natural superiors," and has left no other nexus between man and man than naked self-interest, than callous "cash payment." It has drowned the most heavenly ecstasies of religious fervor, of chivalrous enthusiasm, of philistine sentimentalism, in the icy water of egotistical calculation. It has resolved personal worth into exchange value, and in place of the numberless indefeasible chartered freedoms, has set up that single, unconscionable freedom—Free Trade. In one word, for exploitation, veiled by religious and political illusions, it has substituted naked, shameless, direct, brutal exploitation.

The bourgeoisie has stripped of its halo every occupation hitherto honored and looked up to with reverent awe. It has converted the physician, the lawyer, the priest, the poet, the man of science, into its paid wage laborers.

The bourgeoisie has torn away from the family its sentimental veil, and has reduced the family relation to a mere money relation....

The bourgeoisie has through its exploitation of the world-market given a cosmopolitan character to production and consumption in every country. To the great chagrin of reactionists, it has drawn from under the feet of industry the national ground on which it stood. All old-established national industries have been destroyed or are daily being destroyed. They are dislodged by new industries, whose introduction becomes a life and death question for all civilized nations, by industries that no longer work up indigenous raw material, but raw material drawn from the remotest zones; industries whose products are consumed, not only at home, but in every quarter of the globe. In place of the old wants, satisfied by the productions of the country, we find new wants, requiring for their satisfaction the products of distant lands and climes. In place of the old local and national seclusion and self sufficiency, we have intercourse in every direction, universal interdependence of nations. And as in material, so also in intellectual production. The intellectual creations of individual nations become common property. National one-sidedness and narrowmindedness become more and more impossible, and from the numerous national and local literatures there arises a world-literature.

The bourgeoisie, by the rapid improvement of all instruments of production, by the immensely facilitated means of communication, draws all, even the most barbarian nations, into civilization. The cheap prices of its commodities are the heavy artillery with which it batters down all Chinese walls, with which it forces the barbarians' intensely obstinate hatred of foreigners to capitulate. It compels all nations, on pain of extinction, to adopt the bourgeois mode of production; it compels them to introduce what it calls civilization into their midst, i.e., to become bourgeois themselves. In a word, it creates a world after its own image.

The bourgeoisie has subjected the country to the rule of the towns. It has created enormous cities, has greatly increased the urban population as compared with the rural, and has thus rescued a considerable part of the population from the idiocy of rural life. Just as it has made the country dependent on the towns, so it has made barbarian and semi-barbarian countries dependent on civilized ones, nations of peasants on nations of bourgeois, the East on the West.

The bourgeoisie keeps more and more doing away with the scattered state of the population, of the means of production, and of property. It has agglomerated population, centralized means of production, and has concentrated property in a few hands. The necessary consequence of this was political centralization. independent, or but loosely connected provinces, with separate interests, laws, governments, and systems of taxation, became lumped together in one nation, with one government, one code of laws, one national class-interest, one frontier and one customs' tariff....

The weapons with which the bourgeoisie felled feudalism to the ground are now turned against the bourgeoisie itself.

But not only has the bourgeoisie forged the weapons that bring death to itself; it has also called into existence the men who are to wield those weapons—the modern working class—the proletarians.

In proportion as the bourgeoisie,—that is, as capital, is developed, in the same proportion is the proletariat, the modern working class, developed, a class of laborers who live only so long as they find work, and who find work only so long as their labor increases capital. These laborers, who must sell themselves piecemeal, are a commodity, like every other article of commerce, and are consequently exposed to all the vicissitudes of competition, to all the fluctuations of the market.

Owing to the extensive use of machinery and to division of labor, the work of the proletarians has lost all individual character, and consequently, all charm for the workman. He becomes an appendage of the machine, and it is only the most simple, most monotonous, and most easily acquired knack that is required of him. Hence, the cost of production of a workman is restricted almost entirely to the means of subsistence that he requires for his maintenance, and for the propagation of his race. But the price of a commodity, and also of labor, is equal to its cost of production. In proportion, therefore, as the repulsiveness of the work increases the wage decreases. Nay more, in proportion as the use of machinery and division of labor increase, in the same proportion the burden of toil increases, whether by prolongation of the working hours, by increase of the work enacted in a given time, or by increased speed of the machinery, and so forth.

Modern industry has converted the little workshop of the patriarchal master into the great factory of the industrial capitalist. Masses of laborers, crowded into factories, are organized like soldiers. As privates of the industrial army they are placed under the command of a perfect hierarchy of officers and sergeants. Not only are they the slaves of the bourgeois class and of the bourgeois state, they are daily and hourly enslaved by the machine, by the foreman, and, above all, by the individual bourgeois manufacturer himself. The more openly this despotism proclaims gain to be its end and aim, the more petty, the more hateful and the more embittering it is….

Hitherto every form of society has been based, as we have already seen, on the antagonism of oppressing and oppressed classes. But in order to oppress a class, certain conditions must be assured to it under which it can at least continue its slavish existence. The serf, in the period of serfdom, raised himself to membership in the commune, just as the petty bourgeois, under the yoke of feudal absolutism, managed to develop into a bourgeois. The modern laborer, on the contrary, instead of rising with the progress of industry, sinks deeper and deeper below the conditions of existence to its slave within his slavery, because it cannot help letting him sink into such a state that it has to feed him, instead of being fed by him. Society can no longer live under this bourgeoisie; in other words, its existence is no longer compatible with society….

PROLETARIANS AND COMMUNISTS

…Does it require deep intuition to comprehend that man's ideas, views, and conceptions, in one word, man's consciousness, changes with every change in the conditions of his material existence, in his social relations, and in his social life?

What else does the history of ideas prove than that intellectual production changes in character in proportion as material production is changed? The ruling ideas of each age have ever been the ideas of its ruling class….

The proletariat will use its political supremacy to wrest, by degrees, all capital from the bourgeoisie, to centralize all instruments of production in the hands of the state,—that is, of the proletariat organized as a ruling class; and to increase the total productive forces as rapidly as possible….

When, in the course of development, class distinctions have disappeared, and all production has been concentrated in the hands of a vast association of the whole nation, the public power will lose its political character. Political power, properly so called, is merely the organization power of one class for oppressing another. If the proletariat during its contest with the bourgeoisie is compelled, by the force of circumstances, to organize itself as a class, if, by means of a revolution, it makes itself the ruling class, and, as such, sweeps away by force the old conditions of production, then it will, along with these conditions, have swept away the conditions for the existence of class antagonisms, and of classes generally, and will thereby have abolished its own supremacy as a class.

In place of the old bourgeois society, with its classes and class antagonisms, we shall have an association in which the free development of each is the condition for the free development of all.

Karl Marx and Frederick Engels, *Manifesto of the Communist Party*. Chicago: C. H. Kerr & Company, 1906

Questions:
1. Marx and Engels wrote that "The history of all hitherto existing society is the history of class struggles." What do they mean by class struggles? What historical examples do they use to illustrate their meaning?
2. Who is the "proletariat" and how is the proletariat's status described in the *Communist Manifesto*?
3. Marx and Engels claimed that "man's…consciousness changes with every change in the conditions of his material existence, in his social relations, and in his social life." Do you agree? Why or why not?
4. What parts of their overall argument do you find convincing? With what parts do you disagree? In what ways has history proven their ideas correct or false? Give specific examples.

Charles Darwin: *The Origin of Species*, 1871

The early life of Charles Darwin (1809-1882) showed little promise of his later prominence. As a child, he is reputed to have been something of a daydreamer, who was inordinately fond of collecting seals, postage stamps, and rocks. He performed poorly in high school, was a failure as a medical student at Edinburgh University, and enjoyed an equally lackluster career as a theology student at the University of Cambridge. Indeed, Darwin's father is supposed to have told his son that "you care for nothing but shooting, dogs, and rat-catching, and you will be a disgrace to yourself and your family."

Despite these less than promising beginnings, however, Darwin would go on to revolutionize human knowledge with his theories of organic evolution and its operating principle, natural selection. Serving as the naturalist from 1831 to 1836 on the H.M.S. Beagle, a British ship that was surveying parts of South America and some of the Pacific islands, Darwin collected and surveyed a wide variety of flora and fauna and arrived at a number of radical conclusions regarding human development. In the passages below, which are excerpted from his works regarding the observations and collections that he made during his voyage on the Beagle, Darwin explains his empirical method and his general theory of evolution.

…Again, it may be asked, how is it that varieties, which I have called incipient species, become ultimately converted into good and distinct species which in most cases obviously differ from each other far more than do the varieties of the same species? How do those groups of species, which constitute what are called distinct genera, and which differ from each other more than do the species of the same genus, arise? All these results, as we shall more fully see in the next chapter, follow from the struggle for life. Owing to this struggle, variations, however slight and from whatever cause proceeding, if they be in any degree profitable to the individuals of a species, in their infinitely complex relations to other organic beings and to their physical conditions of life, will tend to the preservation of such individuals, and will generally be inherited by the offspring. The offspring, also, will thus have a better chance of surviving, for, of the many individuals of any species which are periodically born, but a small number can survive. I have called this principle, by which each slight variation, if useful, is preserved, by the term Natural Selection, in order to mark its relation to man's power of selection. But the expression often used by Mr. Herbert Spencer[1] of the Survival of the Fittest is more accurate, and is sometimes equally convenient. We have seen that man by selection can certainly produce great results, and can adapt organic beings to his own uses, through the accumulation of slight but useful variations, given to him by the hand of Nature. But Natural Selection, as we shall hereafter se, is a power incessantly ready for action, and is as immeasurably superior to man's feeble efforts, as the works of Nature are to those of Art....

THE TERM, STRUGGLE FOR EXISTENCE, USED IN A LARGE SENSE

I should premise that I use this term in a large and metaphorical sense including dependence of one being on another, and including (which is more important) not only the life of the individual, but success in leaving progeny. Two canine animals, in a time of dearth, may be truly said to struggle with each other which shall get food and live. But a plant on the edge of a desert is said to struggle for life against the drought, though more properly it should be said to be dependent on the moisture. A plant which annually produces a thousand seeds, of which only one of an average comes to maturity, may be more truly said to struggle with the plants of the same and other kinds which already clothe the ground. The mistletoe is dependent on the apple and a few other trees, but can only in a far-fetched sense be said to struggle with these trees, for, if too many of these parasites grow on the same tree, it languishes and dies. But several seedling mistletoes, growing close together on the same branch, may more truly be said to struggle with each other. As the mistletoe is disseminated by birds, its existence depends on them; and it may methodically be said to struggle with other fruit-bearing plants, in tempting the birds to devour and thus disseminate its seeds. In these several senses, which pass into each other, I use for convenience' sake the general term of Struggle for Existence.

GEOMETRICAL RATIO OF INCREASE

A struggle for existence inevitably follows from the high rate at which all organic beings tend to increase. Every being, which during its natural lifetime produces several eggs or seeds, must suffer destruction during some period of its life, and during some season or occasional year, otherwise, on the principle of geometrical increase, its numbers would quickly become so inordinately great that no country could support the product. Hence, as more individuals are produced than can possibly survive, there must in every case be a struggle for existence, either one individual with another of the same species, or with the individuals of distinct species, or with the physical conditions of life. It is the doctrine of Malthus applied with manifold force to the whole animal and vegetable kingdoms; for in this case there can be no artificial increase of food, and no prudential restraint from marriage. Although some species may be now increasing, more or less rapidly, in numbers, all cannot do so, for the world would not hold them....

Several writers have misapprehended or objected to the term Natural Selection. Some have even imagined that natural selection induces variability, whereas it implies only the preservation of such variations as arise and are beneficial to the being under its conditions of life. No one objects to agriculturists speaking of the potent effects of man's selection; and in this case the individual differences given by nature, which man for some object selects, must of necessity first

---

[1] English philosopher (1820-1903). He applied the doctrine of evolution in his *Principles of Psychology* (1855).

occur. Others have objected that the term selection implies conscious choice in the animals which become modified; and it has even been urged that, as plants have no volition, natural selection is not applicable to them! In the literal sense of the word, no doubt, natural selection is a false term; but who ever objected to chemists speaking of the elective affinities of the various elements?—and yet an acid cannot strictly be said to elect the base with which it in preference combines. It has been said that I speak of natural selection as an active power or Deity; but who objects to an author speaking of the attraction of gravity as ruling the movements of the planets? Every one knows what is meant and is implied by such metaphorical expressions; and they are almost necessary for brevity. So again it is difficult to avoid personifying the word Nature; but I mean by Nature, only the aggregate action and product of many natural laws, and by laws the sequence of events as ascertained by us. With a little familiarity such superficial objections will be forgotten....

Although natural selection can act only through and for the good of each being, yet characters and structures, which we are apt to consider as of very trifling importance, may thus be acted on. When we see leaf-eating insects green, and bark-feeders mottled-grey; the alpine ptarmigan[2] white in winter, the red-grouse the colour of heather, we must believe that these tints are of service to these birds and insects in preserving them from danger. Grouse, if not destroyed at some period of their lives would increase in countless numbers; they are known to suffer largely from birds of prey; and hawks are guided by eyesight to their prey—so much so, that on parts of the Continent persons are warned not to keep white pigeons, as being the most liable to destruction. Hence natural selection might be effective in giving the proper colour to each kind of grouse, and in keeping that colour, when once acquired, true and constant. Nor ought we to think that the occasional destruction of an animal of any particular colour would produce little effect: we should remember how essential it is in a flock of white sheep to destroy a lamb with the faintest trace of black. We have seen how the colour of the hogs, which feed on the "paint-root" in Virginia, determines whether they shall live or die. In plants, the down on the fruit and the colour of the flesh are considered by botanists as characters of the most trifling importance; yet we hear from an excellent horticulturist, Downing, that in the United States, smooth-skinned fruits suffer far more from a beetle, a Curculio, than those with down; that purple plums suffer far more from a certain disease than yellow plums; whereas another disease attacks yellow-fleshed peaches far more than those with other coloured flesh. If, with all the aids of art, these slight differences make a great difference in cultivating the several varieties, assuredly, in a state of nature, where the trees would have to struggle with other trees, and with a host of enemies, such differences would effectually settle which variety, whether a smooth or downy, a yellow or purple fleshed fruit, should succeed....

New York: D. Appleton, 1898

Charles Darwin: *The Descent of Man*, 1871

...The main conclusion arrived at in this work, and now held by many naturalists who are well competent to form a sound judgment, is that man is descended from some less highly-organized form. The grounds upon which this conclusion rests will never be shaken, for the close similarity between man and the lower animals in embryonic development, as well as in innumerable points of structure and constitution, both of high and of the most trifling importance—the

---

[2] grouse—of pheasant family

rudiments which he retains, and the abnormal reversions to which he is occasionally liable—are facts which cannot be disputed. They have long been known, but until recently the told us nothing with respect to the origin of man. Now, when viewed by the light of our knowledge of the whole organic world, their meaning is unmistakable. The great principle of evolution stands up clear and firm, when these groups of facts are considered in connection with others, such as the mutual affinities of the members of the same group, their geographical distribution in past and present times, and their geological succession. It is incredible that all these facts should speak falsely. He who is not content to look, like a savage, at the phenomena of Nature as disconnected, cannot any longer believe that man is the work of a separate act of creation. He will be forced to admit that the close resemblance of the embryo of man to that, for instance, of a dog—the construction of his skull, limbs, and whole frame, independently of the uses to which the parts may be put, on the same plan with that of other mammals—the occasional reappearance of various structures, for instance, of several distinct muscles, which man does not normally possess, but which are common to the Quadrumana—and a crowd of analogous facts—all point in the plainest manner to the conclusion that man is the co-descendant with other mammals of a common progenitor.

We have seen that man incessantly presents individual differences in all parts of his body and in his mental faculties. These differences or variations seem to be induced by the same general causes, and to obey the same laws as with the lower animals. In both cases similar laws of inheritance prevail. Man tends to increase at a greater rate than his means of subsistence; consequently he is occasionally subjected to a severe struggle for existence, and natural selection will have effected whatever lies within its scope. A succession of strongly-marked variations of a similar nature are by no means requisite; slight fluctuating differences in the individual suffice for the work of natural selection. We may feel assured that the inherited effects of the long-continued use or disuse of parts will have done much in the same direction with natural selection. Modifications formerly of importance, though no longer of any special use, will be long inherited. When one part is modified, other parts will change through the principle of correlation, of which we have instances in many curious cases of correlated monstrosities. Something may be attributed to the direct and definite action of the surrounding conditions of life, such as abundant food, heat, or moisture; and lastly, many characters of slight physiological importance, some indeed of considerable importance, have been gained through sexual selection....

Through the means just specified, aided perhaps by others as yet undiscovered, man has been raised to his present state. But since he attained to the rank of manhood, he has diverged into distinct races, or, as they may be more appropriately called, subspecies. Some of these, for instance, the Negro and European, are so distinct that, if specimens had been brought to a naturalist without any further information, they would undoubtedly have been considered by him as good and true species. Nevertheless all the races agree in so many unimportant details of structure and in so many mental peculiarities, that these can be accounted for only through inheritance from a common progenitor; and a progenitor thus characterized would probably have deserved to rank as man....

The main conclusion arrived at in this work, namely, that man is descended from some lowly-organized form, will, I regret to think, be highly distasteful to many persons. But there can hardly be a doubt that we are descended from barbarians. The astonishment which I felt on first seeing a party of Fuegians on a wild and broken shore will never be forgotten by me, for the reflection at once rushed into my mind—such were our ancestors. These men were absolutely naked and bedaubed with paint, their long hair was tangled, their mouths frothed with excitement, and their expression was wild, startled, and distrustful. They possessed hardly any arts, and, like wild animals, lived on what they could catch; they had no government, and were merciless to every one not of their own small tribe. He who has seen a savage in his native land will not feel much shame, if forced to acknowledge that the blood of some more humble creature flows in his veins. For my own part, I would as soon be descended from that heroic little monkey, who braved his dreaded enemy in order to save the life of his keeper; or from that old baboon, who, descending from the mountains, carried away in triumph his young comrade from a crowd of astonished dogs—as from a savage who delights to torture his enemies, offers up bloody sacrifices, practises infanticide without remorse, treat his wives like slaves, knows no decency, and is haunted by the grossest superstitions.

Man may be excused for feeling some pride at having risen, though not through his own exertions, to the very summit of the organic scale; and the fact of his having thus risen, instead of having been aboriginally placed there, may give him hopes for a still higher destiny in the distant future. But we are not here concerned with hopes or feats, only with the truth as far as our reason allows us to discover it. I have given the evidence to the best of my ability; and we must acknowledge, as it seems to me, that man with all his noble qualities, with sympathy which feels for the most debased, with benevolence which extends not only to other men but to the humblest living creature, with his godlike intellect which has penetrated into the movements and constitution of the solar system—with all these exalted powers—Man still bears in his bodily frame the indelible stamp of his lowly origin.

New York: D. Appleton, 1871

Questions:
1. What did Darwin mean by Natural Selection? How did he apply this concept to species he had observed?
2. Thomas Malthus said that population will always grows geometrically while the food supply increases only arithmetically. How did Malthus' ideas influence Darwin's thinking about species?
3. How did Darwin apply his theory to the human species? How did he support his argument? Why did Darwin think that his theory would be "highly distasteful to many persons"?
4. Would Darwin's methods and findings fall within the Enlightenment tradition? Why or why not?

Chapter 24: Europe's "Age of Progress," 1871-1894

Unit 52: The Industrial Revolution, Take Two

The latter part of the nineteenth century witnessed a dramatic increase in European material prosperity. A Second Industrial Revolution fueled by the development of steel, chemicals, electricity, and the internal combustion engine made possible the creation of new products, industries, markets, and transportation systems. All of these industrial developments created new work opportunities, made travel easier, and insured that Europeans of all classes and occupations received more food and manufactured goods. Indeed, the many remarkable scientific and technological achievements of this period convinced a majority of Europeans that theirs was an age of progress, "a brave new world" in which all things were possible. In time, many believed that a new social order would emerge in which poverty was abolished, war ended, and anxiety and boredom would give way to tranquility and amusement. As the readings below make clear, there was certainly grounds for this optimism. Nevertheless, as they also demonstrate, every alteration in the fabric of human affairs, no matter how positive, brings in its wake new challenges and tensions.

Earl Dean Howard: *Industrial Progress in Germany*, 1907

Whereas Britain had been the industrial leader of Europe during the First Industrial Revolution, the new German Empire was unquestionably the principal economic power on the European continent during its second industrial resurgence. While this German "economic wonder" (*Wirtschaftswünder*), was not without the social dislocation, poverty, and environmental degradation that had characterized the First Industrial Revolution, Germany's working class fared considerably better than its counterparts in other European countries. Why German industry was so productive and why its workers appeared less restive than the work forces of other western countries were two of the burning questions at the turn-of-the-last-century. One answer to these questions was provided by the economist Earl Dean Howard.

The ultimate aim in studying the economic conditions of a country is not to establish the amount of imports and exports, or the quantities of iron or textiles produced; these are only means to an end. The real object of all such inquiries is directly or indirectly to ascertain the degree of prosperity enjoyed by the people, and the causes therefore, so that other countries may learn to make use of the same means if they have brought prosperity, or to avoid them if they have proved obstructive.

We have established the fact that Germany has made a great industrial advance; that the amount of goods produced and consumed has enormously increased; that her foreign trade has grown at a greater rate than that of other European countries. But that knowledge requires to be supplemented. We want to know the effect these changes have had on the welfare of the people. Industrial progress is not always synonymous with economic prosperity. The darkest chapter in the economic history of England covers the period during the first half of the nineteenth century, which we know as the period of the Industrial Revolution, when the wealth of that nation was increasing by leaps and bounds, and the great mass of the people were living in the most appalling degradation on the scantiest incomes.

The rate of wages and the amount of incomes tell us much about the economic condition of a people, but with them we must also have some information as to the prices of the common articles of life and the cost of living. Yet even with these facts before us, we cannot draw absolute conclusions. The same money income, possessing the same purchasing power, will secure for one person a comfortable existence, while to his neighbor it will mean poverty. Between the people of different nations this ability to utilize goods and income varies greatly, especially between a wasteful people like the average American and a frugal one like the French.

Furthermore, many of the conditions by which we are surrounded are quite independent of goods which we may purchase with an income. Municipal ordinances, clean and well-lighted streets, public parks, schools, museums, etc., are just as real advantages to those who possess them as the goods which they purchase with money....

The statistics which we have reproduced in this chapter prove conclusively that the rate of wages has risen during the recent past, and has risen more than the price of the necessities of life, showing that the German workingman has shared in the prosperity of the country. Another indication of the improvement of the labor conditions, especially of the lowest class of labor, is the great falling off of emigration during the last decade. There is at present a greater immigration into Germany than emigration from it.

We have refrained from going into the question of the comparative wages of England, the United States, and Germany. Professor von Halle of Berlin, who has intimate personal knowledge of the labor conditions of the United States and England, as well as of those of his own country, says that wage statistics for the purpose of comparing the condition of the workingmen of one country with another are *Schwindel*.[1] Even if it were possible to calculate a sort of "real wage" by mingling together wage statistics with those of the cost of living, we should still lack a suitable basis for conclusions as to the comparative prosperity of the workingmen of the several countries. There are too many elements besides wages and prices to be considered in comparing the condition of one people with that of another, and it would seem to be much more reasonable to draw conclusions from actual observation of conditions as they exist....

There is a surprise in store for every American who visits Germany expecting to see want and misery on every hand. He will search in vain in the large cities for districts which he can compare to the East Side of New York or the Hull House district of Chicago, at least so far as external appearances go. There is in Berlin nothing which is at all like an American slum. At first he will be inclined to attribute this condition to the superior municipal government which makes Berlin the cleanest and best-regulated city in the world. He will still believe that the essential conditions of the slum must exist somewhere, although concealed from the public view behind the white walls of the monotonous rows of flat buildings which, in the poorest quarters of the city, look very little different from those of the fashionable Charlottenburg streets.

He will look for signs of degradation and misery in the people on the streets and the children running about. Of course he will see evidences of poverty, but it is a respectable, dreary dead-level of poverty, which is something quite different from the picturesque loathsomeness to be seen in our slums. He will fail to find that ragged, filthy, drunken depravity which marks so many English cities, as, for example, Liverpool and Manchester. At first he may be tempted to attribute the difference to the German government, and imagine that the extreme poverty is

---

[1] Nonsense.

prevented by large distributions of poor-relief. Authorities will tell him, however, that there is much less expended in purely charitable enterprises in Germany than in England, and that the German pauper class is small compared with that in England. Professor Schmoller[2] says that the burden of public poor-relief is twice as great in Great Britain, as in Germany....

How shall we account for this absence of extreme poverty among the working class in Germany? A difference certainly exists between the German and the Anglo-Saxon in respect to education and training. The German thinks that every person must be educated for his calling in life, no matter how humble that may be; and the opportunity is provided, indeed in most of the cities it is compulsory, for every man to receive instruction in his trade. The continuation schools (*Fortbildungsschulen*) provide instruction evenings and Sundays for those who are employed during the day. The educational system of Germany goes far to eliminate that class of helpless incapables which is the despair of the charitable societies of England and America.

Another cause of the favorable condition of Germany as regards poverty is the greater sobriety of the proletariat, notwithstanding the fact that statistics show the consumption of alcoholic drinks to be much larger in Germany than in England.

CONSUMPTION OF ALCOHOLIC DRINKS PER CAPITA[3]
(Gallons consumed annually)

	Wines	Beer	Spirits
England	0.41	31.9	1.03
Germany	0.77	27.1	1.85

This is not due, however, to the larger consumption of the working classes, but to that of the higher class. While in recent years there has not been wanting temperance agitation in Germany, it has made much less headway than in England and America, and teetotalers are rare. In Germany there is much less drinking of spirits among the working classes, and the large consumption indicated by the statistics arises no doubt from the almost universal habit among the higher classes of drinking liqueurs. Moreover, the German beer is a much milder beverage than the English ale. Drinks of all kinds are much cheaper in Germany than in England, and the German workingman spends far less of his income in this direction than the Englishman or the American. Drunkenness among women, which is so common in England, is as rare in Germany as in America.

If the German workingman spends comparatively little money on drink, he spends still less on gambling. There are no horse-races and pool-rooms for public betting, and few, if any, gambling-rooms of any kind. It is true that the state maintains a lottery, from which it derives a considerable revenue, but it is so arranged, especially in Prussia, as to be as little attractive as possible to the poorer classes. Moreover, this form of gambling is much less harmful than other forms. There is little excitement about it, and men are not likely to be tempted to risk more than they can afford—the worst feature of ordinary gambling. The buying of a lottery ticket is more like an investment, and no doubt often conduces to frugality.

---

[2] *Grundriss der allgemeinen Volkswirtschaftslehre, vol. ii, p. 325*

[3] Board of Trade statistics, 1898

We have observed in Germany a great lack of opportunity for the workman to rise and to better his condition in life. When the German youth has once chosen his Stand [4], he can almost forecast his whole career; he knows almost what his income will be for every year of his life, unless something quite unusual occurs. This settled condition of things is felt by every American who becomes acquainted with Germany as hopelessly depressing; life without the hope of changes of fortune, even when accompanied by the inevitable risks of defeat, seems to him hardly worth the living, especially if he possesses the characteristically American restless, energetic temperament. As he himself would express it, the American wants "a run for his money."

There is, however, a bright side to this picture. The German accepts these settled conditions and knows no other. His philosophy of life teaches him that contentment is the secret of happiness, and all his efforts are directed toward making the best of what he has, since there is little hope of gaining more. Unlike the American, he has not always before him examples of fortunes won by men of his own class who, discontented with their lot, have taken the risk of new enterprises. The German of the lower class lacks enterprise because he has no opportunity to use it; he is wise enough to see that for him frugality and contentment are better.

The introduction of insurance laws protecting the workingman against sickness and accidents, and promising him a pension in his old age, has had the tendency to make the laborer more contented. It does not matter very much that the relief and pension are very small, and that the workingman has paid for most of it himself out of his wages; the real point is that they decrease the chances of misfortune in life. How shall we estimate the psychological effect of his protection in increasing the happiness of the population? Who can say how much it is worth to be rid of anxiety about sustenance in the future? It would be manifestly absurd to try to calculate this effect from the amount of money received by the beneficiaries, or to balance it against the higher wages of the English or American workman.

There is one conspicuous instance in which the German government affords less protection to the workingman than the English or the American. In the latter country the law gives the workman the first lien on the work which he has done. Powerful capitalistic interests have prevented the passage of a similar law by German legislatures. In many cases in the large cities, speculative building companies have undertaken construction on borrowed capital, and have later declared bankruptcy. The lenders of the capital in such cases have taken the building and lost nothing, while employees of the bankrupt company have lost their wages.

We can now begin to appreciate the factors other than wages which enter into consideration in comparing the condition of workingmen of different countries. Lower wages, even lower "real" wages, can be accompanied by just as high or higher standard of happiness. It is often wonderful what a small income can be made to do if its owner concentrates his whole attention to utilizing it to the greatest possible advantage. We may often see this among certain people in our own country who receive fixed incomes which they are powerless to increase. Their energies are not diverted to making more money, but are directed toward making that money which they have bring the greatest results. Here, I think, is the explanation of the German household miracle, the decent maintenance of a family on seventy-five cents to a dollar per day. We don't know *how* it is done, we know only that it *is* done.

---

[4] trade

The government takes an active interest in helping the poor man make the most of his small income. While the taxes are often cruelly heavy, yet they are so scientifically distributed that the burden is as light as possible. The small property-holder or the recipient of a taxable income is spared the indignation of seeing his wealthy neighbor "dodging" his share of the tax. He also has visible evidence always before his eyes of the use to which his contribution is being put, in the clean streets and in the various municipal enterprises....

Besides the greater steadiness in the rate of wages and the absence of such extremes as we find in England and America, there is also less changing of employment and less non-employment in Germany. Men do not change their employment, nor move from one establishment to another so readily. In most cases the law requires at least a two weeks' notice before the employee can be discharged or leave the business.

We may safely say, I think, that the relation between the employer and the employee is less a transaction for the buying and selling of labor force than in laissez-faire England and America. The close interest which Herr Krupp took in the welfare of his employees is duplicated on a smaller scale all over the country. Though the old guild system has practically passed away, yet one of its leading ideas, that the workman has a right to expect his trade to support him, still survives to a large degree. Capitalism has not been able to destroy entirely these old customs; the contributions of the employers to the insurance funds of the workmen testify to the more permanent relation which exists between the employer and the employee than we are accustomed to find in our own country.

The German civil service is the best example of permanency of employment. The young men who enter it expect to remain there all their lives, to receive a pension in their old age, and, if they die or are disabled, to leave their families provided for by the state. They cannot be dismissed without good cause, and promotion comes as a reward for length of service rather than for good work or efficiency. Their hours are short, and they are free after three o-clock in the afternoon, in most of the offices.

The factory legislation of Prussia throws some light on the conditions surrounding the working class....

The law provides that the rules of each factory must be posted up, and that they must state definitely the hours of work, meal-times, time and manner of paying wages, the length of time of notice to quit, punishments, and fines....

Children under thirteen years of age may not be employed. From thirteen to fourteen years they may not be employed longer than six hours per day. From fourteen to sixteen years their working day must not exceed ten hours, with at least one hour at noon and two half-hour recesses, one in the forenoon and one in the afternoon, unless the working day is less than eight hours long....

Women are not allowed by law to do night work, nor must they be employed more than eleven hours per day, and not more than ten hours on Saturdays and days before holidays. If they are also housekeepers, they may demand an extra half hour at noon. Mothers may not be employed for four weeks after confinement, nor for two weeks longer, unless they have a physician's certificate....

As a rule, the factories are kept in a much better condition, and have more arrangements for the comfort of the men, than in the United States. This is the general opinion of writers who compare the conditions prevailing in the two countries, and it seems to be confirmed by direct observation. The factories usually have good light and air, are clean and orderly. The sanitary arrangements and the facilities for washing and changing clothes are splendid. Most of the factories are provided with lockers for the men, so that they need not leave the place in their working-clothes. Very often shower baths are available. The German habit of taking a meal in the forenoon and another in the afternoon during the working-time has led to the establishment of dining-rooms in many factories, where the men may procure a cup of coffee or a glass of beer....

The right of combination[5] is guaranteed by the German law to all employers and employees, except servants, agricultural laborers, and seamen, for the purpose of obtaining a more favorable wage and work conditions. Strikes and lockouts are recognized as legitimate means in industrial disputes;...

Germany was the first nation to introduce successfully a system of workingmen's insurance under the control of the government. We are told that the principal motive behind this social legislation was the desire to limit the spread of socialism among the laboring class. The idea, however, is very congenial to the German mind, which has the habit of expecting the state to do things with no fear of the reproach of paternalism. Moreover, the pension system for all employees of the government and the immobility of the working population furnished the pattern and facilitated the introduction of the system....

The ideas on which the German insurance system is based are compulsory thrift, state aid, and employers' liability. The workingmen are compelled by law to participate in the scheme; the state contributes from the public funds to help bear the expenses of the system, and the employers are to take a large share in organizing and in supporting the system.

The first insurance inaugurated by the state was insurance against sickness, the law being passed in 1883. It was made compulsory in manufacturing, commerce, and trade, and local authorities were empowered to extend it to other classes of the population.

The expenses of this insurance are defrayed from funds which are under the control partly of the state and partly of local associations of employers. The premiums average from 1 1/2 to 3 per cent of the wages of the workmen insured; two thirds is paid by the men and one third by the employers. From nine to ten million persons are insured, and in 1900 four million persons received benefit from the funds, amounting altogether to $42,000,000. The benefit includes free medicine, attendance, and a payment of at least one half of the customary wages, or free treatment in a hospital with half pay to the family. The maximum period for receiving this benefit is thirteen weeks.

The law creating the system of insurance against accident was passed in 1884 at the instigation of Emperor William I. It makes it compulsory for all the employers of a certain district to belong to an association composed of men active in the particular industry. These associations have a legal personality and are self-governed. The funds are maintained by the contributions of the members, the amount being assessed on each one according to the total amount of wages he pays. Payments to the beneficiaries begin only after the thirteenth week from the date of the accident, the first thirteen weeks falling under the care of the sick-insurance funds. The benefit

---

[5] The right of employers and employees to band together in unions and associations and to collectively bargain.

consists of free medical treatment and the receipt of a part of the usual wages up to two thirds, depending upon the seriousness of the injury and the helplessness of the patient. In case death ensues as a result of the accident, a burial allowance of no less than twelve dollars and a pension to the family of from 20 to 60 per cent of the former earnings of the deceased are made. This insurance lays no burdens upon the workingman, since the whole cost falls upon the employers....

from Earl Dean Howard, *Industrial Progress in Germany*. Boston: Houghton Mifflin, 1907.

Questions:
1. According to Earl Dean Howard, how should one measure a country's industrial prosperity? What factors should be taken into consideration?
2. How did Howard depict German labor conditions in the late 1800's? What evidence did he provide to make his points?
3. How is one to account for the differences in English and German conditions for the working classes? Why might the German laborer have been "more contented"?
4. What were the regulations that affected women and child laborers?
5. What government benefits did German workers receive? What do you think Samuel Smiles' reaction to this would have been?

Frederick Winslow Taylor: *The Principles of Scientific Management,* 1915

The development of mechanized transport within plants, in tandem with the invention of precision tools and interchangeable parts, helped make possible the assembly line production of industrial goods during the latter half of the nineteenth century. The introduction of these new assembly lines into factories at this time not only streamlined the industrial production process, but it also enabled industrialists to treble the production levels of their businesses. This new approach to production, however, also underscored the growing need for a well-trained, disciplined, and loyal work force. In order to secure such a labor force, businesses increasingly began to solicit the knowledge and advice of individuals who styled themselves experts in the scientific management of industry.

One of these experts was Frederick Winslow Taylor (1856-1915). An American inventor and engineer, Taylor was in many respects the father of scientific management. Central to his theories of scientifically managed industry was the idea that factory production could be greatly enhanced by eliminating wasted time and motion in the operation of industrial equipment. Indeed, when Taylor's time and motion theories were put into operation, they did prove remarkably effective in increasing industrial production. Moreover, during the early part of the twentieth century, "Taylorism" would be adopted by everyone from Henry Ford to Lenin and Stalin as a means of increasing industrial production. Many intellectuals, economists, and scientists even came to see Taylor's time-motion studies as an all-purpose panacea for the many problems of the developing world.

THE FUNDAMENTALS OF SCIENTIFIC MANAGEMENT

...No one can be found who will deny that in the case of any single individual the greatest prosperity can exist only when that individual has reached his highest state of efficiency; that is, when he is turning out his largest daily output....

If the above reasoning is correct, it follows that the most important object of both the workmen and the management should be the training and development of each individual in the establishment, so that he can do (at his fastest pace and with the maximum of efficiency) the highest class of work for which his natural abilities fit him.

These principles appear to be so self-evident that many men may think it almost childish to state them. Let us, however, turn to the facts, as they actually exist in this country and in England. The English and American peoples are the greatest sportsmen in the world. Whenever an

American workman plays baseball, or an English workman plays cricket, it is safe to say that he strains every nerve to secure victory for his side. He does his very best to make the largest possible number of runs. The universal sentiment is so strong that any man who fails to give out all there is in him in sport is branded as a "quitter," and treated with contempt by those who are around him.

When the same workman returns to work on the following day, instead of using every effort to turn out the largest possible amount of work, in a majority of the cases this man deliberately plans to do as little as he safely can—to turn out far less work than he is well able to do—in many instances to do not more than one-third to one-half of a proper day's work. And in fact if he were to do his best to turn out his largest possible day's work, he would be abused by his fellow-workers for so doing, even more than if he had proved himself a "quitter" in sport. Underworking, that is, deliberately working slowly so as to avoid doing a full day's work, "soldiering," as it is called in this country, "hanging it out," as it is called in England, "ca canae," as it is called in Scotland, is almost universal in industrial establishments, and prevails also to a large extent in the building trades; and the writer asserts without fear of contradiction that this constitutes the greatest evil with which the working-people of both England an America are now afflicted.

It will be shown later in this paper that doing away with slow working and "soldiering' in all its forms and so arranging the relations between employer and employee that each workman will work to his very best advantage and at his best speed, accompanied by the intimate cooperation with the management and the help (which the workman should receive) from the management, would result on the average in nearly doubling the output of each man and each machine....

The elimination of "soldiering" and of the several causes of slow working would so lower the cost of production that both our home and foreign markets would be greatly enlarged, and we could compete on more than even terms with our rivals....

THE PRINCIPLES OF SCIENTIFIC MANAGEMENT

...Perhaps the most prominent single element in modern scientific management is the task idea. The work of every workman is fully planned out by the management at least one day in advance, and each man receives in most cases complete written instructions, describing in detail the task which he is to accomplish, as well as the means to be used in doing the work. And the work planned in advance in this way constitutes a task which is to be solved, as explained above, not by the workman alone, but in almost all cases by the joint effort of the workman and the management. This task specifies not only what is to be done but how it is to be done and the exact time allowed for doing it. And whenever the workman succeeds in doing his task right, and within the time limit specified, he receives an addition of from 30 per cent. to 100 per cent. to his ordinary wages. These tasks are carefully planned, so that both good and careful work are called for in their performance, but it should be distinctly understood that in no case is the workman called upon to work at a pace which would be injurious to his health....

The science which exists in most of the mechanic arts is, however, far simpler than the science of cutting metals. In almost all cases, in fact, the laws or rules which are developed are so simple that the average man would hardly dignify them with the name of a science. In most trades, the science is developed through a comparatively simple analysis and time study of the movements required by the workmen to do some small part of his work, and this study is usually made by a man equipped merely with a stop-watch and a properly ruled notebook. Hundreds of these "time-study" men" are now engaged in developing elementary scientific knowledge where before existed only rule of thumb.... The general steps to be taken in developing a simple law of this class are as follows:

First. Find, say, 10 or 15 different men (preferably in as many separate establishments and different parts of the country) who are especially skillful in doing the particular work to be analyzed.

Second. Study the exact series of elementary operations or motions which each of these men uses in doing the work which is being investigated, as well as the implements each man uses.

Third. Study with a stop-watch the time required to make each of these elementary movements and then select the quickest way of doing each element of the work.

Fourth. Eliminate all false movements, slow movements, and useless movements.

Fifth. After doing away with all unnecessary movements, collect into one series the quickest and best movements as well as the best implements.

This one new method, involving that series of motions which can be made quickest and best, is then substituted in place of the ten or fifteen inferior series which were formerly in use. This best method becomes standard, and remains standard, to be taught first to the teachers (or functional foremen) and by them to every workman in the establishment until it is superseded by a quicker and better series of movements. In this simple way one element after another of the science is developed.

from Frederick Winslow Taylor, The Principles of Scientific Management.
New York: Harper & Brothers, 1915.

Questions:
1. According to Taylor, what was "the greatest evil with which the working-people of both England and America" were afflicted? What examples did Taylor use to support his point?
2. What are the "principles of scientific management," and how might they overcome "soldiering"?
3. What might be the social consequences of implementing Taylor's methods for the worker? Do you think Taylor took this into consideration?

Unit 53: The "Woman Question": The Debate Regarding the Status and Role of Women in the Nineteenth Century

Much of what we regard as "feminism" has its origins in the various debates that raged throughout the nineteenth century over the question of what a woman's legal rights, status, and role should be in modern society. During the nineteenth century, women were denied the right to vote or hold public office, they were subjected to repressive laws governing their bodies and parental rights, and they received unequal pay for the work that they did side by side with men in the new factories, department stores, and offices of the Second Industrial Revolution. In addition to their status as second class citizens, nineteenth century women also found themselves subject to a wide range of conflicting and often contradictory expectations. On the one hand, they were lauded as the "queens" of the domestic sphere whose work was central to the maintenance of family and society. Nevertheless, a woman's domestic activity, i.e. her cooking, cleaning, and child rearing, was unremunerated and regarded as inferior to the husband's "breadwinning" labor. Many middle class women and a majority of their working class counterparts had not only to maintain their homes, but to find additional low paid work in seat shops, factories, stores, or offices in order to keep their families fed and clothed.

A great many women, and not a few men, began to question the prevalent gender attitudes and arrangements. Increasingly, women began to demand protection from abusive spouses, childcare rights in the event of divorce, equal treatment in the workplace, the franchise, and the right to pursue a professional and public life. All of these demands aroused an impassioned debate that continues to the present day.

Madeline Poutret de Mauchamps: "A Petition to the King, to the Deputies from the Departments, and to the Peers of the Realm of France," 1836

In the nineteenth century, most European and American women were without recourse to civil divorce. In the event that a woman could get her husband's consent to dissolve a marriage, she often found herself without any kind of spousal support, and with no right to custody of or even visitation with her children.

Madeleine Poutret de Mauchamps was at the forefront of the struggle to reform these inequitable marriage arrangements in France. She campaigned tirelessly for the revocation of Article 213 of the French Civil Code, a legislative act that had revoked the right of women to seek a civil divorce (a right that had been granted women during the French Revolution and written into France's civil law by Napoleon Bonaparte.)

To obtain the entire and complete suppression of Article 213 of the Civil Code…entitled *Of the respective rights and duties of spouses*, and thus conceived:—A husband owes protection to his wife, a wife obedience to her husband….

Article I of the Charter of 1830 states: The French (*Les Français*)which signifies French men and French women) are equal before the law, whatever their title and their rank.

Before demanding the frank and honest execution of this article of the charter, the spirit. letter, and the legal and social consequences of this article must be well understood.

For, what do these words, *before the law*, mean?

Do not the words *the law* mean *the laws*? Is it not a generic term signifying that French men and French women are equal before the laws, that is to say, that these laws must be binding not only on all French men and women, but further that the obligations, duties, advantages, and prohibitions as well as the authorizations contained in these laws ought to be applicable equally to French women and men, in such a way that both enjoy the same rewards and are held to the same duties….

Now I will offer several commentaries on the subject of the petition I have addressed to you.

Marriage is one of the ameliorations and conditions of the social and civilized state. In the wild or uncivilized state, woman and man are two animals whose bodily strength is unequal, from which it results that the man, being stronger than the woman, subjects her to his will just as he constrains horses and other animals. The intellectual level being nearly zero in the savage state, woman is nothing more than a domestic animal that man uses and abuses according to his whim, having not the right but the power of coercion over her, and even the power of life and death.

But in the social and civilized state, brute force has been reduced to its real value, and industry and mechanics work incessantly to replace the bodily strength of man by that of steam engines or others. Intelligence, the result of instruction, appears in all its splendor and utility; and as this intelligence, which comes from the intellectual faculties, is equal in woman and in man, the laws and institutions based on intelligence ought to accord to woman the same rights as are given to man. In fact, with respect to marriage, an institution unknown to savage peoples, but which in our civilized nation is one of the first requirements of society, marriage is positively considered as an association where the rights and duties are mutual. And for proof of this equality between spouses, suffice it to read Article 212—of the Civil Code.—This article is thus conceived: "The spouses owe each other mutually fidelity, support, and assistance."

And note well, gentlemen, this article says everything. The word *mutually* is the truest expression of the equality of rights and duties of spouses. For if this mutuality no longer exists, if one or the other withdraws, then at that moment the association is flawed and the marriage is dissolved in fact....

Thus we believe the drafting of Article 212 is excellent, and this article summarizes and contains all by itself all the duties of the spouse; nothing more, nothing less.

But if, in fact, this article 212 is the most just and complete conjugal contract, how does one explain, how should one understand, article 213...?

In the former it states: The spouses *owe each other mutually*. And in the latter it states: The wife *owes obedience*....

Gentlemen, you must acknowledge that these two articles are incompatible, and article 213 is *antipathetic* to the Charter of 1830.

It is here that equality before the law should be applied with complete equity. The woman owes no more obedience to her husband than the husband owes to his wife....

from *Women, the Family, and Freedom: The Debate in Documents*. edited by Susan Groag Bell & Karen M. Offen. vol. 1: 1750-1880. Stanford, California: Stanford University Press, 1983.

Questions:
1. What general principle was Mauchamps trying to ensure would be applied to women in France?
2. How did Mauchamps compare the status of women in an uncivilized state with that of a civilized state?
3. Why did she want Article 213 of the French Civil Code to be revoked?

Caroline Sheridan Norton: *The Separation of Mother and Child by the Law of "Custody of Infants," Considered*, 1838

Mauchamps' counterpart in England, Caroline Sheridan Norton, had experienced the inequity of European marriage laws through painful personal experience. Norton's husband had subjected her to savage beatings, thrown her out of their home, kept her property, and took away her three sons while she was still breast-feeding the youngest. Taking up her pen, Norton argued forcefully in a pamphlet for an extension of women's rights over their children. As a result of her campaign, the British Parliament in 1839 passed an Infants' Custody Act.

The law which regulates the Custody of Infant Children, being now under the consideration of the legislature, it is very desirable that the attention of the public and of Members of Parliament in particular, should be drawn towards a subject, upon which so much misconception and ignorance prevails.

It is a common error to suppose that every mother has a *right* to the custody of her child till it attain the age of seven years. By a curious anomaly in law, the mother of a *bastard child HAS this right*, while the mothers of legitimate children are excluded from it,—the law as regards children born in wedlock being as follows.

The custody of legitimate children, is held to be the right of the Father *from the hour of their birth*: to the utter exclusion of the Mother, whose separate claim has no legal existence, and is not recognised by the Courts. No circumstance can modify or alter this admitted right of the father: though he should be living in open adultery, and his wife be legally separated from him on that account. He is responsible to no one for his motives, should he desire entirely to exclude his wife from all access to her children; nor is he accountable for the disposal of the child; that is, the law supposing the *nominal* custody to be with him, does not oblige him to make it a *bona fide* custody by a residence of the child under his roof and protection, but holds 'the custody of the father' to mean, in an extended sense, the custody of whatever stranger the father may think fit to appoint in lieu of the mother; and those strangers can exert his delegated authority to exclude the mother from access to her children; without any legal remedy being possible on her part, by appeal to the Courts or otherwise; the construction of the law being, that they have *no power to interfere* with the exercise of the father's right.

Should it so happen that at the time of separation, or afterwards, the children being in the mother's possession, she should refuse to deliver them up, the father's right extends to forcibly seizing them; *even should they be infants at the breast.* Or he may obtain, on application, a writ of habeas corpus, ordering the mother to produce the child in Court, to be delivered over to him; and should this order be disobeyed, he can cause a writ of attachment to issue against her; or, in other words, cause her to be imprisoned for contempt of court. The fact of the wife being inno-cent and the husband guilty, or of the separation being an unwilling one on her part, does not alter his claim: the law has no power to order that a woman shall even have occasional access to her children, though she could prove that she was driven by violence from her husband's house, and that he had deserted her for a mistress. The Father's right is absolute and paramount, and can no more be affected by the mother's claim, than if she had no existence.

The result of this tacit admission by law, of an individual right so entirely despotic, (the assertion of which *can* only be called for in seasons of family disunion and bitterness of feeling), is exactly what might have been expected. Instances have arisen from time to time in which the power has been grossly and savagely abused. It has been made the means of persecution, and the instrument of vengeance; it has been exerted to compel a disposition of property in favour of the husband, where the wife has possessed an independent fortune; it has been put into force by an adulterous husband to terrify his wife from proceeding in the Ecclesiastical Courts against him; in short, there is scarcely any degree of cruelty which has not been practised under colour of its protection....

Doubtless the claim of a father is sacred and indisputable, but when the mother's claim clashes with it, surely *something* should be accorded to her. There are other laws besides those made by men—what says the holier law, the law of nature?

Does *nature* say that the woman, who endures for nearly a year a tedious suffering, ending in an agony which perils her life, has no claim to the children she bears? Does *nature* say that the woman, who after that year of suffering is over, provides from her own bosom the nourishment which preserves the very existence of her offspring, has no claim to the children she has nursed? Does *nature* say that the woman who has watched patiently through the very many feverish and anxious nights which occur even in the healthiest infancy, has no claim to the children she has tended? And that the whole and sole claim rests with him, who has slept while she watched; whose knowledge of her sufferings is confined to the intelligence that he is a father; and whose love is *at best* but a reflected shadow of that which fills her heart? No! the voice of nature cries out against the inhuman cruelty of such a separation....

Surely in this country, where hatred of all oppression is made a national boast, where if a master were to strike his footboy, an action would lie for assault and damages—where even offensive and violent language subjects a man to a penalty; in this country, and at this time, when all liberal opinions are encouraged and fostered, it is a strange and crying shame, that the only despotic right an Englishman possesses is to wrong the mother of his children! That compelled as he is by the equal and glorious laws of his nation, to govern even the *words in which his anger is expressed* to his fellow men and subjects, he may act what cruelty he pleases by his own fire-side, and he who dares not in the open street lay a finger on the meanest man there, may stand on his own hearth and tear from the very breast of the nursing mother, the little unconscious infant whose lips were drawing from her bosom the nourishment of life!

Is this the vaunted justice—the vaunted mercy of the English code? Shall it be said that there is in England a legal protection for *every* right and *every* claim, natural and artificial, except ONE; and *that* ONE is the tie between mother and child! Over *that* there is no protection; in support of *that* the Courts "have no *power* to interfere"; in making laws for the human race, the mothers of the human race were forgotten!...

> from Caroline Sheridan Norton, *The Separation of Mother and Child by the Law of "Custody of Infants,"*
> *Considered.* London, 1838.

Questions:
1. Who had custody rights of children in England in the early 1800's?
2. What points did Norton make in order to criticize England's custody laws? In theory and practice, how was this law unjust in her eyes? How did she use the "law of nature" to challenge England's contemporary practices?

Karl Marx and Friedrich Engels: *The Communist Manifesto,* 1848

There were Europeans who believed that the only way to secure freedom and equality for women was through a radical restructuring of society. Perhaps the best known proponents of this position were Karl Marx (1818-1883) and Friedrich Engels (1820-1890). In their *Communist Manifesto*, Marx and Engels not only argued for a stateless society in which all property would be held in common, but also for a social order that was free of traditional marriages and family arrangements. Indeed, as the following selection from their manifesto makes clear, both men felt that the inequality and oppression, which were the lot of Europe's female population, were integrally tied up with the domestic ties that were at the very heart of European family life.

But do not dispute with us, while you measure the proposed abolition of Middle-class property, by your Middle-class ideas of freedom, civilization, jurisprudence, and the like. Your ideas are the necessary consequences of the Middle-class conditions of property and production, as your jurisprudence is the Will of your class raised to the dignity of law, a will whose subject is given in the economical conditions of your class. The selfish mode of viewing the question, whereby you confound your transitory conditions of production and property with the eternal laws of Reason and Nature, is common to all ruling classes. What you understand with regard to Antique and Feudal property, you cannot understand with regard to modern Middle-class property.—The destruction of domestic ties! Even the greatest Radicals are shocked at this scandalous intention of the Communists. Upon what rests the present system, the Bourgeois system, of family relationships? Upon Capital, upon private gains, on profit-mongering. In its most perfect form it exists only for the Bourgeoisie, and it finds a befitting complement in the compulsory celibacy of the Proletarians, and in public prostitution. The Bourgeois family system naturally disappears with the disappearance of its complement, and the destruction of both is involved in the destruction of Capital. Do you reproach us that we intend abolishing the using up of children by their parents. We acknowledge this crime. Or that we will abolish the most endearing relationships, by substituting a public and social system of education for the existing private one? And is not your system of education also determined by society? by the social conditions, within the limits of which you educate? by the more or less direct influence of society, through the medium of your schools, and so forth?

The communists do not invent the influence of society upon education; they only seek to change its character, to rescue education from the influence of a ruling class. Middle-class talk about domestic ties and education, about the endearing connection of parent and child, becomes more and more disgusting in proportion as the family ties of the Proletarians are torn asunder, and their children changed into machines, into articles of commerce, by the extension of the modern industrial system. But you intend introducing a community of women, shrieks the whole Middle-class like a tragic chorus. The Bourgeois looks upon his wife as a mere instrument of production; he is told that the instruments of production are to be used up in common, and thus he naturally supposes that women will share the common fate of other machines. He does not even dream that it is intended, on the contrary, to abolish the position of woman as a mere instrument of production. For the rest, nothing can be more ludicrous than the highly moral and religious horror entertained by the Bourgeoisie towards the pretended official community of women among the Communists. We do not require to introduce community of women; it has always existed. Your Middle-class gentry are not satisfied with having the wives and daughters of the Wage-slaves at their disposal—not to mention the innumerable public prostitutes—but they take a particular pleasure in seducing each other's wives. Middle-class marriage is in reality a community of wives. At the most, then, we could only be reproached for wishing to substitute an open, above-board community of women, for the present mean, hypocritical, sneaking kind of community. But it is evident enough that with the disappearance of the present conditions of production, the community of women occasioned by them—namely, official and non-official prostitution—will also disappear.

translated by Helen Macfarlane in "Manifesto of the German Communist Party," *The Red Republican* I, no. 23. London: November 1850.

Questions:
1. Marx and Engels claimed that a woman was a "mere instrument of production." Why? Do you agree or disagree?
2. How might Marx and Engels have responded to Norton's writing?

Jeanne Deroin: "To the Citizens of France," 1849

A far more characteristic, and less radical, statement of the nineteenth century movement for women's equality is that of Jeanne Deroin (1805-1894), a French working-class woman, wife, and mother. Committed to a more evolutionary approach to both socialism and women's rights, Deroin, nevertheless, took an active role in the 1848 revolution that swept away the Orleanist monarchy of Louis-Philippe. In the aftermath of that upheaval, Deroin argued eloquently in favor of both women's suffrage and the right of women to take part in the political life of the Second French Republic.

The reign of brute force has ended; that of morality and intelligence has just begun. The motives that led our fathers to exclude women from all participation in the governance of the State are no longer valid. When every question was decided by the sword, it was natural to

164

believe that women—who could not take part in combat—should not be seated in the assembly of warriors. In those days it was a question of destroying and conquering by the sword; today it is a question of building and of organizing. Women should be called on to take part in the great task of social regeneration that is under way. Why should our country be deprived of the services of its daughters?

Liberty, equality, and fraternity have been proclaimed for all. Why should women be left only with obligations to fulfill, without being given the rights of citizens? Will they be excused from paying taxes and from obeying the laws of the State? Will they be obliged to obey the laws to pay the taxes imposed upon them?

Are they to become the helots[6] of your new Republic? No, citizens, you do not want this; the mothers of your sons cannot be slaves. We address this just demand not merely to the provisional government, which alone cannot decide a question that is of interest to the entire nation. We come to plead our cause—so holy, so legitimate—before the citizens' assembly: our cause is theirs. They will not want to be accused of injustice. When they abolish all privileges, they will not think of conserving the worst one of all and leaving one-half of the nation under the domination of the other half. They will at least give us a role in national representation; some women chosen among the most worthy, the most honorable, the most capable, will be nominated by the men themselves, to come forth in defense of the rights of their sex and the generous principles of our glorious Revolution. Liberty, equality, and fraternity will thus be realized.

from *Women, the Family, and Freedom: The Debate in Documents*, vol. 1. edited by Susan Groag Bell and Karen M. Offen. Stanford, California: Stanford University Press, 1983.

Questions:
1. What arguments did Jeanne Deroin use to demand equality for French women?
2. What rights did she want women to obtain? How would you compare her demands and reasoning with those of Mauchamps?

---

[6] unfree farmers in ancient Sparta.

Chapter 25: Europe on the Eve of World War I

Unit 54: Europe on the Eve of World War I

The horrific slaughter and political chaos of the First World War would lead a great many Europeans to regard the two decades prior to that conflict as a golden age. The period stretching from 1890 to 1914 was characterized by breathtaking breakthroughs in science, daring experiments in art, literature, and music, unprecedented economic growth, European hegemony over most of the globe, and a longstanding, albeit uneasy, peace among the great powers.

Europe at the turn of the last century was also an uneasy and uncertain place to be. The new developments in the arts and sciences raised a number of disturbing questions about human rationality and the ability of our species to improve itself. Economic development continued to bring untold misery to millions. This social suffering, in tandem with the rise of mass politics, kept most of Europe's capitals in a chronic state of political crisis. European imperialism compelled the continent's powers to invest ever more money into armies, navies, and weaponry. Many Europeans sensed the future as an uncertain, dark place, promising only war and chaos.

Bloody Sunday: Father Gapon's Petition to Nicholas II, January 22, 1905

Clamor for serious political reforms in Russia was met by the last two tsars, Alexander III (1881-1894) and Nicholas II (1894-1917) with such Draconian measures as death by hanging or perpetual exile in Siberian labor camps. On January 22, 1905, the tensions between the tsars and their subjects erupted in an event that became known as "Bloody Sunday." Leading a procession of striking workers in St. Petersburg toward the Winter Palace, a pro-Tsarist priest, Father Gapon, attempted to deliver to Nicholas II a petition listing the workers' grievances and wishes. Instead of an audience with his Tsar, Gapon and his petitioners were met by a fusillade of bullets that killed and wounded hundreds of people. This event triggered a revolution, which nearly toppled the regime.

Sovereign!

We, the workers and the inhabitants of various social strata of the city of St. Petersburg, our wives, children, and helpless old parents, have come to you, Sovereign, to seek justice and protection. We are impoverished; our employers oppress us, overburden us with work, insult us, consider us inhuman, and treat us as slaves who must suffer a bitter fate in silence. Though we have suffered, they push us deeper and deeper into a gulf of misery, disfranchisement, and ignorance. Despotism and arbitrariness strangle us and we are gasping for breath. Sovereign, we have no strength left. We have reached the limit of endurance. We have reached that terrible moment when death is preferable to the continuance of unbearable sufferings.

And so we left our work and informed our employers that we shall not resume work until they meet our demands. We do not demand much; we only want what is indispensable to life and without which life is nothing but hard labor and eternal suffering. Our first request was that our employers discuss our needs jointly with us. But they refused to do this; they even denied us the right to speak about our needs, saying that the law does not give us such a right. Also unlawful were our requests to reduce the working day to eight hours; to set wages jointly with us; to examine our disputes with lower echelons of factory administration; to increase the wages of unskilled workers and women to one ruble per day; to abolish overtime work; to provide medical care without insult; to build shops in such a way that one could work there and not die because of awful drafts, rains, and snow.

Our employers and factory administrators considered all this to be unlawful; they regarded every one of our requests as a crime and interpreted our desire to improve our condition as audacity.

Sovereign, there are thousands of us here; outwardly we resemble human beings, but in reality neither we nor the Russian people as a whole enjoy any human right, have any right to speak, to think, to assemble, to discuss our needs, or to take measures to improve our conditions. They have enslaved us and they did it under the protection of your officials, with their aid and with their cooperation. They imprison and (even) send into exile any one of us who has the courage to speak on behalf of the interests of the working class and of the people. They punish us for our good heartedness and sympathy as if for a crime. To pity a down-trodden, disfranchised, and oppressed man is to commit a major crime. All the workers and the peasants are at the mercy of bureaucratic administrators consisting of embezzlers of public funds and thieves who not only disregard the interests of the people but also scorn these interests. The bureaucratic administration has brought the country to complete ruin, has brought upon it a disgraceful war, and continues to lead it further and further into destruction. We, the workers and the people, have absolutely nothing to say in the matter of expenditure of huge taxes that are collected from us. In fact, we do not know where or for what the money collected from the impoverished people goes. The people are deprived of the opportunity to express their wishes and their demands and to participate in determining taxes and expenditures. The workers are deprived of the opportunity to organize themselves in unions to protect their interests.

Sovereign! Is all this compatible with God's laws, by the grace of which you reign? And is it possible to live under such laws? Wouldn't it be better for all of us if we, the toiling people of all Russia, died? Let the capitalist-exploiters of the working class, the bureaucratic embezzlers of public funds, and the pillagers of the Russian people live and enjoy themselves. Sovereign, these are the problems that we face and these are the reasons that we have gathered before the walls of your palace. Here we seek our last salvation. Do not refuse to come to the aid of your people; lead them out of the grave of disfranchisement, poverty, and ignorance; grant them an opportunity to determine their own destiny, and remove from them the unbearable yoke of bureaucrats. Tear down the wall that separates you from your people and let them rule the country with you. You have been placed [on the throne of Russia] for the happiness of the people; the bureaucrats, however, pull this happiness out of our hands and hence it never reaches us; we receive only grief and humiliation. Sovereign, examine our requests attentively and without any anger; they are intended not for any evil but for a good [cause] for both of us. It is not arrogance that forces us to speak but the realization of the need to escape from a situation unbearable for all of us. Russia is too great, her needs too diverse and numerous to be administered by bureaucrats only. It is essential to have a popular representation; it is essential that the people help themselves and that they govern themselves. Only they know their real needs. Do not spurn their help; accept it; decree immediately to summon at once representatives of the Russian land from all classes, from all strata, including workers' representatives. Let there be present a capitalist, a worker, a bureaucrat, a priest, a doctor, and a teacher—let everyone regardless of who they are elect their own representatives. Let everyone be equal and free to elect or be elected, and toward that end decree that the elections to the Constituent Assembly be carried out on the basis of universal, secret, and equal suffrage.

This is our chief request because everything is based within it and upon it; this is the main and the only bandage for our painful wounds; without it they will bleed severely and will soon cause our death.

One measure, however, cannot heal all of our wounds. Other [measures] are indispensable and, Sovereign, we speak about them to you directly and openly, as to our father, in behalf of the entire toiling class of Russia.

[The following measures] are indispensable:

I. Measures to eliminate the ignorance and disfranchisement of the Russian people.

    (a) The immediate release and return [from exile] of all those who have suffered because of their political or religious beliefs, or because of strikes or peasant disturbances.

    (b) An immediate declaration of freedom and inviolability of person, freedom of speech and press, freedom of assembly, and freedom of conscience.

    (c) Universal and compulsory public education, financed by the state.

    (d) Responsibility of Ministers before the people and a guarantee of a law abiding administration.

    (e) Equality before the law for everyone, without exception.

    (f) Separation of the church from the state.

II. Measures to eliminate the poverty of the people.

    (a) Abolition of indirect taxes and the substitution of a direct progressive income tax.

    (b) Abolition of redemption payments, [introduction of] low interest rates, and the gradual transfer of the land to the people.

    (c) Placement of military and naval orders in Russia, not abroad.

    (d) Termination of the war by the will of the people.

III. Measures to eliminate the oppression of labor by capital:

    (a) Abolition of the institution of factory inspectors.

    (b) Establishment at the factories and mills of permanent committees elected by the workers which, jointly with the management, would consider complaints of individual workers. The dismissal of a worker would not take place other than by the decision of this committee.

    (c) Immediate freedom for consumer and trade unions.

    (d) An eight-hour working day and standardization of overtime work.

    (e) Immediate freedom for the struggle between labor and capital.

    (f) Immediate standardization of a minimum wage.

(g) Immediate and continued participation of representatives of the working classes in the preparation of legislation for a state insurance for workers.

Here, Sovereign, are our principal needs with which we came to you. Only if and when they are fulfilled will it be possible to free our country from slavery arid poverty; will it be possible for it to flourish; will it be possible for the workers to organize themselves to protect their interests against the insolent exploitation of the capitalists and the thievish government of bureaucrats who strangle the people. Decree and swear that you will realize these [requests] and you will make Russia happy, famous and will imprint forever your name in our hearts and in the hearts of our descendants. And if you will not decree it, if you will not respond to our plea, we shall die here, in this square, before your palace. We have nowhere else to go and it is useless to go. We have only two roads open to us: one leading to freedom and happiness, the other to the grave. Let our life be a sacrifice for suffering Russia. We do not regret this sacrifice. We offer it willingly.

George Gapon, Priest
Ivan Vasimov, Worker

from *Imperial Russia: A Source Book, 1700-1917,* 3rd edition. Edited by Basil Dmytryshyn. Fort Worth, TX: Holt, Rinehart & Winston, 1990. pp. 409-413. Translation by Basil Dmytryshyn..

Questions:
1. Why were the workers of St. Petersburg petitioning Tsar Nicholas II? What were their grievances, and what remedies were they seeking? Give some specific examples from the document.
2. Who did these workers blame for the burdens they were suffering? Given that this petition was directed toward Tsar Nicholas, what does that suggest about the workers' image of him?

George Kennan, *Siberia and the Exile System*

Supporters of the last Romanovs portrayed all political dissidents as "nihilists," who wanted only to destroy the existing social and political system. George Kennan created a more nuanced portrait of Russian political exiles, dividing them into three "classes."

TSARIST REGULATIONS:

"RULES RELATING TO MEASURES FOR THE PRESERVATION OF NATIONAL ORDER AND PUBLIC TRANQUILITY," 14TH OF AUGUST, 1881.

SECTION 5.

[a] When public tranquillity in any locality shall be disturbed by criminal attempts against the existing imperial form of government, or against the security of private persons and their property, or by preparations for such attempts, so that, for the preservation of order, a resort to the existing permanent laws seems to be insufficient, then that locality may be declared in a state of reinforced safeguard.

[b] When by reason of such attempts the population of a certain place shall be thrown into a state of alarm which creates a necessity for the adoption of exceptional measures to immediately reestablish order, then the said place may be declared in a state of extraordinary safeguard.

SECTION 15. Within the limits of such places [places declared to be in a state of reinforced safeguard] governors-general, governors, and municipal chiefs of police may [a] issue obligatory ordinances relating to matters connected with the preservation of public tranquillity and the security of the Empire, and (b) punish by fine and imprisonment violations of such ordinances.

SECTION 16. Governors-general, governors, and municipal chiefs of police are authorized also [a] to settle by administrative process cases involving violation of the obligatory ordinances issued by them; [b] to prohibit all popular, social, and even private meetings; [c] to close temporarily, or for the whole term of reinforced safeguard, all commercial and industrial establishments; and [d] to prohibit particular persons from residing in places declared to be in a state of reinforced safeguard. [Remark.—Banishment to a specified place, even to one's native place, with obligatory residence there, will be allowed only after communication with the Minister of the Interior. Rules for such banishment are set forth in Sections 32—36.]

SECTION 32. The banishment of a private person by administrative process to any particular locality in European or Asiatic Russia, with obligatory residence there for a specified time, may not take place otherwise than with an observance of the following rules:

SECTION 33. The proper authority, upon becoming convinced of the necessity for the banishment of a private person, shall make a statement to that effect to the Minister of the Interior, with a detailed explanation of the reasons for the adoption of this measure, and also a proposition with regard to the period of banishment. [Remark.—The preliminary imprisonment of a person thus presented for exile to a specified place may be extended, by authority of the Minister of the Interior, until such time as a decision shall be reached in his case.]

SECTION 34. Presentations of this kind will be considered by a special council in the Ministry of the Interior, under the presidency of one of the Minister's associates, such council to consist of two members from the Ministry of the Interior and two members from the Ministry of Justice. The decisions of this council shall be submitted to the Minister of the Interior for confirmation.

SECTION 35. While considering presentations for exile the above-mentioned council may call for supplemental information or explanations, and, in case of necessity, may summon for personal examination the individual nominated for banishment.

SECTION 36. A period of from one to five years shall be designated as the term for continuous residence in the assigned place of exile. [Remark.—The term of banishment may be shortened or lengthened, in the manner prescribed in Section 34, within the limits set by section 36.]

SECTION 245. All persons found guilty of composing and circulating written or printed documents, books, or representations calculated to create disrespect for the Supreme Authority, or for the personal character of the Gossudar [the Tsar], or for the Government of his Empire, shall be condemned, as insulters of Majesty, to deprivation of all civil rights, and to from ten to twelve years of penal servitude. [This punishment carries with it exile in Siberia for what remains of life after the expiration of the hard-labor sentence.]

SECTION 249. All persons who shall engage in rebellion against the Supreme Authority – that is, who shall take part in collective and conspirative insurrection against the Gossudar and the Empire; and also all persons who shall plan the overthrow of the Government in the Empire as a whole, or in any part thereof; or who shall intend to change the existing form of government, or the order of succession to the throne established by law; all persons who, for the attainment of these ends, shall organize or take part in a conspiracy, either actively and with knowledge of its object, or by participation in a conspirative meeting, or by storing or distributing weapons, or by other preparations for insurrection— all such persons, including not only those most guilty, but their associates, instigators, prompters, helpers, and concealers, shall be deprived of all civil rights and be put to death. Those who have knowledge of such evil intentions, and of preparations to carry them into execution, and who, having power to inform the Government thereof, do not fulfil that duty, shall he subjected to the same punishment.

SECTION 250. If the guilty persons have not manifested an intention to resort to violence, but have organized a society or association intended to attain, at a more or less remote time in the future, the objects set forth in Section 249, or have joined such an association, they shall be sentenced, according to the degree of their criminality, either to from four to six years of penal servitude, with deprivation of all civil rights [including exile to Siberia for life] or to colonization in Siberia [without penal servitude], or to imprisonment in a fortress from one year and four months to four years.

KENNAN'S OBSERVATIONS:

THE EXILES:

For the purposes of this chapter I shall divide Russian political exiles into three classes as follows.

1. THE LIBERALS—In this class are included the cool-headed men of moderate opinions, who believe in the gradual extension of the principles of popular self-government; who favor greater freedom of speech and of the press; who strive to restrict the power of bureaucracy; who deprecate the persecution of religious dissenters and of the Jews; who promote in every possible way the education and the moral up-lifting of the peasants; who struggle constantly against official indifference and caprice; who insist pertinaciously upon "due process of law"; who are prominent in all good works; but who regard a complete overthrow of the existing form of government as impracticable at present even if desirable.

2. THE REVOLUTIONISTS—In this class are comprised the Russian socialists, the so-called "peasantists" *[naródniki],* "people's-willists" *[narodovóltsi],* and all reformers who regard the overthrow of the autocracy as a matter of such immediate and vital importance as to justify conspiracy and armed rebellion. They differ from the terrorists chiefly in their unwillingness to adopt the methods of the highwayman and the blood-avenger. If they can see a prospect of organizing a formidable insurrection, and of crushing the autocracy by a series of open blows, fairly delivered, they are ready to attempt it, even at the peril of death on the scaffold; but they do not regard it as wise or honorable to shoot a chief of police from ambush; to wreck an Imperial railroad train; to rob a government sub-treasury; or to incite peasants to revolt by means of a forged manifesto in the name of the Tsar. The objects which they seek to attain are the same that the liberals have in view, but they would attain them by quicker and more direct methods, and they would carry the work of reform to greater extremes. The socialistic revolutionists, for example, would attempt to bring about a redistribution of the land and a more equitable division of the results of labor, and would probably encourage a further development of the principle of association, as distinguished from competition, which is so marked a feature of Russian economic life.

3. THE TERRORISTS— The only difference between the terrorists and the revolutionists is a difference in methods. So far as principles and aims are concerned the two classes are identical; but the revolutionists recognize and obey the rules of civilized warfare, while the terrorists resort to any and every measure that they think likely to injure or intimidate their adversaries. A

terrorist, in fact, is nothing more than an embittered revolutionist, who has found it impossible to unite and organize the disaffected elements of society in the face of a cloud of spies, an immense body of police, and a standing army; who has been exasperated to the last degree by cruel, unjust, and lawless treatment of himself, his family, or his friends; who has been smitten in the face every time he has opened his lips to explain or expostulate, and who, at last, has been seized with the Berserker madness, and has become, in the words of the St. Petersburg *Gólos,* "a wild beast capable of anything."

In point of numerical strength these three classes follow one another in the order in which I have placed them. The liberals, who are the most numerous, probably comprise three-fourths of all the university graduates in the Empire outside of the bureaucracy. The revolutionists, who come next, undoubtedly number tens of thousands, but, under existing circumstances, it is impossible to make a trustworthy estimate of their strength, and all that I feel safe in saying is that, numerically, they fall far short of the liberals. The terrorists never were more than a meager handful in comparison with the population of the country, and they constituted only a fraction even of the anti-Government party; but they were resolute and daring men and women, and they attracted more attention abroad, of course, than a thousand times as many liberals, simply on account of the tragic nature of the roles that they played on the stage of Russian public life. The liberals, who were limited by the censorship and the police on one side, and by their own renunciation of violence on the other, could do very little to attract the attention of foreign observers; but the terrorists, who defied all restrictions, who carried their lives constantly in their hands, and who waged war with dagger, pistol, and pyroxylin bomb, acquired a notoriety that was out of all proportion to their numerical strength.

I met among the political exiles in Siberia representatives of all the classes above described, and I have tried, in the earlier chapters of this work, to convey to the reader the impressions that they made upon me in personal intercourse. I desire now to state, as briefly as I can, my conclusions with regard to their character.

1. THE LIBERALS— So far as I know, it is not pretended by anybody that the Russian liberals are bad men or bad citizens. The Government, it is true, keeps them under strict restraint, prohibits them from making public speeches, drives them out of the universities, forbids them to sit as delegates in provincial assemblies, expels them from St.. Petersburg, suppresses the periodicals that they edit, puts them under police surveillance and sends them to Siberia but, notwithstanding all this, it does not accuse them of criminality, nor even of criminal intent. It merely asserts that they are "politically untrustworthy"; that the "tendency" of their social activity is "pernicious"; or that, from an official point of view, their presence in a particular place is "prejudicial to public tranquillity." These vague assertions mean, simply, that the liberals are in the way of the officials, and prevent the latter, to some extent, from doing what they want to do with the bodies, the souls, or the property of the Russian people....

2. THE REVOLUTIONISTS—The character of the Russian revolutionists is a controverted question, and in order to state the case against them as strongly as possible, and at the same time to show in what manner and upon what grounds the Government proceeds in its dealings with them, I will quote a part of the authorized official report of a political trial.

In February, 1880, a young man named Arsene Boguslavski was brought before a court-martial in the city of Kiev upon the charge of belonging to the revolutionary party and distributing seditious books. General Strelnikof, the prosecuting officer of the Crown, in asking for the condemnation of the accused, made what seemed to be a carefully prepared address, in the course of which he reviewed the history of the revolutionary movement in Russian and expressed the same opinions with regard to the character of the revolutionists that I heard from Colonel Novikof and half a dozen other officers in Siberia. These opinions fairly represent, I think, the Russian official view.

The latter deals with the question of character and motive, is summarized in the authorized report as follows:

> The procureur then referred to the personnel of the revolutionary party, and asked who were these people that had gratuitously taken it upon themselves to reconstruct society and change the whole order of things. He showed that, with a few exceptions, they were mere boys —often minors. The average age of the accused in the Ishutin case, for example, was only twenty-two and a half years, and in the Nechaief case only twenty-three and a half, while the average age of the forty-nine political offenders tried by court-martial up to that time in Kiev was only twenty-four and a half years. The level of their education was extremely low. Out of all the political prisoners brought before the Kiev court-martial, not one had been graduated from the higher educational institutions, and only eight (two of them women) had even completed the course of study of the middle-class schools. The remaining forty-one either had not been at school at all, or had not been graduated. The degree of maturity at which their opinions had arrived was also very low, as might be seen from their publications and from their declarations in the court-room, while their knowledge of the Russian people was limited for the most part to an acquaintance with the waiters in *traktírs* [public tea-houses].... The procureur then passed on to the question of the real object of Russian socialism, showed how that object was made evident by the actions of the party, and cited a surprising number of attempts on the part of socialists to appropriate the goods of others. He referred to a long list of such cases brought to light in connection with previous political trials, beginning with that of Ishutin, and called the attention of the court to the fact that the victims of the crimes of the socialists included even their own comrades. From all that he had previously said the procureur then drew the following conclusions: 1. That "the welfare of the people" was not, by any means, the real aim of the socialistic party. 2. That the destruction of religion, the family, and the state, was only a means of removing obstacles in the way of their real aim. 3. That their real aim was selfish, personal gain. The procureur admitted that, in contravention of these conclusions, it might be argued: first, that not all socialists were so poor as to be in need of other people's property; secondly, that some of them committed their crimes in the face of great and inevitable peril; and thirdly, that in the courtroom and on the scaffold they had shown great bravery. In rejoinder he said that while he believed selfish interest to be the chief aim of the party, he did not assert that it was common to all of its members without exception but only to a majority of them....

It seems to me foolish and impolitic for Russian Government officials to try to make it appear that the revolutionists, as a class, are despicable in point of intellectual ability, or morally depraved. They are neither the one nor the other. So far as education is concerned they are far superior to any equal number of Russian officials with whom, in the course of five years' residence in the Russian Empire, I have been brought in contact. In the face of difficulties and discouragements that would crush most men— in financial distress, in terrible anxiety, in prison, in exile, and in the strait-jacket of the press censorship—they not only "keep their grip," but they fairly distinguish themselves in literature, in science, and in every field of activity that is open to them. Much of the best scientific work that has been done in Siberia has been done by political exiles....

Most of the Russian terrorists were nothing more, at first, than moderate liberals, or, at worst, peaceful socialistic propagandists; and they were gradually transformed into revolutionists, and then into terrorists, by injustice, cruelty, illegality, and contemptuous disregard, by the Government, of all their rights and feelings. I have not a word to say in defense of their crimes. I do not believe in such methods of warfare as assassination, the wrecking of railway trains on which one's enemies are riding, the robbing of Government sub-treasuries, and the blowing up of palaces; but I can fully understand, nevertheless, how an essentially good and noble-natured man may become a terrorist when, as in Russia, he is subjected to absolutely intolerable outrages and indignities and has no peaceful or legal means of redress. It is true, as the Russian Government contends, that after 1878 the terrorists acted in defiance of all the generally accepted principles of civilized combat; but it must not be forgotten that in life and in warfare, as in chess, you cannot disregard all the rules of the game yourself and then expect your adversary to observe them. The Government first set the example of lawlessness in Russia by arresting without warrant; by punishing without trial; by cynically disregarding the judgments of its own courts when such judgments were in favor of politicals; by confiscating the money and property of private citizens whom it merely suspected of sympathy with the revolutionary movement; by sending fourteen-year-old boys and girls to Siberia; by kidnapping the children of "politically untrustworthy" people and exiles and putting them into state asylums; by driving men and women to insanity and suicide in rigorous solitary confinement without giving them a trial; by burying secretly at night the bodies of the people whom it had thus done to death in its dungeons; and by treating as a criminal, *in posse* if not *in esse,* every citizen who dared to ask why or wherefore....

from George Kennan, *Siberia and the Exile System.* vol. 2. New York: The Century Company. 1891.

Questions:
1. How would you describe the decision-making process related to banishment in Russia?
2. How did Kennan describe and compare the effectiveness, methods, size, and social composition of Russian political groups?

Rudyard Kipling "The White Man's Burden," 1899

The mad scramble among the great European powers to establish colonial empires in Africa and Asia at the turn of the last century underscores the fact that the actions of human beings are often motivated by considerations that are not completely rational. To be sure, there were certainly a great many "rational' explanations that were offered by the proponents of the new imperialism to justify their mania for empire building. The one that was bandied about most often was that the white races of Europe were superior to the "black, brown, and yellow" races of Africa and Asia, and had a moral responsibility to rule and civilize these benighted peoples. This argument is most clearly enunciated in the poetry of Britain's Rudyard Kipling (1865-1936).

TAKE up the White Man's burden—
Send forth the best ye breed—
Go bind your sons to exile
To serve your captives' need;
To wait in heavy harness,
On fluttered folk and wild—
Your new-caught, sullen peoples,
Half-devil and half-child.

Take up the White Man's Burden—
In patience to abide,
To veil the threat of terror
And check the show of pride;
By open speech and simple,
An hundred times made plain,
To seek another's profit,
And work another's gain.

Take up the White Man's burden—
The savage wars of peace—
Fill full the mouth of Famine
And bid the sickness cease;
And when your goal is nearest
The end for others sought,
Watch Sloth and heathen Folly
Bring all your hope to nought.

Take up the White Man's burden—
No tawdry rule of kings,
But toil of serf and sweeper—
The tale of common things.

The ports ye shall not enter,
The roads ye shall not tread,
Go make them with your living,
And mark them with your dead.

Take up the White Man's burden—
And reap his old reward:
The blame of those ye better,
The hate of those ye guard—
The cry of hosts ye humour
(Ah, slowly!) toward the light:—
"Why brought ye us from bondage,
"Our loved Egyptian night?"

Take up the White Man's burden—
Ye dare not stoop to less—
Nor call too loud on Freedom
To cloak your weariness;
By all ye cry or whisper,
By all ye leave or do,
The silent, sullen peoples
Shall weigh your Gods and you.

Take up the White Man's burden—
Have done with childish days—
The lightly proffered laurel,
The easy, ungrudged praise.
Comes now, to search your manhood
Through all the thankless years,
Cold, edged with dear-bought wisdom,
The judgment of your peers!

from *Rudyard Kipling's Verse*. New York: Doubleday. 1920.

Questions:
1. How did Kipling depict the indigenous peoples of colonized areas?
2. By contrast, how did Kipling describe the role of Europeans in colonized regions? How did he anticipate Europeans would be received? What advice did he give to the colonizers? Give some specific examples from his writing.

J. A. Hobson "Political Significance of Imperialism," 1902

John Adtkinson Hobson, a British economist (1858-1940) questioned all of the underlying assumptions of his country's imperial policies.

The present condition of the government under which the vast majority of our fellow-subjects in the Empire live is eminently un-British in that it is based, not on the consent of the governed, but upon the will of imperial officials; does indeed betray a great variety of forms, but they agree in the essential of un-freedom. Nor is it true that any of the more enlightened methods of administration we employ are directed towards undoing this character. Not only in India, but in the West Indies, and wherever there exists a large preponderance of coloured population, the trend, not merely of ignorant, but of enlightened public opinion, is against a genuinely representative government on British lines. It is perceived to be incompatible with the economic and social authority of a superior race.

When British authority has been forcibly fastened upon large populations of alien race and colour, with habits of life and thought which do not blend with ours, it is found impossible to graft the tender plants of free representative government, and at the same time to preserve good order in external affairs. We are obliged in practice to make a choice between good order and justice administered autocratically in accordance with British standards, on the one hand, and delicate, costly, doubtful, and disorderly experiments in self-government on British lines upon the other, and we have practically everywhere decided to adopt the former alternative. A third and sounder method of permitting large liberty of self-government under a really loose protectorate, adopted in a few instances, as in Basutoland, part of Bechuanaland, and a few Indian States, meets with no great favour and in most instances seems no longer feasible. It cannot be too clearly recognised that the old Liberal notion of our educating lower races in the arts of popular government is discredited, and only survives for platform purposes when some new step of annexation is urged upon the country.... The decades of Imperialism have been prolific in wars; most of these wars have been directly motivated by aggression of white races upon lower races," and have issued in the forcible seizure of territory. Every one of the steps of expansion in Africa, Asia, and the Pacific has been accompanied by bloodshed; each imperialist Power keeps an increasing army available for foreign service; rectification of frontiers, punitive expeditions, and other euphemisms for war have been in incessant progress. The *Pax Britannica,* always an impudent falsehood, has become a grotesque monster of hypocrisy; along our Indian frontiers, in West Africa, in the Soudan, in Uganda, in Rhodesia fighting has been well-nigh incessant. Although the great imperialist Powers kept their hands off one another, save where the rising empire of the United States found its opportunity in the falling empire of Spain, the self-restraint has been costly and precarious. Peace as a national policy is antagonized not merely by war, but by militarism, an even graver injury. Apart from the enmity of France and Germany, the main cause of the vast armaments which have drained the resources of most European countries is their conflicting interests in territorial and commercial expansion. Where thirty years ago there existed one sensitive spot in our relations with France, or Germany, or Russia, there are a dozen now; diplomatic strains are of almost monthly occurrence between Powers with African or Chinese interests, and the chiefly business nature of the national antagonisms renders them more dangerous, inasmuch as the policy of Governments passes under the influence of distinctively financial *juntos*.[1]

The contention of the *si pacem vis para bellum* school, that armaments alone constitute the best security for peace, is based upon the assumption that a genuine lasting antagonism of real interests exists between the various peoples who are called upon to undergo this monstrous sacrifice.

Our economic analysis has disclosed the fact that it is only the interests of competing cliques of business men— investors, contractors, export manufacturers, and certain professional classes—that are antagonistic; that these cliques, usurping the authority and voice of the people, use the public resources to push their private interests, and spend the blood and money of the

---

[1] small ruling groups

people in this vast and disastrous military game, feigning national antagonisms which have no basis in reality. It is not to the interest of the British people, either as producers of wealth or as tax-payers, to risk a war with Russia and France in order to join Japan in preventing Russia from seizing Corea; but it may serve the interests of a group of commercial politicians to promote this dangerous policy. The South African war, openly fomented by gold speculators for their private purposes, will rank in history as a leading case of this usurpation of nationalism.... The new Imperialism has been, we have seen, chiefly concerned with tropical and sub-tropical countries where large "lower races" are brought under white control. Why should Englishmen fight the defensive or offensive wars of this Empire, when cheaper, more numerous, and better-assimilated fighting material can be raised upon the spot, or transferred from one tropical dominion to another? As the labour of industrial development of tropical resources is put upon the "lower races" who reside there, under white superintendence, why should not militarism be organized upon the same basis, black or brown or yellow men, to whom military discipline will be "a wholesome education," fighting for the British Empire under British officers? Thus can we best economize our own limited military material, keeping most of it for home defence. This simple solution—the employment of cheap foreign mercenary armies—is no new device. The organization of vast native forces, armed with civilized weapons, drilled on "civilized" methods, and commanded by "civilized" officers, formed one of the most conspicuous features of the latest stages of the great Eastern Empires, and afterwards of the Roman Empire. It has proved one of the most perilous devices of parasitism, by which a metropolitan population entrusts the defence of its lives and possessions to the precarious fidelity of conquered races," commanded by ambitious pro-consuls.

One of the strangest symptoms of the blindness of Imperialism is the reckless indifference with which Great Britain, France and other imperial nations embarked on this perilous dependence. Great Britain has gone farthest. Most of the fighting by which we have won our Indian Empire was done by natives; in India, as late in Egypt, great standing armies were placed under British commanders; almost all the fighting associated with our African dominions, except in the southern part, was done for us by natives. How strong the pressure was to reduce the proportion of British soldiers employed in these countries to a bare minimum of safety is amply illustrated in the case of India, when the South African emergency drove us to reduce the accepted minimum by more than fifteen thousand men, while in South Africa itself we established a dangerous precedent by employing large numbers of armed natives to fight against another white race.

Those best acquainted with the temper of the British people and of the politicians who have the direct determination of affairs will understand how readily we may be drawn along this perilous path. Nothing short of the fear of an early invasion of these islands will induce the British people to undergo the onerous experience of a really effective system of compulsory military service; no statesman except under the shadow of a serious menace of invasion will dare to press such a plan. A regular provision for compulsory foreign service will never be adopted when the alternative of mercenary native armies remains. Let these "niggers" fight for the empire in return for the services we render them by annexing and governing them and teaching them "the dignity of labour," will be the prevailing sentiment, and "imperialist" statesmen will be compelled to bow before it, diluting with British troops ever more thinly the native armies in Africa and Asia.

This mode of militarism, while cheaper and easier in the first instance, implies less and less control from Great Britain. Though reducing the strain of militarism upon the population at home, it enhances the risks of wars, which become more frequent and more barbarous in proportion as they involve to a less degree the lives of Englishmen.... As the despotic portion of our Empire has grown in area, a larger and larger number of men, trained in the temper and methods of autocracy as soldiers and civil officials in our Crown colonies, protectorates, the Indian Empire, reinforced by numbers of merchants, planters, engineers, and overseers, whose lives have been those of a superior caste living an artificial life removed from all the healthy restraints of ordinary European society, have returned to this country, bringing back the characters, sentiments, and ideas imposed by this foreign environment. The South and South-West of England is richly sprinkled with these men, many of them wealthy, most of them endowed with leisure, men openly contemptuous of democracy, devoted to material luxury, social display, and the shallower arts of intellectual life. The wealthier among them discover political ambitions, introducing into our Houses of Parliament the coarsest and most selfish spirit of " Imperialism," using their imperial experience and connexions to push profitable companies and concessions for their private benefits, and posing as authorities so as to keep the yoke of Imperialism firmly fixed upon the shoulders of the "nigger." The South African millionaire is the brand most in evidence: his methods are the most barefaced, and his success, social and political, the most redoubtable. But the practices which are writ large in Rhodes, Beit, and their parliamentary confederates are widespread on a smaller scale; the South of England is full of men of local influence in politics and society whose character has been formed in our despotic Empire, and whose incomes are chiefly derived from the maintenance and furtherance of this despotic rule. Not a few enter our local councils, or take posts in our constabulary or our prisons: everywhere they stand for coercion and for resistance to reform. Could the incomes expended in the Home Counties and other large districts of Southern Britain be traced to their sources, it would be found that they were in large measure wrung from the enforced toil of vast multitudes of black, brown, or yellow natives, by arts not differing essentially from those which supported in idleness and luxury imperial Rome.

It is, indeed, a nemesis of Imperialism that the arts and crafts of tyranny, acquired and exercised in our unfree Empire, should be turned against our liberties at home. Those who have felt surprise at the total disregard or the open contempt displayed by the aristocracy and the plutocracy of this land for infringements of the liberties of the subject and for the abrogation of constitutional rights and usages have not taken sufficiently into account the steady reflux of this poison of irresponsible autocracy from our "unfree, intolerant, aggressive" Empire.

from J. A. Hobson, Imperialism: A Study. London: George Allen & Unwin. 1902.

Questions:
1. According to Hobson, how had British publicly-stated motives behind imperialism differed from the actual implementation of imperialism? In what ways were the British imperialists being hypocritical?
2. Who, in Hobson's opinion, were the driving forces behind imperialism?
3. What threat did imperialism pose for Europeans? Why was imperialistic activity hazardous and burdensome to indigenous peoples and Europeans alike?

Chapter 26: World War and Revolution

Unit 55: The Great War and its Aftermath

In the decades that have elapsed since the outbreak of the First World War in 1914, it has become increasingly difficult for people to truly appreciate the significance of this event. Indeed, after a century of world-wide conflicts in which the bombing of civilian populations, genocide, terrorism, and nuclear strategies of "mutual assured destruction" have dulled our sensitivities, it is often hard for us to give much credence to a war that was fought by men in plumed helmets and monocles, who seriously believed that cavalry and massed infantry charges had a place on a battlefield dominated by barbed wire and machine guns. Nevertheless, of all the events that have marked this century, none has more clearly defined it than World War I.

As a result of this conflict some 16 million men lost their lives and another 20 million were maimed and wounded. The experiences of these soldiers in the trenches and pitched battles of the First World War scarred an entire generation, haunted the imaginations of artists and writers years after the war's end, and undermined the widespread belief at the end of the nineteenth century that Europe was progressing toward a scientific and technological utopia. In addition to its psychic toll, the First World War also set into motion political events that reconfigured the map of Europe. Popular dissatisfaction with the war and the governments that had started it sparked revolutions that toppled the thrones of Germany, Austria-Hungary, Turkey, and Russia, and brought into being the present day nations of central and eastern Europe. In addition to these geo-political changes, the revolutions that were sparked by World War I also transformed Russia into a communist state and set the stage for the rise of the Fascist and Nazi mass movements of the 1920s and 30s, events which would once more plunge Europe into crisis and world war. Indeed, if the First World War did not turn out to be "the war to end all wars," it did most certainly prove to be the war that ended a way of life in Europe that had endured for centuries. In many respects, we are still trying to find our way through the ruins that were left behind by that conflict.

The Black Hand: Bylaws, 1911

The crisis that pushed Europe "into the boiling cauldron of war" arose in the Balkans. Its origins lay in the annexation by Austria-Hungary of the Balkan principality of Bosnia-Herzegovina in 1908, an event that was fiercely opposed by Serb nationalists who believed that the region should be part of a Greater Serbia. Among those Serbian groups that were committed to ousting Austria from Bosnia, none was more fanatical than the Union or Death or, as they were more popularly known, the Black Hand. Numbering about 2,500 members, many of whom were officers in the Serbian army, this group shrouded its activities in mystery, initiation rites, and blood oaths. Moreover, as the excerpts from their by-laws printed below make clear, they were capable of any act that they believed necessary in order to realize a union of the south Slavs of Europe. One such act was the assassination of the heir to the Austrian throne Archduke Franz Ferdinand during his state visit to the Bosnian capital of Sarajevo on June 28, 1914. It was the crisis that was precipitated by this deed that would plunge Europe into a world war.

Article 1. This organization is created for the purpose of realizing the national ideal: the union of all Serbs. Membership is open to every Serb, without distinction of sex, religion, or place of birth, and to all those who are sincerely devoted to this cause.

Article 2. This organization prefers terrorist action to intellectual propaganda, and for this reason it must remain absolutely secret.

Article 3. The organization bears the name *Ujedinjenje ili Smirt* (Union or Death).

Article 4. To fulfill its purpose, the organization will do the following:

1. Exercise influence on government circles, on the various social classes, and on the entire social life of the kingdom of Serbia, which is considered the Piedmont of the Serbian nation;

2. Organize revolutionary action in all territories inhabited by Serbs;

3. Beyond the frontiers of Serbia, fight with all means the enemies of the Serbian national idea;

4. Maintain amicable relations with all states, peoples, organizations, and individuals who support Serbia and the Serbian element;

5. Assist those nations and organizations that are fighting for their own national liberation and unification....

Article 24. Every member has a duty to recruit new members, but the member shall guarantee with his life those whom he introduces into the organization.

Article 25. Members of the organization are forbidden to know each other personally. Only members of the central committee are known to each other.

Article 26. In the organization itself, the members are designated by numbers. Only the central committee in Belgrade knows their names.

Article 27. Members of the organization must obey absolutely the commands given to them by their superiors.

Article 28. Each member has a duty to communicate to the central committee at Belgrade all information that may be of interest to the organization.

Article 29. The interests of the organization stand above all other interests.

Article 30. On entering the organization, each member must know that he loses his own personality, that he can expect neither personal glory nor personal profit, material or moral. Consequently, any member who endeavors to exploit the organization for personal, social, or party motives, will be punished. If by his acts he harms the organization itself, his punishment will be death.

Article 31. Those who enter the organization may never leave it, and no one has the authority to accept a member's resignation.

Article 32. Each member must aid the organization, with weekly contributions. If need by, the organization may procure funds through coercion....

Article 33 When the central committee of Belgrade pronounces a death sentence the only thing that matters is that the execution is carried out unfailingly. The method of execution is of little importance.

Article 34. The organization's seal is composed as follows. On the center of the seal a powerful arm holds in its hand an unfurled flag. On the flag, as a coat of arms, are a skull and crossed bones; by the side of the flag are a knife, a bomb and poison. Around, in a circle, are inscribed the following words reading from left to right: "Unification or Death," and at the base "The Supreme Central Directorate."

Article 35. On joining the organization, the recruit takes the following oath:

"I (name), in becoming a member of the organization, 'Unification or Death,' do swear by the sun that shines on me, by the earth that nourishes me, by God, by the blood of my ancestors, on my honor and my life that from this moment until my death, I shall be faithful to the regulations of the organization and that I will be prepared to make any sacrifice for it. I swear before God, on my honor and on my life, that I shall carry with me to the grave the organization's secrets. May God condemn me and my comrades judge me if I violate or do not respect, consciously or not, my oath."

Article 36. These regulations come into force immediately.

Article 37. These regulations must not be changed.

Perry, Marvin, *Sources of the Western Tradition.* Second Edition, Volume II. Copyright©1991 by Houghton Mifflin Company. Used by permission.

Questions:
1. What was the goal of the Black Hand? What methods were its members willing to use in order to achieve their goal?
2. How was the Black Hand organized? What obligations were placed upon members of the Black Hand?

The Treaty of Versailles, May 29, 1919

When World War I ended with the signing of the armistice between the Allies and Germany on November 11, 1918, there were high hopes on both sides of the conflict that a just and fair peace could be worked out, which would insure both an end to war and a new democratic order in Europe. Certainly, this was the kind of peace that was envisioned in the Fourteen Point peace program outlined to the American Congress in 1918 by President Woodrow Wilson. Unfortunately, the Allied statesmen who gathered at the Paris Peace Conference on January 18, 1919 were, by and large, not interested in "doing great, permanent, and noble things." Instead they were largely guided by narrow national interests, greed, and a desire to exact revenge on Germany and its allies. Unfortunately for Europe, the Paris Peace Treaties satisfied no one and in the end they proved to be little more than a guarantee of future tensions and conflicts.

PART V: MILITARY, NAVAL AND AIR CLAUSES

In order to render possible the initiation of a general limitation of the armaments of all nations, Germany undertakes strictly to observe the military, naval and air clauses which follow.

SECTION I: MILITARY CLAUSES
CHAPTER I: EFFECTIVES AND CADRES OF THE GERMAN ARMY
Article 159.

The German military forces shall be demobilised and reduced as prescribed hereinafter.

Article 160.

(1) By a date which must not be later than March 31, 1920, the German Army must not comprise more than seven divisions of infantry and three divisions of cavalry.

After that date the total number of effectives in the Army of the States constituting Germany must not exceed one hundred thousand men, including officers and establishments of depots.

The Army shall be devoted exclusively to the maintenance of order within the territory and to the control of the frontiers.

Article 168.

The manufacture of arms, munitions, or any war material, shall only be carried out in factories or works the location of which shall be communicated to and approved by the Governments of the Principal Allied and Associated Powers, and the number of which they retain the right to restrict.

Within three months from the coming into force of the present Treaty, all other establishments for the manufacture, preparation, storage or design of arms, munitions, or any war material whatever shall be closed down. The same applies to all arsenals except those used as depots for the authorised stocks of munitions. Within the same period the personnel of these arsenals will be dismissed.

Article 169.

Within two months from the coming into force of the present Treaty German arms, munitions and war material, including anti-aircraft material, existing in Germany in excess of the quantities allowed, must be surrendered to the Governments of the Principal Allied and Associated Powers to be destroyed or rendered useless. This will also apply to any special plant intended for the manufacture of military material, except such as may be recongised as necessary for equipping the authorised strength of the Germany Army.

Article 171.

The use of asphyxiating, poisonous or other gases and all analogous liquids, materials or devices being prohibited, their manufacture and importation are strictly forbidden in Germany.

The same applies to materials specially intended for the manufacture, storage and use of the said products or devices.

The manufacture and importation into Germany of armoured cars, tanks and all similar constructions suitable for use in war are also prohibited.

CHAPTER III: RECRUITING AND MILITARY TRAINING
Article 173.

Universal compulsory military service shall be abolished in Germany.

The German Army may only be constituted and recruited by means of voluntary enlistment.

SECTION II: NAVAL CLAUSES
Article 181.

After the expiration of a period of two months from the coming into force of the present Treaty the Germany naval forces in commission must not exceed:

6 battleships of the Deutschland or Lothringen type,

6 light cruisers,

12 destroyers,

12 torpedo boats,

or an equal number of ships constructed to replace them as provided in Article 190.

No submarines are to be included.

All other warships, except where there is provision to the contrary in the present Treaty, must be placed in reserve or devoted to commercial purposes.

SECTION III: AIR CLAUSES
Article 198.

The Armed forces of Germany must not include any military or naval air forces.

Germany may, during a period not extending beyond October 1, 1919, maintain a maximum number of one hundred seaplanes or flying boats, which shall be exclusively employed in searching for submarine mines, shall be furnished with the necessary equipment for this purpose, and shall in no case carry arms, munitions or bombs of any nature whatever.

In addition to the engines installed in the seaplanes or flying boats above mentioned, one spare engine may be provided for each engine of each of these craft.

No dirigible shall be kept.

PART VIII: REPARATION
SECTION I: GENERAL PROVISIONS
Article 231.

The Allied and Associated Governments affirm and Germany accepts the responsibility of Germany and her allies for causing all the loss and damage to which the Allied and Associated Governments and their nationals have been subjected as a consequence of the war imposed upon them by the aggression of Germany and her allies.

Article 232.

The Allied and Associated Governments recognise that the resources of Germany are not adequate, after taking into account permanent diminutions of such resources which will result from other provisions of the present Treaty, to make complete reparation for all such loss and damage.

The Allied and Associated Governments, however, require, and Germany undertakes, that she will make compensation for all damage done to the civilian population of the Allied and Associated Powers and to their property during the period of the belligerency of each as an Allied or Associated Power against Germany by such aggression by land, by sea and from the air, and in general all damage as defined in Annex I hereto.

Article 233.

The amount of the above damage for which compensation is to be made by Germany shall be determined by an Inter-Allied Commission, to be called the Reparation Commission and constituted in the form and with the powers set forth hereunder and in Annexes II to VII inclusive hereto.

This Commission shall consider the claims and give to the German Government a just opportunity to be heard.

The findings of the Commission as to the amount of damage defined as above shall be concluded and notified to the German Government on or before May 1, 1921, as representing the extent of that Government's obligations.

The Commission shall concurrently draw up a schedule of payments prescribing the time and manner for securing and discharging the entire obligation within a period of thirty years from May 1, 1921. If, however, within the period mentioned, Germany fails to discharge her obligations, any balance remaining unpaid may, within the discretion of the Commission, be postponed for settlement in subsequent years, or may be handled otherwise in such manner as the Allied and

Associated Governments, acting in accordance with the procedure laid down in this Part of the present Treaty, shall determine.

SECTION I: GERMAN COLONIES
Article 119

Germany renounces in favour of the Principal Allied and Associated Powers all her rights and titles over her oversea possessions.

SECTION IV: SAAR BASIN
Article 45.

As compensation for the destruction of the coal mines in the north of France and as part payment towards the total reparation due from Germany for the damage resulting from the war, Germany cedes to France in full and absolute possession, with exclusive rights of exploitation, unencumbered and free from all debts and charges of any kind, the coal mines situated in the Saar Basin as defined in Article 48.

from *A History of the Peace Conference of Paris*, volume 2, edited by H. W. V. Temperley.
London: Oxford University Press, 1920.

Question:
What were some of the restrictions placed upon Germany in the Treaty of Versailles?

German Observations on the Treaty of Paris, May 29, 1919

As the German reaction to this agreement makes clear, Germany considered the Versailles treaty to be little more than a harsh, unfair *Diktat*. And given the fact that the former German Empire was saddled with the responsibility for the war, compelled to disarm unilaterally, forced to cede thirteen per cent of its territory, and required to pay an unspecified amount of war reparations, this interpretation was not far from the truth.

'The peace to be concluded with Germany was to be a peace of right, not a peace of might.'

'In his address to the Mexican journalists on the 9th of June, 1918, President Wilson promised to maintain the principle that the interests of the weakest and of the strongest should be equally sacred. "That is what we mean, provided we do so sincerely with understanding and in real knowledge and conception of the subject. If it is indeed and in truth the mutual aim of the Governments allied against Germany and of their nations, in the coming negotiations of peace to bring about a sure and lasting peace, all who sit down at the table of negotiations will be ready and willing to pay the only price for which it can be got. They must also be ready and willing, with manly courage to create the only instrument that can guarantee the execution of the conditions of peace. This price is impartial justice in every item without regard to whose interests may be crossed by it, and not only impartial justice but also satisfaction to all nations whose future is to be decided upon." And in his speech before Congress on the 11th of February 1918, the President described the aim of peace as follows: "What we are striving for is a new international order based upon broad and universal principles of right and justice—no mere peace of shreds and patches.

'The peace document shows that none of these repeated solemn assurances has been kept.

'To begin with the territorial questions:

'In the West, a purely German territory on the Saar with a population of at least 650,000 inhabitants is to be separated from the German Empire for at least fifteen years merely for the reason that claims are asserted to the coal abounding there.

'The other cessions in the West, German-Austria and German-Bohemia will be mentioned in connection with the right of self-determination.

'In Schleswig, the line of demarcation for voting has been traced through purely German districts and goes farther than Denmark herself wishes.

'In the East, Upper Silesia is to be separated from Germany and given to Poland, although it has had no political connexion with Poland for the last 750 years. Contrary to this, the provinces of Posen and almost the whole of West Prussia are to be separated from the German Empire in consideration of the former extent of the old Polish state, although millions of Germans are living there. Again, the district of Memel is separated from Germany quite regardless of its historical past, in the obvious attempt to separate Germany from Russia for economic reasons. For the purpose of securing to Poland free access to the sea, East Prussia is to be completely cut off from the rest of the Empire and thereby condemned to economic and national decay. The purely German city of Danzig is to become a Free State under the suzerainty of Poland. Such terms are not founded on any principle of justice. Quite arbitrarily, here the idea of an imprescribable historical right, there the idea of ethnographical possession, there the standpoint of economic interest shall prevail, in every case the decision being unfavourable to Germany.

'The settlement of the colonial question is equally contradictory to a peace of justice. For the essence of activity in colonial work does not consist in capitalistic exploitation of a less developed human race, but in raising backward peoples to a higher civilization. This gives the Powers which are advanced in culture a natural claim to take part in colonial work. Germany, whose colonial accomplishments cannot be denied, has also this natural claim, which is not recognized by a treaty of peace that deprives Germany of all of her colonies.

'Not only the settlement of the territorial questions but each and every provision of the treaty of peace is governed by the ill-renowned phrase: "Might above Right! "—Here are a few illustrations:

'Under the provisions of Article 117 Germany is to recognize beforehand the full force of all treaties or agreements which may be entered into by her enemies with the states created or to be created in any part of the former Russian Empire, even with respect to her own frontiers.

'According to the provisions of international law as understood on the Continent, the economic war ought to have been considered unlawful, and private property should have been left untouched, even while the war was being carried on. In spite of this, the instrument of peace does not confine itself to demanding, in payment of the public claims of restitution against Germany, the total of German property liquidated by the enemies within their territories. In addition, the enemy Governments monstrously reserve to themselves the right, for an indefinite period after the coming into force of the treaty of peace, to liquidate all German property within their territories without real equivalent and regardless of the time of its importation, or to submit the same to other measures of war at their discretion. This shall apply even to German property in the German colonies, in Alsace-Lorraine, and in the other districts to be ceded.

'The demand is made that German citizens be handed over to courts of the enemy Powers, instead of trying out a new solution, a fruit of the idea of a just peace, of appointing an impartial authority that should settle all violations of international law that have occurred in this war.

'Although President Wilson, in his speech (of October 20th? 1916), has acknowledged that "no single fact caused the war, but that in the last analysis the whole European system is in a deeper sense responsible for the war, with its combination of alliances and understandings, a complicated texture of intrigues and espionage that unfailingly caught the whole family of nations in its meshes," "that the present war is not so simply to be explained and that its roots reach deep into the dark soil of history," Germany is to acknowledge that Germany and her allies are responsible for all damages which the enemy Governments or their subjects have incurred by her and her allies' aggression. This appears all the less tolerable as it is an indisputable historical fact that several of the hostile Powers, such as Italy and Rumania, on their part entered the war for the purpose of territorial conquests. Apart from the consideration that there is no incontestable legal foundation for the obligation for reparation imposed upon Germany, the amount of such compensation is to be determined by a commission nominated solely by Germany's enemies, Germany taking no part in the findings of the commission. The commission is plainly to have power to administer Germany like the estate of a bankrupt.

'As there are natural rights of man, so there are natural rights of nations. The inalienable fundamental right of every state is the right of self-preservation and self-determination. With this fundamental right the demand here made upon Germany is incompatible. Germany must promise to pay an indemnity, the amount of which at present is not even stated. The German rivers are to be placed under the control of an international body upon which Germany's delegates are always to be but the smallest minority. Canals and railroads are to be built on German territory at the discretion of foreign authorities.

'These few instances show that that is not the just peace we were promised, not the peace "the very principle of which, according to a word of President Wilson, "is equality and the common participation in a common benefit. The equality of nations upon which peace must be founded if it is to last must be an equality of rights".'

from *A History of the Peace Conference of Paris*, volume 2, edited by H. w. V. Temperley.
London: Oxford University Press, 1920.

Question:
What was the German reaction to the Treaty of Versailles? Do you agree or disagree with their response?

Chapter 27: Europe During the Interwar Years, 1919-1939

Unit 56: Thunder on the Right: Germany, Hitler, and the Rise of Nazism

Perhaps the key question confronting historians of modern Germany is how a nation renowned for its *Denkers und Dichters* (thinkers and poets) could become a stronghold of Nazi *Henkers und Richters* (executioners and judges) during the 1930s. In the aftermath of World War II, a number of historians suggested that the answer to this question lay in the cultural sphere of German life. According to this theory, German intellectuals, philosophers, and religious figures from Luther and Kant to Hegel and Nietzsche had cultivated within the German people a peculiar "mindset," which glorified war, worshipped the state, and despised the Jews. According to this line of reasoning, much of Hitler's success with the German public during the late 20s and early 30s lay in the fact that his pronouncements on authoritarianism, racism, and war resonated strongly with ideas and opinions that were already deeply ingrained in his audiences. As such, National Socialism was something akin to a serpent's egg, which had been nurtured in the bosom of Germany for centuries, and was merely awaiting the right moment to hatch forth its venomous offspring.

Most contemporary historians are uncomfortable with the idea that the National Socialist triumph can be attributed to Germany's intellectual traditions. They point out, quite rightly, that the vast majority of the thinkers in question (e.g. Luther, Kant, Hegel, et. al.) would have been horrified by Hitler and his party, and that most of Germany's intelligentsia from the seventeenth to the nineteenth centuries were deeply committed to humanism, cosmopolitanism, and liberalism. Nevertheless, it is also true that a great many of the ideas that Hitler would espouse in the 20s and 30s did indeed receive a favorable response from the German people, and that this was due in no small way to the fact that they enjoyed a respectable intellectual provenance. Perhaps the best examples of Nazism's popular intellectual precursors can be found in the following excerpts from the work of the Prussian historian, Heinrich von Treitschke (1834-1896) and the composer Richard Wagner (1813-1883). The writings of these two men were extremely popular and widespread during the nineteenth and early twentieth centuries, and they played a key role in winning over a great many Germans to the banner of national chauvinism, militarism, and anti-Semitism. Indeed, One of those Germans who eagerly embraced many of their ideas was none other than the future Nazi Führer, Adolf Hitler.

Richard Wagner: from *Judaism in Music,* 1850

…It is necessary for us to explain the *involuntary repugnance* we possess for the nature and personality of the Jews…. According to the present constitution of the world, the Jew in truth is already more than emancipate: He rules, and will rule, as long as Money remains the power before which all our doings and our dealings lose their force…. The public art taste has been brought between the busy fingers of the Jews, who preside over an art bazaar…. The Jew's outward appearance always has something disagreeably foreign about it….

The Jew speaks the language of the nation in whose midst he dwells from generation to generation, but he always speaks it as an alien. Our whole European art and civilization have remained to the Jew a foreign tongue. In this speech, its art, the Jew can only after-speak and after-patch—cannot truly make a poem of his words, an artwork of his doings. In the peculiarities of Semitic pronunciation the first thing that strikes our ear as quite outlandish and unpleasant, in the Jew's production of the voice sounds, is a creaking, squeaking, buzzing snuffle. This mode of speaking acquires at once the character of an intolerably jumbled blabber. The cold indifference of his peculiar blubber never by chance rises to the ardor of a higher, heartfelt passion.

The aforesaid qualities of his dialect make the Jew altogether[1] incapable of giving artistic enunciation to his feelings through *talk*; hence it is even more difficult for him to enunciate through *song*, for Song is just Talk aroused to highest passion, and music is the speech of passion.... The Jew who is innately incapable of enouncing himself to us artistically through either his outward appearance or his speech, and least of all through his singing, has, nevertheless, been able in the widest-spread of modern art varieties, to wit, in Music, to reach the rulership of public taste.... Control of money through usury has led the Jews to power, for modern culture is accessible to none but the well-to-do....

Felix Mendelssohn-Bartholdy has shown us that a Jew may have the amplest store of specific talents, the highest and tenderest sense of honor—yet without all these pre-eminences helping him, were it but a single time, to call forth in us that deep, that heart-searching effect which we await from Music.... A far-famed Jewish tonesetter of our day [Meyerbeer] has addressed himself and products to a certain section of our public whose total confusion of musical taste was less to be first caused by him, than worked out to his profit.... The uninspiring, the truly laughable, is the characteristic work whereby this famous composer shows his Jewhood in music....

The Jews have never produced a true poet. [Heinrich Heine] reached the point where he duped himself into a poet, and was rewarded by his versified lies being set to music by our own composers. He was the conscience of Judaism, just as Judaism is the evil conscience of our modern civilization.

translated by William Ashton Ellis, London, 1892-1899. Adapted by Louis L. Snyder in
Documents of German History, Rutgers University Press. 1958.

Questions:
1. How did Wagner depict Jews?
2. What are the possible consequences of Wagner's claim that "the Jew speaks the language of the nation...but he always speaks it as an alien"?

Heinrich von Treitschke: *On the German Character*, c. 1900

ON THE GERMAN CHARACTER

Depth of thought, idealism, cosmopolitan views; a transcendent philosophy which boldly oversteps (or freely looks over) the separating barriers of finite existence; familiarity with every human thought and feeling, the desire to traverse the world-wide realm of ideas in common with the foremost intellects of all nations and all times. All that has at all times been held to be characteristic of the Germans and has always been praised as the essence of German character and breeding.

The simple loyalty of the Germans contrasts remarkably with the unchivalrousness of the English character. This seems to be due to the fact that in England physical culture is sought, not in the exercise of noble arms, but in sports like boxing, swimming, and rowing, sports which undoubtedly have their value, but which obviously tend to encourage a brutal and purely athletic point of view, and the single and superficial ambition of getting a first prize.

---

[1] Wagner later changed this word to "almost".

ON THE STATE

The state is a moral community, which is called upon to educate the human race by positive achievement. Its ultimate object is that a nation should develop in it, a nation distinguished by a real national character. To achieve this state is the highest moral duty for nation and individual alike. All private quarrels must be forgotten when the state is in danger.

At the moment when the state cries out that its very life is at stake, social selfishness must cease and party hatred by hushed. The individual must forget his egoism, and feel that he is a member of the whole body.

The most important possession of a state, its be-all and end-all, is power. He who is not man enough to look this truth in the face should not meddle in politics. The state is not physical power as an end in itself, it is power to protect and promote the higher interests. Power must justify itself by being applied for the greatest good of mankind. It is the highest moral duty of the state to increase its power.

The true greatness of the state is that it links the past with the present and future; consequently, the individual has no right to regard the state as a means for attaining his own ambitions in life. Every extension of the activities of the state is beneficial and wise if it arouses, promotes, and purifies the independence of free and reasoning men; it is evil when it kills and stunts the independence of free men. It is men who make history.

The state does not stand for the whole life of the nation. Its function is essentially protective and administrative. The state does not swallow up everything; it can only influence by external compulsion. It represents the nation from the point of view of power. For in the state it is not only the great primitive forces of human nature that come into play; the state is the basis of all national life. Briefly, it may be affirmed that a state which is not capable of forming and maintaining an external organization of its civilizing activities deserves to perish.

Only the truly great and powerful states ought to exist. Small states are unable to protect their subjects against external enemies; moreover, they are incapable of producing genuine patriotism or national pride and are sometimes incapable of *Kultur* in great dimensions. Weimar produced a Goethe and a Schiller; still these poets would have been greater had they been citizens of a German national state.

ON MONARCHY

The will of the state is, in a monarchy, the expression of the will of one man who wears the crown by virtue of the historic right of a certain family; with him the final authority rests. Nothing in a monarchy can be done contrary to the will of the monarch. In a democracy, plurality, the will of the people, expresses the will of the state. A monarchy excels any other form of government, including the democratic, in achieving unity and power in a nation. It is for this reason that monarchy seems so natural, and that it makes such an appeal to the popular understanding. We Germans had an experience of this in the first years of our new empire. How wonderfully the idea of a united Fatherland was embodied for us in the person of the venerable Emperor! How much it meant to us that we could feel once more: "That man is Germany; there is no gainsaying it!"

ON WAR

The idea of perpetual peace is an illusion supported only by those of weak character. It has always been the weary, spiritless, and exhausted ages which have played with the dream of perpetual peace. A thousand touching portraits testify to the sacred power of the love which a righteous war awakes in noble nations. It is altogether impossible that peace be maintained in a world bristling with arms, and even God will see to it that war always recurs as a drastic medicine for the human race. Among great states the greatest political sin and the most contemptible is feebleness. It is the political sin against the Holy Ghost.

War is elevating because the individual disappears before the great conception of the state. The devotion of the members of a community to each other is nowhere so splendidly conspicuous as in war.

Modern wars are not waged for the sake of goods and chattels. What is at stake is the sublime moral good of national honor, which has something in the nature of unconditional sanctity, and compels the individual to sacrifice himself for it.

ON THE ENGLISH

The hypocritical Englishman, with the Bible in one hand and a pipe of opium on the other, possesses no redeeming qualities. The nation was an ancient robber-knight, in full armor, lance in hand, on every one of the world's trade routes.

The English possess a commercial spirit, a love of money which has killed every sentiment of honor and every distinction of right and wrong. English cowardice and sensuality are hidden behind unctuous, theological fine talk which is to us free-thinking German heretics among all the sins of English nature the most repugnant. In England all notions of honor and class prejudices vanish before the power of money, whereas the German nobility has remained poor but chivalrous. That last indispensable bulwark against the brutalization of society—the duel—has gone out of fashion in England and soon disappeared, to be supplanted by the riding whip. This was a triumph of vulgarity. The newspapers, in their accounts of aristocratic weddings, record in exact detail how much each wedding guest has contributed in the form of presents or in cash; even the youth of the nation have turned their sports into a business, and contend for valuable prizes, whereas the German students wrought havoc on their countenances for the sake of a real or imaginary honor.

ON JEWS

The Jews at one time played a necessary role in German history, because of their ability in the management of money. But now that the Aryans have become accustomed to the idiosyncrasies of finance, the Jews are no longer necessary. The international Jew, hidden in the mask of different nationalities, is a disintegrating influence; he can be of no further use to the world. It is necessary to speak openly about the Jews, undisturbed by the fact that the Jewish press befouls what is purely historical truth.

Snyder, Louis L., *Documents of German History*. Copyright ©1958 by Rutgers, The State University. Reprinted by permission of Rutgers University Press.

Question:
What were von Treitschke's views on the German character, the state, the monarchy, war and the Jews?

Friedrich Kroner: "Overwrought Nerves," 1923

Perhaps if the Weimar Republic had been granted an initial period of political peace and economic stability, it might have been better able to stave off the attacks of those committed to its destruction during the dark days of the Great Depression. Unfortunately, from its inception, the fledgling German republic found itself confronted by a seemingly endless number of internal and external crises. Of these, none was more serious than the Franco-Belgian Invasion and occupation of the German industrial heartland, the Ruhrgebiet, in 1923. Initiated by Paris in an effort to compel the Weimar government to meet its reparations obligations, this ill-considered invasion instead resulted in a decision by the German leadership to order a policy of passive resistance to the French occupation, which shut down all coal, steel, iron, and machine production in the Ruhr. In order to support the workers engaged in this strike the Berlin government began printing more paper money, and this money printing scheme, in tandem with the industrial shutdown, sparked a great inflation that destroyed the value of the German mark. By the end of 1923, Germany's currency fell to a rate of 4.2 trillion marks to the dollar, a development that essentially made everything in German society worthless. As the noted German historian, Alan Bullock, noted, the collapse of the German currency had the effect of "reaching down to and touching every single member of the community in a way which no political event can. The savings of the middle classes and working classes were wiped out at a single blow." What this meant to German moral values and social relationships is poignantly captured in the following accounts by eyewitnesses to this tragic event.

There is not much to add. It pounds daily on the nerves; the insanity of numbers, the uncertain future, today, and tomorrow become doubtful once more overnight. An epidemic of fear, naked need: lines of shoppers, long since an unaccustomed sight, once more form in front of shops, first in front of one, then in front of all. No disease is as contagious as this one. The lines have something suggestive about them: the women's glances, their hastily donned kitchen dresses, their careworn, patient faces. The lines always send the same signal: the city, the big stone city will be shopped empty again. Rice, 80,000 marks a pound yesterday, costs 160,000 marks today, and tomorrow perhaps twice as much; the day after, the man behind the counter will shrug his shoulders, "No more rice." Well then, noodles! "No more noodles." Barley, groats, beans, lentils—always the same, buy, buy, buy. The piece of paper, the spanking brand-new bank note, still moist from the printers, paid out today as a weekly wage, shrinks in value on the way to the grocer's shop. The zeros, *the multiplying zeros!* "Well, zero, zero ain't nothing."

They rise with the dollar, hate, desperation, and need—daily emotions like daily rates of exchange. The rising dollar brings mockery and laughter: "Cheaper butter! Instead of 1,600,000 marks, just 1,400,000 marks." This is no joke; this is reality written seriously with a pencil, hung in the shop window, and seriously read.

It rises with the dollar, the haste to turn that piece of paper into something one can swallow, something filling. The weekend markets overflow with people. City police regulate traffic. The lines consume the produce stands. "I'll have two dozen turnips." "There's only one dozen." Once packed away and the money counted into the hand like at the train ticket window, the next pushes forward from behind: "Two dozen turnips." "There's only one...Next!"

Somewhere patience explodes. Resignation breaks. Not at the turnip man, who is a big fellow. One also swallows the butcher's biting remark, that all cows have to have bones. One pays and staggers off. But then the girl in the dairy store, the one whose face is always pinched, whose way of speaking becomes ever more finicky the fuller her store—this nervous milk maid—she issues regulations: how one is to behave as a customer, that shoving is rude, that everyone should not shout at once. Otherwise she cannot concentrate on the scale. "Come on, when am I finally going to get my butter?" screams a woman. "Your butter? It is not your butter by a long shot. By the time you get to the front of the line, your butter will be all gone." And then comes the umbrella handle, a response crashing through the glass cover on the cream cheese. And the cop standing watch outside pulls a sobbing woman from the store. And there is an uproar. And charges are filed.

from *The Weimar Republic Sourcebook*, edited by Anton Kaes, Martin Jay, and Edward Dimendberg. Berkeley: University of California Press. 1994.

The Nazi Party Program, 1920

Of the many parties of the German right, the one that seemed the least likely to pose a threat to the Weimar Republic was the National Socialist German Workers' Party. founded in 1919 as the German Workers' Party by Anton Drexler, an eccentric Munich locksmith, the nascent Nazi Party was initially little more than a group of twenty to twenty-five ultra-nationalist, rabidly antisemitic cranks. All of this changed, however, when an ill-paid, low level Reichswehr spy, by the name of Adolf Hitler (1889-1945), decided to join Drexler's group and transform it into a vehicle for his own political advancement.

The son of an Austrian customs official, Adolf Hitler's initial ambition was to become an artist, and towards that end he made his way to Vienna. Rejected by the Vienna Academy of Fine Arts, Hitler spent the years from 1908 to 1913 as a bohemian drifter in Austria's capital, and it was here that he became acquainted with the antisemitic, pan-German, and Social Darwinian ideas that would prove to be the core beliefs of his life. Following the outbreak of World War I, Hitler served in the German Army with distinction. After the war, he drifted to Munich, decided to enter politics, and joined Drexler's German Workers' Party. In less than a year, Hitler made himself leader of this group, renamed it the National Socialist German Workers' Party (or Nazi Party for short), and set down its basic political aims in the party program, which is reprinted below. Following an unsuccessful attempt to topple the Weimar government in 1923, Hitler was sentenced to a term of imprisonment, and it was during this period that he wrote what would become the equivalent of the Nazi "bible," *Mein Kampf (My Struggle)*. Both an autobiography and a political tirade, Hitler's work was a collection of half-truths, vicious libels, and out-and-out lies. The following selection from *Mein Kampf* illustrates the central elements of the Hitlerian "worldview," which would plunge Europe once more into war and condemn countless millions to their deaths.

The program is the political foundation of the NSDAP and accordingly the primary political law of the State. It has been made brief and clear intentionally.

All legal precepts must be applied in the spirit of the party program. Since the taking over of control, the Fuehrer has succeeded in the realization of essential portions of the Party program from the fundamentals to the detail.

The Party Program of the NSDAP was proclaimed on the 24 February 1920 by Adolf Hitler at the first large Party gathering in Munich and since that day has remained unaltered. Within the national socialist philosophy is summarized in 25 points:

1. We demand the unification of all Germans in the Greater Germany on the basis of the right of self-determination of peoples.

2. We demand equality of rights for the German people in respect to the other nations; abrogation of the peace treaties of Versailles and St. Germain.

3. We demand land and territory (colonies) for the sustenance of our people, and colonization for our surplus population.

4. Only a member of the race can be a citizen. A member of the race can only be one who is of German blood, without consideration of creed. Consequently no Jew can be a member of the race.

5. Whoever has no citizenship is to be able to live in Germany only as a guest, and must be under the authority of legislation for foreigners.

6. The right to determine matters concerning administration and law belongs only to the citizen. Therefore we demand that every public office, of any sort whatsoever, whether in the Reich, the county or municipality, be filled only by citizens. We combat the corrupting parliamentary economy, office-holding only according to party inclinations without consideration of character or abilities.

7. We demand that the state be charged first with providing the opportunity for a livelihood and way of life for the citizens. If it is impossible to sustain the total population of the State, then the members of foreign nations (non-citizens) are to be expelled from the Reich.

8. Any further immigration of non-citizens is to be prevented. We demand that all non-Germans, who have immigrated to Germany since the 2 August 1914, be forced immediately to leave the Reich.

9. All citizens must have equal rights and obligations.

10. The first obligation of every citizen must be to work both spiritually and physically. The activity of individuals is not to counteract the interests of the universality, but must have its result within the framework of the whole for the benefit of all.

Consequently we demand:

11. Abolition of unearned (work and labour) incomes. Breaking of rent-slavery.

12. In consideration of the monstrous sacrifice in property and blood that each war demands of the people, personal enrichment through a war must be designated as a crime against the people. Therefore we demand the total confiscation of all war profits.

13. We demand the nationalization of all (previous) associated industries (trusts).

14. We demand a division of profits of all heavy industries.

15. We demand an expansion on a large scale of old age welfare.

16. We demand the creation of a healthy middle class and its conservation, immediate communalization of the great warehouses and their being leased at low cost to small firms, the utmost consideration of all small firms in contracts with the State, county or municipality.

17. We demand a land reform suitable to our needs, provision of a law for the free expropriation of land for the purposes of public utility, abolition of taxes on land and prevention of all speculation in land.

18. We demand struggle without consideration against those whose activity is injurious to the general interest. Common national criminals, usurers, Schieber[2] and so forth are to be punished with death, without consideration of confession or race.

19. We demand substitution of a German common law in place of the Roman Law serving a materialistic world-order.

---

[2] a black marketeer or profiteer.

20. The state is to be responsible for a fundamental reconstruction of our whole national education program, to enable every capable and industrious German to obtain higher education and subsequently introduction into leading positions. The plans of instruction of all education institutions are to conform with the experiences of practical life. The comprehension of the concept of the State must be striven for by the school as early as the beginning of understanding. We demand the education at the expense of the State of outstanding intellectually gifted children of poor parents without consideration of position or profession.

21. The State is to care for the elevating national health by protecting the mother and child, by outlawing child-labor, by the encouragement of physical fitness, by means of the legal establishment of a gymnastic and sport obligation, by the utmost support of all organizations concerned with the physical instruction of the young.

22. We demand abolition of the mercenary troops and formation of a national army.

23. We demand legal opposition to known lies and their promulgation through the press. In order to enable the provision of a German press, we demand, that: a. All writers and employees of the newspapers appearing in the German language be members of the race: b. Non-German newspapers be required to have the express permission of the State to be published. They may not be printed in the German language: c. Non-Germans are forbidden by law any financial interest in German publications, or any influence on them, and as punishment for violations the closing of such a publication as well as the immediate expulsion from the Reich of the non-German concerned. Publications which are counter to the general good are to be forbidden. We demand legal prosecution of artistic and literary forms which exert a destructive influence on our national life, and the closure of organizations opposing the above made demands.

24. We demand freedom of religion for all religious denominations within the state so long as they do not endanger its existence or oppose the moral senses of the Germanic race. The Party as such advocates the standpoint of a positive Christianity without binding itself confessionally to any one denomination. It combats the Jewish-materialistic spirit within and around us, and is convinced that a lasting recovery of our nation can only succeed from within on the framework: common utility precedes individual utility.

25. For the execution of all of this we demand the formation of a strong central power in the Reich. Unlimited authority of the central parliament over the whole Reich and its organizations in general. The forming of state and profession chambers for the execution of the laws made by the Reich within the various states of the confederation. The leaders of the Party promise, if necessary by sacrificing their own lives, to support by the execution of the points set forth above without consideration.

from *Nazi Conspiracy and Aggression*, vol. 4. United States Government Printing Office, 1946

Adolf Hitler: Extracts from *Mein Kampf,* 1924

THE JEWS

The Jew of all times has lived in the states of other peoples, and there formed his own state, which, to be sure, habitually sailed under the disguise of 'religious community' as long as outward circumstances made a complete revelation of his nature seem inadvisable. But as soon as he felt strong enough to do without the protective cloak, he always dropped the veil and suddenly became what so many of the others previously did not want to believe and see: the Jew.

The Jew's life as a parasite in the body of other nations and states explains a characteristic which once caused Schopenhauer…to call him the 'great master in lying.' Existence impels the Jew to lie, and to lie perpetually, just as it compels the inhabitants of the northern countries to wear warm clothing.

His life within other peoples can only endure for any length of time if he succeeds in arousing the opinion that he is not a people but a 'religious community,' though of a special sort. And this is the first great lie….

The Jew has always been a people with definite racial characteristics and never a religion; only in order to get ahead he early sought for a means which could distract unpleasant attention from his person. And what would have been more expedient and at the same time more innocent than the 'embezzled' concept of a religious community? For there, too, everything is borrowed or rather stolen. Due to his own original special nature, the Jew cannot possess a religious institution, if for no other reason because he lacks idealism in any form, and hence belief in a hereafter is absolutely foreign to him. And a religion in the Aryan sense cannot be imagined which lacks the conviction of survival after death in some form….

The Jew also becomes liberal and begins to rave about the necessary progress of mankind.

Slowly he makes himself the spokesman of a new era.

Also, of course, he destroys more and more thoroughly the foundations of any economy that will really benefit the people. By way of stock shares he pushes his way into the circuit of national production which he turns into a purchasable or rather tradable object, thus robbing the enterprises of the foundations of a personal ownership. Between employer and employee there arises that inner estrangement which later leads to political class division.

Finally, the Jewish influence on economic affairs grows with terrifying speed through the stock exchange. He becomes the owner, or at least the controller, of the national labor force.

To strengthen his political position he tries to tear down the racial and civil barriers which for a time continue to restrain him at every step. To this end he fights with all the tenacity innate in him for religious tolerance….

While on the one hand he organizes capitalist methods of human exploitation to their ultimate consequence, [the Jew] approaches the very victims of his spirit and his activity and in a short time becomes the leader of their struggle against himself. 'Against himself' is only figuratively speaking; for the great master of lies understands as always how to make himself appear to be the pure one and to heap the blame on others. Since he has the gall to lead the masses, it never even enters their heads that this might be the most infamous betrayal of all times.

And yet it was.

Scarcely has the [proletariat] grown out of the general economic shift than the Jew, clearly and distinctly, realizes that it can open the way for his own further advancement. First, he used the bourgeoisie as a battering-ram against the feudal world, then the worker against the bourgeois world. If formerly he knew how to swindle his way to civil rights in the shadow of the bourgeoisie, now he hopes to find the road to his own domination in the worker's struggle for existence….

With satanic joy in his face, the black-haired Jewish youth lurks in wait for the unsuspecting girl whom he defiles with his blood, thus stealing her from her people. With every means he tries to destroy the racial foundations of the people he has set out to subjugate. Just as he himself systematically ruins women and girls, he does not shrink back from pulling down the blood barriers for others, even on a large scale. It was and it is Jews who bring the Negroes into the Rhineland, always with the same secret thought and clear aim of ruining the hated white race by the necessarily resulting bastardization, throwing it down from its cultural and political height, and himself rising to be its master....

The Jewish train of thought in all this is clear. The Bolshevization of Germany—that is, the extermination of the national folkish...intelligentsia to make possible the sweating of the German working class under the yoke of Jewish world finance—is conceived only as a preliminary to the further extension of this Jewish tendency of world conquest. As often in history, Germany is the great pivot in the mighty struggle. If our people and our state become the victim of these blood-thirsty and avaricious Jewish tyrants of nations, the whole earth will sink into the snares of this octopus; if Germany frees herself from this embrace, this greatest of dangers to nations may be regarded as broken for the whole world....

THE STATE

All these views have their deepest root in the knowledge that the forces which create culture and values are based essentially on racial elements and that the state must, therefore, in the light of reason, regard its highest task as the preservation and intensification of the race, this fundamental condition of all human cultural development....

It is, therefore, the first obligation of a new movement, standing on the ground of a folkish world view, to make sure that its conception of the nature and purpose of the state attains a uniform and clear character.

Thus the basic realization is: *that the state represents no end, but a means. It is, to be sure, the premise for the formation of a higher human culture, but not its cause, which lies exclusively in the existence of a race capable of culture.* Hundreds of exemplary states might exist on earth, but if the Aryan culture-bearer died out, there would be no culture corresponding to the spiritual level of the highest peoples of today. We can go even farther and say that the fact of human state formation would not in the least exclude the possibility of the destruction of the human race, provided that superior intellectual ability and elasticity would be lost due to the absence of their racial bearers.

This glorious creative ability was given only to the Aryan, whether he bears it dormant within himself or gives it to awakening life, depending whether favorable circumstances permit this or an inhospitable Nature prevents it.

From this the following realization results:

The state is a means to an end. Its end lies in the preservation and advancement of a community of physically and psychically homogeneous creatures. This preservation itself comprises first of all existence as a race and thereby permits the free development of all the forces dormant in this race. Of them a part will always primarily serve the preservation of physical life, and only the remaining part the promotion of a further spiritual development. Actually the one always creates the precondition for the other.

States which do not serve this purpose are misbegotten, monstrosities in fact. The fact of their existence changes this no more than the success of a gang of bandits can justify robbery...

Thus, the highest purpose of a folkish state is concern for the preservation of those original racial elements which bestow culture and create the beauty and dignity of a higher mankind. We, as Aryans, can conceive of the state only as the living organism of a nationality which not only assures the preservation of this nationality, but by the development of its spiritual and ideal abilities leads it to the highest freedom....

The folkish state must make up for what everyone else today has neglected in this field. It must set race in the center of all life. It must take care to keep it pure. It must declare the child to be the most precious treasure of the people. It must see to it that only the healthy beget children; that there is only one disgrace: despite one's own sickness and deficiencies, to bring children into the world, and one highest honor: to renounce doing so. And conversely it must be considered reprehensible: to withhold healthy children from the nation. Here the state must act as the guardian of a millennial future in the face of which the wishes and the selfishness of the individual must appear as nothing and submit. It must put the most modern medical means in the service of this knowledge. It must declare unfit for propagation all who are in any way visibly sick or who have inherited a disease and can therefore pass it on, and put this into actual practice. Conversely, it must take care that the fertility of the healthy woman is not limited by the financial irresponsibility of a state regime which turns the blessing of children into a curse for the parents. It must put an end to that lazy, nay criminal, indifference with which the social premises for a fecund family are treated today, and must instead feel itself to be the highest guardian of this most precious blessing of a people. Its concern belongs more to the child than to the adult....

excerpts from *Mein Kampf* by Adolf Hitler, translated by Ralph Mannheim. Copyright © 1943, renewed 1971 by Houghton Mifflin Co. Reprinted by permission of Houghton Mifflin Co. All rights reserved.

Questions:
1. What are some of the principles outlined in the Nazi Party Program?
2. What role did race and anti-Semitism play in Hitler's *Mein Kampf?* What function should the state serve, according to Hitler?

Elections to the German Reichstag, 1924-1932

There is little question but that the Great Depression, which began in late 1929, was the single most important factor in the Nazi rise to power. From a relatively small and insignificant party with no more than twelve members in the German Reichstag, the Nazi share of the vote went from 810,000 in 1928 to 6,407,000 in 1930. As the election chart reprinted below makes clear, the reason for this dramatic reversal in the Nazi party's political fortunes can be attributed in no small way to the fact that an ever increasing number of Germans found themselves without employment from 1930 to 1933. What these numbers do not reveal, however, is what this actually meant for the millions of Germans who found themselves unemployed and homeless.

Elections to the German Reichstag, 1924-1932					
	May 4, 1924	December 7, 1924	May 20, 1928	September 14, 1930	July 31, 1932	November 6, 1932
Number of eligible voters (in millions)	38.4	39.0	41.2	43.0	44.2	44.2
Votes Cast (in millions)	29.7	30.7	31.2	35.2	37.2	35.7
National Socialist German Workers Party	1,918,000 6.6%	908,000 3%	810,000 2.6%	6,407,000 18.3%	13,779,000 37.3%	11,737,000 33.1%
German Nationalist People's Party (Conservative)	5,696,000 19.5%	6,209,000 20.5%	4,382,000 14.2%	2.458,000 7%	2,187,000 5.9%	3,131,000 8.8%
Center Party (Catholic)	3,914,000 13.4%	4.121,000 13.6%	3.712,000 12.1%	4.127,000 11.8%	4,589,000 12.4%	4,230,000 11.9%
Democratic Party (The German State Party)	1,655,000 5.7%	1,921,000 6.3%	1,506,000 4.9%	1,322,000 3.8%	373,000 1%	339,000 1%
Social Democratic Party	6,009,000 20.5%	7,886,000 26%	9,153,000 29.8%	8,576,000 24.5%	7,960,000 21.6%	7,251,000 20.4%
Communist Party	3,693,000 12.6%	2,712,000 9%	3,265,000 10.6%	4,590,000 13.1%	5,370,000 14.3%	5,980,000 16.9%

Unemployment in Germany, 1924-1932					
	1924	1928	1930	July 31, 1932	October 31, 1932	
	978,000	1,368,000	3,076,000	5,392,000	5,109,000	

from *The Nazi Years: A Documentary*, edited by Joachim Remak. Englewood Cliffs, N.J.: Prentice-Hall, 1969

Raymond H. Geist, "The Nazi Conspiracy," 1945

Despite their electoral breakthrough during the early thirties, the Nazis never did win a popular majority in any of the many elections that they contested during this time. Nevertheless, through a series of behind-the-scenes political deals and a campaign of terror and intimidation they managed to win power and establish Adolf Hitler as undisputed Führer of the German Reich in March 1933. Over the next six years, the Nazis and their leader established a ruthless authoritarian regime that was dedicated to the establishment of German hegemony in Europe. In the following testimony of Raymond H. Geist, the American Consul in Berlin from 1933-1939, we are given a rather comprehensive view of what life in Hitler's thousand year Reich was like during the years immediately preceding the outbreak of World War II.

RAYMOND H. GEIST, BEING FIRST DULY SWORN, DEPOSES AND SAYS:

I came to Berlin in December, 1929, as Consul and continued in that capacity, exercising my official functions until the end of 1939. In 1938 I was appointed First Secretary of the Embassy and continued in that office discharging at the same time my duties as consul. During the entire period of ten years my work was of such character that I frequently came into contact with many officials of the German Government. After the Nazis came to power in 1933, these contacts increased owing to the much more frequent occasions on which it was necessary to intervene with German officials in order to protect the rights of American citizens and their properties. During this period I not only had many official contacts but also friends and acquaintances, both in Berlin and elsewhere in Germany. My work permitted and occasionally required travel in Germany....

I also saw the preparations being made for building up the new army. I visited the camps of the compulsory labor service, the *Arbeitsdienst*, which was well under way by the end of 1933, with camps established all over Germany. Though this was ostensibly a labor service, it was essentially military in character, as is well known. I saw the men working on reclamation projects and was informed that they worked two hours in the morning and two hours in the afternoon, the balance of the time being spent in military tactics and in instruction in Nazi ideology. So that when conscription went into effect in 1935 through the medium of these camps, it was possible for the Germans to put a trained army of at least 3,500,000 men, which formed the nucleus of the future army of aggression.

Particularly through the years 1933 and 1934 the hordes of storm troopers SA were much in evidence practicing military exercises. They were being converted into a military organization. I frequently encountered the storm troopers deployed in fields and in forests engaged in military technical exercises. This was all the part of a general plan to prepare Germany's manpower for war.

I witnessed, too, scores of times, the training of the Hitler Youth, which included boys from 14 to 17, who dressed in their uniforms, were likewise generally in evidence wherever I chose to travel. I frequently saw them in the woods near Berlin, deployed in ravines, in fields, woods and hillsides staging mock attacks, employing the technique of actual maneuvers. Frequently they were under the direction of uniformed leaders and at times under officers of the Reichswehr.[3] This type of training of the youth extended everywhere in Germany. Frequently my route of travel had to be changed in order not to find myself in the midst of some maneuvers which

---

[3] Army.

required the use of roads or paths along which I was riding. It was not considered wise to get too close to these operations, particularly if they were on an extensive scale.

The *Deutsche Jungvolk* (boys from the ages of 6 to 14) was also the vehicle for military training. They were also in evidence throughout the country. I frequently met them marching. I saw them engaged in military exercises in the school yards during the school recesses, particularly throwing hand grenades usually under expert adult leadership. Often I have seen these children in large numbers engaged in what were obviously military maneuvers, and under the direction of adult uniformed officers.

I had occasion, at times, to witness the organizations which were created for the girls that were part of the Hitler Youth and were also incorporated in the so-called *Arbeitsdienst*, usually located somewhere near the camps for men. The resultant illegitimate children were a definite planned result of the program; they were part of the manpower and the army for the next generation. The shame and the grief of parents over this program fostered and urged by the Nazis, although it existed, was seldom openly expressed on account of dangers to which the parents might expose themselves....

By the middle of 1934 it had become obvious that the rearmament program, though in its beginning, was being planned on a vast scale so that it could not possible be considered as defensive armament but only as a weapon for offensive war. This was, however, not a conclusion of my own; but it was openly stated as such to me. Graffenstein told me in 1934, during the conversations to which I have already referred, that the purpose of the program was an aggressive war. He told me that he had been so informed by General Goettke in particular. This statement was borne out by other persons who were in the know in Germany at that time. I confirmed his statements by my own conversations with the generals who gathered in his house. They intimated to me, not only that Germany was embarked upon an inevitable program toward war but even gave me indications of the general plan, namely, the drive to the East and the attack upon Russia, after Poland, Czechoslovakia, and Austria had been eliminated. This was a early as 1934, and I had many similar conversations along the same line at Graffenstein's house during the following years.

Similar information was constantly being confirmed from other sources at later dates. For instance, in December 1938, I had a conversation with General Franz Halder, who was then Chief of Staff, at the house of Dr. Etscheit, a prominent Berlin lawyer. Halder stated to me: "You must take into account the National Socialist program in the East. If you, the Western powers, oppose our program in the East, we shall have to go to war with you." During this conversation he made it clear to me that the program of the Nazis for expansion in the East was unalterably fixed and decided upon. It included the attack on Poland, the annexation of Austria, territorial expansion in Yugoslavia, Czechoslovakia, Rumania, and Russia, particularly in the Ukraine. The latter provinces would have to be German. When I replied to Halder that I was positive the Western powers would never tolerate any such aggressive program and that inevitably it would not only mean war with England and France but with the United States as well Halder replied: "That is a pity."...

I also had a good deal of personal experience with and first-hand knowledge of the internal policies from 1935 to 1939...

For a period I dealt directly with Herr Heinrich Himmler, then subsequently with Herr Reinhard Heydrich and often with Dr. Werner Best....

As I have stated, my frequent contacts with this entire Gestapo organization began with the first wave of terrorist acts in the week of March 6-13, 1933. That wave was accompanied by universal mob violence. Since 1925, one of the cries of the Nazi party had been "Jude Verrecke" (Death to the Jews) and when the Nazi party won the elections in March, 1933, on the morning of the sixth, the accumulated passion blew off in wholesale attacks on the Communists, Jews, and those who were suspected of being either. Mobs of S.A. men roamed the streets, beating up, looting, and even killing persons....

For the Germans who were taken into custody by the Gestapo, chiefly Communists at that time, there was, from my experience and from the information that I had from all sources, a regular pattern of brutality and terror. Upon arrest, the victims would be systematically subjected to indignities and brutalities such as beatings, kicking, pushing downstairs, deprivation of food and all comforts, and threats of much worse. After the victims had been imprisoned—usually in cellars, since both the headquarters at No. 8 Albrechtstrasse and the S.A. meeting places usually had them—they would be beaten with various degrees of severity. If the Gestapo believed that the victim—particularly Communist leaders—had information as to other alleged accomplices they would give systematic beatings, usually when stripped and tied on a table. This would go on often for many days until they had extracted the information they wanted or killed the victim.

Based on all of the reports which I had from many sources, my judgment is that the victims were numbered in the hundreds of thousands all over Germany. Many of them were ultimately released. I can state with certainty that the contemporaneous accounts in foreign newspapers, such as the London Times and the American newspapers which I have seen, are accurate.

The second wave of terror was not so systematic nor so concentrated as to point of time. It was directed chiefly against the Jews, and was chiefly the result of the ruthless and occasionally violent enforcement of numerous decrees and orders, such as the Nuremberg Decrees. After the initial out-break in March, 1933, and all through that year and the next, the Jews still in Germany had, in many cases, come to believe that things might become a little better and that they could live in some sort of peaceable relationship with the Nazis, even though they were reduced to the status of second or third class citizens. In 1935, however, the pressure on them began to increase and they began to be excluded completely from certain civil activities. The terrorism was continued all the time to some degree; but the enforcement of the new decrees in 1935 was characterized by such brutality and ruthlessness that it warrants special attention. Inadvertent violators were dealt with, for example, with great severity.

The 1938 wave of terror was a very pronounced and definite one. Again the object was the Jews, particularly the wealthy ones. The ostensible occasion was the murder of the German diplo-mat, von Rieth, by a French Jew, but the violence was in no sense spontaneous. Dr. Best, the Administrative Officer of the Gestapo, told me that the terror had been decided upon and ordered by Hitler himself, and that he, Dr. Best, could, therefore, do nothing about it. Actually that statement corroborated what everyone knew. Innumerable persons with whom I talked and who witnessed the violence told me that at all of the synagogues, which had been set on fire by the Nazis, the fire departments were always present, but never acted except to prevent the fires from spreading to neighboring non-Jewish properties. Nor did the police interfere with any of these acts of vandalism and incendiarism....

On another occasion I was given considerable information by a high official of the Gestapo as to the policy of the Nazis with respect to the Jews. I had had a considerable contact with the head of the Jewish section of the Gestapo, known as the "Judische Abteilung der Gestapo," one Dr. Hassel-bacher, in connection with making arrangements for official representatives of the American Joint Distribution Committee to visit certain Jewish centers throughout Germany, for which visits, of course, the permission of the Gestapo was necessary. These negotiations brought me frequently in touch with Dr. Hasselbacher, whom I came to know very well. He told me that Germany will be made "Judenrein," that is clean of Jews. He said that all the Jews who failed to leave Germany would be exterminated. That statement was made in 1938 before the extermination camps were established, but the statement of Hasselbacher clearly indicated the eventual emergence of exter-mination camps in accordance with the general Nazi plan; for certainly the Jews were unable to leave Germany, even if they had been permitted to do so by the Nazis, as no world-wide arrangement had been made to receive them in other countries....

from *Nazi Conspiracy and Aggression*, vol. 4. Washington: United States
Government Printing Office, 1946.

Questions:
1. What observations did Geist make of Nazi Germany? In what ways was Germany violating the Treaty of Versailles?
2. What internal developments did Geist witness in Germany? That is, what activities were such groups as the SA and the Gestapo engaged in during the 1930s? Who were the targets of these actions?

Chapter 28: World War II and the Holocaust, 1939-1945

Unit 57: "The Blood-Dimmed Tide is Loosed": World War II

Many historians see the entire period stretching from 1914 to 1945 as a single all-encompassing period of prolonged "crisis," a kind of latter day "Thirty Years' War." Certainly, as we have already noted, the treaties that ended World War I in many respects did little more than set the stage for a continuation of that conflict at a later date. Nevertheless, few people in the interwar years really believed that Europeans would be so foolish as to allow themselves to be dragged into yet another round of bloodletting. Unfortunately, this would prove to be an illusion, and on September 1, 1939, the unprovoked German Invasion of Poland triggered what would come to be known as the Second World War.

No less than the First World War, the second one had catastrophic consequences for Europe and the world. Russian military deaths from this conflict were estimated at over 7 million, German at 3.5 million, Chinese at 2.2 million, Japanese at 1.3 million; British and Commonwealth losses were in the range of 350,000, American at 300,000, and France lost about 200,000 soldiers. Horrifying as these dry military statistics are, however, they cannot even begin to convey the suffering that was endured by Europe's civilian populations who were forced to endure aerial bombings, famines, epidemics, deportations, and mass-extermination programs. Some estimate that as many as 35 to 40 million men, women, and children lost their lives either directly or indirectly from the military operations and state terrorism that were unleashed by the Second World War. As Yeats would doubtless have agreed, "the blood-dimmed tide" had indeed been loosed.

The Atlantic Charter, August 14, 1941

The overwhelming consensus in America today is that if there was a "righteous" war that the United States was completely justified in waging, it was most certainly World War II. Of course, this was not the popular attitude among Americans at the beginning of 1941. Indeed, on the eve of the bombing of pearl Harbor, some 80% of the American people were solidly against U.S. Involvement in either the European or Asian conflicts.

No one was more conscious of and troubled by this isolationist sentiment than the American president of that time, Franklin D. Roosevelt. Aware of the fact that an Axis victory would leave the United States an isolated democracy vulnerable to attack, Roosevelt did everything in his power to enlarge and modernize America's armed forces and to assist Great Britain in its lone battle against the Nazi Reich. Indeed, the Atlantic Charter, which is reprinted below, was a joint declaration by Roosevelt and the British Prime Minister, Winston Churchill, in which the two men outlined the common aims and principles of the American and British democracies vis-a-vis the "Nazi tyranny." Noble as these shared aims were, however, it ultimately took a surprise attack by the Japanese Empire on the United States fleet at Pearl Harbor to bring a reluctant America into World War II. In a dramatic meeting off Newfoundland, President Roosevelt and Winston Churchill formulated this statement of common war aims.

The President of the United States of America and the Prime Minister, Mr. Churchill, representing His Majesty's Government in the United Kingdom, being met together, deem it right to make known certain common principles in the national policies of their respective countries on which they base their hopes for a better future for the world.

First, their countries seek no aggrandizement, territorial or other;

Second, they desire to see no territorial changes that do not accord with the freely expressed wishes of the peoples concerned;

Third, they respect the right of all peoples to choose the form of government under which they will live; and they wish to see sovereign rights and self government restored to those who have been forcibly deprived of them;

Fourth, they will endeavor, with due respect for their existing obligations, to further the enjoyment by all States, great or small, victor or vanquished, of access, on equal terms, to the trade and to the raw materials of the world which are needed for their economic prosperity;

Fifth, they desire to bring about the fullest collaboration between all nations in the economic field with the object of securing, for all, improved labor standards, economic advancement and social security;

Sixth, after the final destruction of the Nazi tyranny, they hope to see established a peace which will afford to all nations the means of dwelling in safety within their own boundaries, and which will afford assurance that all the men in all the lands may live out their lives in freedom from fear and want'

Seventh, such a peace should enable all men to traverse the high seas and oceans without hindrance;

Eighth, they believe that all of the nations of the world, for realistic as well as spiritual reasons must come to the abandonment of the use of force. Since no future peace can be maintained if land, sea or air armaments continue to be employed by nations which threaten, or may threaten, aggression outside of their frontiers, they believe, pending the establishment of a wider and permanent system of general security, that the disarmament of such nations is essential. They will likewise aid and encourage all other practicable measures which will lighten for peace-loving peoples the crushing burden of armaments.

Franklin D. Roosevelt
Winston S. Churchill
White House News Release, August 14, 1941

from *Documents of American History*. Edited by Henry Steele Commager. New York:
Appleton-Century-Crofts,, 1948.

Question:
What were the principles set forth in the Atlantic Charter? What is the relevant historical context that might explain this document?

Franklin D. Roosevelt: Request for Declaration of War, December 7, 1941

The day after the attack on Pearl Harbor, President Roosevelt appeared before Congress and asked for a declaration of war against Japan. Congress responded that same afternoon, without a dissenting vote.

Yesterday, December 7, 1941—a date which will live in infamy—the United States of America was suddenly and deliberately attacked by naval and air forces of the Empire of Japan.

The United States was at peace with that nation and, at the solicitation of Japan, was still in conversation with its Government and its Emperor looking toward the maintenance of peace in the Pacific. Indeed, one hour after Japanese air squadrons had commenced bombing in Oahu, the Japanese Ambassador to the United States and his colleague delivered to the Secretary of State a formal reply to a recent American message. While this reply stated that it seemed useless to continue the existing diplomatic negotiations, it contained no threat or hint of war or armed attack.

It will be recorded that the distance of Hawaii from Japan makes it obvious that the attack was deliberately planned many days or even weeks ago. During the intervening time the Japanese Government has deliberately sought to deceive the United States by false statements and expressions of hope for continued peace.

The attack yesterday on the Hawaiian Islands has caused severe damage to American naval and military forces. Very many American lives have been lost. In addition American ships have been reported torpedoed on the high seas between San Francisco and Honolulu.

Yesterday the Japanese Government also launched an attack against Malaya. Last night Japanese forces attacked Hong Kong. Last night Japanese forces attacked Guam. Last night Japanese forces attacked the Philippine Islands. Last night the Japanese attacked Wake Island. This morning the Japanese attacked Midway Island.

Japan has, therefore, undertaken a surprise offensive extending throughout the Pacific area. The facts of yesterday speak for themselves. The people of the United States have already formed their opinions and well understand the implications to the very life and safety of our nation.

As Commander-in-Chief of the Army and Navy, I have directed that all measures be taken for our defense.

Always will we remember the character of the onslaught against us.

No matter how long it may take us to overcome this premeditated invasion, the American people in their righteous might will win through to absolute victory.

I believe I interpret the will of the Congress and of the people when I assert that we will not only defend ourselves to the uttermost but will make very certain that this form of treachery shall never endanger us again.

Hostilities exist. There is no blinking at the fact that our people, our territory and our interests are in grave danger.

With confidence in our armed forces—with the unbounded determination of our people— we will gain the inevitable triumph—so help us God.

I ask that the Congress declare that since the unprovoked and dastardly attack by Japan on Sunday, December seventh, a state of war has existed between the United States and the Japanese Empire.

White House News Release, December 8, 1941.

from *Documents of American History*. Edited by Henry Steele Commager. New York: Appleton-Century-Crofts,, 1948.

Question:
How did President Roosevelt describe the bombings by Japan in December 1941?

U.S. Strategic Bombing Survey: On the Effects of Bombing, 1945 and 1948

Perhaps the most tragic aspect of World War II was the toll that it took on the civilian populations of the countries involved in the conflict. Indeed, the Second World War was the first human conflict in which civilian centers were subjected to sustained and heavy aerial bombardments. Axis and Allied air raids leveled millions of buildings and were responsible for countless deaths. Of course, as the following document regarding the atomic bombing of Hiroshima and Nagasaki makes clear, these "conventional" bombing raids were nothing in comparison to the destruction that could be unleashed on a civilian population by a nuclear device.

BOMBING OF GERMAN CITIES

SEPTEMBER 30, 1945

...For residential areas,...fire was the chief cause of the damage that resulted from bombing. In many incidents ignition followed the use of high-explosive bombs, as, for example, when highly combustible materials were released and then ignited by the hot gases of the explosion, or when electrical equipment was short-circuited, or when stoves and heaters were overturned. In addition, in certain high-temperature, high-pressure processes, the hot liquids and gases ignited spontaneously when released. But the principal weapon for setting fires was the incendiary bomb. This weapon was most effective in causing destruction in city residence areas. When used in industrial attacks the effectiveness varied from good, to fair, to poor.

Many German cities presented partial areas of vast devastation. Perhaps the outstanding example was Hamburg, where a series of attacks in July and August of 1943 destroyed 55 to 60 per cent of the city, did damage in an area of 30 square miles, completely burned out 12.5 square miles, wiped out 300,000 dwelling units, and made 750,000 people homeless. German estimates range from 60,000 to 100,000 persons killed, many of them in shelters where they were reached by carbon-monoxide poisoning. The attacks used both high-explosive and incendiary bombs as it was thought by the Air Forces and later confirmed that the former created road blocks, broke water mains, disrupted communications, opened buildings, broke windows, and displaced roofing. Most important, they kept the fire fighters in shelters until the incendiaries became effective. But, of the total destruction, 75 to 80 per cent was due to fires, particularly to those in which the so-called fire storm phenomenon was observed.

Fire-storms occurred in Hamburg, Kassel, Darmstadt, and Dresden....

EFFECT OF ATOMIC BOMBS ON HIROSHIMA AND NAGASAKI

...The morning of 6 August 1945 began bright and clear. At about 0700 there was an air-raid alarm and a few planes appeared over the city. Many people within the city went to prepared air-raid shelters, but since alarms were heard almost every day the general population did not seem to have been greatly concerned. About 0800 an all-clear was sounded after the planes had disappeared. At this hour of the morning many people were preparing breakfast. This fact is probably important since there were fires in charcoal braziers in many of the homes at this time. Some of the laboring class were at work but most of the downtown business people had not gone to work. Consequently, a large percentage of the population was in their homes and relatively few were in the more strongly constructed business buildings.

After the all-clear sounded, persons began emerging from air-raid shelters and within the next few minutes the city began to resume its usual mode of life for that time of day. It is related by some survivors that they had watched planes fly over the city. At about 0815 there was a blinding flash. Some described it as brighter than the sun, others likened it to a magnesium flash. Following the flash there was a blast of heat and wind. The large majority of people within 3,000 feet of ground zero were killed immediately. Within a radius of about 7,000 feet almost every Japanese house collapsed. Beyond this range and up to 15,000-20,000 feet many of them collapsed and others received serious structural damage. Persons in the open were burned on exposed surfaces, and within 3,000-5,000 feet many were burned to death while others received severe burns through their clothes. In many instances clothing burst into spontaneous flame and had to be beaten out. Thousands of people were pinned beneath collapsed buildings or injured by flying debris. Flying glass particularly produced many non-lethal injuries and the distances at which they occurred are discussed in the following chapter, but the foregoing presentation was necessary for one to appreciate the state of the population immediately after the bomb exploded.

Shortly after the blast fires began to spring up over the city. Those who were able made a mass exodus from the city into the outlying hills. There was no organized activity. The people appeared stunned by the catastrophe and rushed about as jungle animals suddenly released from a cage. Some few apparently attempted to help others from the wreckage, particularly members of their family or friends. Others assisted those who were unable to walk alone. However, many of the injured were left trapped beneath collapsed buildings as people fled by them in the streets. Pandemonium reigned as the uninjured and slightly injured fled the city in fearful panic. Teams which had been previously organized to render first aid failed to form and function. Those closer to ground zero were largely demobilized due to injuries and death. However, there were physically intact teams on the outskirts of the city which did not function. Panic drove these people from the city just as it did the injured who could walk or be helped along. Much of the city's firefighting equipment was damaged beyond use so that soon the conflagrations were beyond control.

In Nagasaki a similar but slightly less catastrophic picture occurred. The blast was not centered over the main business section of the city but was up the valley about 2 miles. There were large industrial plants, hospitals, the medical school and partially built-up residential areas near the ground zero. The terrain in this area was uneven with large hills which shielded certain areas. Due to the shielding factor and the distance of the explosion from the center of the city, Nagasaki was less completely destroyed than Hiroshima and the panic was apparently less....

An amazing feature of the Atomic bombings to one going into the areas later was the poor recuperative powers of the population towards the restoration of all types of facilities. Though this was probably less so in the medical field than in others it was still alarmingly apparent. The panic of the people immediately after the bombing was so great that Hiroshima was literally deserted. It was apparently less true of Nagasaki and this was probably due to the fact that the city was less completely destroyed, but the same apathy was there. The colossal effects of the bombs and the surrender following shortly thereafter seemed to have completely stunned the people. The effects of the typhoons of September and early October may have contributed to this psychological reaction.

Since the most outstanding feature of the atomic bombs was the high rate of human casualties, it was natural that this was the greatest problem in the areas following the bombing. But even in this regard the progress was astoundingly slow and haphazard. Other evidences of restoration were almost completely absent. For instance, at the time the Medical Division visited

Hiroshima, 3 months after the bombing, the first street car was beginning operation, people wandered aimlessly about the ruins, and only a few shacks had been built as evidence of reoccupation of the city. No system for collection of night soil or garbage had been instituted. Leaking water pipes were seen all over the city with no evidence of any attention. It was reported that following the bombing several days were required for disposal of the dead and they were simply piled into heaps and burned without attempts at identification or enumeration. Street cars were burned as a method of cremating the bodies within. All in all, there appeared to be no organization and no initiative.

The care of the wounded immediately after the bombing was essentially nil in Hiroshima. Beyond the sphere of family ties there seemed to be little concern for their fellow man. It is true that essentially all of the medical supplies were destroyed by the bombing and that there were no hospitals and little with which to work. For the first 3 days there was no organized medical care. At the end of this time the Prefectural Health Department was successful in getting a portion of the surviving physicians together and to begin ministering to the wounded who remained in the city. Up until this time all nursing and medical care had been on an individual basis. The more seriously injured were placed in the few remaining public buildings on the outskirts of the city. Many of them died but many seriously burned cases remained. Small stocks of medical supplies which had been stored in caves outside the city were brought out but were soon exhausted. With all medical supplies gone and practically none being brought in, the treatment of the injured seems to have consisted largely of offering a place of refuge. There is no doubt that many died who might have been saved by modern, competent medical care....

The effects of the atomic bombing of Nagasaki were very similar to those in Hiroshima. Even though it followed the bombing of Hiroshima by 3 days, wartime secrecy, general confusion and the short lapse of time did not allow the population of Nagasaki any particular advantage from the previous experience. The psychological reaction of the people was essentially the same and the chaos in the city seems to have been almost as great. A very important difference between the two cities was that Nagasaki was not so completely destroyed. Further, the bomb blast was centered over a more industrial area and the character of the buildings resulted in less extensive fires. But from the medical standpoint the bombing was particularly catastrophic because the bulk of the city's hospital facilities were located within a radius of 3,000 feet of the center of the explosion. The destruction of the University Hospital and the Medical College was so great that the buildings left standing could not be reoccupied even for emergency medical care. Other hospitals and clinics, including the Tuberculosis Sanatorium, had burned to a heap of ashes. The only remaining facilities were small, private clinics and hospitals and many of them were seriously damaged. Essentially no organized medical care was carried out for several days after the bombing. The Shinkosen Hospital was established in an old school building for the care of bomb victims, but it was woefully inadequate. At one time it harbored over 500 victims. Fortunately, there was a large medical depot at Omura, 20 miles away. Such large stocks of supplies were on hand here that Nagasaki did not suffer in this respect as did Hiroshima. Another school building was converted into an infectious disease hospital.

At the time the Allied Military Government entered Nagasaki, about 1 October, the population was found to be apathetic and profoundly lethargic. Even at this time the collection of garbage and night soil had not been re-established, restoration of other public utilities was lacking, and the hospital facilities were inadequate. Through the initiative of the Military Government, a system of reporting infectious diseases was instituted, the collection of garbage and night soil was re-established, and attempts were made to increase the supply of safe water. A survey of the remaining hospitals and clinics at this time by Captain Horne of American Military Government revealed such obvious inadequacies that the survey was not even completed....

The devastating effects of the atomic bombs upon medical facilities can be appreciated in the light of the foregoing presentation. Not only were the existing facilities almost completely destroyed but there was extreme apathy toward the restoration of hospitals and the care of the injured.

The United States Strategic Bombing Survey, Over-All Report. Washington, 1945.

Question:
What were the effects of U.S. bombing of German and Japanese cities? What do you learn about the social consequences of war for civilian populations?

Unit 58: "Why Did the Heavens Not Darken?" The Holocaust

The most horrific aspect of World War II was the effort by the Nazi regime and its allies to murder every single Jewish man, woman, and child under their control. Indeed, the Nazi-engineered slaughter of some 6 million Jews, or two-thirds of the estimated Jewish population of Europe as a whole, was so unprecedented that it was necessary after the war to coin the germ *genocide* (from the Greek *genos*, meaning "race," "nation," or "tribe," and the Latin *cide*, meaning "killing") to describe the deliberate and systematic attempt to destroy a whole group of people simply because of their racial, religious, or ethnic identity. Moreover, the fact that this genocide was carried out by one of the world's most advanced nations in the heart of what was believed to be a civilized and enlightened Europe, called into question a whole range of western assumptions regarding human rationality, progress, and the possibility that peoples of different cultures and persuasions might be able to coexist peacefully with one another.

Given the enormity of this crime, and the troubling questions that it has raised for western society, it is critical that we attempt to arrive at some understanding of what Karl Schleunes has termed the "twisted path to Auschwitz." In the following testimonies, speeches, memoirs, and reports, we will attempt to trace the various ways in which Jews, and other victims of the Nazis, were identified, demonized, despoiled, concentrated in ghettos or camps, and then systematically murdered by gunfire, gas, and forced labor. Only by coming to an understanding of how the Nazis were able to murder 6 million Jewish innocents, as well as an estimated 9 to 10 million non-Jews, e.g. Poles, Sinti/Roma Gypsies, Soviet POWs, German homosexuals, and Jehovah's Witnesses, can we hope to insure the prevention and suppression of any future attempts at genocide.

The Nuremberg Laws, 1935

As Joseph Goebbels remarks in the article reprinted below make clear, Hitler and his Nazis regarded the Jews as Germany's principal enemy and they intended their Reich to be *Judenrein* or "Jew-free." Nor were these pronouncements an empty exercise in Jew-baiting for the benefit of the more rabid antisemites in the Nazi Party. From 1933 to 1935, Germany's Jews found themselves officially and legally driven out of their positions in state and national government, expelled from the nation's universities, and, under the terms of the so-called Nuremberg Laws, transformed into a racially distinct group of second-class citizens. Furthermore, as Hitler moved his country closer to war, the situation for German Jews continued to deteriorate. Between 1938 and 1939, the one-third of the German Jewish population that had not fled Germany found their property confiscated, their movements rigorously regulated, and their existence completely separated from that of their fellow non-Jewish Germans. The first steps to Auschwitz had been taken.

THE REICH CITIZENSHIP LAW OF 15 SEPTEMBER 1935

The Reichstag has adopted unanimously, the following law, which is herewith promulgated.

Article 1

1. A subject of the State is a person, who belongs to the protective union of the German Reich, and who, therefore, has particular obligations towards the Reich.

2. The status of the subject is acquired in accordance with the provisions of the Reich- and State law of Citizenship.

Article 2

1. A citizen of the Reich is only that subject, who is of German or kindred blood and who, through his conduct, shows that he is both desirous and fit to serve faithfully the German people and Reich.

2. The right to citizenship is acquired by the granting of Reich citizenship papers.

3. Only the citizen of the Reich enjoys full political rights in accordance with the provision of the laws.

Article 3

The Reich minister of the Interior in conjunction with the Deputy of the Fuehrer will issue the necessary legal and administrative decrees for the carrying out and supplementing of this law.

FIRST REGULATION TO THE REICHS CITIZENSHIP LAW OF 14 NOVEMBER 1935

On the basis of Article 3, Reichs Citizenship Law, of 15 September 1935 the following is ordered:

Article 1

1. Until further issue of regulations regarding citizenship papers, all subjects of German or kindred blood, who possessed the right to vote in the Reichstag elections, at the time the Citizenship Law came into effect, shall, for the time being, possess the rights of Reich citizens. The same shall be true of those whom the Reich Minister of the Interior, in conjunction with the Deputy of the Fuehrer, has given the preliminary citizenship.

2. The Reich Minister of the Interior, in conjunction with the Deputy of the Fuehrer, can withdraw the preliminary citizenship.

Article 2

1. The regulations in Article 1 are also valid for Reichs subjects of mixed, Jewish blood.

2. An individual of mixed Jewish blood, is one who descended from one or two grandparents who were racially full Jews, insofar as he does not count as a Jew according to Article 5, paragraph 2. One grandparent shall be considered as full-blooded if he or she belonged to the Jewish religious community.

Article 3

Only the Reich citizen, as bearer of full political rights, exercises the right to vote in political affairs, and can hold a public office. The Reich Minister of the Interior, or any agency empowered by him, can make exceptions during the transition period, with regard to occupying public offices. The affairs of religious organizations will not be touched upon.

Article 4

1.   A Jew cannot be a citizen of the Reich. He has no right to vote in political affairs, he cannot occupy a public office.

2.   Jewish officials will retire as of 31 December 1935. If these officials served at the front in the World War, either for Germany or her allies, they will receive in full, until they reach the age limit, the pension to which they were entitled according to last received wages; they will, however, not advance in seniority. After reaching the age limit, their pension will be calculated anew, according to the last received salary, on the basis of which their pension was computed.

3.   The affairs of religious organizations will not be touched upon.

4.   The conditions of service of teachers in Jewish public schools remain unchanged, until new regulations of the Jewish school systems are issued.

Article 5

1.   A Jew is anyone who descended from at least three grandparents who were racially full Jews. Article 2, paragraph 2, second sentence will apply.

2.   A Jew is also one who descended from two full Jewish [grand]parents, if: (a) he belonged to the Jewish religious community at the time this law was issued, or who joined the community later; (b) he was married to a Jewish person, at the time the law was issued, or married one subsequently; (c) he is the offspring from a marriage with a Jew, in the sense of Section 1, which was contracted after the Law for the protection of German blood and German honor became effective; (d) he is the offspring of an extramarital relationship, with a Jew, according to Section 1, and will be born out of wedlock after July 31, 1936.

Article 6

1.   As far as demands are concerned for the pureness of blood as laid down in Reichs law or in orders of the NSDAP[1] and its echelons—not covered in Article 5—they will not be touched upon.

2.   Any other demands on pureness of blood, not covered in Article 5, can only be made with permission from the Reich Minister of the Interior and the Deputy of the Fuehrer. If any such demands have been made, they will be void as of 1 January 1936, if they have not been requested from the Reich Minister of the Interior in agreement with the Deputy of the Fuehrer. These requests must be made from the Reich Minister of the Interior.

---

[1] The Nazi party

Article 7

The Fuehrer and Reichs Chancellor can grant exemptions from the regulations laid down in the law.

from Nazi Conspiracy and Aggression, vol. 4. Office of United States Chief of Counsel for
Prosecution of Axis Criminality. Washington: U.S. Government Printing Office, 1946.

Question:
How was citizenship defined by the Nuremberg Laws? How were Jews affected by these laws?

Joseph Goebbels, "The Jews Are to Blame!" 1941

World Jewry's historic guilt for the outbreak and extension of this war has been so abundantly proven that no additional words need to be lost over the matter. The Jews wanted their war. Now they have it. But what is also coming true for them is the Führer's prophecy which he voiced in his Reichstag speech of January 30, 1939. It was that if international financial Jewry succeeded in plunging the nations into another world war, the result would not be the Bolshevization of the world and thus the victory of Jewry, but the destruction of the Jewish race in Europe.

We now are witnessing the acid test of this prophecy, and thus Jewry is experiencing a fate which is hard but more than deserved. Pity or even regrets are entirely out of place here. World Jewry, in starting this war, made an entirely wrong estimate of the forces at its disposal, and is now suffering the same gradual process of destruction which it had planned for us, and which it would apply without hesitation were it to possess the power to do so. It is in line with their own law, "An eye for an eye, a tooth for a tooth," that the ruin of the Jews is now taking place.

In this historic conflict every Jew is our enemy, no matter whether he is vegetating in a Polish ghetto, or still supporting his parasitical existence in Berlin or Hamburg, or blowing the war trumpet in New York or Washington. By reason of their birth and race, all Jews are members of an international conspiracy against National Socialist Germany. They wish for its defeat and destruction, and do whatever is in their power to help bring it about. That in Germany itself, the means at their disposal toward this end are small, certainly is not due to their being loyal here, but solely to the fact that we took those measures against them which we judged to be proper.

One of those measures is the introduction of the Jew's star, which every Jew is obliged to wear visibly. This is designed to mark him externally, too, above all so that if he should make the least attempt to injure the German national community, he can immediately be recognized as a Jew. It is an extraordinarily humane order, a prophylactic health measure, as it were, designed to keep the Jew from creeping into our ranks, unrecognized, to saw disunion among us.

When the Jews, a few weeks ago, appeared in the streets of Berlin adorned with their Jew's stars, the first impression among the capital's citizens was one of general amazement. Only a very small number among us knew that there were still so many Jews in Berlin. Everyone discovered, in his district or his neighborhood, some fellow who acted as though he could not harm a fly, who had, it was true, attracted some occasional attention by his griping and complaining, but whom no one would have suspected of being a Jew. Who among us, please, had any idea that the enemy was standing right next to him that he was a silent, or a cleverly prompting, listener to conversations in the street, in the subway, or in the line that was forming in front of the tobacco shop? There are Jews who can hardly be told apart any more by their looks. As much as they could, they have assimilated themselves in this respect too. They are the most dangerous ones. It is symptomatic that any measure we take against the Jews is reported the very next day in the British and American press. The Jews, then, even now have their secret lines of communication to the enemy nations, and use them not only in their own cause, but in all matters that are militarily vital to the Reich. Thus the enemy is right in our midst. What, therefore, is more obvious than to make him at least externally recognizable to every citizen?

…How sad, compared with this international problem which has bothered mankind for millennia, are the stupid, sentimentally thoughtless arguments of some still extant pals of the Jews! How their eyes, noses, and mouths would fly open if they ever saw their dear Jews in the possession of power. But then it would be too late. And therefore it is the duty of a national leadership to make sure, by the means it deems proper, that this will never come to pass. There is a difference between humans and humans, just as there is a difference between animals and animals. We know good and bad humans, just as we know good and bad animals. The fact that the Jew still lives among us is no proof that he is one of us, no more than the flea's domestic residence makes him a domestic animal. If Herr Bramsig or Frau Knöterich feel a touch of pity as they look upon an old woman wearing a Jew's star, let them remember please that a distant cousin of this old lady, Nathan Kaufman by name, is sitting in new York and has prepared a plan according to which all Germans under 60 would be sterilized. Let them remember that the son of her distant uncle is a warmonger by the name of Baruch or Morgenthau or Untermayer, who is standing behind Mr. Roosevelt, urging him to go to war, and if he should succeed in that aim, some decent but ignorant American soldier might shoot Herr Bramsig's or Frau Knöterich's son quite dead—all to the greater glory of Jewry, of which this old woman is a part, too, no matter how fragile or pity-inspiring she might act.…

So, superfluous though it might be, let me say once more:

1. The Jews are our destruction. They provoked and brought about this war. What they mean to achieve by it is to destroy the German state and nation. This plan must be frustrated.

2. There is no difference between Jew and Jew. Every Jew is a sworn enemy of the German people. If he fails to display his hostility against us, it is merely out of cowardice and slyness, but not because his heart is free of it.

3. Every German soldier's death in this war is the Jews' responsibility. They have it on their conscience; hence they must pay for it.

4. Anyone wearing the Jew's star has been marked as an enemy of the nation. Any person who still maintains social relations with him is one of them, and must be considered a Jew himself and treated as such. He deserves the contempt of the entire nation, which he has deserted in its gravest hour to join the side of those who hate it.

5. The Jews enjoy the protection of the enemy nations. No further proof is needed of their destructive role among our people.

6. The Jews are the messengers of the enemy in our midst. Anyone joining them is going over to the enemy in time of war.

7. The Jews have no claim to pretend to have rights equal to ours. Wherever they want to open their mouths, in the streets, in the lines in front of the stores, or on public transportation, they are to be silenced. They are to be silenced not only because they are wrong on principle, but because they are Jews and have no voice in the community.

8. If Jews pull a sentimental act for you, bear in mind that they are speculating on your forgetfulness. Show them immediately that you see right through them and punish them with contempt.

9. A decent enemy, after his defeat, deserves our generosity. But the Jew is no decent enemy. He only pretends to be one.

10. The Jews are to blame for this war. The treatment we give them does them no wrong. They have more than deserved it....

from The Nazi Years: A Documentary History. Edited by Joachim Remak.
Englewood Cliffs, N.J.: Prentice Hall, 1969.

Questions:
1. According to Goebbels, for what were the Jews to be blamed? How would you compare Goebbels' views of the Jews with that of Hitler's in *Mein Kampf*?
2. How would the Nuremberg Laws and writings like that of Goebbels contribute to the isolation of the Jews?

Dr. T. Lang: "Detailed Statement on the Murdering of Ill and Aged People in Germany," 1941

As we have already noted in our examination of Hitler's *Mein Kampf*, at the heart of National Socialism was a kind of crude racial Social Darwinism. Indeed, a key element of the Nazi worldview was that the "Aryan" race must be improved upon by weeding out undesirable traits and elements in the German gene pool. Towards that end, Hitler's government passed a number of so-called "eugenics" laws in the 1930s, and also began investigating ways of dealing with the problem of those Germans it regarded as "unfit for life," i.e. the mentally handicapped, the disabled, the aged, and psychiatric patients of Germany's asylums and sanitoria. The solution that Hitler and his lieutenants in the SS came up with for dealing with this "disability question" was the T-4 program of "euthanasia" or "mercy killing," which involved rounding up Germany's disabled people, transporting them to so-called "medical institutes," and then marching them into carbon monoxide gas chambers disguised as showers. Afterward, anything that might be economically useful about the bodies, such as gold fillings and human hair, would be removed. The Nazi euthanasia program would serve as the model for the "final solution" of the "Jewish question" as well.

1. The murdering can be traced back to a secret law which was released sometime in Summer 1940....

3. As I have already stated, there were/after careful calculation/ at least 200,000 mainly mentally deficient, imbeciles, besides neurological cases and medically unfit people/ these were not only incurable cases/, and at least 75,000 aged people.

4. The murders were mainly accomplished in Muensingen/Wuerttemberg and Linz 0/Danube; several gas-chambers with cremation chambers directly attached were constructed there. As the gas-chambers are next to the training grounds of the troops in Muensingen, it is believed that the mentally deficient who were murdered there, were used for experimenting with new poison-gases.

5. The transport from the institutions to the gas-chambers is carried out by SS Kommandos. These call themselves "Gemeinnuetzige Transport A. G., Berlin, Luetzowufer." This Limited Company also stores the individual medical case histories of the murdered inmates of the institutions.

6. The inmates of the many smaller and middle-sized institutions were murdered almost without exception. The larger institutions are partly—to keep up the pretence to the outside world—still at hand, but they now only have a fraction of the original number of their inmates...

from *Nazi Conspiracy and Aggression*, vol. 4. Office of United States Chief of Counsel for Prosecution of Axis Criminality. Washington: U.S. Government Printing Office, 1946.

Estimated Savings From The T-4 Program

On the assumption that the level of nutrition of the inmates of asylums will remain the same as at present even after the end of the war, the savings in foodstuffs in the case of 70,273 disinfected persons with an average life expectancy of ten years would be as follows:

Type of foodstuff	Kg.
Potatoes	189,737,160
Meat and sausage products	13,492,440
Bread	59,029,320
Flour	12,649,200
Butter	4,216,440
Butter fat	421,680
Margarine	3,794,760
Bacon	531,240
Ouark	1,054,080
Cheese	1,054,080
Special Foods	1,686,600
Pastry Products	1,475,766
Sago, etc.	421,608
Coffee substitute	3,373,080
Jam	5,902,920
Sugar	7,589,520
Eggs	33,731,040 items
Vegetables	88,540,040
Pulses	4,216,440
Salt and spice substitutes	1,054,080
Total	400,244,520 Kg.

=141,775,573.80RM

On the basis of an average daily cost (per patient) of RM 3.50 there will be

1. a daily saving of RM	245,955.50
2. a yearly saving of RM	88,543,980.00
3. with a life expectancy of ten years	885,439,800.00

In words: eight hundred and eighty-five million four hundred and thirty-five thousand and eight hundred Reich marks.

i.e., This sum will be or has been saved up to 1 September 1941 through the disinfection of 70,273 persons carried out so far.

from *Nazism: A History in Documents and Eyewitness Accounts, 1919-1945*, Vol. 2. Edited by J. Noakes and G. Pridham. New York: 1988

Questions:
What were the Nazis' motivations for and consequences of targeting disabled individuals?

Hermann Göring: "Order to Reinhard Heydrich Regarding a Total Solution to the Jewish Problem," July 31, 1941

While there is some debate as to exactly when and why the Nazi leadership decided to effect a "final solution" to the "Jewish question" in Europe, which involved the extermination of every Jewish man, woman, and child on the continent, there is a consensus that the decision in favor of a program of mass murder against the Jews was taken soon after the German invasion of the Soviet Union. Certainly, the order reprinted below, from Reich Marshal Hermann Göring, Hitler's designated successor, to the Chief of the SS Security Service, Reinhard Heydrich, strongly indicates that the Nazi leadership had concluded during the summer of 1941 that emigration was no longer a viable of dealing with the millions of Jews that had fallen under their control throughout Europe.

The Reich Marshal of the Greater German Reich
Commissioner for the Four Year Plan
Chairman of the Ministerial Council for National Defense Berlin, 31 July 1941

To: The Chief of the Security Police and the Security Service;
SS-Gruppenfuehrer Heydrich

Complementing the task that was assigned to you on 24 January 1939, which dealt with the carrying out of emigration and evacuation, a solution of the Jewish problem, as advantageous as possible, I hereby charge you with making all necessary preparations in regard to organizational and financial matters for bringing about a complete solution of the Jewish question in the German sphere of influence in Europe.

Wherever other governmental agencies are involved, these are to cooperate with you.

I charge you furthermore to send me, before long, an overall plan concerning the organizational, factual and material measures necessary for the accomplishment of the desired solution of the Jewish question.

signed GOERING

from *Nazi Conspiracy and Aggression*, vol. 3. Office of United States Chief of Counsel for Prosecution of Axis Criminality. Washington: U.S. Government Printing Office, 1946.

Minutes of the Wannsee Conference, January 20, 1942

Of course, even after the decision to murder European Jewry had been taken there remained the question of how it was to be effected. One such solution had already suggested itself during the early days of the Russian campaign of 1941 when SS "special task forces," or *Einsatzgruppen*, had moved in behind the advancing Wehrmacht and begun to systematically round up and shoot any and all Soviet officials, officers, and "partisans" that fell into their hands. It was decided to expand these killing operations to include the Jewish communities of the Soviet Union.

While these *Einsatzgruppen*-engineered mass shootings did succeed in murdering some 1.5 million Soviet Jews, as well as thousands of Communist government officials and party workers, they were not without their problems. Aside from requiring a considerable amount of ammunition, they also necessitated the assistance of Wehrmacht soldiers, many of whom just could not handle playing a role in the massacre of unarmed, helpless civilians. Furthermore, mass shootings tended to attract a considerable number of unwanted witnesses. Consequently, Reinhard Heydrich and his assistants decided in the fall of 1941 to establish a series of death camps in occupied Poland where Europe's Jewish communities would be shipped, and either gassed, or worked to death for the benefit and profit of the Reich's war industries, as well as the various enterprises of the SS. Towards this end, Heydrich convened a conference of high level SS officials, Gauleiters, and state functionaries in the Berlin suburb of Wannsee on January 20, 1942, for the purpose of drawing up and coordinating the total annihilation of European Jewry. The minutes of that meeting are reprinted below.

SECRET REICH BUSINESS!

Protocol of Conference

II. At the beginning of the meeting the Chief of the Security Police and the SD, SS Ober-gruppenfiihrer *Heydrich,* announced his appointment by the Reich Marshal, as Plenipotentiary for the Preparation of the Final Solution of the European Jewish Question, and pointed out that this conference had been called to clear up fundamental questions. The Reich Marshal's request to have a draft sent to him on the organizational, substantive, and economic concerns on the final solution of the European Jewish question necessitates prior joint consideration by all central agencies directly concerned with these questions, with a view to keeping policy lines parallel.

Primary responsibility for the handling of the final solution of the Jewish question, the speaker stated, is to lie centrally, regardless of geographic boundaries, with the Reichsführer SS and the Chief of the German Police.

The Chief of the Security Police and the SD then gave a brief review of the struggle conducted up to now against this enemy. The most important aspects are:

a. Forcing the Jews out of the various areas of life of the German people;
b. Forcing the Jews out of the living space of the German people.

In carrying out these efforts, acceleration of the emigration of the Jews from Reich territory, being the only possible provisional solution, was undertaken in intensified and systematic fashion.

By decree of the Reich Marshal, a Reich Central Office for Jewish Emigration was set up in January 1939, and its direction was entrusted to the Chief of the Security Police and the SD. In particular, its tasks were:

a. To take all measures toward *preparation* for intensified emigration of the Jews;
b. To *direct* the stream of emigration;
c. To expedite emigration *in individual cases....*

Financing of the emigration was handled by the Jews or Jewish political organizations them-selves. To avoid a situation where only the proletarianized Jews would remain behind, the principle was followed that well-to-do Jews had to finance the emigration of destitute Jews. To this end, a special assessment or emigration levy, staggered by property levels, was decreed, the proceeds being used to meet financial obligations in connection with the emigration of destitute Jews.

In addition to the funds raised in German marks, foreign currency was needed for the moneys which emigrants were required to have and for landing fees. To conserve the German supply of foreign currencies, Jewish financial institutions abroad were prompted by the Jewish organizations in this country to see to it that appropriate funds in foreign currencies were obtained. Through these foreign Jews, a total of approximately $9,500,000 was made available by way of gifts up to October 30, 1941.

Since then, in view of the dangers of emigration during wartime and in view of the possibilities in the East, the Reichsführer SS and Chief of the German Police has forbidden the emigration of Jews.

III. Emigration has now been replaced by evacuation of the Jews to the East as a further possible solution, in accordance with previous authorization by the Führer.

However, these actions are to be regarded only as provisional options; even now practical experience is being gathered that is of major significance in view of the coming final solution of the Jewish question....

Under appropriate direction, in the course of the final solution, the Jews are now to be suitably assigned to labor in the East. In big labor gangs, with the sexes separated, Jews capable of work will be brought to these areas, employed in roadbuilding, in which task a large part will undoubtedly disappear through natural diminution.

The remnant that may eventually remain, being undoubtedly the part most capable of resistance, will have to be appropriately dealt with, since it represents a natural selection and in the event of release is to be regarded as the germ cell of a new Jewish renewal. (Witness the experience of history).

In the course of the practical implementation of the final solution, Europe is to be combed through from west to east. The Reich area, including the Protectorate of Bohemia and Moravia, will have to be handled in advance, if only because of the housing problem and other socio-political necessities.

The evacuated Jews will first be brought, group by group, into so-called transit ghettos, to be transported from there farther to the East....

from *A Holocaust Reader*. Edited by Lucy S. Dawidowicz. New York: Behrman House, 1976.
Reprinted with permission of the publisher, Behrman House, Inc.

Rudolf Höss: Affidavit Regarding the Operation of Auschwitz, 1946

The main death centers for the implementation of the Nazi "Final Solution" were in occupied Poland at Lublin-Majdanek, Auschwitz, Belzec, Sobibor, and Treblinka. As the expression "death camp" indicates, the principal mission of these camps was mass murder. From 1942 through the summer of 1944, twenty-four hours a day, seven days a week, millions of Jews and other individuals deemed "undesirable" were transported via sealed cattle cars to these camps, robbed of their possessions, stripped naked, and herded into gas chambers. Between 4.2 million to 6 million Jews were murdered in this fashion and with them eighty to ninety per cent of the pre-war Jewish populations of Poland, Czechoslovakia, Latvia, Lithuania, Yugoslavia, Greece, Holland, and Germany.

As these documents also indicate, however, in addition to being death centers, these camps were vast slave labor complexes and experimental laboratories as well. Indeed, millions perished not only in the gas chambers of these centers but also from being worked to death in the plants that were set up outside of, or as part of, these camp complexes. Auschwitz, for example, boasted plants by such German firms as Krupp, Siemens, I.G. Farben and Borsig. Furthermore, these camps, and others, such as Dachau, were also used by "scientists," such as Dr. Josef Mengele, in order to carry out medical experiments that involved the freezing, burning, disemboweling, suffocation, and poisoning of living human beings, many of whom were children.

In the following testimonies by both perpetrators and victims, you can get some idea of the horror that was the reality of the Nazi industry of death.

I, Rudolf Franz Ferdinand Hoess being *first* duly sworn, depose and say as follows:

1. I am forty-six years old, and have been a member of the NSDAP since 1922; a member of the SS since 1934; a member of the Waffen-SS since 1939. I was a member from 1 December 1934 of the SS Guard Unit, the so-called Deathshead Formation [*Totenkopf Verband*].

2. I have been constantly associated with the administration of concentration camps since 1934, serving at Dachau until 1938; then as Adjutant in Sachenhausen from 1938 to May 1, 1940, when I was appointed Commandant of Auschwitz. I commanded Auschwitz until 1 December 1943, and estimate that at least 2,500,000 victims were executed and exterminated there by gassing and burning, and at least another half million succumbed to starvation and disease making a total dead of about 3,000,000. This figure represents about 70% or 80% of all persons sent to Auschwitz as prisoners, the remainder having been selected and used for slave labor in the concentration camp industries. Included among the executed and burnt were approximately 20,000 Russian prisoners of war (previously screened out of Prisoner of War cages by the Gestapo) who were delivered at Auschwitz in Wehrmacht transports operated by regular Wehrmacht officers and men. The remainder of the total number of victims included about 100,000 German Jews, and great numbers of citizens, mostly Jewish, from Holland, France, Belgium, Poland, Hungary, Czechoslovakia, Greece, or other countries. We executed about 400,000 Hungarian Jews alone at Auschwitz in the summer of 1944.

4. Mass executions by gassing commenced during the summer 1941 and continued until fall 1944. I personally supervised executions at Auschwitz until the first of December 1943 and know by reason of my continued duties in the Inspectorate of Concentration Camps WVHA[2] that these mass executions continued as stated above. All mass executions by gassing took place under the direct orders, supervisions, and responsibility of RSHA.[3] I received all orders for carrying out these mass executions directly from RSHA.

6. The "final solution" of the Jewish question meant the complete extermination of all Jews in Europe. I was ordered to establish extermination facilities at Auschwitz in June 1941. At that time, there were already in the general government three other extermination camps; Belzek, Treblinka, and Woizek. These camps were under the Einsatzkommando of the Security Police and SD. I visited Treblinka to find out how they carried out their extermination. The Camp Commandant at Treblinka told me that he had liquidated 80,000 in the course of one-half year. He was principally concerned with liquidating all the Jews from the Warsaw ghetto. He used monoxide gas and I did not think that his methods were very efficient. So when I set up the extermination building at Auschwitz, I used Cyclon B, which was a crystallized prussic acid which we dropped into the death chamber from a small opening. It took from 3 to 15 minutes to kill the people in the death chamber depending upon climatic conditions. We knew when the people were dead because their screaming stopped. We usually waited about

---

[2] Central Economic Administrative Office of the SS.

[3] Reich Central Security Office.

one-half hour before we opened the doors and removed the bodies. After the bodies were removed our special commandos took off the rings and extracted the gold from the teeth of the corpses.

7. Another improvement we made over Treblinka was that we built our gas chambers to accommodate 2,000 people at one time, whereas at Treblinka their 10 gas chambers only accommodated 200 people each. The way we selected our victims was as follows: we had two SS doctors on duty at Auschwitz to examine the incoming transports of prisoners. The prisoners would be marched by one of the doctors who would make spot decisions as they walked by. Those who were fit for work were sent into the Camp. Others were sent immediately to the extermination plants. Children of tender years were invariably exterminated since by reason of their youth they were unable to work. Still another improvement we made over Treblinka was that at Treblinka the victims almost always knew that they were to be exterminated and at Auschwitz we endeavored to fool the victims into thinking that they were to go through a delousing process. Of course, frequently they realized our true intentions and we sometimes had riots and difficulties due to that fact. Very frequently women would hide their children under the clothes but of course when we found them we would send the children in to be exterminated. We were required to carry out these exterminations in secrecy but of course the foul and nauseating stench from the continuous burning of bodies permeated the entire area and all of the people living in the surrounding communities knew that exterminations were going on at Auschwitz.

8. We received from time to time special prisoners from the local Gestapo office. The SS doctors killed such prisoners by injections of benzine. Doctors had orders to write ordinary death certificates and could put down any reason at all for the cause of death.

9. From time to time we conducted medical experiments on women inmates, including sterilization and experiments relating to cancer. Most of the people who died under these experiments had been already condemned to death by the Gestapo....

I understand English as it is written above. The above statements are true; this declaration is made by me voluntarily and without compulsion; after reading over the statement, I have signed and executed the same at Nuremberg, Germany, on the fifth day of April 1946.

[signed] Rudolf Hoess

from *Nazi Conspiracy and Aggression*, vol. VI. Office of United States Chief of Counsel for Prosecution of Axis Criminality. Washington: U.S. Government Printing Office, 1946.

Dr. S. Rascher: On Medical Experiments at Dachau, 1942

INTERMEDIATE REPORT ON INTENSE CHILLING EXPERIMENTS IN THE DACHAU CAMP, STARTED ON 15 AUGUST 1942

The experimental subjects (V P) were placed in the water, dressed in complete flying uniform, winter or summer combination, and with an aviator's helmet. A life jacket made of rubber or kapok was to prevent submerging. The experiments were carried out at water temperatures varying from 2.5° to 12°. In one experimental series, Occiput and brain stem protruded above the water, while in another series of experiments the Occiput (brain stem) and back of the head were submerged in water.

Electrical measurements gave low temperature readings of 26.4° in the stomach and 26.5° in the rectum. Fatalities occurred only when the brain stem and the back of the head were also chilled. Autopsies of such fatal cases always revealed large amounts of free blood, up to ½ liter, in the cranial cavity. The heart invariably showed extreme dilation of the night chamber. As soon as the temperature in these experiments reached 28°, the experimental subjects (VP) died invariably, despite all attempts at resuscitation. The above discussed autopsy finding conclusively proved the importance of a warming protective device for head and Occiput when designing the planned protective clothing of the foam type.

Other important findings, common in all experiments, to be mentioned. Marked increase of the viscosity of the blood, marked increase of hemoglobin, an approximate five fold increase of the leukocytes, invariable rise of blood sugar to twice its normal value. Auricular fibrillation made its appearance regularly at 30°.

During attempts to save severely chilled persons, it was shown that rapid re-warming was in all cases preferable to slow rewarming, because after removal from the cold water, the body temperature continued to sink rapidly. I think that for this reason we can dispense with the attempt to save intensely chilled subjects by means of animal heat.

Rewarming by animal warmth—animal bodies or women's bodies—would be too slow. As auxiliary measures for the prevention of intense chilling, improvements in the clothing of aviators come alone into consideration. The foam suit with suitable neck protector which is being prepared by the German Institution for textile research [*Deutsches Textilforschungsinstitut*] Muenchen-Gladbach deserves first priority in this connection. The experiments have shown that pharmaceutical measures are probably unnecessary if the flier is still alive at the time of rescue.

(signed) Dr. S. Rascher

from *Nazi Conspiracy and Aggression*, vol. 4. Office of United States Chief of Counsel for Prosecution of Axis Criminality. Washington: U.S. Government Printing Office, 1946.

Question:
What were the conditions under which prisoners were forced to labor for the Nazis? For those who were selected for immediate death, what methods did the Nazis use?

Heinrich Himmler: "Combating the Gypsy Nuisance," December 8, 1938

As already mentioned, while the Jews were the principal target of the Nazi program of persecution and murder, they were not the only victims of the Hitler regime. As Himmler makes clear in his circular on the "gypsy nuisance," Europe's Sinti and Roma were also regarded by the Nazis as a race with alien and inferior blood that had to be rounded up and exterminated. Indeed, it is estimated that out of a population of one million, some forty per cent of Europe's Gypsies were killed in the Nazi death camps.

Experience gained in combatting the Gypsy nuisance, and knowledge derived from race-biological research, have shown that the proper method of attacking the Gypsy problem seems to be to treat it as a matter of race. Experience shows that part-Gypsies play the greatest role in Gypsy criminality. On the other hand, it has been shown that efforts to make the Gypsies settle have been unsuccessful, especially in the case of pure Gypsies, on account of their strong compulsion to wander. It has therefore become necessary to distinguish between pure and part-Gypsies in the final solution of the Gypsy question.

To this end, it is necessary to establish the racial affinity of every Gypsy living in Germany and of every vagrant living a Gypsy-like existence.

I therefore decree that all settled and non-settled Gypsies, and also all vagrants living a Gypsy-like existence, are to be registered with the Reich Criminal Police Office-Reich Central Office for Combatting the Gypsy Nuisance.

The police authorities will report (via the responsible Criminal Police offices and local offices) to the Reich Criminal Police Office-Reich Central Office for Combatting the Gypsy Nuisance all persons who by virtue of their looks and appearance, customs or habits, are to be regarded as Gypsies or part-Gypsies.

Because a person considered to be a Gypsy or part-Gypsy, or a person living like a Gypsy, as a rule confirms the suspicion that marriage (in accordance with clause 6 of the first decree on the implementation of the Law for the Protection of German Blood and Honor…or on the basis of stipulations in the law on Fitness to Marry) must not be contracted, in all cases the public registry officials must demand a testimony of fitness to marry from those who make such an application to be married.

Treatment of the Gypsy question is part of the National Socialist task of national regeneration. A solution can only be achieved if the philosophical perspectives of National Socialism are observed. Although the principle that the German nation respects the national identity of alien peoples is also assumed in combatting the Gypsy nuisance, nonetheless the aim of measures taken by the State to defend the homogeneity of the German nation must be the physical separation of Gypsydom from the German nation, the prevention of miscegenation and finally the regulation of the way of life of pure and part-Gypsies. The necessary legal foundation can only be created through a Gypsy Law, which prevents further intermingling of blood, and which regulates all the most pressing questions which go together with the existence of Gypsies in the living space of the German nation.

from The Racial State: Germany 1933-1945. Edited by Michael Burleigh and Wolfgang Wipperman.
New York, 1991.

Despite the abundance of documented evidence—films, photographs, testimonies, memoirs, etc.—there are still individuals that either argue that the Holocaust did not happen, or that its many atrocities were actually isolated acts of sadism about which the Nazi leadership was ignorant. The following remarks by Heinrich Himmler and the Commandant of Auschwitz, Rudolf Höss, make abundantly clear that everyone involved in the Nazi Final Solution knew that it was Hitler's express wish that Europe's Jews be destroyed.

Rudolf Höss: from *Death Dealer*, 1946-47[4]

Over and over I had to hear from the prisoners in Dachau, "Why does the SS hate us so? We are human beings too." This alone should suffice to clarify the general relationship between the SS and prisoners.

---

[4] Höss wrote his memoirs while in prison between 1946 and 1947.

I do not believe that Eicke personally hated and despised these dangerous ENEMIES OF THE STATE, as he continuously tried to make the troops believe. I am more convinced that his constant priming only served to force the SS men to their utmost alertness and constant readiness. What he caused by this, and what effect his hounding had on everyone, he never realized. And so, raised and trained in the spirit of Eicke, I had to perform my duty in the concentration camp, as a block leader, a duty officer, and as supply administrator. I must now admit, I conscientiously and attentively performed my duty to everyone's satisfaction. I didn't let the prisoners get away with anything. I was firm and often hard. But I had been a prisoner for too long for me not to notice their needs. It was not without inner sympathy that I faced all of the occurrences in the camp. Outwardly I was cold, even stone-faced, but inwardly I was moved to the deepest. I saw many crimes, suicides, or those shot while trying to escape. I was close enough to determine if they were real situations or set up by the guards. I viewed the work accidents, those who died by running into the electrified wire. I was present at the legal identification of bodies in the autopsy room, during disciplinary beatings, and during the punishments Loritz ordered done and often observed himself. These were Loritz's punishment assignments and his way of fulfilling a sentence. By looking at the stone mask on my face he was firmly convinced that he didn't have to "toughen me up," as he loved to do with the SS men who seemed to him to be too weak.

This is when my guilt really begins.

It had become clear to me that I was not suited for this kind of service because in my heart I did not agree with the conditions and the practices of the concentration camp as demanded by Eicke.

My heart was tied to the prisoners because I had suffered their kind of life much too long and had also experienced their needs. Right then I should have gone to Eicke or Himmler and explained that I was not suited for service in the concentration camp because I had too much compassion for the prisoners.

I did not have the courage to do this.

I did not want to reveal myself because I didn't want to admit my sensitivity. I was too stubborn to admit that I had made the wrong decision when I gave up my plans to farm.

I had volunteered to join the active SS. The black uniform had become too precious to me and I didn't want to take it off in this way. If I admitted that I was too soft for the SS, 1 would have been expelled, or at least been dismissed without ceremony. I did not have the heart for that.

So I fought between my inner conviction and my sense of duty. And I struggled with my loyalty oath of the SS and my allegiance to Hitler. Should I become a deserter? Even today my wife knows nothing of this inner conflict. I have kept it to myself until now.

As an old-time member of the Nazi Party, I believed in the need for the concentration camps. The real ENEMIES OF THE STATE had to be put away safely; the asocials and the professional criminals who could not be locked up under the prevailing laws had to lose their freedom in order to protect the people from their destructive behavior.

I was also firmly convinced that only the SS, the guardians of the new state, could perform this job. But 1 did not agree with Eicke's views about inmates and his method of enraging the basest feelings of hate among the guard troops. I did not agree with his personnel policy of leaving the prisoners with incompetent people; I did not agree with his practice of unsuitable people in their positions. I was *not* in agreement with the length of sentencing depending on someone's whim.

But by staying in the concentration camp, I adopted the views, orders, and decrees which were in force there. I accepted my fate, which 1 had voluntarily chosen, even though deep inside I quietly hoped to find another kind of duty in the service in the future. At that time, however, this was unthinkable because Eicke said I was very much suited for prison duty.

Even though I became accustomed to all of the occurrences of the concentration camp, I never became insensitive to human suffering. I always saw it and felt it. But I always had to walk away from it because I was not allowed to be soft. I wanted to have the reputation of being hard. I did not want to be thought of as a weak person.

from Steven Paskuly (ed.), *Death Dealer: The Memoirs of the SS Kommandant at Auschwitz*. (Amherst, NY: Prometheus Books). Copyright 1992. Reprinted by permission of the publisher.

Heinrich Himmler: "Speech of the Reichsfuehrer-SS at the Meeting of SS Major-Generals at Posen," 1943

One basic principle must be the absolute rule for the SS man: we must be honest, decent, loyal, and comradely to members of our own blood and to nobody else. What happens to a Russian, to a Czech does not interest me in the slightest. What the nations can offer in the way of good blood of our type, we will take, if necessary by kidnapping their children and raising them here with us. Whether nations live in prosperity or starve to death interests me only in so far as we need them as slaves for our Kultur; otherwise, it is of no interest to me. Whether 10,000 Russian females fall down from exhaustion while digging an anti-tank ditch interests me only in so far as the anti-tank ditch for Germany is finished. We shall never be rough and heartless when it is not necessary, that is clear. We Germans, who are the only people in the world who have a decent attitude towards animals, will also assume a decent attitude towards these human animals. But it is a crime against our own blood to worry about them and give them ideals, thus causing our sons and grandsons to have a more difficult time with them. When somebody comes to me and says, "I cannot dig the anti-tank ditch with women and children, it is inhuman, for it would kill them," then I have to say, "You are a murderer of your own blood because if the anti-tank ditch is not dug, German soldiers will die, and they are sons of German mothers. They are our own blood." That is what I want to instill into the SS and what I believe I have instilled into them as one of the most sacred laws of the future. Our concern, our duty is our people and our blood. It is for them that we must provide and plan, work and fight, nothing else. We can be indifferent to everything else. I wish the SS to adopt this attitude to the problem of all foreign, non-Germanic peoples, especially Russians. All else is vain, fraud against our own nation and an obstacle to the early winning of the war.

THE CLEARING OUT OF THE JEWS

I also want to talk to you, quite frankly, on a very grave matter. Among ourselves it should be mentioned quite frankly, and yet we will never speak of it publicly. Just as we did not hesitate on June 30th, 1934 to do the duty we were bidden, and stand comrades who had lapsed, up against the wall and shoot them, so we have never spoken about it and will never speak of it. It was that tact which is a matter of course and which I am glad to say, is inherent in us, that made us never discuss it among ourselves, never to speak of it. It appalled everyone, and yet everyone was certain that he would do it the next time if such orders are issued and if it is necessary.

I mean the clearing out of the Jews, the extermination of the Jewish race. It's one of those things it is easy to talk about— "The Jewish race is being exterminated", says one party member, "that's quite clear, it's in our program—elimination of the Jews, and we're doing it, extermin-ating them." And then they come, 80 million worthy Germans, and each one has his decent Jew. Of course the others are vermin, but this one is an A-1 Jew. Not one of all those who talk this way has witnessed it, not one of them has been through it. Most of *you* must know what it means when 100 corpses are lying side by side, or 500 or 1000. To have stuck it out and at the same time—apart from exceptions caused by human weakness—to have remained decent fellows, that is what has made us hard. This is a page of glory in our history which has never been written and is never to be written, for we know how difficult we should have made it for ourselves, if—with the bombing raids, the burdens and the deprivations of war—we still had Jews today in every town as secret saboteurs, agitators and trouble-mongers. We would now probably have reached the 1916/17 stage when the Jews were still in the German national body.

We have taken from them what wealth they had. I have issued a strict order, which SS-Obergruppenfuehrer Pohl has carried out, that this wealth should, as a matter of course, be handed over to the Reich without reserve. We have taken none of it for ourselves. Individual men who have lapsed will be punished in accordance with an order I issued at the beginning, which gave this warning; Whoever takes so much as a mark of it, is a dead man. A number of SS men—there are not very many of them—have fallen short, and they will die, without mercy. We had the moral right, we had the duty to our people, to destroy this people which wanted to destroy us. But we have not the right to enrich ourselves with so much as a fur, a watch, a mark, or a cigarette or anything else. Because we have exterminated a bacterium we do not want, in the end, to be infected by the bacterium and die of it. I will not see so much as a small area of sepsis appear here or gain a hold. Wherever it may form, we will cauterize it. Altogether however, we can say, that we have fulfilled this most difficult duty for the love of our people. And our spirit, our soul, our character has not suffered injury from it.

from Nazi Conspiracy and Aggression, vol. 4. Office of United States Chief of Counsel for
Prosecution of Axis Criminality. Washington: U.S. Government Printing Office, 1946.

Adolf Hitler: from "Political Testament," 1945

More than thirty years have now passed since I in 1914 made my modest contribution as a volunteer in the first world-war that was forced upon the Reich.

In these three decades I have been actuated solely by love and loyalty to my people in all my thoughts, acts, and life. They gave me the strength to make the most difficult decisions which have ever confronted to mortal man. I have spent my time, my working strength, and my health in these three decades.

It is untrue that I or anyone else in Germany wanted the war in 1939. It was desired and instigated exclusively by those international statesmen who were either of Jewish descent or worked for Jewish interests. I have made too many offers for the control and limitation of armaments, which posterity will not for all time be able to disregard for the responsibility for the outbreak of this war to be laid on me. I have further never wished that after the first fatal world war a second against England, or even against America, should break out. Centuries will pass away, but out of the ruins of our towns and monuments the hatred against those finally responsible whom we have to thank for everything, International Jewry and its helpers, will grow.

Three days before the outbreak of the German-Polish war I again proposed to the British ambassador in Berlin a solution to the German-Polish problem—similar to that in the case of the Saar district, under international control. This offer also cannot be denied. It was only rejected because the leading circles in English politics wanted the war, partly on account of the business hoped for and partly under influence of propaganda organized by international Jewry.

I also made it quite plain that, if the nations of Europe are again to be regarded as mere shares to be bought and sold by these international conspirators in money and finance, then that race, Jewry, which is the real criminal of this murderous struggle, will be saddled with the responsibility. I further left no one in doubt that this time not only would millions of children of Europe's Aryan peoples die of hunger, not only would millions of grown men suffer death, and not only hundreds of thousands of women and children be burnt and bombed to death in the towns, without the real criminal having to atone for this guilt, even if by more humane means.

After six years of war, which in spite of all set-backs, will go down one day in history as the most glorious and valiant demonstration of a nation's life purpose, I cannot forsake the city which is the capital of this Reich. As the forces are too small to make any further stand against the enemy attack at this place and our resistance is gradually being weakened by men who are as deluded as they are lacking in initiative, I should like, by remaining in this town, to share my fate with those, the millions of others, who have also taken upon themselves to do so. Moreover I do not wish to fall into the hands of an enemy who requires a new spectacle organized by the Jews for the amusement of their hysterical masses.

I have decided therefore to remain in Berlin and there of my own free will to choose death at the moment when I believe the position of the Fuehrer and Chancellor itself can no longer be held....

Above all I charge the leaders of the nation and those under them to scrupulous observance of the laws of race and to merciless opposition to the universal poisoner of all peoples, international Jewry.

Given in Berlin, this 29th day of April 1945. 4:00 a.m.

Adolf Hitler

from *Nazi Conspiracy and Aggression*, vol. 6. Office of United States Chief of Counsel for Prosecution of Axis Criminality. Washington: U.S. Government Printing Office, 1946.

Questions;
1. What does Höss' statement reveal about his motivations? Do you find contradictions in his testimony?
2. How did Himmler justify in his mind the murder of civilians? How did he try to suppress any acts of compassion directed toward Jews?
3. How did Hitler try to rationalize the actions he had taken during World War II?

Chapter 29: The Postwar World, 1945-1970

Unit 59: The Bitter Harvest

The Yalta Conference, February 1945

From the end of 1943 through the summer of 1945, there were three major Allied conferences at Teheran, Yalta, and Potsdam. These conferences coordinated Allied war strategy and also addressed the whole question of postwar political arrangements around the world. Of these three conferences, the one that was held at Yalta in February 1945 held out the most hope for a new world order free of "exclusive alliances and spheres of influence."

The Crimea Conference of the heads of the Governments of the United States of America, the United Kingdom, and the Union of Soviet Socialist Republics, which took place from Feb. 4 to 11, came to the following conclusions:

I. WORLD ORGANIZATION

It was decided:

1. That a United Nations conference on the proposed world organization should be summoned for Wednesday, 25 April, 1945, and should be held in the United States of America.

2. The nations to be invited to this conference should be:

    (a) The United Nations as they existed on 8 Feb., 1945; and

    (a) Such of the Associated Nations as have declared war on the common enemy by 1 March, 1945. (For this purpose, by the term "Associated Nations" was meant the eight Associated Nations and Turkey.) When the conference on world organization is held, the delegates of the United Kingdom and United States of America will support a proposal to admit to original membership two Soviet Socialist Republics, i.e., the Ukraine and White Russia.

3. That the United States Government, on behalf of the three powers, should consult the Government of China and the French Provisional Government in regard to decisions taken at the present conference concerning the proposed world organization.

4. That the text of the invitation to be issued to all the nations which would take part in the United Nations conference should be as follows:

    "The Government of the United States of America, on behalf of itself and of the Governments of the United Kingdom, the Union of Soviet Socialist Republics and the Republic of China and of the Provisional Government of the French Republic, invite the Government of _____ to send representatives to a conference to be held on 25 April, 1945, or soon thereafter, at San Francisco, in the United States of America, to prepare a charter for a general international organization for the maintenance of international peace and security.

    "The above-named Governments suggest that the conference consider as affording a basis for such a Charter the proposals for the establishment of a general international organization which were made public last October as a result of the Dumbarton Oaks conference and which have now been supplemented by the following provisions for Section C of Chapter VI:...

II. DECLARATION ON LIBERATED EUROPE

The following declaration has been approved:

The Premier of the Union of Soviet Socialist Republics, the Prime Minister of the United Kingdom and the President of the United States of America have consulted with each other in the common interests of the peoples of their countries and those of liberated Europe. They jointly declare their mutual agreement to concert during the temporary period of instability in liberated Europe the policies of their three Governments in assisting the peoples liberated from the domination of Nazi Germany and the peoples of the former Axis satellite states of Europe to solve by democratic means their pressing political and economic problems.

The establishment of order in Europe and the rebuilding of national economic life must be achieved by processes which will enable the liberated peoples to destroy the last prestiges of nazism and fascism and to create democratic institutions of their own choice. This is a principle of the Atlantic Charter—the right of all peoples to choose the form of government under which they will live—the restoration of sovereign rights and self-government to those peoples who have been forcibly deprived of them by the aggressor nations.

To foster the conditions in which the liberated peoples may exercise these rights, the three Governments will jointly assist the people in any European liberated state or former Axis satellite state in Europe where, in their judgment conditions require, (a) to establish conditions of internal peace; (b) to carry out emergency measures for the relief of distressed peoples; (c) to form interim governmental authorities broadly representative of all democratic elements in the population and pledged to the earliest possible establishment through free elections of Governments responsive to the will of the people; and (d) to facilitate where necessary the holding of such elections.

The three Governments will consult the other United Nations and provisional authorities or other Governments in Europe when matters of direct interest to them are under consideration.

When, in the opinion of the three Governments, conditions in any European liberated state or any former Axis satellite state in Europe make such action necessary, they will immediately consult together on the measures necessary to discharge the joint responsibilities set forth in this declaration.

By this declaration we reaffirm our faith in the principles of the Atlantic Charter, our pledge in the Declaration by the United Nations and our determination to build in cooperation with other peace-loving nations world order, under law, dedicated to peace, security, freedom and general well-being of all mankind...

U. S. State Department. Quoted in the *New York Times*, March 15, 1945

Questions:
1. What was the stated purpose of the United Nations?
2. What were the main principles expressed at Yalta in the "Declaration on Liberated Europe"?

The Truman Doctrine

The war of words between the former members of the Grand Alliance was soon transformed into a more heated and dangerous contest of formal government programs, alliances, and international policies in 1947. When a civil war in Greece and economic chaos in Turkey opened the whole of the eastern Mediterranean to Soviet expansion, President Harry S. Truman (1945-1953) announced that it must be American policy to "support free peoples who are resisting attempted subjugation by armed minorities or by outside pressures." This Truman Doctrine, which was backed up by over $400 million in aid to Greece and Turkey, essentially committed the United States to providing material and military assistance to any country that was thought to be threatened by Communist expansion.

MR. PRESIDENT, MR. SPEAKER, MEMBERS OF THE CONGRESS OF THE UNITED STATES:

The gravity of the situation which confronts the world today necessitates my appearance before a joint session of the Congress.

The foreign policy and the national security of this country are involved.

One aspect of the present situation, which I present to you at this time for your consideration and decision, concerns Greece and Turkey.

The United States has received from the Greek Government an urgent appeal for financial and economic assistance. Preliminary reports from the American Economic Mission now in Greece and reports from the American Ambassador in Greece corroborate the statement of the Greek Government that assistance is imperative if Greece is to survive as a free nation.

I do not believe that the American people and the Congress wish to turn a deaf ear to the appeal of the Greek Government.

Greece is not a rich country. Lack of sufficient natural resources has always forced the Greek people to work hard to make both ends meet. Since 1940, this industrious, peace loving country has suffered invasion, four years of cruel enemy occupation, and bitter internal strife.

When forces of liberation entered Greece they found that the retreating Germans had destroyed virtually all the railways, roads, port facilities, communications, and merchant marine. More than a thousand villages had been burned. Eighty-five percent of the children were tubercular. Livestock, poultry, and draft animals had almost disappeared. Inflation had wiped out practically all savings.

As a result of these tragic conditions, a militant minority, exploiting human want and misery, was able to create political chaos which, until now, has made economic recovery impossible.

Greece is today without funds to finance the importation of those goods which are essential to bare subsistence. Under these circumstances the people of Greece cannot make progress in solving their problems of reconstruction. Greece is in desperate need of financial and economic assistance to enable it to resume purchases of food, clothing, fuel and seeds. These are indispensable for the subsistence of its people and are obtainable only from abroad. Greece must have help to import the goods necessary to restore internal order and security so essential for economic and political recovery.

The Greek Government has also asked for the assistance of experienced American administrators, economists and technicians to insure that the financial and other aid given to Greece shall be used effectively in creating a stable and self-sustaining economy and in improving its public administration.

The very existence of the Greek state is today threatened by the terrorist activities of several thousand armed men, led by Communists, who defy the government's authority at a number of points, particularly along the northern boundaries. A Commission appointed by the United Nations Security Council is at present investigating disturbed conditions in northern Greece and alleged border violations along the frontier between Greece on the one hand and Albania, Bulgaria, and Yugoslavia on the other.

Meanwhile, the Greek Government is unable to cope with the situation. The Greek army is small and poorly equipped. It needs supplies and equipment if it is to restore authority to the government throughout Greek territory.

Greece must have assistance if it is to become a self-supporting and self-respecting democracy.

The United States must supply this assistance. We have already extended to Greece certain types of relief and economic aid but these are inadequate.

There is no other country to which democratic Greece can turn.

No other nation is willing and able to provide the necessary support for a democratic Greek government.

The British Government, which has been helping Greece, can give no further financial or economic aid after March 31. Great Britain finds itself under the necessity of reducing or liquidating its commitments in several parts of the world, including Greece.

We have considered how the United Nations might assist in this crisis. But the situation is an urgent one requiring immediate action, and the United Nations and its related organizations are not in a position to extend help of the kind that is required...

Greece's neighbor, Turkey, also deserves our attention.

The future of Turkey as an independent and economically sound state is clearly no less important to the freedom-loving peoples of the world than the future of Greece. The circumstances in which Turkey finds itself today are considerably different from those of Greece. Turkey has been spared the disasters that have beset Greece. And during the war, the United States and Great Britain furnished Turkey with material aid.

Nevertheless, Turkey now needs our support.

Since the war Turkey has sought additional financial assistance from Great Britain and the United States for the purpose of effecting that modernization necessary for the maintenance of its national integrity...

I am fully aware of the broad implications involved if the United States extends assistance to Greece and Turkey, and I shall discuss these implications with you at this time.

One of the primary objectives of the foreign policy of the United States is the creation of conditions in which we and other nations will be able to work out a way of life free from coercion. This was a fundamental issue in the war with Germany and Japan. Our victory was won over countries which sought to impose their will, and their way of life, upon other nations.

To ensure the peaceful development of nations, free from coercion, the United States has taken a leading part in establishing the United Nations. The United Nations is designed to make possible lasting freedom and independence for all its members. We shall not realize our objectives, however, unless we are willing to help free peoples to maintain their free institutions and their national integrity against aggressive movements that seek to impose upon them totalitarian regimes. This is no more than a frank recognition that totalitarian regimes imposed upon free peoples, by direct or indirect aggression, undermine the foundations of international peace and hence the security of the United States.

The peoples of a number of countries of the world have recently had totalitarian regimes forced upon them against their will. The Government of the United States has made frequent protests against coercion and intimidation, in violation of the Yalta agreement, in Poland, Rumania, and Bulgaria. I must also state that in a number of other countries there have been similar developments.

At the present moment in world history nearly every nation must choose between alternative ways of life. The choice is too often not a free one.

One way of life is based upon the will of the majority, and is distinguished by free institutions, representative government, free elections, guarantees of individual liberty, freedom of speech and religion, and freedom from political oppression.

The second way of life is based upon the will of a minority forcibly imposed upon the majority. It relies upon terror and oppression, a controlled press and radio, fixed elections, and the suppression of personal freedoms.

I believe that it must be the policy of the United States to support free peoples who are resisting attempted subjugation by armed minorities or by outside pressures.

I believe that we must assist free peoples to work out their own destinies in their own way.

I believe that our help should be primarily through economic and financial aid which is essential to economic stability and orderly political processes.

The world is not static, and the status quo is not sacred. But we cannot allow changes in the status quo in violation of the Charter of the United Nations by such methods as coercion, or by such subterfuges as political infiltration. In helping free and independent nations to maintain their freedom, the United States will be giving effect to the principles of the Charter of the United Nations.

It is necessary only to glance at a map to realize that the survival and integrity of the Greek nation are of grave importance in a much wider situation. If Greece should fall under the control of an armed minority, the effect upon its neighbor, Turkey, would be immediate and serious. Confusion and disorder might well spread throughout the entire Middle East.

Moreover, the disappearance of Greece as an independent state would have a profound effect upon those countries in Europe whose peoples are struggling against great difficulties to maintain their freedoms and their independence while they repair the damages of war.

It would be an unspeakable tragedy if these countries, which have struggled so long against overwhelming odds, should lose that victory for which they sacrificed so much. Collapse of free institutions and loss of independence would be disastrous not only for them but for the world.

Discouragement and possibly failure would quickly be the lot of neighboring peoples striving to maintain their freedom and independence.

Should we fail to aid Greece and Turkey in this fateful hour, the effect will be far reaching to the West as well as to the East.

We must take immediate and resolute action.

I therefore ask the Congress to provide authority for assistance to Greece and Turkey in the amount of $400,000,000 for the period ending June 30, 1948. In requesting these funds, I have taken into consideration the maximum amount of relief assistance which would be furnished to Greece out of the $350,000,000 which I recently requested that the Congress authorize for the prevention of starvation and suffering in countries devastated by the war.

In addition to funds, I ask the Congress to authorize the detail of American civilian and military personnel to Greece and Turkey, at the request of those countries, to assist in the tasks of reconstruction, and for the purpose of supervising the use of such financial and material assistance as may be furnished. I recommend that authority also be provided for the instruction and training of selected Greek and Turkish personnel.

Finally, I ask that the Congress provide authority which will permit the speediest and most effective use, in terms of needed commodities, supplies, and equipment, of such funds as may be authorized.

If further funds, or further authority, should be needed for the purposes indicated in this message, I shall not hesitate to bring the situation before the Congress. On this subject the Executive and Legislative branches of the Government must work together.

This is a serious course upon which we embark.

I would not recommend it except that the alternative is much more serious.

The United States contributed $341,000,000,000 toward winning World War II. This is an investment in world freedom and world peace.

The assistance that I am recommending for Greece and Turkey amounts to little more than 1/10 of 1 percent of this investment. It is only common sense that we should safeguard this investment and make sure that it was not in vain.

The seeds of totalitarian regimes are nurtured by misery and want. They spread and grow in the evil soil of poverty and strife. They reach their full growth when the hope of a people for a better life has died.

We must keep that hope alive.

The free peoples of the world look to us for support in maintaining their freedoms.

If we falter in our leadership, we may endanger the peace of the world—and we shall surely endanger the welfare of this Nation.

Great responsibilities have been placed upon us by the swift movement of events.

I am confident that the Congress will face these responsibilities squarely.

from *Public Papers of the Presidents of the United States: Harry S. Truman: 1947.*
Washington: U.S. Government Printing Office, 1963.

Questions:
1. What was the cause of political chaos in Greece in 1947?
2. According to Truman, what motivations did the United States have in giving economic assistance to Greece? Were there any historical examples that Truman could call upon to support his position? Do you agree or disagree with his view of the situation in Greece and the possible consequences of that circumstance?

The Marshall Plan, 1947

The policy of assistance to anti-Communist governments outlined in the Truman Doctrine was further strengthened by the European Recovery Program, better known as the Marshall Plan, which provided $13 billion for the economic recovery of western Europe. From the following excerpts, it is readily apparent that the days of American isolationism were most definitely at an end.

I need not tell you gentlemen that the world situation is very serious. That must be apparent to all intelligent people. I think one difficulty is that the problem is one of such enormous complexity that the very mass of facts presented to the public by press and radio make it exceedingly difficult for the man in the street to reach a clear appraisement of the situation. Furthermore, the people of this country are distant from the troubled areas of the earth and it is hard for them to comprehend the plight and consequent reactions of the long-suffering peoples, and the effect of those reactions on their governments in connection with our efforts to promote peace in the world.

In considering the requirements for the rehabilitation of Europe, the physical loss of life, the visible destruction of cities, factories, mines, and railroads was correctly estimated, but it has become obvious during recent months that this visible destruction was probably less serious than the dislocation of the entire fabric of European economy. For the past 10 years conditions have been highly abnormal. The feverish preparation for the war and the more feverish maintenance of the war effort engulfed all aspects of national economies. Machinery has fallen into disrepair or is entirely obsolete. Under the arbitrary and destructive Nazi rule, virtually every possible enterprise was geared into the German war machine. Long-standing commercial ties, private institutions, banks, insurance companies and shipping companies disappeared, through loss of capital, absorption through nationalizations or by simple destruction. In many countries, confidence in the local currency has been severely shaken. The breakdown of the business structure of Europe during the war was complete. Recovery has been seriously retarded by the fact that two years after the close of hostilities a peace settlement with Germany and Austria has not been agreed upon. But even given a more prompt solution of these difficult problems, the rehabilitation of the economic structure of Europe quite evidently will require a much longer time and greater effort than had been foreseen.

There is a phase of this matter which is both interesting and serious. The farmer has always produced the foodstuffs to exchange with the city dweller for the other necessities of life. This division of labor is the basis of modern civilization. At the present time it is threatened with breakdown. The town and city industries are not producing adequate goods to exchange with the food-producing farmer. Raw materials and fuel are in short supply. Machinery is lacking or worn out. The farmer or the peasant cannot find the goods for sale which he desires to purchase. So the sale of his farm produce for money which he cannot use seems to him an unprofitable transaction. He, therefore, has withdrawn many fields from crop cultivation and is using them for grazing. He feeds more grain to stock and finds for himself and his family an ample supply of food, however short he may be on clothing and the other ordinary gadgets of civilization. Meanwhile people in the cities are short of food and fuel. So the governments are forced to use their foreign money and credits to procure these necessities abroad. This process exhausts funds which are urgently needed for reconstruction. Thus a very serious situation is rapidly developing which bodes no good for the world. The modern system of the division of labor upon which the exchange of products is based is in danger of breaking down.

The truth of the matter is that Europe's requirements for the next three or four years of foreign food and other essential products—principally from America—are so much greater than her present ability to pay that she must have substantial additional help, or face economic, social, and political deterioration of a very grave character.

The remedy lies in breaking the vicious circle and restoring the confidence of the European people in the economic future of their own countries and of Europe as a whole. The manufacturer and the farmer throughout wide areas must be able and willing to exchange their products for currencies the continuing value of which is not open to question.

Aside from the demoralizing effect on the world at large and the possibilities of disturbances arising as a result of the desperation of the people concerned, the consequences to the economy of the United States should be apparent to all. It is logical that the United States should do whatever it is able to do to assist in the return of normal economic health in the world, without which there can be no political stability and no assured peace. Our policy is directed not against any country or doctrine but against hunger, poverty, desperation, and chaos. Its purpose should be the revival of a working economy in the world so as to permit the emergence of political and social conditions in which free institutions can exist. Such assistance, I am convinced, must not be on a piecemeal basis as various crises develop. Any assistance that this Government may render in the future should provide a cure rather than a mere palliative. Any government that is willing to assist in the task of recovery will find full cooperation, I am sure, on the part of the United States Government. Any government which maneuvers to block the recovery of other countries cannot expect help from us. Furthermore, governments, political parties, or groups which seek to perpetuate human misery in order to profit therefrom politically or otherwise will encounter the opposition of the United States.

It is already evident that, before the United States Government can proceed much further in its efforts to alleviate the situation and help start the European world on its way to recovery, there must be some agreement among the countries of Europe as to the requirements of the situation and the part those countries themselves will take in order to give proper effect to whatever action might be undertaken by this Government. It would be neither fitting nor efficacious for this Government to undertake to draw up unilaterally a program designed to place Europe on its feet economically. This is the business of the Europeans. The initiative, I think, must come from Europe. The role of this country should consist of friendly aid in the drafting of a European program and of later support of such a program so far as it may be practical for us to do so. The program should be a joint one, agreed to by a number, if not all European nations.

An essential part of any successful action on the part of the United States is an understanding on the part of the people of America of the character of the problem and the remedies to be applied. Political passion and prejudice should have no part. With foresight, and a willingness on the part of our people to face up to the vast responsibility which history has clearly placed upon our country, the difficulties I have outlined can and will be overcome.

from *Department of State Bulletin*. Vol. XVI #415. Washington, June 15, 1947, Washington.

Questions:
1. What were the economic problems Europe faced in the aftermath of World War II?
2. What motives did the United States have in providing aid to Europe?

Daniel Goldy: "Report on Italy," April 15, 1952

You can get some idea of what the Marshall Plan involved from the following report by Dan Goldy (b. 1915), a Marshall Plan economic consultant charged with addressing the various ways in which postwar American aid might assist Italy in overcoming its unemployment.

GENERAL DESCRIPTION OF SURVEY

1. This is a report on my recent trip to Italy, during which I attempted a brief, preliminary survey of the possibilities for solving the Italian unemployment problem through the development of Italy's resources potentials. Theretofore the United States has accepted it as a fact that Italy has had a surplus population. It, along with other nations, has attempted to cooperate with Italy to solve this problem by promoting Italian emigration.

CONCLUSIONS

5. b. It is clear that current efforts to solve the unemployment problem through Italian emigration have been ineffective. While an analysis of the specific impediments to migration was obtained from the ILO[1] and the IRO[2] in Geneva and Italian and U.S. officials in Rome, it appears that even if the specific known obstacles were overcome, it would be unlikely that sufficient migration could occur soon enough to affect materially the internal problems of Italy. On the other hand, if a vigorous program were undertaken by the Italian government to utilize the basic resources of the country to raise living standards—particularly in the South—the opportunities for Italian migration would undoubtedly increase as the internal pressure for migration decreased.

    c. Italy has a resources base which, if properly developed and utilized, would be adequate to support its population at a substantially higher standard of living and higher levels of employment than now prevail. If Italy were to undertake the programs necessary to make full use of its physical resources potentials, it would probably need all its population for the amount of work involved. On the other hand, some alleviation of the immediate unemployment problem through migration might be necessary—particularly in industrial areas—during the initial period while Italy was overhauling the industrial portions of its economy.

    d. Italy is not as poor in basic resources as is commonly supposed—but the poverty of large segments of the population is greater than is generally known. While Italy does not posses as much under-developed wealth as some of its European neighbors, e.g. France, the principal obstacle to a more prosperous Italy is not lack of basic opportunity, but a set of political and economic institutions that frustrate progress toward full development.

---

[1] International Labor Office.

[2] International Refugee Organization.

FINDINGS

    17. Political and Economic Institutions

        a. The basic impediments to the full development of Italy's resources potentials in the agricultural, mineral, energy and industrial fields and to a solution of the unemployment problem within Italy are the political and economic institutions under which Italy is operating. These institutions are characterized by: absence of competition and a free market; lack of incentive for risk-taking and new investment by private capital; high cost of credit and limitations placed on new investment by government, presumably for the purpose of controlling inflation; high prices, high profits, limited output and low wages; a highly regressive tax system, which falls with crushing force on the poor and leaves the rich relatively unburdened by taxes;...

As is to be expected in such a society, there are thousands of ways in which the basic institutions are reflected in conditions which would be deemed unsatisfactory in the United States. It serves no useful purpose to attempt a complete enumeration of these conditions. It is sufficient to point out that many of these conditions would soon change in an economy which was dedicated to raising the standards of living of all its people, instead of one dedicated to maximizing the profits of a few large monopolists. An economy dedicated to the latter purpose actually accomplishes neither. The result is a poor country—of which Italy is certainly a prime example....

[But] the basic change required is that of dedicating the institutions of the country to increasing the standard of living of its people. Were the government aggressively to undertake the pursuit of this goal, it could find many more opportunities for effecting improvements and changes than could any outsider making a survey of the Italian potentials. Were an aggressive policy of this sort to be undertaken, it appears certain that the basic resources of Italy, physical, industrial and human, are such as to make it possible to absorb in gainful employment those persons who by any reasonable standards should be in the labor force. Moreover, the basic resource capacities make possible a higher standard of living. A higher standard of living in turn should make feasible the retirement of over-aged workers and the rigorous enforcement of child labor and compulsory education laws. These latter measures alone would do a great deal toward eliminating Italian unemployment.

Daniel L. Goldy. U. S. Government: National Archives and Records Administration.
April 15, 1952.

Question:
George C. Marshall claimed that "Our policy is directed not against any country or doctrine but against hunger, poverty, desperation, and chaos." Using Goldy's report on Italy, evaluate Marshall's claim.

George Kennan: "The Sources of Soviet Conduct," July 1947

    In the aftermath of the Truman Doctrine and the Marshall Plan, American foreign policy vis-a-vis the Soviet Union and its allies was increasingly focused on the idea of "containing" Communist aggression. The underpinnings of this policy have their origins in a very influential article in the journal *Foreign Affairs*, which was published in July 1947 by George Kennan, a well-known American diplomat and historian of Russia. In the following excerpt from that article, Kennan explains the rationale for a policy of containment against further Soviet aggressive moves.

...Of the original ideology, nothing has been officially junked. Belief is maintained in the basic badness of capitalism, in the inevitability of its destruction, in the obligation of the proletariat to assist in that destruction and to take power into its own hands. But stress has come to be laid primarily on those concepts which relate most specifically to the Soviet regime itself: to its position as the sole truly Socialist regime in a dark and misguided world, and to the relationships of power within it.

The first of these concepts is that of the innate antagonism between capitalism and Socialism. We have seen how deeply that concept has become imbedded in foundations of Soviet power. It has profound implications for Russia's conduct as a member of international society. It means that there can never be on Moscow's side any sincere assumption of a community of aims between the Soviet Union and powers which are regarded as capitalist. It must invariably be assumed in Moscow that the aims of the capitalist world are antagonistic to the Soviet regime, and therefore to the interests of the peoples it controls. If the Soviet Government occasionally sets its signature to documents which would indicate the contrary, this is to be regarded as a tactical maneuver permissible in dealing with the enemy (who is without honor) and should be taken in the spirit of *caveat emptor*. Basically, the antagonism remains. It is postulated. And from it flow many of the phenomena which we find disturbing in the Kremlin's conduct of foreign policy: the secretiveness, the lack of frankness, the duplicity, the wary suspiciousness, and the basic unfriendliness of purpose. These phenomena are there to stay, for the foreseeable future. There can be variations of degree and of emphasis. When there is something the Russians want from us, one or the other of these features of their policy may be thrust temporarily into the background; and when that happens there will always be Americans who will leap forward with gleeful announcements that "the Russians have changed," and some who will even try to take credit for having brought about such "changes." But we should not be misled by tactical maneuvers. These characteristics of Soviet policy, like the postulate from which they flow, are basic to the internal nature of Soviet power, and will be with us, whether in the foreground or the background, until the internal nature of Soviet power is changed.

This means that we are going to continue for a long time to find the Russians difficult to deal with. It does not mean that they should be considered as embarked upon a do-or-die program to overthrow our society by a given date. The theory of the inevitability of the eventual fall of capitalism has the fortunate connotation that there is no hurry about it. The forces of progress can take their time in preparing the final *coup de grace*. Meanwhile, what is vital is that the "Socialist fatherland"—that person of the Soviet Union—should be cherished and defended by all good Communists at home and abroad, its fortunes promoted, its enemies badgered and confounded. The promotion of premature, "adventuristic" revolutionary projects abroad which might embarrass Soviet power in any way would be an inexcusable, even a counter-revolutionary act. The cause of Socialism is the support and promotion of Soviet power, as defined in Moscow.

This brings us to the second of the concepts important to contemporary Soviet outlook. That is the infallibility of the Kremlin. The Soviet concept of power, which permits no focal points of organization outside the Party itself, requires that the Party leadership remain in theory the sole repository of truth. For if truth were to be found elsewhere, there would be justification for its expression in organized activity. But it is precisely that which the Kremlin cannot and will not permit.

The leadership of the Communist Party is therefore always right, and has been always right ever since in 1929 Stalin formalized his personal power by announcing that decisions of the Politburo were being taken unanimously....

These considerations make Soviet diplomacy at once easier and more difficult to deal with than the diplomacy of individual aggressive leaders like Napoleon and Hitler. On the one hand it is more sensitive to contrary force, more ready to yield on individual sectors of the diplomatic front when that force is felt to be too strong, and thus more rational in the logic and rhetoric of power. On the other hand it cannot be easily defeated or discouraged by a single victory on the part of its opponents. And the patient persistence by which it is animated means that it can be effectively countered not by sporadic acts which represent the momentary whims of democratic opinion but only by intelligent long-range policies on the part of Russia's adversaries—policies no less steady in their purpose, and no less variegated and resourceful in their application, than those of the Soviet Union itself.

In these circumstances it is clear that the main element of any United States policy toward the Soviet Union must be that of a long-term, patient but firm and vigilant containment of Russian expansive tendencies. It is important to note, however, that such a policy has nothing to do with outward histrionics: with threats or blustering or superfluous gestures of outward "toughness." While the Kremlin is basically flexible in its reaction to political realities, it is by no means unamenable to considerations of prestige. Like almost any other government, it can be placed by tactless and threatening gestures in a position where it cannot afford to yield even though this might be dictated by its sense of realism. The Russian leaders are keen judges of human psychology, and as such they are highly conscious that loss of temper and of self-control is never a source of strength in political affairs. They are quick to exploit such evidences of weakness. For these reasons, it is a *sine qua non* of successful dealing with Russia that the foreign government in question should remain at all times cool and collected and that its demands on Russian policy should be put forward in such a manner as to leave the way open for a compliance not too detrimental to Russian prestige.

In the light of the above, it will be clearly seen that the Soviet pressure against the free institutions of the western world is something that can be contained by the adroit and vigilant application of counter-force at a series of constantly shifting geographical and political points, corresponding to the shifts and maneuvers of Soviet policy, but which cannot be charmed or talked out of existence. The Russians look forward to a duel of infinite duration, and they see that already they have scored great successes....

It is clear that the United States cannot expect in the foreseeable future to enjoy political intimacy with the Soviet regime. It must continue to regard the Soviet Union as a rival, not a partner, in the political arena. It must continue to expect that Soviet policies will reflect no abstract love of peace and stability, no real faith in the possibility of a permanent happy coexistence of the Socialist and capitalist worlds, but rather a cautious, persistent pressure toward the disruption and weakening of all rival influence and rival power.

Balanced against this are the facts that Russia, as opposed to the western world in general, is still by far the weaker party, that Soviet policy is highly flexible, and that Soviet society may well contain deficiencies which will eventually weaken its own total potential. This would of itself warrant the United States entering with reasonable confidence upon a policy of firm containment, designed to confront the Russians with unalterable counter-force at every point where they show signs of encroaching upon the interests of a peaceful and stable world.

But in actuality the possibilities for American policy are by no means limited to holding the line and hoping for the best. It is entirely possible for the United States to influence by its actions the internal developments, both within Russia and throughout the international Communist movement, by which Russian policy is largely determined. This is not only a question of the modest measure of informational activity which this government can conduct in the Soviet Union and elsewhere, although that, too, is important, It is rather a question of the degree to which the United States can create among the peoples of the world generally the impression of a country which knows what it wants, which is coping successfully with the problems of its internal life and with the responsibilities of a World Power, and which has a spiritual vitality capable of holding its own among the major ideological currents of the time. To the extent that such an impression can be created and maintained, the aims of Russian Communism must appear sterile and quixotic, the hopes and enthusiasm of Moscow's supporters must wane, and added strain must be imposed on the Kremlin's foreign policies. For the palsied decrepitude of the capitalist world is the keystone of Communist philosophy. Even the failure of the United States to experience the early economic depression which the ravens of the Red Square have been predicting with such complacent confidence since hostilities ceased would have deep and important repercussions throughout the Communist world....

It would be an exaggeration to say that American behavior unassisted and alone could exercise a power of life and death over the Communist movement and bring about the early fall of Soviet power in Russia. But the United States has it in its power to increase enormously the strains under which Soviet policy must operate, to force upon the Kremlin a far greater degree of moderation and circumspection than it has had to observe in recent years, and in this way to promote tendencies which must eventually find their outlet in either the break-up or the gradual mellowing of Soviet power. For no mystical, Messianic movement—and particularly not that of the Kremlin—can face frustration indefinitely without eventually adjusting itself in one way or another to the logic of that state of affairs.

Thus the decision will really fall in large measure in this country itself, The issue of Soviet-American relations is in essence a test of the over-all worth of the United States as a nation among nations. To avoid destruction the United States need only measure up to its own best traditions and prove itself worthy of preservation as a great nation.

Surely, there was never a fairer test of national quality than this. In the light of these circumstances, the thoughtful observer of Russian-American relations will find no cause for complaint in the Kremlin's challenge to American society. He will rather experience a certain gratitude to a Providence which, by providing the American people with this implacable challenge, has made their entire security as a nation dependent on their pulling themselves together and accepting the responsibilities of moral and political leadership that history plainly intended them to bear.

from "The Sources of Soviet Conduct," By X (George Kennan) *Foreign Affairs*, Vol. 25, # 4. July, 1947.
New York: Council on Foreign Relations.